THOMAS HARDY REAPPRAISED:
ESSAYS IN HONOUR OF MICHAEL MILLGATE

EDITED BY KEITH WILSON

Thomas Hardy Reappraised: Essays in Honour of Michael Millgate

UNIVERSITY OF TORONTO PRESS
Toronto Buffalo London

© University of Toronto Press Incorporated 2006
Toronto Buffalo London
Printed in Canada

ISBN-13: 978-0-8020-3955-2
ISBN-10: 0-8020-3955-3

Printed on acid-free paper

Library and Archives Canada Cataloguing in Publication

Thomas Hardy reappraised : essays in honour of Michael
Millgate / edited by Keith Wilson.

Includes bibliographical references and index.
ISBN 0-8020-3955-3

1. Hardy, Thomas, 1840–1928 – Criticism and interpretation.
I. Millgate, Michael   II. Wilson, Keith (Keith G.)

PR4754.T495 2006   823'.8   C2005-907375-6

University of Toronto Press acknowledges the financial assistance to
its publishing program of the Canada Council for the Arts and the
Ontario Arts Council.

University of Toronto Press acknowledges the financial support for
its publishing activities of the Government of Canada through the
Book Publishing Industry Development Program (BPIDP).

Contents

Acknowledgments

My main thanks go to the authors of these essays, all of whom responded with such warmth and enthusiasm to the invitation to express in this way their appreciation for Michael Millgate's contributions to Hardy studies. Pamela Dalziel in particular was a firm and wise supporter of this project from its inception and I thank her for her assistance in bringing it to fruition. I am grateful also to the generous support provided by the Faculty of Arts at the University of Ottawa and the Faculty of Arts and Science at the University of Toronto. At Ottawa, Antoni Lewkowicz, former Associate Dean of Arts (Research), and David Rampton, Chair of English, provided invaluable assistance, as did Brian Corman, Chair of English at the University of Toronto, and I am greatly indebted to all three. I also thank my colleagues Ina Ferris and April London for, as always, their sage advice. Jill McConkey of the University of Toronto Press helped at every stage of this book's advance to publication and I am most indebted to her, as I am to Barb Porter for her work as editor. Miriam Skey was an exemplary copy-editor, and I am very grateful to her.

Keith Wilson
Ottawa
February 2006

Introduction

KEITH WILSON

This collection of new essays written by fifteen of the world's most eminent Hardy scholars in honour of Michael Millgate, University Professor of English Emeritus at the University of Toronto, offers in the frequency with which his name is invoked in its bibliographical citations graphic testimony to the magnitude of his contribution to the study of the life and work of Thomas Hardy. Most of the textual, critical, and biographical resources that these essays take for granted as an essential context for serious discussion of Hardy's work did not exist when Michael Millgate began his career as a Hardy scholar. The fact that they do now owes much to his remarkable contributions to the field. His first book on Hardy, *Thomas Hardy: His Career as a Novelist* (1971), an exceptionally acute reading of all the novels enabled by extensive familiarity with the biographical, historical, and archival background (and a seemingly instinctive feel for what can most productively be made of it), is still in print, nearly thirty-five years after its initial publication. His *Thomas Hardy: A Biography* (1982; recently revised as *Thomas Hardy: A Biography Revisited*, 2004) is the most authoritative life – meticulously researched, temperate, and unerring in its capacity to relate documentable fact to plausible speculation without any confusion between the two. His seven-volume edition, coedited with Richard Little Purdy, of the *Collected Letters* (1978–88) is one of the great scholarly editions of literary correspondence, a sign of its accomplishment being the frequency with which its authority is cited in sale catalogues, and the corresponding infrequency with which a dealer can experience the pleasure of being able to annotate one of his offerings 'Not in Millgate and Purdy.' Recoverer of Hardy's intended text for *The Life and Work of Thomas Hardy* (1985), editor of *Letters of Emma and*

Florence Hardy (1996) and of *Thomas Hardy's Public Voice: The Essays, Speeches and Miscellaneous Prose* (2001), coeditor with one of our contributors of *Thomas Hardy's 'Studies, Specimens, &c.' Notebook* (1994), and compiler of the website 'Thomas Hardy's Library at Max Gate: Catalogue of an Attempted Reconstruction' (http://www.library.utoronto.ca/fisher/hardy/ established August 2003), Michael Millgate has produced scholarship of a transformative kind, providing the firm historical and biographical ground on which fellow Hardy scholars now stand at the same time as making his findings accessible to the worldwide community of nonacademic Hardy enthusiasts. Generous in his willingness to assist and share his knowledge with other scholars, ever willing to respond to the calls on his time that the automatic association of his name with Hardy's inevitably occasions, he is held in such universal respect and affection in Hardy circles that the comment of one of the contributors to the present volume upon responding with immediate enthusiasm to the invitation to participate in this project can be allowed to stand for the general sentiment: 'Nobody in the Thomas Hardy world better deserves celebration than Michael Millgate.'

It now requires a retentive memory in the older scholar and an act of imaginative will in the younger to try to reclaim a sense of what Hardy studies were like around the time that Michael Millgate was beginning his contributions to them. Just five years before the publication of *Thomas Hardy: His Career as a Novelist*, Philip Larkin (who would shortly give a substantial boost to what he regarded as Hardy's sadly neglected poetic reputation by making him the most generously represented poet in his selections for *The Oxford Book of Twentieth-Century Verse* [1973]),[1] had famously complained in the pages of *Critical Quarterly* about what he saw as the continued inadequacies, nearly forty years after Hardy's death, of the kind of criticism his work attracted, advancing his case for the prosecution under the deliberately provocative title 'Wanted: Good Hardy Critic.'[2] The ostensible occasion for the announcement of this desideratum was a review of two recent books on Hardy: a revised edition of the biocritical study *Hardy of Wessex* by the prolific American Hardy scholar Carl J. Weber, prime begetter of the important Colby College Hardy collection, and Roy Morrell's *Thomas Hardy: The Will and the Way*. Both were of their kind useful books, by scholars who had made substantial contributions to Hardy scholarship, and Morrell's in particular had some claim to being a genuinely original, if rather obsessively insistent, revisionist analysis that set out to challenge what it saw as longstanding but wrong-headed received opinion. Neither book really warranted the spikily Larkinesque trouncing they both received ('Why doesn't Hardy attract people who can write?'),[3] nor was it true that there was not already available a solid body of informed and perceptive Hardy criticism. But it was certainly the case that Hardy scholarship had often seemed oddly mixed in quality, uncertain in focus, and on occasion grudging to the point of condescension, especially when seen against the kind of attention that other Victorian and modern writers of his stature attracted.[4] To misappropriate the phrasing of the unwise judgment that Matthew Arnold made on the romantics, it sometimes appeared that Hardy criticism was attempting to proceed 'without having its proper data, without sufficient materials to work with. In other words ... [it] did not know enough,'[5] although it often thought it knew a very great deal, particularly about those points of natural intersection between Hardy's personal life, his evocation of the rural experience of southwest England, his supposed autodidacticism, and the dominant ideas (easily invocable as something called the 'Hardy philosophy') that informed his writing.

At the time of the appearance of Larkin's article, Hardy biographical scholarship, one of the areas in which Michael Millgate has had his most profound influence, was revealing itself as spectacularly vulnerable to the charge of not knowing enough. This was partly because most of what it knew was still more or less what Hardy had wanted it to know and had artfully told it, under Florence Hardy's name, in the *Life*, that tantalizing combination of apparent scrupulous detail and evasiveness. The presumed concealments behind the overt revelations of the *Life*, coupled with the well-documented tales of Max Gate bonfires and the relentlessness with which Hardy's texts seemed given to exacting their 'full look at the Worst,' fed the supposition that there must have been much worth concealing. The year of Larkin's 'wanted' posting saw also the publication of one of the strangest exercises in biographical speculation ever inflicted upon a major author, Lois Deacon's notorious *Providence and Mr. Hardy* (London: Hutchinson, 1966), coauthored with Terry Coleman. At this distance in time, it is easy to forget that some of the more sensational assertions about the nature and consequences of Hardy's relationship with his cousin Tryphena Sparks were still receiving significant credence in serious academic circles well into the 1970s. In the same year that *Thomas Hardy: His Career as a Novelist* appeared, for example, another critical work on Hardy, F.R. Southerington's *Hardy's Vision of Man*, accepted Deacon's authority more or less wholesale, even down to the unwise reproduction of a photograph confidently labelled, without a hint of tentativeness or caution, 'Randal, son of Hardy and Tryphena Sparks.'[6] Between them F.B. Pinion, Robert Gittings, and Michael Millgate gradually advanced the verdict from not proven to inherently unlikely to 'there was certainly no child, probably no formal engagement, and perhaps not even a dramatic parting,'[7] but not before mainstream Hardy scholarship had begun to identify Tryphena as the hidden presence in an implausible array of imaginative contexts, most notably those poems relating to disappointment in love.[8]

Another idiosyncratic venture that seems in retrospect quaintly representative of the temper of the times in Hardy biographical work was the Toucan Press monograph series, in the third of which Lois Deacon's impassioned speculations had first found their way into print. We have good reason to be grateful for the foresight of J. Stevens Cox in preserving these reminiscences of the rapidly declining number of people who had known Hardy personally, if not in the main particularly well (given Hardy's constitutional reserve, it was unlikely that his gardener, parlourmaid, or barber would have gleaned much of great substance from the socially imbalanced occasions on which their paths crossed). But illuminating though some of them were, such offerings could by their nature be no more than they modestly claimed to be: variously useful 'Materials for a Study of His Life, Times and Works,' rather than the study itself. Nor could the correspondence fill out the life very much at that time. Only small subgroupings of letters had appeared in print, notably those that had attracted the attention of Carl Weber.[9] And while Evelyn Hardy had published as early as 1955 an erratically transcribed and partial edition of two of Hardy's 'Memoranda' notebooks, the only Hardy notebook to have appeared in a reliable published form was the 'Architectural Notebook,' edited by C.J.P. Beatty.[10]

It was not only in matters biographical that Hardy scholarship seemed to lack much of its proper data. The editions in which Hardy's works came before their public had not yet received much sustained attention from textual scholars, although the forms in which his published writings had originally appeared and the collected editions appearing during his lifetime had been admirably documented in Richard Little Purdy's *Thomas Hardy: A Bibliographical Study*.[11] For the novels, the Hardy-approved Wessex Edition of 1912 was conventionally regarded as definitive, and Macmillan, confident of being the natural guardians of this venerable name and preparing for their imminent (1978) loss of Hardy copyright, would soon be producing volumes of the fiction in something optimistically designated the 'New Wessex Edition.' While these would have perceptive introductions by established scholars, and a scattering of notes, they had no pretensions to be critically established scholarly editions. But the situation of the poems was far worse. The standard edition of the *Collected Poems* was still the old 1930 'Fourth Edition,' reprinted so many times as to have taken on the appearance of being generated by processes seemingly designed to create in the cramped and faded typography an appropriately Hardyesque evocation of the relentlessness of 'Time's unflinching rigour.'

In the decade following publication of *Thomas Hardy: His Career as a Novelist* the situation changed dramatically. Reliable editions of the Hardy notebooks began to appear, first Lennart A. Björk's preliminary partial edition of the *Literary Notes* (1974), and then Richard H. Taylor's edition of *The Personal Notebooks* (1978).[12] Robert Gittings produced two volumes of biography that constituted genuine, well-researched complements to Hardy's own *Life*.[13] Under the 'New Wessex' designation, James Gibson first made the *Complete Poems* available in a comprehensive and readable edition, and then in what was termed a Variorum format (1979).[14] And by the first year of the new decade, two volumes of the *Collected Letters* were already in print. Thus by 1980, Hardy biographical and textual scholarship had taken on a much more purposive direction, not least because with Macmillan's loss of copyright, primary texts had become available to other publishers, notably Oxford University Press, who were prepared to make some investment in the preparation of genuine scholarly editions. Dale Kramer's Clarendon edition of *The Woodlanders* appeared in 1981, followed in 1983 by Juliet Grindle and Simon Gatrell's edition of *Tess of the d'Urbervilles*, bracketing between them the exceptional harvest of Hardy scholarship that was garnered in 1982: the third volume of the *Collected Letters*, the Millgate *Biography*, and the first volume of Samuel Hynes's magnificent edition of *The Complete Poetical Works*.

There is still much textual work to be done, notably on the novels, but the scholarly and critical context surrounding the emergent Hardy scholar today is very different from that encountered by Michael Millgate when he first turned his attention to Hardy. Subsequent developments have continued the consolidation that began in the 1970s, to such a degree that now Hardy, far from being a misrepresented writer still in need of a good critic or two, is so well served by scholarship and criticism of every editorial, political, theoretical, historical, aesthetic, and philosophical orientation as to occupy an assured position at the very centre of contemporary literary and cultural studies. Michael

Millgate's own contribution to that transformation has been unrivalled, and this group of friends and colleagues who have themselves played important roles in the process are very pleased to be able to offer him this volume of their own work as a token of their great appreciation for his.

Given the biographical emphasis of so much of Michael's work, it is fitting that the opening essay in this collection, Pamela Dalziel's 'The Gospel According to Hardy,' should take the form of a major new contribution to our understanding of Hardy's early spiritual biography. Making available in print for the first time a sermon written by the eighteen-year-old Hardy, Dalziel invites us to rethink the nature of his youthful religious formation in ways that illuminate the paradoxes of his lifelong relationship with Christianity. In later life, and in response to the various pejorative terms that had been attached to his state of nonbelief, Hardy famously referred to himself as 'churchy; not in an intellectual sense, but in so far as instincts and emotions ruled.'[15] The authorship of what Dalziel typifies as 'an orthodox Evangelical sermon' provides evidence of the young Hardy's intellectual engagement also with doctrinal matters and seems to offer some support to the claim, implicit in the correspondence of his Baptist friend Henry Bastow, that Hardy once, if only briefly, had a faith somewhat closer to Evangelical- ism than to the High-Church Anglicanism practised at his family's home parish at Stinsford. Hardy's own account of his doctrinal position in these years suggests, after some investigation of the argument for adult baptism, a vigorous resistance to the attempted suasions of both Bastow and the two sons of Dorchester's Baptist minister, whose polemical aid Bastow enlisted in his proselytizing.[16] But whatever the truth of the matter, the sermon, as Dalziel asserts, 'provides a unique glimpse into his early religious beliefs,' and a clear indication of the extent to which his secularized ethical ideals were founded in early immersion in scriptural text.

This unveiling of an important new discovery illuminating Hardy's early relationship with religious modes of apprehension leads naturally into Mary Rimmer's '"My Scripture Manner": Reading Hardy's Biblical and Liturgical Allusion,' which further elaborates on the complex reso- nances attaching to the term 'belief' for a writer whose much-invoked unsuccessful fifty-year search for God is perhaps more significant for its inclination to seek than its failure to find. The rich allusiveness of Hardy's writing has long been recognized. Rimmer's essay identifies and elaborates on the generative intermixture of sacred and secular resonances in his allusions, with their frequent articulation of doubt in the language and cadences of faith. This tonal ambiguity and the generic heterogeneity of the literary contexts in which Hardy uses scriptural allusion in themselves indicate the centrality of sacred text to a consciousness conventionally regarded as being resiliently secular in its articles of faith and doubt.

Michael Millgate's recent establishment of the 'Thomas Hardy's Library at Max Gate' website makes particularly appropriate the continuance of the motif of allusion in the next two essays. Hardy's reading always lies close to the surface of his own writing, sometimes sufficiently self-consciously to have evoked those somewhat condescending early references to him as an autodidact.[17] After the Bible and the Book of Common Prayer, the works of Shakespeare constitute the literary texts that make their intellectual and emotional presence felt most assertively in Hardy's writing. In 1916, Hardy claimed, 'I read S[hakespeare]. more closely from 23 to 26 than I have ever done since, or probably ever shall again.'[18] No Shakespeare play echoes more widely through his work than *Hamlet*. Drawing on the evidence of Hardy's annotated copies of Shakespeare, most particularly the 1856 Singer edition now held in the Dorset County Museum, Dennis Taylor's 'Hardy and *Hamlet*' makes an attempted reconstruction of the constituent stages of Hardy's reading and re-reading of *Hamlet*, as a prelude to considering the recurrent influence of his immersion in this play on his own creative work. As Taylor remarks, it is perhaps not an overstatement to say that this 'play about ghost possession' haunted and possessed Hardy, and his close attention to it reflects something of the way in which the literary tradition more generally might have been said to possess him. The motif of haunting, so recurrent in Hardy's work in both literal and figurative, explicit and implicit manifestations provides a suggestive image for his relationship to a literary past that he constantly remakes in his own creative present.

As the Dalziel and Millgate edition of *Thomas Hardy's 'Studies, Specimens &c' Notebook* reveals, Hardy's familiarity with more contemporary poets is no less marked. The implication of Hardy's reading in the referential power of his own writing forms the subject matter of Barbara Hardy's essay 'Literary Allusion: Hardy and Other Poets,' which explores Hardy's intertextual conversations not only with nineteenth-century but also with classical writers, 'a dialogue crossing cultures and centuries.' The range is remarkable, Browning, Shelley, Keats, Meredith,

Barnes, Swinburne, Wordsworth, Tennyson, Sophocles, and Horace comprising the primary touchstones. Not reluctant to identify those laboured moments when allusions are little more than 'unassimilated name-or-quote-dropping' that manifests Hardy's occasional 'bad habit of piling up allusion,' Barbara Hardy's spirited assessment shows a poet's eye for those more charged referential convergences when originary text and Hardy's reformulation generate 'a participation in ritual.'

After consideration of these scriptural and literary presences, the collection moves to engagement with three recurrent cultural reference points in Hardy's writing, all of which have yet to receive the degree of attention they warrant. Given Hardy's well-documented affection for children, some irony attaches to the fact that his fictional children tend to be viewed as sharing with Dickens's Paul Dombey the characteristics of the 'old-fashioned' child, not least when – as with Little Father Time – they are made to carry the burden of precocious anticipation of the shape of adult consciousnesses to come. Hardy's own childhood memory of '[r]eflecting on his experiences of the world so far as he had got' and coming to 'the conclusion that he did not wish to grow up,'[19] shapes the temperaments of more Hardyan children than just the young Jude. Notwithstanding the propensity of the best known of Hardy's literary children to be disconcertingly unchildlike, Hardy scholarship has recently been fascinated by the possibility that his poetic canon might need expansion to incorporate a group of deceptively simple poems, previously assumed to have been written by his second wife Florence, that Hardy himself may have written specifically for children.[20] This is therefore a fitting time for U.C. Knoepflmacher to be addressing in 'Hardy's Subterranean Child' the complex question of 'the nature of [Hardy's] engagement with childhood.' Knoepflmacher explores the qualification to the familiar Blakean binary of Innocence and Experience that Hardy's view of childhood invites, much as it relies on the familiar typology that it subverts. He encourages us to see that Hardy also creates children, in both his fiction and his poetry, whose 'subversive roles ... differ from the one he assigns to Father Time,' roles that can 'even challenge the disenchantments of our adult constructions of meaning.'

As ubiquitous as the protean child in Hardy's work is the elemental and unyielding substance with which Hardy's own childhood as the son of a stonemason and builder, and his early years as an architect, made him very familiar. Marjorie Garson's 'Written in Stone: Hardy's Grotesque Sublime' discusses Hardy's recurrent preoccupation with stone in its various forms – geological, architectural, and memorial. In a richly evocative study, she explores stone's potential to embody not only distinctively Hardyesque anxieties about the body but also to suggest spiritual possibilities that transcend bodily circumstance. This essay reengages in suggestive ways with that paradoxical relationship between an impervious material world and the aspirant sublimity of human response to it implicit in the opening essays' explorations of Hardy's religious sensibility.

Simon Gatrell's 'The Erotics of Dress in *A Pair of Blue Eyes*' also considers the rendering of bodily identity in Hardy's writing, as mediated through the iconography of clothing. While scholarship in the field of material culture has recently been addressing the social and psychological significance of fashion in a range of historically theorized ways, the subject has received little attention in relation to the pointed foregrounding of dress in Hardy's work. Whether invoked in tragic terms, as in Lucetta Templeman's identification through dress style with the skimmity-ride effigy or Tess's repossession by Alec as figured in the finery in which he has clothed her, or in the comic ironic terms of such poems of sexual irregularity as 'The Ruined Maid' or 'In the Days of Crinoline,' clothing is recurrently used by Hardy to provide external designation of sexual circumstance. By considering the erotics of dress in relation to one of Hardy's earlier novels, Gatrell's essay opens up a field of speculation whose emergence in Hardy studies is particularly timely given the recent increasing interest in, and accessibility of, the illustrations that accompanied original publication of much of his fiction.

The next four essays focus on individual novels, all in their different ways locating terms of analysis within the textured biographical and historical specifics to which Michael Millgate's scholarship has so variously contributed. Ruth Bernard Yeazell's 'Hardy's Rural Painting of the Dutch School' takes its direction from the subtitle of Hardy's *Under the Greenwood Tree*. Her raising of the question 'what did it mean to identify a novel with Dutch painting?' leads to consideration of Hardy's relationship with 'realism,' and those rhythms of community interaction that the genre ratifies. In a period inclined to associate realism with visual representation of the quotidian, particularly as photography gradually supplanted representational painting as the measure of mimetic fidelity, this early emphasis is understandable. But as Yeazell indicates, it is also of relatively brief duration, and Hardy's work would rapidly move away from the focus on 'ordinary experience' that made the sub-title of his second published novel appropriate, directing his attention increasingly to those exceptional and tortured figures whose aspirations and failures transcend the 'ordinary.'

Prominent among these are the central characters of *The Return of the Native*, the subject of J. Hillis Miller's essay 'Individual and Community in *The Return of the Native*: A Reappraisal,' which further explores the relationship between individual and community in the light of Clym Yeobright's compulsion to return 'home.' While Yeazell places *Under the Greenwood Tree*'s emphasis on the collective that 'nearly doubles as a protagonist,' Miller locates the evocation of community in *The Return of the Native* within opposed terms theorized by Martin Heidegger and Raymond Williams. The heath dwellers are shown to constitute a genuine community, but Miller's analysis crucially complicates any meaningful application of the concept of community to the main protagonists, who form 'a non-community of distinctive individuals who interact with one another destructively and without mutual understanding.' The contentment of the Egdon community is purchased at the expense of ignorance, while the protagonists' 'self-conscious awareness of their specific situations' exacts the toll of discontent and frustrated purpose.

This diagnosis of a destructive and rootless self-consciousness as the inevitable condition of modernity leads appropriately into George Levine's '*The Woodlanders* and the Darwinian Grotesque,' which considers the influence of Darwinian thought on another novel in which outsiders and returned natives exist in overt alienation from a rooted community. Levine's cocontributor, Dennis Taylor, was one of the first commentators to encourage us to think of Hardy in relation to the grotesque, reaching towards Ruskin to define its generic mix 'of caricature and seriousness, the ludicrous and the fearful.'[21] Levine attempts to make sense of *The Woodlanders*' 'generic chaos' by identifying its version of a distinctively Victorian 'romantic and highly moralized organicism,' whose 'connections' are unintentional in a 'quite Darwinian way,' product as they are of 'the overlaying of the ideal work of human consciousness on the regardlessness and mindlessness of nature.' The resulting, and disturbing, strangeness of the book makes sense when seen 'in the light of the pervasive presence of Darwin in Hardy's imagination.' The match between 'Darwin's questioning of species categorization' and Hardy's temperamental predisposition to see this 'as demonstrating that categories are fictions' encourages a juxtaposition of incompatibilities that helps account for the distinctive generic nature – by turns tragic, comic, farcical, and melodramatic – of Hardy's novel.

Levine's invocation of Michael Millgate's claim for the ease with which the young Hardy could range 'ideas newly derived from Darwin and Huxley' with 'the necessitarian views already instilled in him by both the peasant fatalism of his upbringing and the tragic patterns of the Greek dramatists'[22] points us nicely in the direction of the final article on Hardy's fiction, Jeremy Steele's 'Plato and the Love Goddess: Paganism in Two Versions of *The Well-Beloved*.' The two versions in question are the text as it appeared in 1897 as Hardy's last published novel and the serial version, *The Pursuit of the Well-Beloved*, as it had appeared five years earlier in the *Illustrated London News*. Steele's essay returns to the focus on allusion with which this collection began, with Hardy's readings in Plato as the primary informing influence here. The shift in narrative direction between the serial and book versions allows for another perspective on the continued generic instabilities of Hardy's fiction at the point at which he was preparing to take his departure from it.

The three essays on the poetry approach their subjects from very different viewpoints. Contemporary readers of Hardy's poetry are so used to reading it either as part of a collected edition or in the piecemeal form necessitated by anthology selection that it is difficult to imagine it into existence in the forms in which it was collected for an early readership: individual books of verse, each with an organizational principle of its own, however compromised by the exigencies of drawing together individual poems written as often as not over an extended period of time. William W. Morgan's 'Aesthetics and Thematics in Hardy's Volumes of Verse: The Example of *Time's Laughingstocks*' considers the volume of verse as book, the only context for a relational presentation of a number of poems over which the poet himself might be said to have some degree of control. While we never will read *Time's Laughingstocks* as a book in a way fully analogous to that in which we read *Tess of the d'Urbervilles*, Morgan's approach opens to view principles of structure within the volume – and by extension other volumes of poetry – that were fundamental to Hardy's presentational conception of his work.

Samuel Hynes's essay, 'Hardy and the Battle God,' discusses Hardy as a war poet, taking its direction from the paradox that he is rarely thought of as one, so routinely is the designation applied only to those who fight in wars as well as write poems about them. Yet his lifetime saw such changes in the nature of both wars and ways of thinking about them that his attitudes to a subject that both horrified and fascinated him were in their way as contradictory as his responses to religious belief. Hynes's identification of two Hardy voices, one the more familiar articulator of war's pity, the other 'the martial voice in love with the old wars,' is located poignantly against those conflicts, primarily the Boer War and the First World War, through which he lived.

Norman Page's 'Opening Time: Hardy's Poetic Thresholds' completes this grouping of essays on Hardy's poetry by exploring their openings. Hardy's poetry is so frequently associated with endings – the parting of lovers, death, the recurrent cadences of closure at the end of volumes of verse any one of which could so easily have been his last, the slow inevitability of the movement to his final resolution to say no more – that this focus on strategies of beginning is a novel and suggestive one. Page identifies tonal and lexical idiosyncrasies that by seeming to emphasize the fragmentary complicate the relationship between speaker, supposed interlocutor, and eavesdropping reader. The obliquities and evasions, despite the ubiquity of the first-person pronoun, suggest the reticence of Hardy's temperament, even as he embarks on the communicative act of writing poetry of a kind that gives public expression, at times almost obsessively, to private emotion. Page identifies a distinctive Hardyan poetic voice 'so restrained as to be ... barely audible,' rendering its enduring power to speak across the generations all the more remarkable.

The volume closes with a return to the biographical and contextual, not as we began, in consideration of those authors and texts, sacred and secular, by which Hardy was influenced, but in relation to the family of younger writers who became collectively another literary voice of 'Wessex,' and for whom Hardy was a revered inspirational presence. W.J. Keith's 'Thomas Hardy and the Powyses' provides not only an expansive sense of Hardy's relationship with this singular fraternity of writers but also an adumbration of his wider influence on modernism, a modernism 'typical of a world torn between the opposed challenges of progressivism and radical conservation.' Given the starting point of this collection, Keith's speculation that 'the Powyses admired Hardy for his example in the delicate area of religious belief and practice' is a telling one. The Powys brothers might be said to share with Hardy what Keith terms in relation to the atheistic Llewelyn Powys 'a life-affirming religion that does not depend upon belief.'

It is to the life-affirming qualities of Hardy's writing that Hardy scholars and enthusiasts always seem to find themselves vigorously attesting, even in the face of the copious textual evidence of his sceptical view of a universe that seems to offer limited possibilities for human felicity. There is an obvious irony in the fact that the same writer who feelingly laments the loss of 'primal rightness' after 'the disease of feeling germed' and yearns for the reaffirmation of nescience can also, with equal conviction, imagine himself remembered for an exceptional responsiveness to the fleeting visual gifts of a quasi-sacramental natural world – as a man who 'used to notice such things.'[23] In such paradoxes is seen the complexity of the sensibility with which these new essays engage, to the understanding of which Michael Millgate has contributed so much.

On his eighty-first birthday, Hardy received a congratulatory address from 106 younger writers expressing their gratitude for his work: 'We thank you, Sir, for all that you have written ... but most of all, perhaps, for *The Dynasts*.'[24] We live in a less confident critical world and are therefore a little uncomfortable with affirming distinctions of value that time has an unfortunate habit of rearranging. It would be a rash commentator on Michael Millgate's work who would attempt to give convincing primacy to any single aspect of his many contributions – biographical, editorial, scholarly, and critical – to Hardy studies. Thus our final words of thanks to Michael, while echoing those made to Hardy, will stop cautiously at the ellipsis marks. We simply thank him for all that he has written. We also anticipate with great pleasure what is still to come.

NOTES

1 A year before the appearance of Larkin's new anthology, Donald Davie had paved the way for its foregrounding of Hardy by challengingly advancing in the first sentence of his *Thomas Hardy and British Poetry* (New York: Oxford University Press, 1972) the novel thesis 'that in British poetry of the last fifty years ... the most far-reaching influence, for good and ill, has been not Yeats, still less Eliot or Pound, not Lawrence, but *Hardy*' (3).
2 Philip Larkin, 'Wanted: Good Hardy Critic,' *Critical Quarterly* 8 (1966): 174–9.
3 Ibid., 178. Morrell eventually replied to this review when Larkin collected it in *Required Writing: Miscellaneous Pieces 1955–82* (1983): see Roy Morrell, 'Mr Philip Larkin, Tess and Thomas Hardy,' *The Thomas Hardy Journal* 1 (1985): 40–6.
4 As was so often the case, the benchmark for grudgingness had long since

been enduringly established by F.R. Leavis, who having proclaimed early that 'his rank as a major poet rests upon a dozen poems' (*New Bearings in English Poetry* [1932; Harmondsworth: Penguin 1963], 53) later reined in this uncustomary generosity and reduced it to half a dozen ('Hardy the Poet,' *Southern Review* 6 [1940]: 87–98).

5 'The Function of Criticism at the Present Time,' *Essays in Criticism: First Series* (1865; London: Macmillan, 1932), 7.

6 F.R. Southerington, *Hardy's Vision of Man* (London: Chatto & Windus, 1971), facing 136.

7 Michael Millgate, *Thomas Hardy: A Biography* (Oxford: Oxford University Press, 1982), 106. For key stages in the demolition of the Tryphena's-son-by-Hardy story see F.B. Pinion, *A Hardy Companion* (London: Macmillan, 1968), 435–40; Robert Gittings, 'Thomas Hardy and Tryphena Sparks,' *Times Literary Supplement* 27 April 1973, 477–8, and Gittings, *Young Thomas Hardy* (London: Heinemann, 1975), 223–9.

8 She was, for example, omnipresent throughout J.O. Bailey's expansive *The Poetry of Thomas Hardy: A Handbook and Commentary* (Chapel Hill: University of North Carolina Press, 1970), which was particularly unfortunate since it was only the fifth book ever to have been written on Hardy's poetry, and in its worthy aim of providing at least some commentary, however brief, on every Hardy poem it might, unencumbered with Tryphena and allied biographical will-o'-the-wisps, have been a more useful one.

9 *The Letters of Thomas Hardy, Transcribed from the Original Autographs Now in the Colby College Library*, ed. Carl J. Weber (Waterville, ME: Colby College Press, 1954 [1970]), and *'Dearest Emmie': Thomas Hardy's Letters to His First Wife*, ed. Carl J. Weber (London: Macmillan, 1963). See also *Thomas Hardy's Correspondence at Max Gate: A Descriptive Check List*, ed. Carl J. Weber and Clara Carter Weber (Waterville, ME: Colby College Press, 1968). To these was later added *One Rare Fair Woman: Thomas Hardy's Letters to Florence Henniker 1893–1922*, ed. Evelyn Hardy and F.B. Pinion (London: Macmillan, 1972).

10 *Thomas Hardy's Notebooks, and Some Letters from Julia Augusta Martin*, ed. Evelyn Hardy (London: Hogarth Press, 1955) and *The Architectural Notebook of Thomas Hardy*, ed. C.J.P. Beatty (Dorchester: Dorset Natural History and Archaeological Society, 1966).

11 Richard Little Purdy, *Thomas Hardy: A Bibliographical Study* (Oxford: Clarendon, 1954). This has recently been reissued with an introduction and supplement by Charles P.C. Pettit (London: The British Library, 2002).

12 *The Literary Notes of Thomas Hardy*, ed. Lennart A. Björk, 2 vols (Göteborg:

Acta Universitatis Gothoburgensis, 1974). The full edition of these note-
books was later published as *The Literary Notebooks of Thomas Hardy*, ed.
Lennart A. Björk, 2 vols (London: Macmillan, 1985). The two 'Memoranda'
notebooks, the 'Schools of Painting Notebook,' and 'The Trumpet-Major
Notebook,' appeared as *The Personal Notebooks of Thomas Hardy*, ed. Richard
H. Taylor (London: Macmillan, 1978). The most recent Hardy notebook to
be made available is *Thomas Hardy's 'Facts' Notebook: A Critical Edition*, ed.
William Greenslade (Aldershot: Ashgate, 2004).

13 Robert Gittings, *Young Thomas Hardy* (London: Heinemann, 1975) and *The
Older Hardy* (London: Heinemann, 1978).

14 *The Complete Poems of Thomas Hardy*, ed. James Gibson (London:
Macmillan, 1976), and *The Complete Poems of Thomas Hardy: A Variorum
Edition*, ed. James Gibson (London: Macmillan, 1979).

15 *The Life and Work of Thomas Hardy*, ed. Michael Millgate (London:
Macmillan, 1984), 407. Hereafter cited as *LW*.

16 *LW*, 33–4.

17 F.A. Hedgcock's reference to him in *Thomas Hardy, penseur et artiste* (1911)
as '*ce Saxon autodidacte*' provoked Hardy into a marginal annotation in his
own copy of Hedgcock's book: 'This is not literary criticism, but imperti-
nent personality & untrue, as he was taught Latin & French at School and
college' (see Michael Millgate, *Thomas Hardy: His Career as a Novelist*
(London: Bodley Head, 1971), 38.

18 Thomas Hardy to J.W. Mackail, 13 August 1916, *The Collected Letters of
Thomas Hardy*, ed. Richard Little Purdy and Michael Millgate, 7 vols
(Oxford: Clarendon, 1978–88), 5:174.

19 *LW*, 20.

20 See *Fifty-Seven Poems by Thomas Hardy*, ed. Bernard Jones (Gillingham,
Dorset: Meldon House, 2002).

21 Dennis Taylor, *Hardy's Poetry, 1860–1928* (London: Macmillan, 1981), 105.

22 Millgate, *Biography*, 132.

23 'Before Life and After' and 'Afterwards,' in *The Complete Poetical Works of
Thomas Hardy*, ed. Samuel Hynes, 5 vols (Oxford: Clarendon, 1982–95),
1:333 and 2:308–9.

24 *LW*, 446.

THOMAS HARDY REAPPRAISED:
ESSAYS IN HONOUR OF MICHAEL MILLGATE

1 The Gospel According to Hardy

In February 1920, when he was in his eightieth year, Hardy received an invitation to be included in Joseph McCabe's *A Biographical Dictionary of Modern Rationalists*. His reply, sent over Florence Hardy's signature, no doubt surprised McCabe: '[Mr Hardy] says he thinks he is rather an irrationalist than a rationalist, on account of his inconsistencies. He has, in fact, declared as much in prefaces to some of his poems where he explains his views as being mere impressions that frequently change. Moreover, he thinks he could show that no man is a rationalist, and that human actions are not ruled by reason at all in the last resort.'[1] Hardy's inclusion of the letter in *Life and Work* makes it part of the 'official' record, part of the self-portrait that he created in his late seventies and eighties in the hope that it would become the standard, unchallenged account of both his life and his work.[2] The prefaces that he invokes – written not only for several poetry volumes but also for some of the prose – further contribute to this self-portrait. Like *Life and Work*, they were written in the wake of the furore caused by the publication of *Tess of the d'Urbervilles* and especially of *Jude the Obscure*.

Hardy's earliest insistence that a literary work is 'an impression, not an argument,' in fact appears in his highly defensive preface to the so-called Fifth Edition of *Tess* published in 1892.[3] Three years later he (unsuccessfully) attempted to forestall outraged response to *Jude* by concluding the preface to the first volume edition with a similar disclaimer: 'Like former productions of this pen, *Jude the Obscure* is simply an endeavour to give shape and coherence to a series of seemings, or personal impressions, the question of their consistency or their discordance, of their permanence or their transitoriness, being regarded as not of the first moment.'[4] Similar statements subsequently appeared in the prefaces to *Poems of the Past and the Present* (1901) and *The Dynasts, Part First* (1903), the general preface to the Wessex Edition (1911), the prefatory note to *Life and Work* (c. 1917–19), and the 'Apology' in *Late Lyrics and Earlier* (1922). It is therefore not surprising that Hardy's final prefatory word, the introductory note he drafted for *Winter Words* (published posthumously in 1928), should conclude: 'I also repeat what I have often stated on such occasions, that no harmonious philosophy is attempted in these pages – or in any bygone pages of mine, for that matter.'[5]

Hardy was of course quite correct to insist that an author's literary works, individually and collectively, can give expression to any number of (contradictory) views and that novels and poems are not intended to be read as philosophical treatises. More problematic is his insistence on his own inconsistencies, since his personal views, philosophical and otherwise, seem to have been fundamentally consistent throughout most of his adult life. It is true that our sense of those views depends primarily upon published and archival materials from Hardy's later years: by the 1890s, when he was in his fifties, Hardy was a well-established if somewhat notorious literary figure who felt able to articulate his views more directly in essays, speeches, and – in spite of what the prefaces might suggest – verse; during these years of celebrity his correspondence also increased substantially and much more of it was preserved; and *Life and Work*, not begun until 1917, inevitably emphasizes the elderly Hardy's opinions, which equally inevitably would have dictated both the selection for inclusion and the representation of autobiographical material from his earlier years.[6] Nonetheless, these late articulations of Hardy's philosophical position are not contradicted by the surviving letters and other documentary materials of the 1870s and 1880s, and therefore probably constitute a reasonably accurate representation of his adult views, at least from the point during his young manhood at which he ceased to believe in Christian orthodoxy until his death at eighty-seven. With his loss of orthodox belief came an acknowledged inability to comprehend 'the Whence and the Wherefore of things,' but he had no doubt about the existence of 'the *Cause of Things*, whatever that cause may be,' and whatever it may be called: God, the Prime or First Cause, the Invariable Antecedent, the Will, and so forth.[7] Hardy accordingly maintained that 'no modern thinker can be an atheist in the modern sense, while all modern thinkers are atheists in the ancient and exploded sense,' having rejected belief in 'a tribal god, man-shaped, fiery-faced and tyrannous.'[8] Hardy also rejected the 'Good-

God theory,' his acute identification with the world's suffering rendering him incapable of either emotional or intellectual belief in a benevolent, omnipotent God, and ultimately leading him to conclude that the
Cause of Things must be unconscious, 'neither moral nor immoral, but
*un*moral,' like the 'purblind Doomsters' in one of his earliest poems,
'Hap,' dated 1866, or the 'Aimless' Causer in 'A Philosophical Fantasy,'
dated 1920 and 1926 and published a year before his death.[9] In a letter
of 1907 Hardy defined this 'philosophy of life,' most recently articulated in *The Dynasts, Part First and Part Second*, as 'that which I had
shaped out in my previous volumes of verse (& to some extent prose),
as being a generalized form of what the thinking world had gradually
come to adopt, myself included.'[10]

The process of writing *The Dynasts* also led Hardy to develop his
personal belief that the Unconscious Will was evolving, gradually becoming conscious and 'ultimately, it is to be hoped, sympathetic,'[11] as
predicted by the final *Dynasts* Chorus:

> *a stirring thrills the air*
> *Like to sounds of joyance there*
> *That the rages*
> *Of the ages*
> *Shall be cancelled, and deliverance offered from the darts that were,*
> *Consciousness the Will informing, till It fashion all things fair!*
>
> (After Scene, ll. 105–10, *CPW*, 5:255)

Hardy's references in his letters to the Will's evolution – and his insistence on the originality of the idea – suggest the centrality of this
optimistic concept to his philosophical thought.[12] In *Life and Work*,
however, he claimed not only that the 'mad and brutal' world war had
destroyed his long-held 'belief in the gradual ennoblement of man' but
also that 'he would probably not have ended *The Dynasts* as he did end
it if he could have foreseen what was going to happen within a few
years' (*LW*, 398). It is certainly true that during his final decade – the
years in which he was writing *Life and Work* – Hardy's belief in evolutionary progress of any kind was considerably shaken. His birthday
reflections of both 1919 and 1920 led him to lament that material and
scientific development had resulted in so little 'real improvement in the
world': 'People are not more humane ... Disinterested kindness is less.'[13]
Even so, two years later in the *Late Lyrics* 'Apology' Hardy was once
again able to express his hope – a perhaps 'forlorn hope' – in the world's

progress: 'if it be true, as Comte argued, that advance is never in a straight line, but in a looped orbit, we may, in the ... ominous moving backward, be doing it *pour mieux sauter*, drawing back for a spring' (*CPW*, 2:325). If none of Hardy's surviving postwar letters refers to the Will's parallel evolution and advance, the last of his extended philosophical speculations in verse, 'A Philosophical Fantasy,' reiterates all the essentials of his prewar thought. The 'Causer' defines itself as 'Aimless,' 'unconscious,' *'purposeless propension* ... Along lines of least resistance,' and insists that it has no ethical sense (ll. 19, 65, 128, 142–4, 103–7, *CPW*, 3:235–8). It also claims, however, both that it is willing to learn and that its state of unconsciousness may already be evolving:

> – I would add that, while unknowing
> Of this justice earthward owing,
> Nor explanation offering
> Of what is meant by suffering,
> Thereof I'm not a spurner,
> Or averse to be a learner.
>
> ...
>
> Aye, to human tribes nor kindlessness
> Nor love I've given, but mindlessness,
> Which state, though far from ending,
> May nevertheless be mending.   (ll. 116–21, 130–3, *CPW*, 3:237–8)

'A Philosophical Fantasy' is of course an imaginative work and, as Hardy himself repeatedly insisted, there is a 'vast difference between the expression of fancy and the expression of belief.'[14] Still, that Hardy considered the poem to be important – and perhaps even representative of his personal views – is suggested by his publishing it in the *Fortnightly Review* as his 1927 new year's poem, by his extensive revision of both the manuscript and the published text, and especially by his citation in *Life and Work* of its most optimistic lines (130–3, quoted above) and definition of its philosophy as 'much as he had set forth before,' with 'a ray of hope ... for the future of mankind.'[15]

Even as Hardy criticized the reading of his works of art as if they were both an expression of his personal convictions and 'a scientific system of philosophy' (*LW*, 406), he inevitably pointed to those same works of art when asked to clarify his philosophical views. Thus, in contradicting the poet Alfred Noyes's assumption that Hardy's 'pessimism' necessitated a belief in a malign Power, the eighty-year-old Hardy emphasized that 'a writer's opinions should be judged as a whole, and not from picked passages that contradict them as a whole,' and that he had 'defined in scores of places,' in '"The Dynasts" as well as in short poems,' his own conviction that the Cause of Things 'neither good nor evil knows.'[16] Writing to John Addington Symonds more than thirty years earlier, Hardy had similarly acknowledged the correspondence between his fictional work and his personal world view:

> The tragical conditions of life imperfectly denoted in The Return of the Native & some other stories of mine I am less & less able to keep out of my work. I often begin a story with the intention of making it brighter & gayer than usual; but the question of conscience soon comes in; & it does not seem right, even in novels, to wilfully belie one's own views. (14 April 1889, *CL* 1:190)

Critics past and present therefore can perhaps be forgiven for attempting to infer Hardy's philosophy from his literary works and indeed for labelling him, as he lamented in *Life and Work*, 'Nonconformist, Agnostic, Atheist, Infidel, Immoralist, Heretic, Pessimist or something else equally opprobrious in their eyes,' but never 'what they might have called him much more plausibly – churchy; not in an intellectual sense, but in so far as instincts and emotions ruled' (*LW*, 407).

Hardy's instinctual and emotional 'churchiness' has in fact been discussed by a number of recent critics, most notably Timothy Hands, who rightly draws attention to Hardy's family associations with the Church of England, his conviction that the church was – and should remain – the social, ethical, and educational centre of a community, his lifelong love of church music and the language of the Bible and the Book of Common Prayer, his continued, if irregular, attendance at church services, and his wistful expression in such poems as 'The Impercipient' and 'The Oxen' of a desire for traditional belief.[17] On the other hand, there has been virtually no acknowledgment of how intellectually 'churchy' Hardy was, especially during his young manhood, but also, in some respects, after his movement away from orthodox belief. This critical oversight can be attributed both to the paucity of surviving documentary materials from Hardy's early years and to the influence of his retrospective self-representation in *Life and Work*. It is, after all, Hardy himself who insisted that he was not 'churchy' in an intellectual sense, and his acknowledgment later in that same *Life and Work* passage of his childhood dream of becoming a parson and his youthful attempts to realize this dream by reading for Cambridge is qualified by his positioning himself as one of the 'many people brought up under Church-of-England influences' who wished that 'modern ideas' could be given 'liturgical form' and expressed in 'the same old buildings that had already seen previous reforms successfully carried out' (*LW*, 407). Earlier in *Life and Work* he claimed that his idea of becoming 'a curate in a country village' was a 'curious scheme' formulated during his mid-twenties in order to enable him to combine poetry and the Church, and that the plan fell through 'less because of its difficulty than from a conscientious feeling, after some theological study, that he could hardly take the step with honour while holding the views that on examination he found himself to hold' (*LW*, 53). *Life and Work* never suggests that Hardy underwent a classic Victorian loss of faith or indeed that he ever had a sustained, personal faith to lose.

It is therefore not surprising that Michael Millgate – and numerous others following his lead – should conclude that Hardy's 'attraction to the Church seems always to have depended not so much upon intellectual conviction as upon the emotional appeal of its rituals,' and that 'his early adherence to Anglican principles was largely automatic, taken for granted upon the basis of family and local example.'[18] The surviving documentary evidence, however, points to a different conclusion. On 24 October 1858, the eighteen-year-old Hardy wrote the following sermon, published here for the first time:

Galatians III.13. Christ hath redeemed us from the curse of the law, being made a curse for us –

On first reading this passage we should naturally ask why is the law a curse to us? How was Christ made a curse for us? Why did he thus redeem us? The better to understand our text I shall divide it into these three divisions[:] first – The law is a curse to us. Now it is well known that the law was given by God to the Children of Israel on Mount Sinai as a rule for their lives but he well knew that it was impossible that any descendant of Adam should keep this law[,] for St Paul says[,] If ye break one of my Commandments ye are guilty of All[,] & we all see that though it may be possible to keep some of his commandments[,] as Thou shalt do no murder, Thou shalt not steal, yet who can plead innocent to those of the heart, as Thou shalt not covet, Remember the sabbath day &c. – Who has never wronged the Sabbath by thought or deed? Who has not looked with envy upon his neighbour. Not one of us my brethren. Thus we see that we are all condemned by that law and under the curse of sin & death –

Secondly. Christ was made a curse for us. Now we have seen that we cannot keep the law & therefore should have been eternally condemned had not God in his infinite mercy opened his bowels of compassion for us[,] & sent his only Son Jesus to bear all the punishment the law inflicted[.] He was made a curse for us[,] all the weight of our sins were put upon him for us[,] he suffered all the indignity man could heap upon him & lastly suffered death upon the cross, between two thieves[,] with the burden of the sins of the whole world upon him which in the anguish of his spirit caused him to cry My God! why hast thou forsaken me! Truly he was made a curse for us, was bruised for our iniquities & the chastisement of our peace was upon him[;] he was made the scape goat for us, sacrificed for us in the same manner as the goat the priest sacrificed for the sins of the Israelites: this goat being a type of him and all for us unworthy creatures.

Thirdly why did he thus redeem us? There was no selfish calculation in all this[:] it was pure, unbounded love, love for the creatures he had made[,] fallen as they were, love for you & me my brethren. How can we then reject him[,] crucify him afresh, put him to an open shame. Oh turn to him & live, believe on him, take his burden upon you[,] for he hath said my yoke is easy & my burden is light. There is no fear of being rejected, Whosoever cometh to me I will in no wise cast out. My hearers there is no other way[.] Through him & him alone can we hope to be saved[.] Accept his invitation[.] Come to me all ye that labour & are heavy laden & I will give you rest. Do not delay brethren. The night is far spent[,] the day is at hand[.] Put ye on the whole armour of light.[19]

On first reading this passage we should naturally ask (to return to its opening words): can Hardy have written this? A more un-Hardyan composition in terms of either style or content seems difficult to imagine. The only surviving literary work from Hardy's teenage years is 'Domicilium,' identified by Hardy as his *earliest known production in verse* and dated *'between 1857 and 1860,'*[20] though not published until 1916 – and presumably then only after extensive revision by the septuagenarian poet. Unlike 'Domicilium,' the sermon has little literary merit. That it is Hardy's work cannot, however, be disputed. Its numerous false starts, revisions, insertions, and so forth,[21] indicate that it is a creative work in progress rather than a reconstruction of someone else's reflections, and it is both signed and dated.

In October 1858 Hardy was in the third year of his articles to John Hicks, a Dorchester architect; among his personal friends were his fellow pupil Henry Bastow, an ardent Baptist, and Henry, George, Charles, Handley, and especially Horace Moule, sons of Henry Moule, the Evangelical vicar of Fordington, much admired for his social activism, practical inventions, and powerful preaching. Theological discussion was evidently a common feature of Hardy's youthful friendships: Bastow, having been baptized in September 1858, evinced all the zealous concern for Hardy's personal salvation that would later lead to heated arguments about paedo-baptism and, after Bastow's departure for Tasmania in 1860, to reiterated pleas for Hardy to stand firm in the faith; the Moule brothers discussed the issues of the day with Hardy and gave him several books, both conventional and controversial, including (in the latter category) Horace's April 1858 gift of Gideon Algernon Mantell's *The Wonders of Geology*, the original acquisition of which had led to a Moule family conflict similar to that depicted in *Tess of the d'Urbervilles* when Angel orders an irreligious book.[22]

It was within this context of discussion and debate, then, that Hardy on Sunday, 24 October 1858, wrote an orthodox Evangelical sermon, remarkable primarily for its brevity and its integration of so many Christian clichés and stock quotations, including Isaiah 53:5 ('he was bruised for our iniquities ...'), Matthew 11:28–30 ('Come unto me, all ye that labour and are heavy laden ...'), and Romans 13:12 ('The night is far spent, the day is at hand ...'). On the other hand, the text for Hardy's sermon, Galatians 3:13, is not a stock quotation; nor was Galatians 3 one of the lessons for 24 October 1858. Galatians 3 was, however, one of the Evening Prayer lessons the previous Sunday, and Hardy may have heard it read at that service or, if he was following the lectionary in his private devotions, he may have read it at home that day. In any case, the following Sunday found him – appropriately enough given his desire to take holy orders – attempting to develop his sermon-writing skills and to come to terms with a difficult theological concept. The very few markings in the Bible (published in 1819) that Hardy was using in 1858[23] reveal – as does the sermon – a fascination with Judeo-Christian concepts of sin, judgment, and redemption. Hardy marked, for example, Jeremiah 36:7 ('It may be they will present their supplication before the Lord, and will return every one from his evil way: for great is the anger and the fury that the Lord hath pronounced against this people'), Matthew 7:19 ('Every tree that bringeth not forth good fruit is hewn down, and cast into the fire'), and Galatians 2:19–20 ('For I through the law am dead to the law, that I might live unto God. I am crucified with Christ: nevertheless I live; yet not I, but Christ liveth in me: and the life which I now live in the flesh I live by the faith of the Son of God, who loved me, and gave himself for me'). In 1861 Hardy acquired a new Bible (published in 1859), which he used for nearly forty years, marking passages and often dating his reading and his church atten-dance.[24] Numerous markings in this Bible confirm the continuing sig-nificance of sin, judgment, and redemption for Hardy, at least during what he would later refer to as his 'theological days' (the early 1860s),[25] when he marked a number of doctrinal passages in Romans, including 6:23 ('For the wages of sin is death; but the gift of God is eternal life through Jesus Christ our Lord') and 8:1 ('There is therefore now no condemnation to them which are in Christ Jesus, who walk not after the flesh, but after the Spirit').

Hardy's sermon and Bible markings support Bastow's claim – hith-erto regarded with some scepticism – that Hardy as a young man had a personal faith of a distinctly Evangelical cast. Bastow's letters, written from Tasmania during the early 1860s, exhort Hardy to be faithful, both to Jesus and to Evangelical teaching:

> You know as well as I that you once professed to love a crucified saviour – and to know him as yours – oh: cling to him. – be faithful.
>
> Dear old Tom dont you let your eye get off Jesus. – I did hear a whisper that *you* had begun to think that *works may do something* in the way of salvation – but dear fellow if you think so – dont oh dont for a moment let it prevent your leaning for all your salvation on 'Him.'[26]

Although Hardy allowed the correspondence with Bastow to lapse in the mid-1860s, he kept Bastow's letters all his life and two months before his death expressed a desire to see again the friend of his youth (*LW*, 478). Such acts bear witness to the importance of the friendship to Hardy – and perhaps also to the importance of those lost 'theological' days.'

Hardy's sermon, read in conjunction with his Bible markings and Bastow's letters, provides a unique glimpse into his early religious beliefs. As such, it is of considerable biographical significance. Timothy Hands claims that Hardy's interest in Evangelical churchmanship be-gan before the end of 1860 but after he left Bockhampton to live in Dorchester during the week, returning home only on weekends (an arrangement which Hands dates to 1859, though it was probably somewhat later).[27] Scholars have hitherto assumed that in 1858 Hardy was still worshipping regularly at Stinsford, the parish of his childhood, and that his churchmanship, like the vicar Arthur Shirley's, was moderately High. Their assumption is once again based upon Hardy's retrospective self-portrait in *Life and Work*, where he associates himself only with Stinsford, noting that in the mid-1850s he and Shirley's two sons taught the Sunday School and that a few years later he turned to Shirley for assistance in defending the Church's practice of paedo-baptism against the Bible-based arguments of Bastow and the Perkins brothers, sons of the local Baptist minister (*LW*, 30, 33). Hardy's sermon, however, indicates that he was both familiar with and sympathetic to Evangelical churchmanship as early as 1858. His knowledge of Evangelical preaching, demonstrated by his use of such exhortations as 'Oh turn to him & live, believe on him,' 'Do not delay brethren,' is not in itself surprising, given his friendship with the Moule family, but his explicit articulation and implicit acceptance of Evangelical belief seem distinctly un-Hardyan. And Hardy's comments in *Life and Work* about wishing to be a curate in a country village, being 'churchy,' and determining to 'stick to his own [Church] side' in debate with Bastow and the Perkinses, all suggest a kind of gentlemanly, unimpassioned faith, more social than religious, and fundamentally different from the Evangelical – and indeed evangelistic – zeal embodied in his sermon.[28]

As Hands has noted, however, Hardy's Bible markings indicate that Hardy was attending Evangelical services – as well as High Church services – from 1859 through the mid-1860s, and that at 10:45 PM on 17 April 1861 he evidently underwent some kind of religious experience that resulted in daily Bible reading.[29] What the sermon adds to this picture is evidence of Hardy's being already sympathetic to Evangelicalism by October 1858, of his taking sufficiently seriously his so-called dream of ordination to practise writing a sermon, and, most significantly, of his having a personal faith that was both ardent and orthodox. Thus Hardy's abandonment of his clerical ambitions – to say nothing of his loss of faith – must have involved more of a struggle than *Life and Work* suggests in its brief and rather dismissive account: 'he could hardly take the step [of taking holy orders] with honour while holding the views that on examination he found himself to hold' (*LW*, 53). Even the claim that this realization was made 'on examination' implies that Hardy did not experience a dramatic loss of faith, but that his views quietly evolved – or even that they were always present and not closely examined. Hardy, however, marked in both his 1819 Bible and his 1859

Bible Colossians 2:8 ('Beware lest any man spoil you through philosophy and vain deceit, after the tradition of men, after the rudiments of
the world, and not after Christ'),[30] a passage frequently turned to during the Victorian period when orthodox faith was challenged by scientific discoveries or philosophical thought, and it is tempting to speculate
that Hardy too sought reassurance from these words upon first encountering evolutionary theory and biblical criticism. *Life and Work* maintains that Hardy was one of the 'earliest acclaimers' of Darwin's *On the
Origin of Species* (1859) and that he had been 'impressed ... much' by the
notorious Broad Church collection *Essays and Reviews* (1860), but his
acceptance of such unorthodox views must have come only after a personal struggle and been accompanied by a sense of loss (*LW*, 158, 37).

   Thus one of the ironies of Hardy's self-representation in *Life and Work*
is that, while it insists on his philosophical inconsistencies, it in fact
creates an essentially consistent self-portrait, quietly passing over the
fervently Evangelical youth who would seem to have had little in
common with the author of *Jude the Obscure* and *The Dynasts*. Paradoxically, however, what is most striking about Hardy's 'non-Hardyan'
sermon is that even as it foregrounds the fundamental shift in his
religious beliefs it also demonstrates that his central preoccupations
remained unchanged throughout his entire life. The three points of the
sermon focus respectively on the law as curse, on suffering, and on
the saving force of love – all of which sounds very Hardyan indeed. The
eighteen-year-old Hardy, who already understood the consequences of
humanity's inability to keep the law ('Who has never wronged the
Sabbath by thought or deed? Who has not looked with envy upon his
neighbour ... [W]e are all condemned by that law'), would in his later
years fight in a multitude of ways against the death-dealing condemnation of the law, whether it be in publishing *Jude the Obscure*, with its
provocative epigraph 'The letter killeth' (2 Corinthians 3:6, which continues, 'but the spirit giveth life'), or in lamenting to his rationalist
friend Edward Clodd the 'deplorable ... effect of that terrible, dogmatic
ecclesiasticism – Christianity so called (but really Paulinism *plus* idola-
try) – on morals & true religion: a dogma with which the real teaching
of Christ has hardly anything in common' (17 January 1897, *CL*, 2:143).

   For the Hardy who could no longer subscribe to Christian orthodoxy,
that 'real teaching of Christ' was 'an ethical ideal'[31] based upon 'loving-
kindness' (the term Hardy used to describe selfless, compassionate
love, essentially synonymous with the Christian concept of charity). For
the Evangelical Hardy of eighteen, on the other hand, the 'real teaching

of Christ' centred on humanity's redemption through Christ's suffering, but that suffering, significantly enough, is defined as the embodiment of 'pure, unbounded love.' It is not surprising that the Hardy who spent seventy years reflecting upon life's 'general drama of pain' in creative works from *The Poor Man and the Lady* to *Winter Words* should as a youth have been moved by Christ's suffering, or that the Hardy who believed that 'pain to all ... tongued or dumb, shall be kept down to a minimum by loving-kindness' should have focused upon the love inherent in the gospel story.[32]

In many respects, Hardy, so often condemned as an atheist, remained throughout his life profoundly Christian, not only culturally and emotionally, but also ethically and even to some extent theologically. As Hardy in *Life and Work* wrote of the bishop who supposedly burnt *Jude the Obscure*, 'if the bishop could have known him as he was, he would have found a man whose personal conduct, views of morality, and of the vital facts of religion, hardly differed from his own' (*LW*, 295). In his 1922 'Apology' Hardy expressed his hope for a rational religion within the Church of England, which seemed to be 'showing evidence of "removing those things that are shaken,"' in accordance with the wise Epistolary recommendation to the Hebrews' (*CPW*, 2:324). Four years later, writing to a young ordinand who had publicly pointed out that many members of the Church could not give literal assent to all elements of the creeds, Hardy suggested that 'a simpler plan than that of mental reservation ... would be just to abridge the creeds & other primitive parts of the Liturgy, leaving only the essentials': 'if a strong body of young Reformers were to make a bold stand, in a sort of New Oxford Movement, they would have a tremendous backing from the thoughtful laity, & might overcome the retrogressive section of the Clergy.'[33] Hardy's letter suggests that he was sympathetic to Broad Church theology, even while his intellectual integrity prevented him from remaining within the Church. As he wrote in some notes (dated 1907 and included in *Life and Work*) for an 'ephemeral article,' entitled 'The Hard Case of the Would-be-Religious,' 'By Sinceritas':

> We enter church, and ... we say the established words full of the historic sentiment only, mentally adding, 'How happy our ancestors were in repeating in all sincerity these articles of faith!' But we perceive that none of the congregation recognizes that we repeat the words from an antiquarian interest in them, and in a historic sense, and solely in order to keep a church of some sort afoot – a thing indispensable; so that we are pretend-

ing what is not true; that we are believers. This must not be; we must leave. And if we do, we reluctantly go to the door, and creep out as it creaks complainingly behind us. (*LW*, 357–8)

If Hardy was not an orthodox Christian believer, he was not a rationalist either. In 1915, five years before he declined to be included in McCabe's *A Biographical Dictionary of Modern Rationalists*, he wrote to Caleb Saleeby, who had sent him a copy of Henri Bergson's *Creative Evolution*: 'You must not think me a hard-headed rationalist ... Half my time (particularly when I write verse) I believe – in the modern use of the word – not only in things that Bergson does, but in spectres, mysterious voices, intuitions, omens, dreams, haunted places, &c., &c.'[34] Hardy's belief in the Unconscious Will's becoming conscious and ultimately sympathetic is not, after all, a rationalist theory; rather, it is a theory that suggests that the darkling thrush may have some basis for its 'blessed Hope.'

The existence of pain remained the insurmountable problem in Hardy's desire to believe in an omnipotent, loving power. Responding to a suggestion in the *Daily News* of 14 March 1908 that his 'pessimism' must lead to despair, Hardy confessed: 'What does often depress me is the sight of so much pain in the world, constant pain; & it did just as much when I was an orthodox Churchman as now; for no future happiness can remove from the past sufferings that have been endured.'[35] The previous year, in his notes for 'The Hard Case of the Would-be-Religious,' he had reflected: 'We enter church, and ... we have to sing, "My soul doth magnify the Lord," when what we want to sing is, "O that my soul could find some Lord that it could magnify! Till it can, let us magnify good works, and develop all means of easing mortals' progress through a world not worthy of them"' (*LW*, 358). As a writer, Hardy's 'good works' were his literary works: 'What are my books but one plea against "man's inhumanity to man" – to woman – and to the lower animals?'[36] If theodicean issues prevented him from being able to fulfil Christ's first commandment – 'Thou shalt love the Lord thy God with all thy heart, and with all thy soul, and with all thy mind, and with all thy strength' – his life and work certainly strove towards the second: 'Thou shalt love thy neighbour as thyself' (Mark 12:30, 31). As one admirer of *The Dynasts* wrote in a letter that Hardy chose for inclusion in *Life and Work*, 'You have carried me on to the mountain with Jesus of Nazareth, and, viewing with him the great conflict below, one chooses with him to side with the Spirit of the Pities, in the belief that they will ultimately triumph; and even if they do not we at least will do our little to add to the joy rather than to the woe of the world' (*LW*, 363).

NOTES

1 18 February 1920, *The Collected Letters of Thomas Hardy*, ed. Richard Little Purdy and Michael Millgate, 7 vols (Oxford: Clarendon, 1978–88), 7:162. Hereafter cited as *CL*. This letter is also included in *The Life and Work of Thomas Hardy*, ed. Michael Millgate (London: Macmillan, 1984), 432. Hereafter cited as *LW*.

2 Most of *Life and Work* was written 1917–19, but the process of revision and composition concluded only with Hardy's death; see Millgate, introduction to *LW*, xii–xviii.

3 *Tess of the d'Urbervilles* (London: Osgood, McIlvaine, 1892), viii.

4 *Jude the Obscure* (London: Osgood, McIlvaine, 1896 [1895]), vi.

5 *The Complete Poetical Works of Thomas Hardy*, ed. Samuel Hynes, 5 vols (Oxford: Clarendon, 1982–95), 3:166. Hereafter cited as *CPW*.

6 That Hardy did not hesitate to revise his notebook entries and letters before including them in *Life and Work* can be demonstrated from surviving primary materials; see Millgate, introduction to *LW*, xiv–xvi.

7 General preface to the Wessex Edition, *Tess of the d'Urbervilles* (London: Macmillan, 1912), xlii; *LW*, 406.

8 *LW*, 406. The note is dated 1917; critics seeking support for Hardy's alleged atheism often cite an earlier note (dated 29 January 1890): 'I have been looking for God 50 years, and I think that if he had existed I should have discovered him' (*LW*, 234). They neglect to mention, however, that the 1890 note specifically defines 'God' in this context 'As an external personality, of course,' and that a note dated less than three months later assumes the existence of 'the Prime Cause or Invariable Antecedent' (*LW*, 234, 235). An 1899 note further states: 'It would be an amusing fact, if it were not one that leads to such bitter strife, that the conception of a First Cause which the theist calls "God," and the conception of the same that the so-styled atheist calls "no-God," are nowadays almost exactly identical' (*LW*, 326).

9 *LW*, 406; Hardy to Alfred Noyes, 20 December 1920, *CL*, 6:54 (also included in *LW*, 439); 'Hap,' l. 13, *CPW*, 1:10; 'A Philosophical Fantasy,' l. 65, *CPW*, 3:236. The earliest reference in *Life and Work* to the unconsciousness of the Cause of Things (identified as 'Law') is dated 9 May 1881 (153). For Hardy's rejection of theodicean arguments, see his letter published in *Academy and Literature*, 17 May 1902, in *Thomas Hardy's Public Voice: The*

Essays, Speeches, and Miscellaneous Prose, ed. Michael Millgate (Oxford: Clarendon, 2001), 175–6 (also included in *LW,* 338–9). See also Jon Roberts, 'Mortal Projections: Thomas Hardy's Dissolving Views of God,' *Victorian Literature and Culture* 31 (2003): 43–66.

10 Hardy to Edward Wright, 2 June 1907 (Hardy's sixty-seventh birthday), *CL,* 3:255 (also included in *LW,* 361). In *Life and Work* Hardy maintained that 'He had written his poems entirely because he liked doing them, without any ulterior thought; because he wanted to say the things they contained and would contain – mainly the philosophy of life afterwards developed in *The Dynasts'* (325).

11 Hardy to Wright, 2 June 1907, *CL,* 3:255.

12 Hardy to Wright, 2 June 1907; to Edward Clodd, 20 February 1908; to Valery Larbaud, 1 November 1908; and to Caleb Saleeby, 21 December 1914, *CL,* 3:255, 298, 351, and 4:70.

13 Hardy to Florence Henniker, 5 June 1919, *CL,* 5:309; *LW,* 435.

14 Hardy to Noyes, 20 December 1920, *CL,* 6:54.

15 *LW,* 470. Although Millgate claims that the concluding two chapters of *Life and Work* were 'written entirely by Florence Hardy,' he also notes that they incorporated 'much material her husband had left for just such a purpose' and that Hardy continued to work on the manuscript until his death (introduction, xxxiii and xviii). Moreover, the style of most of the passages in those two chapters, excluding 'Notes by F.E.H.' and the account of Hardy's last days, suggests that they were primarily Hardy's work. For Hardy's revision of 'A Philosophical Fantasy,' see *CPW,* 3:344–51.

16 Hardy to Noyes, 20 December 1920, *CL,* 6:54.

17 Timothy Hands, *Thomas Hardy: Distracted Preacher?* (Basingstoke: Macmillan, 1989) and the entries on 'religion' and 'hymns and metrical psalms' in *Oxford Reader's Companion to Hardy,* ed. Norman Page (Oxford: Oxford University Press, 2000). See also Jan Jędrzejewski, *Thomas Hardy and the Church* (Basingstoke: Macmillan, 1996).

18 Michael Millgate, *Thomas Hardy: A Biography* (Oxford: Oxford University Press, 1982), 91. Hereafter cited as *Biography.*

19 The sermon is written on the final two leaves of a notebook, catalogued as 'Copper-plate writing book. Some dates 1855. Ms. pencilled notes in rear Feb [*sic*] 24/58, signed "Thos Hardy" on text from Galatians III, 13' (Lock Collection, Dorset County Museum). I am grateful to the Trustees of the Estate of the late Miss E.A. Dugdale for permission to publish the sermon in its entirety.

20 Note on the manuscript (cited in *CPW,* 3:335).

21 For example, in the opening sentence 'should naturally ask' is a revision

of 'are struck by the words "the curse of the law,"' and in the second paragraph the following passage is an addition marked for insertion: 'he was made the scape goat for us, sacrificed for us in the same manner as the goat the priest sacrificed for the sins of the Israelites: this goat being a type of him.'

22　*Biography*, 63–8.

23　Dorset County Museum. Timothy Hands refers to this Bible as the 'Bastow Bible' (*Thomas Hardy*, 14), following Michael Millgate's assumption that the sheet of verses from the hymn 'Just as I am' written out by Bastow and inserted within this Bible functioned as a gift inscription (*Biography* 63–4, 65n.). However, in a conversation of 23 February 2004, Professor Millgate acknowledged it to be unlikely that Bastow would have given Hardy a second-hand Bible.

24　Dorset County Museum. The 1859 Bible was replaced by Emma Hardy's gift of a Bible on Hardy's fifty-ninth birthday, 2 June 1899 (Dorset County Museum).

25　On 20 February 1906 Hardy wrote to R. Bosworth Smith: 'I used to read the Gk. Testt [purchased in 1860] in my younger & theological days' (*CL*, 3:197).

26　23 December 1863 and 23 May 1862 (Dorset County Museum).

27　Hands, *Thomas Hardy*, 11, 13; see also *LW*, 40, and *Biography*, 61.

28　*LW*, 53, 407, 33. Note that Hardy's insistence on his being 'churchy' is preceded by his list of 'slurs' cast upon him by 'invidious critics' and that the list begins with 'Nonconformist.' Evangelical churchmen were by definition not Nonconformists, but they did hold similar theological views and were sometimes subject to similar social ostracism. Henry Moule's Evangelical enthusiasm, for example, initially alienated the Dorset gentry, who 'ostracised him as a Methodist' (Hands, *Thomas Hardy*, 18).

29　Hands, *Thomas Hardy*, 14–24. Hardy annotated Ephesians 5 'Wednesday night, April 17th/61, ¼ to 11'; his dating of Colossians 1 ('April 22nd 1861') and Titus 3 ('very warm – 16/5/61') suggests that he was reading a chapter a day (1819 Bible).

30　In the 1859 Bible only the first clause ('Beware lest any man spoil you through philosophy') is marked.

31　Hardy to Clodd, 27 February 1902, *CL*, 3:5. The letter articulates Hardy's long-held belief (compare, for example, his 20 November 1885 letter to John Morley, *CL*, 1:136–7) that 'If the doctrines of the supernatural were quietly abandoned to-morrow by the Church, & "reverence & love for an ethical ideal" alone retained, not one in ten thousand would object to the readjustment, while the enormous bulk of thinkers excluded by the old teaching would be brought into the fold, & our venerable old churches & cathedrals would become the centres of emotional life that they once were.'

32 *The Mayor of Casterbridge* (Oxford: Oxford University Press, 2004), 310; 'Apology,' *CPW*, 2:319.

33 Hardy to Roy McKay, 27 April 1926, *CL*, 7:21.

34 2 February 1915, *CL*, 5:79 (also included in *LW*, 400).

35 Hardy to A.G. Gardiner, 19 March 1908, *CL*, 3:308.

36 William Archer, 'Real Conversations: Conversation II. – With Mr. Thomas Hardy,' *Pall Mall Magazine* 22 (1901): 535.

2 'My Scripture Manner': Reading Hardy's Biblical and Liturgical Allusion

MARY RIMMER

Hardy's always complex relationships to texts and culture become still more complex when the text in question is the Bible or the Book of Common Prayer. To quote from or allude to a sacred text, even to the extent of a single resonant term, necessarily brings the concept of the sacred into play, and for Hardy that concept was fraught with difficulty, because he was always travelling away from belief in the sacred without ever quite leaving it behind. His 1890 note, 'I have been looking for God 50 years, and I think that if he had existed I should have discovered him,' is usually taken as a bleak statement of his loss of faith, but such a reading erases the idea of the fifty-year search: like so many of Hardy's statements about religion, this one foregrounds uncertainty and contingency ('I think that,' 'if he had existed I should have') as much as disbelief.[1] Moreover, for Hardy the words of Bible and prayer book were bound up with memories of his childhood, with family traditions of church music – in short with the 'old association'[2] that was so powerfully evocative for him, and intimately connected with his creative imagination. His early immersion in the Bible and his frequent use of it by no means make him an oddity among Victorians, for whom scriptural allusion was a 'habit of mind.'[3] Most writers of the period drew readily on the Bible, confident that any reasonably alert reader would decode their allusions. From Dissenters and Evangelicals who seasoned every discourse with biblical references, to agnostics such as Matthew Arnold whose texts reveal the impress of the Bible they no longer saw as revealed truth, Victorians were steeped in biblical language, and for those raised in the Church of England the prayer book too was a common source of vocabulary and allusion.[4] What sets Hardy's allusions apart is their shiftiness: the sacred and the secular mix freely in them, and they can be moving, ironic, playful and irreverently mocking, sometimes almost simultaneously; as Timothy Hands points out, Hardy 'uses Scriptural allusion like an Evangelical and agnostic combined.'[5] His allusions to Bible and prayer book at once reflect and resist the complex web of pieties that those texts represented to him, so that he may verge on blasphemy at times, and yet remain 'churchy,' to use the word he applied to himself in the *Life*.[6]

Even in a poem like 'God's Funeral,' whose very title would seem to rule belief out of the question, the haunting allusiveness of the language plays back and forth across the boundaries of belief. Using biblical words such as 'wrought,' 'loving-kindness,' and 'longsuffering,' or the cadence of hymns, as in 'ages rolled,' or echoes of both prayer book and Bible, as in 'mercies manifold,' Hardy couches varying shades of doubt in the phrases of faith.[7] The words, especially in the mourners' chant (VI–XII), invoke the sweetness of 'years far hied' (XI), when the mourners used to start the day with prayer and 'lie down liegely at the eventide / And feel a blest assurance he was there' (XI), lines that recall the last verse of Psalm 4, often used as an evening prayer: 'I will lay me down in peace, and take my rest:. for it is thou, Lord, only, that makest me dwell in safety.'[8] Still more explicitly, Psalm 137 ('By the waters of Babylon ...') becomes the basis of the mourners' plaint that they are 'Sadlier than those who wept in Babylon, / Whose Zion was a still abiding hope' (X).

These plangent echoes deepen the poem's uncertainties, and make it difficult to interpret a more subdued set of allusions to Matthew Arnold. Echoing Arnold's 'Dover Beach,' the 'twilit plain' (stanza I) and 'Darkling' (X) progress of the funeral procession seem to place the poem within the tradition of High Victorian agnosticism; Arnold might be identified with the mourners the speaker ultimately decides to follow, 'of whom / Some were right good, and many nigh the best ...' (XVII), although they form that most un-Arnoldian of groupings, a 'crowd' (XVII). The mourners, however, are not alone on the twilit plain; they are checked by two other groups, 'Some in the background' who call the funeral a 'counterfeit of straw' (XIII), and 'A certain few' who stand 'aloof' and point to a 'small light' (XVI) on the horizon. The speaker sympathizes with each group, recalling his past affinities with the faithful, following the procession as one of the mourners, and seeing the light even before the 'certain few' point it out: 'to my growing sight there seemed / A pale yet positive gleam low down behind' (XV).[9] 'Gleam' is perhaps another echo of 'Dover Beach,' but in Arnold's poem the light is deemphasized, appearing in the third line only to be quenched: 'on the French coast the light / Gleams and is gone.'[10] Though the Dover cliffs 'stand, / Glimmering and vast (4–5),' the light is soon forgotten as the poem turns towards the roar of grating shingle which figures misery and retreat from faith. The mental landscape of Arnold's 'darkling plain' (35) comes to dominate 'Dover Beach,' obscuring any hint of light or solace except that within human relationships. In 'God's Funeral,' by contrast, the gleam is persistent and unsettling, even though the speaker finally falls in with the mourners who cannot see it: 'Thus dazed and puzzled 'twixt the gleam and gloom / Mechanically I followed with the rest' (XVII).

Ending 'God's Funeral' with this move appears to align the speaker with the mourners and settle the issue in favour of God's demise, but since he goes along 'mechanically,' as a 'dazed' and 'puzzled' follower of a crowd, he hardly seems to make an active choice. The ending can no more settle the issue than the corpse, which shifts from a 'man-like' shape to 'an amorphous cloud of marvellous size, / At times endowed with wings of glorious range' (III), can settle into one form. It remains unclear whether 'this phantasmal variousness' (IV) in the mourned object comes from the speaker's 'blurred eyes' (III), from the darkness, from the possibility that the faithful are right – or from whatever the 'gleam' may mean. Rather than straightforward lack of conviction, the poem offers perhaps the purest type of agnosticism, in which the doubting subject is unsure of his own doubts. 'Dover Beach' ends by opposing human love to an external world which 'Hath really neither joy, nor love, nor light' (33), but Hardy's poem refuses such a resolution, providing neither a definitive statement of faith lost nor the consolation of a soulmate.[11]

The play of meaning around the Bible and questions of religious faith is inevitably social as well as personal. Given the Bible's centrality in Victorian culture, knowledge of and attitudes towards it were heavily inflected by class concerns. As Joss Marsh's study of nineteenth-century blasphemy has demonstrated, judgments in blasphemy trials frequently upheld the 'decent' language of the middle and upper classes (even when that language expressed atheism or agnosticism) against lower-class irreverence, transforming blasphemy into a class crime – a 'linguistic insurrection.'[12] Ironically, fears of such an insurrection were initially spurred by the many schools for the poor, started in the late eighteenth and early nineteenth centuries to make Bible-readers of the illiterate.[13] These schools may have enabled insurrectionary writing and reading, but they also made the Bible widely accessible. Moreover, the association they forged between literacy and Bible reading turned knowledge of the Bible into a marker of upward social mobility, the hallmark of decency and respectability.[14]

In Hardy's novels detailed biblical knowledge often gives its possessor social distinction. Consider for instance the final paragraph of *Far from the Madding Crowd*, where Joseph Poorgrass applies a quotation to Gabriel's and Bathsheba's marriage: 'I were once or twice upon saying to-day with holy Hosea in my scripture manner which is my second nature, "Ephraim is joined to idols: let him alone."'[15] R.H. Hutton is certainly both snobbish and inaccurate when he criticizes Hardy for giving his rustics more 'profane-minded familiarity with the Bible' than is consistent with the 'heavy, bovine character' of rural English workfolk, but Joseph's carefully nonchalant claim about his 'scripture manner' suggests a sense that biblical knowledge is praiseworthy, and by no means 'second nature' to anyone else in his circle.[16] To know one's Bible connotes at least literacy, and perhaps also an orientation towards middle-class values – or even upward social mobility. In Joseph's case social advance is probably stalled by his liking for alcohol, and consequent affliction by 'multiplying eye' (251), but as Gabriel points out, Joseph's biblical tags give him a useful cover even when he drinks, because he does his 'wicked deeds in such confoundedly holy ways' (251). Joseph's sense of scripture is almost talismanic rather than reverent: on this occasion, having left Fanny Robin's coffin outside the Buck's Head inn while he drinks himself tipsy, he tries to fend off Gabriel's anger with garbled references to 'King Noah' and to biblical texts (e.g., 'from my getting up to my going down of the same'), much as he kneels and recites all he knows 'out of book' (52) from the service of Morning Prayer to persuade a recalcitrant gate to open.[17]

Although Joseph may naively believe in the power of sacred words to raise his status and get him out of trouble, he sees no fundamental incongruity between his 'scripture manner' and his 'multiplying eye,' or between the prayer book and the stuck gate: his use of texts seems innocent rather than sacrilegious. In this he may be an alter-ego for Hardy, along with many other rustic characters for whom mixing 'holy ways' with 'wicked deeds,' or at least secular deeds, seems 'second nature.' Like Joseph, Hardy regards the Bible and prayer book as available to him for any purpose: he can readily draw on them as sources of powerful but familiar words that a good memory can make serviceable in all kinds of homely ways.

The extent of that serviceableness comes into sharper focus with Ethelberta Petherwin in Hardy's next novel – a character from a background not far removed from Joseph's but using secular and sacred words to assist a much more self-conscious and ambitious social ascent. A 'Comedy in Chapters,' as *The Hand of Ethelberta* is subtitled, seems an even odder place to find biblical allusion than the Buck's Head, but although Ethelberta draws on a variety of texts in her cultural and social performances, she and other characters come back frequently to the Bible, as does the narrator. Here the biblical references are darker than in *Far from the Madding Crowd*, often contributing an ironic counterpoint to the comic plot. Christopher Julian, for instance, finding his sister Faith in the British Museum's Assyrian gallery, tries to tell her about his break with Ethelberta; he interrupts her reverie about Sennacherib's attacks on Israel and on 'the fenced cities of Judah' (2 Kings 18:13), forcing her to exclude 'Sennacherib there and then from Christopher's affairs by the firm settlement of her features to a present-day aspect.'[18] There are comic overtones here, especially given the consonance between these 'deserted antiques' in the Museum basement and Faith's 'homely suit' of 'rusty black' (177), yet the contrast between the story of Sennacherib (which involves the destruction of whole communities) and Christopher's need for her as 'something to talk at' (176) also makes his woes seem petty.

Ethelberta's own biblical language is also sombre, though she invokes its elegiac possibilities in more complex and perhaps more self-indulgent ways than Faith. She uses the story of Lazarus and the rich man (Luke 16:19–31) to compare the impenetrable politeness of her society friends with the direct manners of her brothers: 'Between these and my poor crude Sol and Dan how great a gulf is fixed!' (198).[19] The reference implicitly critiques the idle socialites, who may find themselves in hell after death, like the rich man, separated by a great gulf from heaven, where Lazarus is rewarded for his earthly suffering. Yet the brothers do not fit the part of Lazarus. They are not helpless beggars, but skilled and increasingly successful workmen; a few pages earlier we have heard that they are changing under the influence of London, becoming 'less spontaneous and more comparative; less genial, but smarter' (190), though still loyal to their family. Ethelberta seems to type them nostalgically according to a fixed model rooted in memory, as though she has failed to notice, or does not wish to see, that Sol and Dan too are in flux, not static points against which she can measure her own meteoric rise. She focuses on her own lost connection to them and the open manners 'familiar to her in childhood, though impracticable now' (198); the greatest 'gulf' may be between Ethelberta and her own past.

Another elegiac biblical reference appears a few pages later, where Sol and Dan, waiting for Ethelberta at the Royal Academy, seem to her as 'big as the Zamzummims of old time' (179; Deuteronomy 2:20).[20] The phrase neatly registers her condescension towards her brothers, with their unpolished manners and 'painfully lavish exhibition of large new gloves' (179). Although the allusion does give them a dignity the fashionable Academy crowds lack, it is the dignity of temporal defeat: the Zamzummims, 'A people great, and many, and tall' (Deuteronomy 2:21), are said to have been destroyed by God and their land given to Lot's descendents. Again Ethelberta has used allusion to place Sol and Dan as she wants to see them: they resemble the ill-fated giants only in bulk, having clearer prospects before them than their precariously fashionable sister does. Her biblical references merge her childhood and family into the 'old time' of the Bible, both being at once emotionally resonant and largely inaccessible. This rhetorical move allows her to express her love for her relatives but also to suppress their agency in favour of her own as their guide and provider.

When Ethelberta retreats to Knollsea for a seaside holiday with her younger sisters, she becomes 'again Berta Chickerel as of old' (234), and for a while allusions retreat as well. But her encounter with Lord Mountclere and the Imperial Archaeological Association at Coomb Castle brings them back with a vengeance.[21] On her way there she sees the sunlit Channel on her right looking like 'a New Jerusalem' (237; Revelation 3:12, 21:2), contrasting with 'dark and cloudy weather' on her left, and reads the struggle between cloud and sun as 'typical of her own fortunes' (237), though cloud, metaphor, and allusion disappear quickly upon a change in the wind. The donkey she rents from a passing boy and has to hide from her 'four-wheeled friends' (236) is an apt emblem of 'Berta Chickerel,' a role now again pushed aside for that of the celebrated Mrs Petherwin. She pretends to know nothing of the animal, who looks at her 'as though he would say, "Why don't you own me, after safely bringing you over those weary hills?"' (241). The scene seems almost a parody of St Peter's denial of Christ, and the donkey a stray bit of the 'old time': as one Association member muses, 'the humble creature looks so aged and is so quaintly saddled that we may suppose it to be only an animated relic of the same date as the other remains' (239).[22] Ethelberta has joined the Association's expedition in part because the past attracts her, allowing her to contemplate 'the attenuating effects of time even upon great struggles' and so to correct 'the apparent scale of her own' (235). In the event, however, she abandons the donkey, the contemplation of history, and the possibility of reconnecting with her family 'as of old,' devoting herself anew to the struggle for 'the entry of drawing-rooms' (235), acquiescing in Mountclere's arthritic flirtation, and feeling 'The enjoyment of power in a new element' (248) when he cuts down elm trees he has planted in his boyhood to gratify her whimsical desire for a view of the sea from the ruins.

When Ethelberta returns to Knollsea, the complex tensions between her social ambition and family loyalty are again marked by biblical quotations. Fresh from juggling suitors at Coomb Castle, and finding that she has missed Christopher's visit by going there, she exclaims that there is nothing but 'vanity and vexation' (249; Ecclesiastes 1:14) in England and that she will go on to Normandy. The Ecclesiastes verse as a whole (a well-known one) underlines the futility of her decision: 'I have seen all the works that are done under the sun; and, behold, all is vanity and vexation of spirit.' To think of escaping such a universal 'vexation of spirit' by crossing the Channel is either to miss the point, or to assume that one's own history will somehow rise above the mortal condition. Ethelberta's perspective is further ironized when the children return from their day on the beach and begin to tell her 'of the wonders of the deep' (250; Psalms 107:24). Like the Ecclesiastes passage, this is a famous one: 'They that go down to the sea in ships: and occupy their business in great waters; These men see the works of the Lord: and his wonders in the deep.' Ethelberta's somewhat petulant quotation from Ecclesiastes contrasts sharply with the psalm's sense of awe. Like the psalmist, the children seem in touch with the sea as an elemental force, while for Ethelberta the sea has been merely a personal symbol, first of her struggle to keep her social place, and then, as it appears behind Mountclere's falling elms, of her power over an aged, infatuated lover.

Yet for all this, the biblical contexts given to both Ethelberta's and her siblings' perceptions suggest the enduring connections binding the family together. Even Sol, the most radical member of the Chickerel family, who stands aloof from Ethelberta's ambitions and denounces her marriage to Mountclere as 'A creeping up among the useless lumber' (376) of the nation, can invoke the Bible in a moment of passion, as he does when he calls Mountclere 'a d— old Philistine' (352). Sol may well see Ethelberta's frequent use of the Bible as part of her social performance, a display of the respectable knowledge that has earned her a provisional place among the wealthy, but he too finds the privileged text useful, if only for attacking the privileged. His father, though he acquiesces more readily in Ethelberta's plans, may be doing something similar when he tells Christopher how she has conquered the opposition she faces from Mountclere's servants and relatives after her marriage: 'one by one they got to feel there was somebody among them whose little finger, if they insulted her, was thicker than a Mountclere's loins' (403).

The ramifications of this allusion are complex. In Kings and Chronicles, Rehoboam, Solomon's son, is asked on his father's death to lighten the heavy burdens that Solomon has placed on the people; ignoring the older men, his father's counsellors, who advise him to comply, he listens instead to the young men, who tell him to increase the people's load and to say to them, 'My little finger shall be thicker than my father's loins' (1 Kings 12:10, 2 Chronicles 10:10). For Ethelberta the analogy with Rehoboam is ominous, since he not only shows bad judgment here, and loses a good part of his kingdom in consequence, but also later brings further punishment on the remnant, trusting in his fortifications rather than in God, and consequently suffering an Egyptian invasion. Although God spares him full punishment because he humbles himself, his record remains largely one of failure through arrogance, and the summing-up of his reign in Chronicles is negative: 'he did evil, because he prepared not his heart to seek the Lord' (2 Chronicles 12:14).[23] For Chickerel himself the quotation has uncomfortable ironies: a powerless patriarch long subject to his daughter's energetic management, he uses the passage to define her dominance of another older man, her noble husband – dominance which in the Bible turns on the association of manliness ('my father's loins') and the power of rule.

Ethelberta, already said by Christopher's gossipy driver to have become 'my lord and my lady both' (399), has beaten the odds stacked against her by gender and by class, but her father's comment perhaps unwittingly casts a shadow over the future of her hard-won kingdom, which we see only from a distance, at second hand. Like other biblical allusions in the novel, this valedictory one seems to twist in the hand, gesturing towards a threatening past of betrayal and defeat, and hinting at potential retribution for those who, as Sol puts it, have 'worked to false lines' (376). These suggestions lurk at the boundaries of the comedy of manners, suggesting the ultimate inability of polite fiction to keep the dark undercurrents hidden.[24]

Biblical allusion in *Far from the Madding Crowd* and *The Hand of Ethelberta* turns in one way or another on what Hands calls 'The suggestion of a stable community,' one located in 'years far hied,' but still linked to the present.[25] To move from these to a novel like *Jude the Obscure*, then, is initially to feel oneself in a very different fictional context, for Jude seems cut off from the past even more emphatically than Ethelberta, who like the mourners in 'God's Funeral' can at least remember what she no longer has. In *Jude*, by contrast, the past remains virtually inaccessible except for stray remarks from Aunt Drusilla and Mrs Edlin. Acquired through a brief and almost accidental contact with a village schoolmaster, Jude's hankering after Christminster, learning, and biblical knowledge is bare of 'old association.' No family habits of biblical quotation, no memories of a communal past, nor of fathers and grandfathers in parish choirs, wooing their future wives by 'Bowing "New Sabbath" or "Mount Ephraim,"'[26] link Jude to Bible or church, as Hardy was linked and as most of his characters are. An orphan boy with little awareness of his family's history, he lives in a parish where thatched cottages have been pulled down, trees felled, and the old church replaced 'by a certain obliterator of historic records who had run down from London and back in a day.'[27]

The absence of a resonant past may account for *Jude*'s connections to nineteenth-century blasphemy debates. To Marsh, who has persuasively demonstrated those connections, the root cause of late-century blasphemy prosecutions was that publications such as the secularist *Freethinker* attempted quite self-consciously to debunk what its editor called 'the deceitful glamour' of 'Bible English' – by parodying it, often in irreverent cartoons, by mixing sacred and profane language, and by subtly reworking familiar phrases 'to give echoes that are slightly "off."'[28] Although many of Hardy's biblical references have at least an element of that debunking spirit, in most cases they are constrained by the memory of past reverence, or by a community in which a scriptural context is taken for granted. In *Jude*, however, the constraints are stripped away and the result is a 'novel that makes no compensatory amends and supplies no alibi for its heretical nastiness.'[29] The characters subject the Bible to physical dismemberment as well as irreverent quotation: Sue Bridehead literally cuts it up, rearranging it in a textual parody.[30] Even 'restoring' the Word becomes a kind of parody when Sue, pregnant and unmarried, helps Jude to clean and repaint the Commandments on the wall of a church. Jude makes an irreverent spectacle of liturgical language by drunkenly reciting the Latin Nicene Creed in a public house, to an audience who would not know the difference between the Creed in Latin and 'the Ratcatcher's Daughter in double Dutch' (122); he will later borrow biblical language with sharper (and sober) blasphemous intent when he responds to Sue's banishing him from her bed by throwing one of the pillows on the floor and exclaiming, 'Then let the veil of our temple be rent in two from this hour!' (354; Matthew 27:51, Mark 15:38).

Despite the storm of protest when *Jude the Obscure* came out, Hardy was never prosecuted for blasphemy, and as Marsh acknowledges, 'Bible English' in the novel remains 'precariously viable,' though Hardy's 'painful trace of lingering faith' ironically makes him more of a blasphemer, because more conscious of the crime.[31] Hardy verges on thoroughgoing blasphemy here and Jude increasingly misapplies biblical quotations, 'wrenching them to appropriateness,' as Patricia Ingham puts it.[32] Yet some vestige of 'churchiness' remains in the author, and in the protagonists, and Jude's death scene still suggests both the precariousness and the lingering viability of the Bible in the novel.

The precariousness may initially be more obvious, as Hardy plays on that staple of Victorian fiction, the reverent deathbed scene. Jude's death fits at best awkwardly within that tradition, for his quotation of Job is despairing rather than redemptive. Drawing only from the earlier part of the book, where Job asks, 'Why died I not from the womb?' (403; Job 3:11) he implicitly cancels Job's later redemption.[33] By preceding his quotation with a reference to Sue as 'defiled' in her remarriage to Phillotson – an act which most churchmen would see instead as her penitential return to her lawful husband – he also emphasizes his heretical position on marriage. The narrator adds one last heterodox twist by interspersing the quoted verses with 'hurrahs' from the Remembrance games, making it clear that the Christminster establishment Jude has studied so hard to join cares nothing for him and his class. Like his earlier recitation of the creed, this quotation is 'blaspheming, or next door to it' (123).[34] It 'wrenches' the sacred from its context to fit his purpose, and points to the futility of a 'scripture manner' when there is no stable community to make it meaningful. Yet these words from Job, spoken by a man dying in painful solitude, do acquire solemnity, if not exactly reverence, from their very bleakness, especially since they are juxtaposed with Arabella's decidedly secular holiday making and her brisk moves to secure her next husband. By contrast, Jude is still seeking words to make sense of failure and despair and, in a final irony, he reaches for them in the Bible. In adding this quotation for the first volume edition of the novel in 1895, Hardy seems to want to register not only the irony, but also Jude's continuing reliance on what he tries to reject.

To make sense of failure is also the apparent aim of one of Hardy's most peculiar poems, 'After Reading Psalms XXXIX., XL., etc.' He dates this work to the 1870s, which means that he would have written it when he reached an age a little beyond Jude's at his death, when 'the bumping of near thirty years' (405) ceases. If we suppose that the poem's speaker is about the same age, then he is looking back at a life that has lasted about as long as Jude's. Like Jude, he appropriates biblical phrases to sum up a less than successful career; like Jude, he knows his ecclesiastical Latin, well enough to borrow from the Vulgate Bible. The merest glance at the poem, though, with its playful English/Latin rhymes and ingenious manipulations of the Vulgate phrases to get them to fit the syntax and metre of the poem, makes the contrast between these two bookish figures stand out sharply. The poem's speaker seems a kind of reverse-image double of Jude. Though he certainly uses scripture for secular purposes, commenting on everything from his youth, simplicity, and ignorance of 'gallant tryst' and 'High adventure' to his failure at 'fervid rhymes,' the result seems less blasphemous than humorous, even jaunty.[35]

Taken together, the two psalms mentioned in the title can be applied (with a little wrenching) to a young man who has tried to make his way as a poet. Psalm 39 focuses on not speaking; Hardy paraphrases one of its best-known passages in his third line: 'Even from good words held my tongue' ('I kept silence, yea, even from good words'). Psalm 40, on the other hand, emphasizes speaking; the petitions to God which seem to go unheard in 39 get a response in the first verse of 40: 'I waited patiently for the Lord: and he inclined unto me, and heard my calling.' The psalmist goes on to speak freely, saying 'I have declared thy righteousness in the great congregation: lo, I will not refrain my lips, O Lord' (Psalms 40:11). The rhythm of suffering, petition, and despair, followed by release into rejoicing and song, is typical of the psalms as a whole, and most of the poem follows a similar pattern, moving from the speaker's hapless situation in the first three lines of each stanza to a statement of God's providential action in the Latin phrases that come in every fourth line: '*Quoniam Tu fecisti!*' (for it was thy doing), '*me deduxisti!*' (thou leddest me), *Me suscepisti!*' (thou upholdest me), '*Dies ... / Meos posuisti!*' (thou hast made my days), and '*Domine, Tu scisti!*' (Lord ... thou knowest).[36] The interesting exception here is the Latin phrase in the last line, *Quem elegisti?* (Whom have you chosen?), a question in the poem but part of a statement in the psalm where it appears: 'Blessed is the man, whom thou choosest' (Psalms 65:4, Vulgate Psalms 64:5). The plaintive interrogation of that last line and the stanza of which it forms a part is the closest the poem gets to the 'pain and grief' (Psalms 39:3) that mark Psalm 39, the mood of deep sorrow that makes it appropriate as one of the set psalms in the prayer-book burial service.

It is the absence of such sorrow that makes this speaker a complete contrast to Jude: the contrast may stem in part from their different degrees of misfortune, but it also reflects a difference in temperament. Both begin naively, keeping 'no gallant tryst' (2), their work with silent words taking the place of 'Love-lore' (10) and worldly knowledge. The sense of this naivety echoes through the first three stanzas, though we can assume that the speaker now has the experience lacking at his 'start by Helicon' (9). Yet even his older self, as he turns to recount his failures in the fourth stanza, seems too taken with his ingenious placing of the Latin phrase to notice his own shift from innocence to discouragement:

> When I failed at fervid rhymes
>   'Shall', I said, 'persist I?'
> '*Dies*' (I would add at times)
>   '*Meos posuisti!*'   (13–16)

It is difficult to get through this stanza without smiling, and that reaction has little to do with the meaning: it is the sheer verbal ingenuity, the fussy parenthetical phrase, the almost ridiculous rhyming of 'persist I/ *posuisti*' and the preposterousness of the poem's whole project (now it is pushed over the top like this) that raises the smile.

Hands suggests that the poem is an uneasy combination of 'latter-day Tate and Brady, quoting or paraphrasing the Scriptures in a common hymn metre,' and 'tongue-in-cheek semi-burlesque.'[37] It takes a funeral psalm for its starting point, ends on a searching question directed to a doubtful audience at dead of night and yet, with these *Jude*-like materials, it produces something that is at least on the edge of humour. The effect, as Hands puts it, is to make the 'problem of interpretation ... unsettlingly acute,' and, interestingly, to make many commentators and anthologists fight shy of discussing or including the poem.[38] To see Hardy as an agnostic and track the impact of his loss of faith in books like *Jude* is relatively easy for the twenty-first-century reader, no longer shocked by pessimistic or even blasphemous ideas, and accustomed to the notion that great art makes serious, sombre claims on its audience. But to see Hardy as someone who could make the words of a funeral psalm into a technical game, and delight in the skill that carried it out, attacks a different set of pieties, precisely because it does not seem quite 'serious.' Even the last stanza's hint that Providence may not after all have 'chosen' him issues in a pained but whimsical question, still constrained by the rhyme that, in Isobel Grundy's words, joins 'archaic and often feeble verbs' in English with 'the strong, confident Latin.'[39] Of all Hardy's uses of the Bible, this sort of half-comic virtuoso performance may be the most unsettling.

Hardy's shifting attitudes towards and uses of the Bible raise a 'problem of interpretation' because they refuse consistency. He creates a Joseph Poorgrass, an Ethelberta, a Jude – and the irrepressible speaker of 'After Reading Psalms XXXIX., XL., etc.' Yet all his Bible-conscious characters resemble each other (and Hardy himself) in their sense of Biblical and prayer-book texts, even in Latin, as personal possessions, well-worn tools with many uses. Familiarity is not reverence, of course, and familiarity with a sacred text need not imply belief, but there is still a lurking sense of affection in this persistent habit of drawing on the Bible in all kinds of situations and moods.

Few agnostics present such vexed and contradictory attitudes towards the sacred as Hardy: the man who in his last illness could ask his wife to read him the gospel accounts of 'the Nativity and ... the Massacre of the Innocents' and comment when she was finished 'that there was not a grain of evidence that the gospel story was true in any detail,' was one for whom the Bible remained a fascinating text.[40] Several decades after his gradual loss of religious faith, though he could not receive the Bible as truth, he still recognized, and had to assert himself against, its claim to be true. His mixing of sacred words and secular emotions may aim at a 'denigration of religion,' as Hands contends, but it simultaneously registers a residual sense of possible belief.[41] If Hardy's novels, in Bharat Tandon's words, 'flicker, disorientingly, between different understandings of causality,'[42] so biblical language in Hardy's texts flickers along the spectrum of belief, nostalgic reverence, humour, and mockery.

NOTES

1 Thomas Hardy, *The Life and Work of Thomas Hardy*, ed. Michael Millgate (London: Macmillan, 1985), 234. Hereafter cited as *LW*. Millgate, in *Thomas*

Hardy: A Biography (Oxford: Oxford University Press, 1982), 91, points out that because Hardy's original attachment to the church was emotional rather than a matter of 'intellectual conviction,' and his 'early adherence to Anglican principles ... taken for granted upon the basis of family and local example,' his loss of conviction was an 'erosion ... a gradual process rather than the consequence of a single moment of crisis.' Timothy Hands, in *Thomas Hardy: Distracted Preacher?* (Basingstoke: Macmillan, 1989), concurs with this judgment, and notes that Hardy was rather a 'not-knower' than an agnostic in his inability to 'set clearly defined limits to his beliefs and doubts' (35–6).

2 Thomas Hardy, *The Woodlanders,* ed. Patricia Ingham (1887; London: Penguin, 1998), 125.

3 Michael Wheeler, *The Art of Allusion in Victorian Fiction* (London: Macmillan, 1979), 16.

4 See Hands, *Thomas Hardy,* 37–8, for a discussion of Evangelical allusive practice and its impact on Hardy.

5 Ibid., 122.

6 Hardy, *LW,* 407. Henry Anthony Trevor Johnson's 'Churchy Hardy: A Study of the Influence of the Anglican Liturgy on the Novels and Lyrical Poetry of Thomas Hardy O.M.' (PhD thesis, University of Manchester, 1998) is a thoughtful and detailed discussion of Hardy's 'churchiness' and its traces in his work.

7 Hardy, 'God's Funeral,' in *The Complete Poetical Works of Thomas Hardy,* ed. Samuel Hynes, 5 vols (Oxford: Clarendon, 1982–95), 2:34–7, stanzas II, IV, VII (this poem hereafter cited parenthetically by stanza; *Poetical Works* cited as *CPW*). 'Wrought,' 'loving-kindness,' and 'longsuffering' appear in many places in the Authorized Version of the Bible. 'Ages rolled' is a poetic formula especially frequent in hymns, such as the one Charles Wesley wrote on the death of George Whitefield, 'Servant of God, – Well Done' (1770), lines 23–4: 'Long as eternal ages roll / Thou seest thy Saviour's face.' (Note the present tense, commonly used for this phrase in hymns to refer to an eternal, Providential time scale, in contrast to the past-tense human time the mourners invoke in stanza VII.) In the 'Prayer of Humble Access' in the prayer-book Communion Service, communicants prepare to receive the Sacrament, affirming their trust in God's 'manifold and great mercies' rather than in their own righteousness. 'Manifold mercies' also occurs in Nehemiah (9:19 and 9:27), and 'Mercies manifold' in several religious poems and hymns.

8 I have throughout quoted psalms from the Coverdale Psalter, as found in the Book of Common Prayer. This version of the psalms, taken largely from the Great Bible commissioned by Henry VIII (1539; trans. Miles Coverdale),

is close to the Authorized Version, the Great Bible being one of the texts synthesized into the Authorized, but the two are not identical.

9 Deborah Collins, in *Thomas Hardy and his God: A Liturgy of Unbelief* (Basingstoke: Macmillan, 1990), identifies the gleam as 'the light of positivism rising for the first time above a universe freshly emancipated by the decease of God' (26). F.B. Pinion also reads the gleam as a reference to positivism in *A Commentary on the Poems of Thomas Hardy* (1976; New York: Barnes and Noble, 1976), 100, but to me such a reading sorts out the poem's contradictory impulses too neatly.

10 Matthew Arnold, 'Dover Beach,' in *The Poems of Matthew Arnold*, 2nd ed., ed. Kenneth Allott and Miriam Allott (1965; London: Longman, 1979), 253–7, lines 3–4 (hereafter cited parenthetically by line).

11 Hands, *Thomas Hardy*, 117, sees Hardy's 'insecurity of doubt' as similar to Arnold's, but Hardy's insecurity seems far more apparent.

12 Joss Marsh, *Word Crimes: Blasphemy, Culture, and Literature in Nineteenth-Century England* (Chicago: University of Chicago Press, 1998), 160–2, 83. The relationship between class and religion in the Victorian age is a much-debated one, and the 'insurrection' may have existed primarily in the minds of those who feared it. Hugh McLeod, in *Religion and Society in England, 1850–1914* (New York: St Martin's, 1996), offers a useful overview of the debate and argues for 'a relatively high degree of religious consensus' (1) in Victorian and Edwardian England.

13 Marsh, *Word Crimes*, 85.

14 Ibid., 86, points out that there was at least as much pressure from below for education as philanthropic/religious effort from above, and that many working-class families preferred to avoid schools set up to inculcate respectable and Bible-oriented obedience. No doubt, however, many took advantage of the systems on offer, as Thomas Hardy's family did, with varying degrees of adherence to and influence by the schools' religious approaches. McLeod regards secularists and agnostics as 'a small minority' who yet 'had considerable influence' (*Religion and Society*, 47).

15 Hardy, *Far from the Madding Crowd*, ed. Rosemarie Morgan (1874; London: Penguin, 2000), 353. Hereafter cited parenthetically by page number.

16 R.H. Hutton, review of *Far from the Madding* Crowd, *The Spectator*, 19 December 1874, rpt. in *Thomas Hardy: The Critical Heritage*, ed. R.G. Cox (New York: Barnes and Noble, 1970), 22. In *LW*, Hardy records his memory of a dairymaid in his Sunday-school class, later the model for Marian in *Tess of the d'Urbervilles*, who 'had a marvellous power of memorizing whole chapters in the Bible' and used to recite them, 'to his boredom' (30): this memory may give the lie to Hutton's assumption that the working

class is Bible-illiterate, but it also suggests that the dairymaid thought of her achievement as rare and impressive – as even her bored teacher apparently did.

17 In the Buck's Head episode Joseph is probably recalling Psalm 50:1 ('... from the rising up of the sun, unto the going down thereof') and/or Malachi 1:11 ('... from the rising of the sun even unto the going down of the same'). Hands, *Thomas Hardy*, 93–6, argues that Hardy constructs a 'parodic religion of drink' with Joseph and several other fictional characters.

18 Hardy, *The Hand of Ethelberta*, ed. Tim Dolin (1876; London: Penguin, 1996), 177, 178. Hereafter cited parenthetically by page number.

19 The parable is the basis for many popular songs, most called 'Dives and Lazarus,' and as a girl Ethelberta may have first encountered it in this form, along with the subversive subtext that the rich are heading for apocalyptic punishment.

20 The phrase belongs formally to the narrator, but this seems to be an instance of free indirect speech following Ethelberta's thoughts. Marlene Springer, in *Hardy's Use of Allusion* (Lawrence: University Press of Kansas, 1983), 78, calls this one of Hardy's 'teasingly obscure' allusions, pointing out in a note that there is only one, parenthetical, reference to the Zamzummims in the Bible (181, n. 27). The obscurity, however, may suggest both the extent of Ethelberta's Bible reading, and her tendency (or Hardy's?) to seek out references with elegiac overtones.

21 'Coomb' Castle is Corvsgate in editions from 1896 on.

22 Paul Turner, in *The Life of Thomas Hardy: A Critical Biography* (Oxford, Blackwell 1998), suggests that Ethelberta's entrance into the castle also mimics 'that of Jesus into Jerusalem, "lowly, and riding upon an ass"' (55; see Zechariah 9:9 and Matthew 21:5). The shifting role this idea assigns to Ethelberta (from Christ to Peter) is characteristic of the twists in Hardy's allusions.

23 There is no summary statement about Rehoboam's reign in Kings, though the chapters dealing with him present a similarly negative view. The episode from 2 Chronicles is summarized in Hardy's 'Literary Notes I' notebook under the heading 'Taking counsel.' *The Literary Notebooks of Thomas Hardy*, ed. Lennart A. Björk, 2 vols (Basingstoke: Macmillan, 1985), 1:13, n. 93; Björk makes the connection with Ethelberta in his annotation to this note, 254.

24 *Ethelberta* has often been read as a novel which uses the 'front' of fiction to half-expose hidden anxieties; see for instance Peter Widdowson's chapter on this book in *Hardy in History: A Study in Literary Sociology* (London: Routledge, 1989), 155–97.

25 Hands, *Thomas Hardy*, 46. Hands argues that Hardy's biblical allusions help to create that sense of a stable community, especially in *Far from the Madding Crowd*.

26 Hardy, 'A Church Romance,' in *CPW*, 1:306, line 14. Hardy makes the link between this poem and his parents in *LW*, 18–19.

27 Thomas Hardy, *Jude the Obscure*, ed. Dennis Taylor (1895; London: Penguin, 1998), 12. Hereafter cited parenthetically by page number.

28 Marsh, *Word Crimes*, 251. Marsh is quoting G.W. Foote.

29 Ibid., 278. Marsh has taken up the concept of the 'alibi' in a conference lecture on the reception of *Tess* and *Jude*, 'Angelic Appeasement and Aesthetic Alibi,' Fifteenth International Thomas Hardy Conference, Dorchester, U.K., July 2002. Her argument in *Word Crimes* about the blasphemous elements of *Jude* is too complex to summarize here, but one of her points involves the connections between Jude and Thomas Pooley, a Cornish well-sinker convicted of blasphemy in 1857 (296–319).

30 Marjorie Garson, in *Hardy's Fables of Integrity: Woman, Body, Text* (Oxford: Clarendon, 1991), reads this dismembering of the Bible suggestively, arguing that Sue's various attacks on the Word ultimately make a scapegoat of her, dramatizing 'as female scattiness the breakdown of logocentric security' (165).

31 Marsh, *Word Crimes*, 278. Many of the reviewers, perhaps luckily for Hardy, focused instead on what they saw as the book's indecency and its attack on marriage.

32 Patricia Ingham, introduction to *Jude the Obscure* (1895; Oxford: Oxford University Press, 1985), xvi.

33 The Job quotation is not in the manuscript or serial; it was added for the first book edition. Hardy seems to have been revising to further complicate the status of the Bible in the novel. See Ingham, introduction xix, for comments on a similar process of complication with respect to Sue's emotions and desires. A good example of a reverent fictional deathbed is that of John Barton in Elizabeth Gaskell's *Mary Barton* (1848; ed. Edgar Wright [Oxford: Oxford University Press, 1987], 436–9). Barton, murderer and erstwhile scornful hater of the rich, offers 'earnest, passionate, broken words of prayer'; when he can no longer speak, a rich man, the father of the man he has murdered, takes up the prayer, begging forgiveness for himself and Barton in the words of Luke 18:13 and the Lord's Prayer.

34 Richard Nemesvari, in 'Appropriating the Word: *Jude the Obscure* as Subversive Apocrypha,' *Victorian Review* 19:2 (winter 1993): 56–7, notes that Jude Fawley's namesake, the writer of the Epistle of Jude, inveighs

against precisely such personal uses of scripture as 'turning the grace of our God into lasciviousness' (Jude 4).

35 Hardy, 'After Reading Psalms XXXIX., XL., etc.' in *CPW*, 2:484–5, lines 2, 6, 13. Hereafter cited parenthetically by line.

36 Psalm phrase translations are from the Coverdale Psalter. Note that Vulgate psalm and verse numbering often differs from that in the Coverdale Psalter and the Authorized Version; I give the Vulgate numbers in square brackets here. '*Quoniam tu fecisti*' (Psalms 39:10 [38:10]); '*me deduxisti*' (Psalms 77:20; [76:21]; the object is not *me* but *populum*, thy people); '*Me suscepisti*' (Psalms 41:12 [40:13]; '*Dies meos posuisti*' (Psalms 39:6; Vulgate *posuisti dies meos* [38:6]); *Domine tu scisti* (Psalms 40:11; [39:10]).

37 Hands, *Thomas Hardy*, 122.

38 Ibid., 122.

39 Isobel Grundy, 'Hardy's Harshness,' in *The Poetry of Thomas Hardy*, ed. Patricia Clements and Juliet Grindle (London: Vision, 1980), 4. In her brief but astute commentary on this poem, a notable exception to the general critical silence, Grundy points out that the rhymes render both the 'gulf between [Hardy's] own and the Psalmist's thinking, and the astonishing fact that contact is made across the gulf.'

40 Hardy, *LW*, 479; Hardy asked for the reading on 26 December 1927; he died on 11 January 1928.

41 Hands, *Thomas Hardy*, 51; Hands's study does as a rule acknowledge such a possibility, as for instance when he identifies 'three predominant qualities – fascination, rejection and sentimental illogicality' in Hardy's religious outlook (80).

42 Bharat Tandon, 'The Fossil in the Cliff: How Thomas Hardy Took a Microscope to the Tiniest Clues to Life,' review article, *The Times Literary Supplement*, 5 Dec. 2003, 3.

3 Hardy and *Hamlet*

DENNIS TAYLOR

If Shakespeare was the writer who most influenced Thomas Hardy's literary work, *Hamlet* was the most influential play. It is cited in at least nine novels (and three short stories), more perhaps than any other play, except *Romeo and Juliet*.[1] Hardy began early as a *Hamlet* critic, when at age twelve he read 'Shakespeare's tragedies for the plots only, not thinking much of *Hamlet* because the ghost did not play his part up to the end as he ought to have done.'[2] Here the schoolboy's disappointment at the let-down of a ghost story coincides with one of the critical cruxes of the play.[3] In residence in London from 1862 to 1867, Hardy started attending Shakespeare plays starring the Keans, and ended attending plays starring Samuel Phelps (*LW*, 44, 54), an experience that would result in the poem 'To an Impersonator of Rosalind' (dated '21st April 1867'; *CPW*, 1:286); either this or an 1890 performance may have inspired the poem 'The Two Rosalinds' (*LW*, 239; *CPW*, 1:247–50), printed in 1909. About the Phelps performances, which he attended with a companion, Hardy said: 'They used to carry a good edition of the play with them, and be among the first of the pit queue, holding the book edgewise on the barrier in front during the performance – a severe enough test for the actors if they noticed the two enthusiasts.' At the end of his stay in London, 'he had formed an idea of writing plays in blank verse – and had planned to try the stage as a supernumerary for six or twelve months, to acquire technical skill in their construction ... Nothing however came of the idea' (*LW*, 55). During this period, in 1863, he purchased and began marking the ten-volume collected edition of Shakespeare's plays, *The Dramatic Works of William Shakespeare*, edited by Samuel Weller Singer (London: Bell and Daldy,

1856). This set of the Singer edition is now in the Dorset County Museum.

Hamlet is included in volume 9 of the Singer edition. The first volume, with a red bookplate inserted by Sydney Cockerell, is signed by Hardy and inscribed '16 Westbourne Park Villas 1863.' Various other dates are inscribed in the volumes, signalling some of Hardy's later readings of various plays: 1870, 1871, 1892, and 1917. Hardy apparently owned other copies of *Hamlet*, including two single editions: an 1895 *The Tragedy of Hamlet*, picked up at Stratford, and *The Tragedy of Hamlet* (Temple Classics Edition 1905).[4] Hardy also may have owned *Hamlet* in two other collected editions: *Mr. William Shakespeare's Comedies, Histories, and Tragedies Faithfully Reproduced in Facsimile from the Edition of 1623* (London: Methuen, 1910), a presentation copy from Samuel Cockerell in 1918; and Shakespeare's *Works* (London: Knight's Illustrated Edition, 1859), probably Emma Hardy's childhood copy, as remembered by her and noted in the Hodgson sales catalogue; also perhaps, *The Works of William Shakespere*, 12 vols, ed. H.A. Doubleday et al. (London: Constable, 1893–8).

The Singer is the key edition, however. It is bound in handy volumes, more or less octavo with measurements of 7 by 4½ inches, easily portable. It is probably the 'good edition' which Hardy perched against the boards of the London theatres. It is a scholarly edition with prefatory notes, critical essays, and footnotes, among which Hardy would make annotations, in addition to those he made in the main text. The volumes are marked throughout, showing various stages of reading, as Hardy kept returning to the texts. Volume 9 contains *Macbeth*, *Hamlet*, and *King Lear*.

We can speculate on the stages of Hardy's reading of *Hamlet* in the 1860s and beyond. An ur-reading perhaps soon after purchase in 1863 is present in various erasures of marginal lines and underlinings which are still just barely discernible in the text. These erasures show that Hardy was intrigued by Claudius's paradoxes, 'With mirth in funeral, and with dirge in marriage,' etc. He also noted the electric early dialogue between Hamlet and his friends waiting for the ghost: '*Ham* ... but this troubles me. / Hold you the watch to-night? / *All*. We do, my lord.' Hardy noted Hamlet's 'solid flesh' soliloquy and was also struck by his 'there is nothing either good or bad, but thinking makes it so.' He noted Hamlet's flippant reply ('Sir, a whole history') to Guildenstern's 'Good my lord, vouchsafe me a word with you.' He marked Polonius's directions to Ophelia ('we do sugar o'er / The devil himself') and also Hamlet's comment on Polonius dead, 'Who was in life a foolish prating knave.' He marked Claudius's 'Is there not rain enough in the sweet heavens, / To wash it white as snow?'; also Horatio on Ophelia strewing 'Dangerous conjectures in ill-breeding minds'; and the clown's 'gallows' speech. He noted Laertes' Herodian rhetoric, 'Now pile your dust upon the quick and dead.' Some of the underlinings of specimens are erased, like 'happy cause,' or 'th' offender's scourge is weigh'd, / But never the offence.' For whatever reason, Hardy erased what were perhaps initial notations.

For the next stage of Hardy's reading of *Hamlet*, we might turn to his purchase of William Dodd's compilation, *The Beauties of Shakespeare* (Halifax: Milner and Sowerby, 1863), signed by Hardy in 1865. The book includes extensive quotations from the various plays, and Hardy makes many underlinings throughout (although some of the marginal marks are made by Emma, to whom Hardy gave the book in 1870). The underlinings of words, however, seem to follow Hardy's usual pattern. Interestingly, they constitute rather elementary word choices as though Hardy was still learning basic vocabulary (the underlinings in the Singer edition are of more sophisticated locutions). In the Dodd selections from *Hamlet*, there are various marginal lines, many of which may be Hardy's. Hardy makes only one underlining (apparently his) within the text, as indicated below:

> enterprises of great pith and moment,
> With this regard, their currents turn awry,
> And <u>lose</u> the name of action.[5]   (3.1.86–8)

A next stage of reading perhaps coincides with the *Studies, Specimens &c.* notebook, subtitled '1865 Notes,' signed by Hardy in 1865 and 1867 (with late entries of 1868 and 1869), in which he recorded words, phrases, and sections from various literary authors, most from Shakespeare (some fifteen of the eighty-eight manuscript pages worth).[6] The keeping of the *Studies, Specimens &c.* notebook, as a mine of literary vocabulary, coincided with Hardy's beginning an early (1865–7) course of writing Shakespearean sonnets, influenced by the copy of Palgrave's *The Golden Treasury* that Horace Moule gave him in 1862; then or later Hardy marked several of the Shakespeare sonnets. The *Studies, Specimens &c.* notebook has the following entry for *Hamlet*, with fifteen specimens:

Shak – <u>niggard</u> of question : edge [on] :
colour – (give its nature to) <u>smart</u> lash :
   shock : awry : as lief : cope with
loth : mich (slink) : tax him home :
bound to [hence e.g. bound <u>for</u> pleasure – &c]
            (win)
to buy out [or to buy^ e.g. buy a kiss with truth]
bow [the knee] : <u>wring</u> your heart :   (22–3)

While Hardy does not underline these specimens in the Singer text, the relevant 'colour,' 'shock,' 'awry,' and 'mich' passages are given marginal lines in the Singer edition.[7]

Coincident, either earlier or later, with such notations in *Studies, Specimens &c.* is Hardy's underlining of specimens in various literary texts that he purchased in the 1860s.[8] In his Singer edition of Shakespeare, Hardy underlined in total about 230 words, phrases, or sentences (sixty-five of these underlinings are erased), and inserted many marginal lines, interspersed throughout the ten volumes, and made at different times. In *Hamlet* specifically (with its commentary), Hardy underlined about seventy-six words or phrases (two of which underlinings are erased). If we were to compile a *Studies, Specimens &c.* style summary of these specimens (including Hardy's parenthetical commentary), it would be as follows:

exhibited : Wits Miserie : World's Madnesse : sometimes (i.e. aforetime) ; at issue about : vailed lids : river in the eye : will most incorrect : heart unfortified : For ... his favour (=itism) : Forward, not permanent – sweet, not lasting : waxes : no soil : greatness weigh'd : unvalued persons : choice be circumscribed : sits in the shoulder : express'd in fancy : the apparel oft proclaims the man : Have of your audience been most free and bounteous : tenders of : puh : die : of a doubt : leave her to heaven : encompassment and drift : Take you (some knowledge) : breathe his faults so quaintly : taints of : unreclaimed blood : fetch : He closes with you : addition : bait of falsehood takes this carp of truth : we of wisdom and of reach : assays of bias : indirections find directions out : have me : No hat upon his head; his stockings foul'd, Ungarter'd, and down-gyved to his ankle : Pale as his shirt : knees knocking : Put ... into command ... to entreaty : effect, defective : not art to reckon my groans : sigh gratis; the humorous man shall end his part in peace : barmy jacket of a beer-brewer : exclaim against their own succession : went to cuffs : his picture in little : writ (wit?) :

sugar o'er : enterprizes of great pith : that darke cloudie lande : so sweet breath : thoughts to put them in : make (call the reason of) : Th' expectancy and rose of the fair state : of (i.e. by) : expel : tear a passion to tatters : o'erdoing Termagant : suffer not thinking on, with the hobby-horse : Purpose is but the slave to memory : May one be pardon'd, and retain th' offence : wicked prize : to be demanded of a sponge : Hide fox : inform against me : fust.

    some craven scruple
  Of thinking too precisely on th' event, –
  A thought, which, quarter'd, hath but one part wisdom,
  And, ever, three parts coward.
And that our drift look through our bad performance : co-mere (Qy 'calmer') : let a beast be lord of beasts, and his crib shall stand at the king's mess.

Most of these specimens are clearly philological, as in the *Studies, Specimens &c.* notebook, which explores vocabulary and phrasing. It is possible that Hardy made most of his underlinings in the Singer *Hamlet* in the middle to late 1860s. In the Singer edition Hardy also inserts various marginal lines and comments, perhaps inserted shortly after the 'specimens' approach, as he turned to the larger meanings of the text. He may have begun making such commentary annotations when he took the volume with him to the Phelps performances of Shakespeare's plays in 1867, or in 1868 when, as noted in *Life and Work*, he conducted an extensive reading of the plays. Later, in a 1926 letter to *The Times*, Hardy said of the 'dram of eale' passage: 'in the eighteen-sixties I worked at elucidating it, and marked in the margin of a copy I used my own conjectural reading.'[9] In 1870 Hardy may have purchased Cowden-Clarke, *The Complete Concordance to Shakespeare* (rev. ed. London: W. Kent, 1870), which he signed and lightly annotated.[10] The sorts of notebooks Hardy began to keep in the 1870s were no longer philological but literary. So the marking of whole passages by marginal lines may have begun with his leisurely reading of Shakespeare in 1868, the year after he left London, an exercise he noted again for 1870 (*LW*, 61, 80). In this same year, next to Hamlet's 'Thou wouldst not think, how ill all's here about my heart: but it is no matter ... we defy augury; there's a special providence in the fall of a sparrow,' etc., Hardy wrote 'Dec. 15, 1870'; he also alluded to this signature and highlighted passage in *Life and Work* (85). But this does not settle the question of the precedence of the 'specimens' notations. Looking back in 1916, Hardy will say: 'I read S. more closely from 23 to 26 than I have ever done since.'[11] Periodically throughout his life, Hardy will refer to attending Shakespeare plays and readings, and at any time he might have added annotations. Also, as indicated below, the novels show a flurry of *Hamlet* allusions (four or more) in *A Pair of Blue Eyes*, then in *The Woodlanders*, and finally in *Tess*. So the writing of these three novels, in 1872–3, 1885–6, and 1888–90 respectively, might have occasioned more annotations in the Singer edition of *Hamlet*.

Hardy's comments in the Singer edition fall into three broad categories: philological observations, directorial insights, and textual interpretations. It is tempting to think that the directorial insights are the earliest, since they seem the least sophisticated (although lack of expressive sophistication would seem not to typify the young Hardy, who could write a poem as tonally assured as 'Neutral Tones' as early as 1867). I consider the three categories in turn.

Philological Observation. For some of the underlined words, Hardy noted parallels in the Wessex dialect. 'Hide fox,' he noted, is the Dorset 'hide-ye-buck.'[12] Ophelia's 'dupp'd the chamber door' is interpreted by Singer as 'open the door,' but Hardy notes that the Dorset idiom 'do the door' means 'bar the door.'[13] He also noted that 'miching mallecho' is 'still in use in Dorset'; he probably means that 'miching' is from the verb 'mitch,' meaning 'to slink,' the meaning noted in the *Studies, Specimens &c.* notebook.[14]

Directorial Insights. Some of Hardy's notations reflect insights, some more perceptive than others, about the motives behind various speeches. When Hamlet says 'Methinks, I see my father,' and Horatio responds, 'O, where, My lord?' Hardy notes that 'Horatio is mindful of the ghost.' In a similar vein, when Hamlet starts to reveal the ghost's message to his friends, but then says 'There's ne'er a villain, dwelling in all Denmark / But he's an arrant knave,' Hardy notes: 'Hamlet alters his mind – he had been going to tell them.' When Hamlet starts to stab Polonius through the arras ('*Ham.* How now! a rat? ... Dead, for a ducat, dead'), Hardy notes that Hamlet is 'Thinking it the king.'

Textual Interpretations. When Horatio says that in Julius Caesar's time, 'The graves stood tenantless, and the sheeted dead / Did squeak and gibber in the Roman streets; / As, stars with trains of fire, and dews of blood, / Disasters in the sun,' Hardy notes that the last phrases are not simply a list, but constitute a new thought: he thus suggests the addendum: 'As stars with trains of fire, and dews of blood [did usher] / Disasters in the sun.' About the line, 'A little more than kin, and less than kind,' Hardy proposes the interpretation: 'Though you are doubly kin to me your / kind expressions are more than you feel.' About the famous crux as given in Singer, 'The dram of base / Doth all the noble substance of a doubt, / To his own scandal,' Hardy suggests: 'The dram of ill / Doth all the noble substance leaven down / To his own scandal.'[15] This is the interpretation remembered in the 1926 letter to *The Times*. Where Polonius warns Ophelia against 'the trifling of his favour,' Hardy interposes a clarification: 'the trifling of his favouritism.' When the Ghost complains that he has been 'Doom'd for a certain term to walk the night; / And, for the day, confined to lasting fires,' Hardy changes this last to the more purgatorial and active 'confinéd fast in fires,' and adds an accent to save the metre. In another case, Hardy fiddles with the metre when he adds the accent: 'That lend a tyrannous and a damnéd light.' When Hamlet cautions his friends not to reveal their evening with the ghost, or make hints about it, he concludes: 'This not to do; / So grace and mercy at your most need help you! / Swear'; Hardy notes: 'i.e. "Swear not to do this – ."' When Hamlet scarifies Ophelia and screams that 'you jig ... and make your wantonness your ignorance,' Hardy emends: 'you jig ... and call the reason of your wantonness your ignorance.' When Ophelia in turn mourns Hamlet as 'Th' observ'd of all observers,' Hardy suggests: 'Th' observ'd by all observers.' When Polonius praises the actors for achieving balance, 'For the law of writ and the liberty,' Hardy suggests: 'For the law of wit and the liberty.' When Hamlet opines that a great man 'must build churches then: or else shall he suffer not thinking on, with the hobby-horse,' Hardy suggests the clarification: 'shall he have to undergo not being thought of, like the hobbyhorse.' When Claudius in his closet mouths that 'the wicked prize itself / Buys out the law,' Hardy suggests: 'the prize won by being wicked / Buys out the law.' When Hamlet tells Horatio about the English plot, 'Ere I could make a prologue to my brains,' Hardy emends: 'Ere I could make a prologue suit to my brains.' When Hamlet forges the royal letter ordering England to kill Rosencrantz and Guildenstern, 'As peace should still ... stand a co-mere 'tween their amities' (in Singer's version), Hardy suggests tentatively: 'stand a calmer 'tween their amities.'

Several of the underlinings thus seem to represent a later stage of reading, occasioning commentary ('at issue about,' 'of a doubt,' 'effect, defective,' 'writ', 'suffer not thinking on, with the hobby-horse,' 'wicked prize,' 'Hide fox'). But it has to be said that it is finally impossible to make absolute distinctions between earlier and later notations.

We can now trace the influence of this early reading of *Hamlet* on Hardy's later creative work. In a letter of 10 September 1868 asking for news about *The Poor Man and the Lady* (later rejected), Hardy wrote to Alexander Macmillan:

> I become anxious to hear from you again. As the days go on, & you do not write, & my production begins to assume that small & unimportant shape everything one does assumes as the time & mood in which one did it recedes from the present I almost feel that I don't care what happens to the book, so long as something happens. The earlier fancy, that *Hamlet* without Hamlet would never do turns to a belief that it would be better than closing the house. (*CL*, 1:8)

This apparently reflects the suggestion that the heart of the novel, its social criticism, be removed; Hardy will keep open the 'house' of his fiction by writing about 'rural scene & humble life' in a novel to come. Here he associates Hamlet with the heart of his creative work.

In *Desperate Remedies* (1871), Hardy described his hero, Edward Springrove (a figure, Millgate notes, much like Hardy himself),[16] as one who 'knows Shakespeare to the very dregs of the foot-notes'(24),[17] while in *Under the Greenwood Tree* (1872), Dick Dewy at the gypsy party, missing his beloved, 'danced with the rival in sheer despair of ever being able to get through that stale, flat, and unprofitable afternoon in any other way' (136).

A Pair of Blue Eyes (1873) contains numerous references to *Hamlet*. Henry Knight is characterized as follows: 'the brow and face ... were getting sicklied o'er by the unmistakable pale cast' (143); Hardy had made a notation about the relevant lines in the *Studies, Specimens &c.* notebook and in his Singer edition. And Stephen says to Knight: 'You out-Hamlet Hamlet in morbidness of mood' (401). Hardy had underlined 'o'erdoing Termagant ' in his Singer edition. The title page ominously quotes Laertes' advice to Ophelia about Hamlet's love, a passage partly underlined in Hardy's Singer edition: 'A violet in the youth of primy nature, / Forward, not permanent, sweet, not lasting, / The perfume and suppliance of a minute; / No more.'[18] Elfride's father complains about Stephen's low origins and compares him to Osric: 'Yes. "Let a beast be lord of beasts, and his crib shall stand at the king's mess"'(91), a passage partly underlined in Hardy's Singer edition. To Elfride, afraid to tell Knight of her earlier elopement with Stephen, is applied the Player Queen's fear for her husband: 'Where love is great, the littlest doubts are fear; / Where little fears grow great, great love grows there' (291). Hardy put a marginal line against these lines in his Singer edition. Elfride, ashamed to be seen with her new lover before her old, is described as 'yet unwilling to renounce him; so that her glove merely touched his sleeve. "Can one be pardoned, and retain the offence?" quoted Elfride's heart then' (298). Hardy had underlined the line in his Singer edition. Finally, the famous scene in the vault (chapter 27) where the labourers discuss the burial of Lady Luxellian is an acclaimed Hardy version of the graveyard scene from *Hamlet*. In his Singer edition, Hardy erased the marginal lines which he had earlier drawn next to this scene.

In *Far From the Madding Crowd* (1874), Hardy contrasted stolid Gabriel Oak to those more mercurial 'men of towns who are more to the manner born' (11), echoing Hamlet's 'I am native here, / And to the manner born,' which ends in the 'dram of eale' passage which Hardy marked. Later Oak is described as being 'Like Guildenstern ... happy in that he was not over happy' (167); Hardy put a marginal line next to this line in his Singer edition. Bathsheba, foolish in love, 'could show others the steep and thorny way, but "reck'd not her own reed"' (215), echoing Ophelia's rebuke to Laertes. For Ethelberta in *The Hand of Ethelberta* (1876), the possibility of disgrace and the pressure to marry 'were driving her to a Hamlet-like fanaticism and defiance of augury' (293). In 1876 Hardy cites and pastes into his scrapbook an article, 'The Wessex Labourer' (*Examiner*, 15 July 1876), which says: 'the clowns in *Hamlet* are no anachronism if placed in a west country village of our own day.' Hardy will later cite this as the first article to take up his term 'Wessex.'[19] In *The Trumpet-Major* (1880), Matilda scorns John Loveday because she thinks him 'a stale and unprofitable personality' (327). Earlier his attempt at entertainment fails when she feels faint: 'There was a regular collapse of the tea-party, like that of the Hamlet play scene' (149). When John interferes with his brother's love life, the act 'showed that John had been temporarily cruel to be ultimately kind' (166).

In *Two on a Tower* (1882), Swithin's mood changes from despair when Viviette agrees to marry him; she chides him: 'There is nothing either good or bad, but thinking makes it so' (119), a passage with an erased marginal line in the Singer edition. When she seeks him out after their separation, her brother thought her conduct the outcome of mistaken pity and 'such a kind gain-giving as would trouble a woman' (274), another passage given a marginal line in the Singer edition. In the story 'A Mere Interlude' (1885), the lover proposes elopement: 'An enterprise of such pith required, indeed, less talking than consideration' (*A Changed Man*, 273); Hardy had early underlined and erased his underlining ('lose the name of action') from this passage in *'The Beauties of Shakespeare,'* then cited 'awry' in the *Studies, Specimens &c.* notebook, and then had underlined 'enterprizes of great pith' in the Singer edition, and added a marginal line.

In *The Woodlanders* (1887), Melbury is cheered up by news from his daughter, showing that 'a soul's specific gravity constantly re-asserts itself as less than that of the sea of troubles into which it is thrown'(30), echoing the Hamlet soliloquy, which is given a marginal line by Hardy. Giles appeals to Mrs Charmond by letter and is 'left alone to the suspense of waiting for a reply from the divinity who shaped the ends of the Hintock population' (125). Notwithstanding his misfortunes, Giles 'had, like Hamlet's friend, borne himself throughout his scathing "As one, in suffering all, that suffers nothing," investing himself thereby with a real touch of sublimity' (264). As mentioned in *Life and Work* (262), Hardy would later mark this passage in the play with a marginal line and add the notation: 'Character of Thomas Hardy Senr – Died July 20 1892.' Fitzpiers, trying to reconnect with his wife, writes to her: 'You may call my fancies whimsical; but remember, sweet, lost one, that "nature is fine in love, and where 'tis fine it sends some instance of itself"' (405), quoting Laertes' address to the mad Ophelia. In the story 'The Waiting Supper' (1888), Nicholas is said to have 'never ceased to be a lover; no personal worries had as yet made him conscious of any staleness, flatness, or unprofitableness in his admiration of Christine' (*A Changed Man*, 45), the third use of this quotation by Hardy.

In *Tess of the d'Urbervilles* (1891), Angel Clare defends his sceptical respect for old families: 'Some of the wise even among themselves "exclaim against their own succession," as Hamlet put it' (213), a line Hardy had underlined in his Singer edition. Country lovers like Tess do not calculate: 'in the fields and pastures to "sigh gratis" is by no means deemed waste; love-making being here more often accepted inconsiderately and for its own sweet sake' (224), echoing the line underlined by Hardy in which Hamlet assures the players that they will not 'sigh gratis' as lovers. Angel, feeling betrayed, then bore 'the face of a man who was no longer passion's slave' (300), again evoking the Horatio passage which Hardy associated with his father. Angel exclaims that he and Tess should never have children: 'Don't you think we had better endure the ills we have than fly to others?' (310–11); Hardy had put a marginal line next to Hamlet's speech, 'bear those ills ...'[20] In the 1892 preface, defending the novel against attack, Hardy concluded: 'So densely is the world thronged that any shifting of positions, even the best warranted advance, galls somebody's kibe' (xx), a quote from Hamlet's graveyard scene.[21] As a final echo of *Hamlet* in Hardy's thinking about *Tess of the d'Urbervilles,* many years later (1921), he told a correspondent, 'There was very slight foundation for the story of 'Tess' ... So I fear you must assume the novel to be but "the figment of a dream"' (*CL,* 6: 75), alluding apparently to Guildenstern on Hamlet's ambition as 'the shadow of a dream.'

In *Jude the Obscure* (1895), Phillotson, agreeing to let Sue go to Jude, tells Gillingham: 'She little thinks I have out-Sued Sue in this' (279), again echoing Hamlet's 'out-herods Herod' line. Jude, horrified at Sue's giving herself to Phillotson, exclaims, 'she, so sensitive, so shrinking, that the very wind seemed to blow on her with a touch of deference' (484), evoking Hamlet's soliloquy on his father: 'so loving to my mother / That he might not beteem the winds of heaven / Visit her face too roughly.' As the youthful shouts of the Oxford students echo in Jude's death chamber, his books 'roughened with stone-dust ... seemed to pale to a sickly cast at the sounds' (493), with Hardy using the line he had applied to Henry Knight in *A Pair of Blue Eyes.*

In the years after his turn to poetry and away from the writing of fiction, Hardy continued to use Hamlet as an associational reference point. In 1896 he visited Stratford and picked up a copy of *The Tragedy of Hamlet* (London: Dent, 1895), which he slightly annotated.[22] In 1899, in connection with his poem 'A Christmas Ghost-Story,' he notes: 'Hamlet's father, impliedly martial in life, was not particularly brave as a spectre. In short, and speaking generally, these creatures of the imagination are uncertain, fleeting, and quivering, like winds, mists, gossamer-webs, and fallen autumn leaves; they are sad, pensive, and frequently feel more or less sorrow for the acts of their corporeal years.'[23] In 1904 Hardy read a review of *The Dynasts* and said: 'Your critic is as absolute as the gravedigger in *Hamlet*'; and also noted: 'As with a certain King, the reverse of worthy, in the case of another play, some people ask, "Have you read the argument? Is there no offence in't?"'[24] In 1905 he notes the passing of the poet, Violet Nicolson: 'for her, in poetry as in all else, the rest is silence.'[25] On a much more personal level, in designing

Emma's tombstone after her death in late 1912, Hardy 'said he could not make up his mind about the inscription – "THIS FOR REMEM-BRANCE" – which was partly from Shakespeare and partly from the Bible, and where to put it, at the head or the side'[26] – thus poignantly evoking Ophelia. And in relation to more public events, in 1914 he writes a friend, 'With the Germans, (apparently) only a week from Paris, the native hue of resolution is sicklied o'er with the pale cast of thought' (*CL*, 5:44), which is the fifth instance we have cited of Hardy's connection with this passage. In 1915 Hardy records in his *Poetical Matter* notebook, under a list of epitaphs, '"For Remembrance". Ham-let –.' Finally, in 1918, after reading about the revival of spiritualism in a book by his friend Edward Clodd,[27] Hardy wrote to Clodd: 'What a set-back this revival of superstition is! It makes one despair of the human mind. Where's Willy Shakespeare's "So noble in reason" now!' (*CL*, 5:247).

The continuing significance of *Hamlet* for Hardy cannot be theorized adequately here, but a few remarks might be ventured. Hardy uses *Hamlet* to articulate various observations about life, to help define some of his main characters (Henry Knight, Ethelberta, Giles Winterborne, Angel Clare, Jude), and also to define some key moments in his own emotional life. But perhaps this play's most suggestive resonance in Hardy's life and work relates to his self-definition as a haunted writer, and in this Hardy's interest in King Hamlet's ghost was seminal, continuing from his boyhood fascination through to his annotation of the *Hamlet* ghost scenes, as well as the graveyard scenes, in the 1860s. There are not many overt references to Shakespeare in the poems,[28] but we may say that Hardy's earlier interest in Shakespeare's classic ghost, along with the ghosts from Gothic fiction, spilled into the many ghosts and general ghostliness of his poetry.[29] Hamlet, caught between the ghost of the past and the present world, is like Jude caught between 'mediævalism' and 'the world around him' (99); and in turn, like Hardy himself, haunted by the ghost of the past.[30] Hardy is also, like Ophelia, driven by 'remembrance,' the motivating theme of his 'Poems of 1912–13' and of his burial epitaph for Emma (see above). We have seen that Hardy discussed King Hamlet's ghost and compared it to imagination itself: 'these creatures of the imagination are uncertain, fleeting, and quivering, like winds, mists, gossamer-webs ...' And he used a characteristic applied to Hamlet the son to characterize the novel, *Tess*, as the 'figment of a dream.' Hardy's sense of himself as primarily a poet rather than a novelist[31] is like his defence of Shakespeare as primarily a poet, something Hardy felt so strongly that he opposed a memorial to Shakespeare as dramatist.

If *Hamlet* is a play about ghost possession, it is also a play that possessed Hardy, and is a synecdoche of the way Shakespeare, and the literary tradition in general, also possessed him. One of Hardy's most fascinating Shakespeare comments is the one recorded around 1880 in his *Poetical Matter* notebook: 'At the end of a historical play, the ghosts of the real chars. appear on stage (say Macbeth or R'. III) & avenge themselves – say by burning theatre. They have already destroyed Sh.'s soul.' Just as Hamlet had been haunted by the ghost of his father, Shakespeare had been haunted by the ghosts of his characters (at least of these two evil characters). This authorial burden passes on to Hardy, haunted since childhood by Shakespeare and the allure of literature, an allure whose danger he discerns in this 1880 note. The 1613 conflagration of the Globe Theatre, during a performance of *Henry VIII*, is here made emblematic of the way literature can invade and possess the self, literature replacing life, and life taking its revenge, leaving only smouldering embers, *'veteris vestigia flammae.'*[32]

NOTES

1 Some tentative comparative statistics can be offered for the novels next most quoted: *Romeo and Juliet* is quoted in nine novels; *Twelfth Night* in eight; *Macbeth* and *The Tempest* in six; *Othello* and *As You Like It* in five. However these are only approximate statistics. We do not yet have a definitive listing of Shakespeare references in Hardy. The two best sources are F.B. Pinion, *A Hardy Companion* (London: Macmillan, 1968), 215–17, and Carl J. Weber, *Hardy of Wessex* (New York: Columbia UP, 1940), 246–57, the latter to be treated with caution. To the Pinion and Weber lists can be added, for now, the following allusions (included in the above totals): *As You Like It* in *Desperate Remedies* (72) and in 'The House of Silence' (*The Complete Poetical Works of Thomas Hardy*, ed. Samuel Hynes, 5 vols [Oxford: Clarendon, 1982–95], 2:213–14. All further references to this edition cited parenthetically as *CPW*); *Hamlet* in *A Pair of Blue Eyes* (91), in *Two on a Tower* (274), and in 'Our Exploits at West Poley' (*An Indiscretion in the Life of an Heiress and Other Stories*, ed. Pamela Dalziel [Oxford: Oxford University Press, 1994], 129. All further references to this volume cited parenthetically as *Indiscretion*); *I Henry IV* in 'The Thieves Who Couldn't Help Sneezing' (*Indiscretion*, 40); *Julius Caesar* in *A Laodicean* (227); *Macbeth* in *A Pair of Blue Eyes* (242), *The Return of the Native* (397), *Two on a Tower* (53, 128,

304), *The Well-Beloved* (109), and 'A Pump Complaining' (printed in Richard Little Purdy, *Thomas Hardy: A Bibliographical* Study [Oxford: Clarendon, 1954], 291–2); *The Merchant of Venice* in *Desperate Remedies* (335) and *A Laodicean* (352); *A Midsummer Night's Dream* in *A Laodicean* (283); *Othello* in *Two on a Tower* (233); *Romeo and Juliet* in *Two on a Tower* (139) and 'A Pump Complaining' (Purdy, 292); sonnet 57 in *Desperate Remedies* (258), sonnet 115 in *Two on a Tower* (103), sonnet 111 in *The Woodlanders* (8); *The Taming of the Shrew* in 'The Spectre of the Real' (*Indiscretion*, 184); *Twelfth Night* in *An Indiscretion in the Life of an Heiress* (66); Shakespeare in *Jude the Obscure* (93, 176).

2 Thomas Hardy, *The Life and Work of Thomas Hardy*, ed. Michael Millgate (London: Macmillan, 1984), 29. Hereafter cited parenthetically as *LW*.

3 The earliest evidence of Hardy's use of any Shakespeare may be a youthful skit, 'A Pump Complaining,' *The Dorset County Chronicle*, 6 March 1856, where the town pump complains that it was 'crabbed [cabined], cribbed, confined' (*Macbeth*) in an undersized housing, and appeals for a little oil to avoid 'being prematurely consigned to the "tomb of all the capulets"' (*Romeo and Juliet*; see Purdy, 292). The present essay is concerned mainly with Hardy's use of *Hamlet*, and does not consider the manifold references in Hardy to other Shakespeare plays. For a summary of some general relations of Shakespeare to Hardy's art, see Michael Thorpe, 'William Shakespeare' in *Oxford Reader's Companion to Hardy*, ed. Norman Page (Oxford: Oxford University Press, 2000), 390–2. Weber has a good comparison of the lives of Shakespeare and Hardy (*Hardy of Wessex*, 248–9).

4 For bibliographical details and locations (where known) of the books from Hardy's library, see Michael Millgate, '*Thomas Hardy's Library at Max Gate: Catalogue of an Attempted Reconstruction*' (http://www.library.utoronto.ca/fisher/hardy/). Millgate lists a variety of books which mention Shakespeare. That Hardy owned the 1905 edition is dependent on a brief note by Gabriel Austin, in *Four Oaks Library* (Somerville, NJ. n.p., 1967), 103. The 1893–8 edition is dependent on its listing in the Hodgson sales catalogue.

5 Quoted from *The Beauties of Shakespeare*. All other quotations from Shakespeare in this essay are taken from the Singer edition. A typographical version of the pages of Hamlet as seen and marked by Hardy is presented in my 'Hardy's Copy of Hamlet,' *Thomas Hardy Journal* 20 (October 2004): 87–112.

6 *Thomas Hardy's 'Studies, Specimens &c.' Notebook*, ed. Pamela Dalziel and Michael Millgate (Oxford: Clarendon, 1994).

7 The editors provide the Shakespeare line references for these specimens (113).

8 For an account of such textual markings, see Dennis Taylor, Appendix,

'Hardy's *Studies, Specimens &c. Notebook*,' in his *Hardy's Literary Language and Victorian Philology*, rev. ed. (Oxford: Clarendon, 1998); Taylor, 'Hardy's Copy of *The Golden Treasury*,' *Victorian Poetry* 37 (1999):165–91; and Taylor, 'Hardy's Missing Poem and His Copy of Milton,' *Thomas Hardy Journal* 6 (Feb. 1990): 50–60.

9 The letter is collected in *Thomas Hardy's Public Voice: The Essays, Speeches, and Miscellaneous Prose*, ed. Michael Millgate (Oxford: Clarendon, 2001), 449–50.

10 Millgate, '*Library*.'

11 To J.W. Mackail, 13 August 1916, *The Collected Letters of Thomas Hardy*, ed. Richard Little Purdy and Michael Millgate, 7 vols (Oxford: Clarendon, 1978–88), 5:174. Hereafter cited parenthetically as *CL*.

12 *The English Dialect Dictionary*, ed. Joseph Wright, 6 vols (London: Frowde, 1898–1905; repr. Oxford University Press, 1961) records the Dorset 'hide buck' in a list that includes the Kentish 'hide-and-fox, the game of hide-and-seek' (3:154).

13 Wright lists Hardy, from the story 'Wessex Folk,' as the unique example of this reading; Wright also interprets Ophelia's phrase as meaning 'shut' not 'open' (2:99).

14 'Slink' is the first meaning Wright gives, but without a Dorset citation. Thus Hardy's note in his Singer edition is the unique Dorset evidence for this usage.

15 Hardy's additional notation, 'over-lout [6. v. 1 Henry VI.]' is hard to discern and puzzling to me. In 1 *Henry VI*, 'I am lowted by a traitor' (4.3.13) is given a long footnote by Singer discussing 'To *lowt*, i.e. to *treat with contempt* ...' (Singer, 6:83–4).

16 Michael Millgate, *Thomas Hardy: A Biography* (New York: Oxford University Press, 1982), 118.

17 All references to the novels are taken from the Wessex Edition (London: Macmillan, 1912). Page references will be given parenthetically in the text.

18 '[T]he epigraph alone seems sufficient to suggest that Hardy saw Knight as the romantic intellectual whose essential nobility of soul cannot prevent him from bringing disaster upon himself and others. Knight's obsessions, like Hamlet's, emerge in indecision, morbidity, and disgust, and his internal struggle between an established dedication to the intellectual life and a late-emerging and perhaps ambiguous sexuality is strongly brought out' (Michael Millgate, *Thomas Hardy: His Career as a Novelist* [New York: Random House, 1971], 69).

19 Millgate, *Career*, 96–7.

20 Some interesting connections between Angel and Hamlet are made by

William F. Hall, 'Hawthorne, Shakespeare and Tess: Hardy's Use of Allusion and Reference,' *English Studies* 52 (1971): 533–42.

21 In the year of *Tess*'s publication, Hardy went to a theatre tavern in London and noted that 'Shakespeare.is largely quoted at the tables; especially "How long will a man lie i' the earth ere he rot"' (*LW*, 249–50), again citing Hamlet in the graveyard scene. Other glancing references around this time include the description in 'Our Exploits at West Poley' (1892) of Leonard agreeing to keep his friend's secret ('Steve made me swear, in the tone of Hamlet to the Ghost' [*Indiscretion*, 129]) and, more notoriously, Hardy's reference to Henry James and Robert Louis Stevenson as 'the Polonius and the Osric of novelists' (*LW*, 259).

22 As noted in the Elkin Mathews sale catalogue, according to Millgate, '*Library*.' The book was later given by Florence Hardy to Granville Barker, the great Shakespeare critic.

23 'A Christmas Ghost Story,' *Public Voice*, 158.

24 '*The Dynasts*: A Rejoinder' and '*The Dynasts*: A Postscript,' *Public Voice*, 195, 199.

25 '[Unpublished Preface to Posthumous Poems of Laurence Hope,]' *Public Voice*, 222.

26 Millgate, *Biography*, 526.

27 Edward Clodd, *The Question: 'If a Man Die, Shall He Live Again?': A Brief History and Examination of Modern Spiritualism* (London: Grant Richards, 1917).

28 The few overt allusions include the form of the Shakespearean sonnets, the epigraph to 'Sapphic Fragment' ('Tombless, with no remembrance' [*CPW*, 1:222]), 'The House of Silence' ('mankind in its ages seven' [*CPW*, 2:214]), 'Meditations on a Holiday' (*CPW*, 2:383–6), 'To Shakespeare' (*CPW*, 2:173–4), and the two Rosalind poems cited above. *The Dynasts*, of course, has a relation to Shakespeare's history plays too complex to engage with here.

29 This theme is pervasive in Hardy criticism, notably in J. Hillis Miller, *Thomas Hardy: Distance and Desire* (Cambridge, MA.: Harvard University Press, 1970); Dennis Taylor, 'Hardy's Apocalypse' (chapter 5), in his *Hardy's Poetry, 1860–1928*, 2nd ed. (London: Macmillan, 1989); and Tim Armstrong, *Haunted Hardy: Poetry, History, Memory* (London: Palgrave, 2000), in which he cites both Derrida's and Torok/Abraham's discussions of *Hamlet* (11, 179n6).

30 See, for example, Hardy quoted in William Archer, *Real Conversations* (London: Heinemann, 1904), 37: 'I should think I am cut out by nature for a ghost-seer ... people say I am almost morbidly imaginative.'

31 See Dennis Taylor, 'Thomas Hardy and Thomas Gray: The Poet's Currency,' *ELH* 65 (1998): 451–77. Hardy quoted Shakespeare (*King Lear*) to reinforce his argument about the superiority of his poetry over 'those novels written in the past on conventional lines for magazine editors – "to keep base life afoot"' (*CL*, 7:155).

32 I am grateful to the Thomas Hardy Memorial Collection Trustees for permission to quote from Hardy's marginalia.

4 Literary Allusion: Hardy and Other Poets

Hardy's cultural allusion is lavish and uneven, sometimes superfluous and naive, sometimes enriching and resonant. The range of his references to poets includes arbitrary or superficial allusion, pondered quotation or reminiscence, and imaginative engagement or dialogue with writers and texts.

In *The Life of Thomas Hardy* Paul Turner spots literary allusion everywhere, in plot, subject, and characters.[1] His examples valuably illustrate Hardy's wide reading but tell us little about the quality or resonance of the allusion. Looking at influences rather than sources in the poetry, Samuel Hynes and Kenneth Marsden use different criteria and material to conclude that Hardy's extensive reading is thoroughly digested.[2] As Marsden says: 'The sources, largely sources of technique, are ultimately unimportant because they have been absorbed and often transformed by the creative personality of the poet.'[3]

Hardy's transformations are often imperceptible because he makes the source so much his own, but his allusions are often unassimilated name-or-quote-dropping. Such reference can be particularly distracting in his stories, where it is not only literary allusion which is cursory, but psychology and language too. A Shakespearean image in 'The Marchioness of Stonehenge' is typical of its shallow story. The Marchioness is worn out by 'That anguish that is sharper than a serpent's tooth,'[4] but if ever child had a right to give its parent a bite it is her son, preferring the humble foster-mother to whom he was selfishly handed over as a baby. This serpent does much less with *King Lear* and for Hardy than *The Return of the Native*'s real adder, which bites Mrs Yeobright when she is desolate on a wild heath mistakenly regretting a thankless child.

At the beginning of 'The Melancholy Hussar of the German Legion' there is a neat quotation from *Hamlet*: 'A divinity still hedged kings here and there; and war was considered a glorious thing' (*CSS*, 35). This curt irony comes aptly from a narrator, more literary and learned than his characters, to introduce the strange sad story of war and love which Phillis told him 'with her own lips' when she was seventy-five and he fifteen.

There is less relevant Shakespeare at the end of another good story, 'The Three Strangers,' where the sheep-stealer's brother is distractingly associated with Macbeth :

> the little man was released offhand; but he looked nothing the less sad on that account, it being beyond the power of magistrate or constable to raze out the written troubles in his brain, for they concerned another whom he regarded with more solicitude than himself. (*CSS*, 26)

This is rapidly followed by more *Macbeth* when the baby whose christening party welcomed three strangers becomes 'a matron in the sere and yellow leaf' (*CSS*, 27). The constable and attendant crime-catchers, however, are worthy descendants of the Watch and Dogberry in *Much Ado About Nothing* whose blundering justice gets their man – in Hardy's case, lets him escape inhumane law. Like *Lear* in *The Return of the Native*, this is influence not allusion.[5]

Hardy quotes Browning's 'The Statue and the Bust' from *Men and Women* in *Desperate Remedies*, but its fickle unlucky lovers are nothing like Browning's and the quotations, while not inept, sound no echo of Browning's marmoreally inert characters. Their deceptively animated meeting is used to dignify Hardy's lovers:

> He looked at her as a lover can;
> She looked at him as one who awakes –
> The past was a sleep, and her life began.[6]

This moment is integrated with the flow of feeling, neatly introduced, 'like the Great Duke Ferdinand in "The Statue and the Bust"' and firmly concluded with Edward Springrove's impulsive invitation and the narrator's Thackerayan comment, 'How blissful it all is at first' (chapter 3, 70). In chapter 13 Cytherea Graye quotes the same poem less happily:

> The world and its ways have a certain worth,
> And to press a point where these oppose
> Were a simple policy.   (257)

Hardy makes an unrhymed stanza out of lines from two rhymed stanzas, changes a dash to full stop, and loses Browning's irony about worldly lovers who enjoy as well as defer to the world's worth. The broken extract is relevant but unnecessary, seeming to come in pat from a commonplace book.

He made amends when he repeated this adapted quotation in 'The Waiting Supper,' published in *'A Changed Man' and Other Tales*. This story, like *Desperate Remedies*, uses material from the discarded first novel, *The Poor Man and the Lady*, and it is possible that the poem was quoted there first. To point his theme he praises the 'new-risen' Browning, new-risen indeed since *Men and Women* had not been published at the time of the action: the story was probably written in 1887 and set 'fifty years ago'; F.B. Pinion points out the anachronism and Browning's influence in his notes (*CSS*, 924). Whether Hardy is criticizing or endorsing her judgment or not, his cultivated Christine tells her 'rural swain' that Browning is 'sensible,' repeating the rejigged nonrhyming stanza with irony removed, putting a colon instead of Hardy's earlier comma in the first line and a comma for Browning's dash after 'policy,' omitting his 'a' before 'policy,' and adding 'Better wait' to underline title and theme:

> I can bear whatever comes, for social ruin is not personal ruin or even personal disgrace. But as a sensible, new-risen poet says, whom I have been reading this morning: –
>
> The world and its ways have a certain worth:
> And to press a point while these oppose
> Were simple policy. Better wait.   (*CSS*, 607)

The story is melodramatic and shallow but, like Browning's, it is about separation, compromise, endless waiting, and unconsummated love. It resembles the poem most interestingly in having a ruling image: the disappointed ritual of that waiting supper, an uneaten wedding-eve meal on a spread table with cloth and candles, less profound, harsh, and ironically suggestive than the statue and bust but a solid social symbol with critical point, the best thing in the story.

He returned to this favourite poem in his last novel, *Jude the Obscure*, quoting it twice. Jude says he is not one of 'The soldier-saints who, row on row, / Burn upward each to his point of bliss' (book 4, chapter 5, 253). Later on Sue brings in 'the world and its ways have a certain worth,' adding '(I suppose),' (book 6, chapter 4, 368) : Jude's quotation is apt but Sue does not need hers to say what she means, and other Browning allusions in the novel are neither pointed nor resonant.

Hardy could use Browning without caring much for his meanings and feelings, even his stanza and rhyme, but he obviously found his dramatic narrative and language congenial, and assimilated their models. He knew the poet as well as his poems, and the day before his death asked Florence to read the optimistic 'Rabbi Ben Ezra.' His erratic appropriations of 'The Statue and the Bust' show a long attachment to Browning at his least optimistic, most radically ironic.

A group of Hardy's poems about literature engage with other writers in not only quotation but also strong lyrical response. The prevailing feeling is not always admiring: 'Shelley's Skylark' tacitly takes issue with the original, reimagining the abstracted symbol of Shelley's 'To a Skylark,' 'Shall I call thee bird?' Hardy writes an affectionate counter-poem asserting the bird's particularity, arguing that it was a real bird, 'A little ball of feather and bone,' still existing somewhere as dust.[7] Hardy's literal-mindedness comes into its own, recalling and revising romantic symbolism, making us remember or reread Shelley.

His *hommages* to other poets are marked by sympathetic reachings out to life behind art. 'At Lulworth Cove a Century Back' remembers the dead poet as man as well as great name (*CPW*, 2:371). Hardy cunningly withholds that name to retrieve Keats's sometime anonymity: 'That man goes to Rome – to death, despair, / And no one notes him now ...' The oblique allusion to 'Bright Star! would I were steadfast as thou art ' is not quite buried in common human experience: 'He looks up at a star, As many do.' The omission and suggestion of 'but wrote, as the many do not' delicately indicates poetry's transformations. The allusion to one sonnet, the last, which Hardy wrongly thought Keats wrote at Lulworth, particularizes a fellow-feeling for neglected genius. Place was always important for Hardy, and here specific location gives him and his time-traveller a spot to inhabit, a physical link with the famous dead. The dialogue of Time and the man in a hurry (like Coleridge's wedding guest) uses the strange image of Time's finger, to halt a reluctant listener and compel a cold truth.

'At a House in Hampstead' evokes Keats's absent bird in 'never a nightingale pours one / Full-throated sound,' quotation assimilated to colloquial style (*CPW*, 2:340). In 'The Selfsame Song' Hardy subdues the method of 'Shelley's Skylark,' never mentioning but tacitly apostrophizing Keats's immortal bird not born for death to make a frank materialist claim for mortality (*CPW* 2:367). He entertains the romantic image:

A pleasing marvel is how
A strain of such rapturous rote
Should have gone on thus till now
   Unchanged in a note !

The marvel must be dismissed. Of course it is not 'the selfsame song': the title sounds positive then turns out to be negative. The poem is less about Keats than about involuntary memory but it argues with Keats's symbol and would not have been written without the pleasing marvel. Keats himself doubted its reliability: 'Was it a vision, or a waking dream? / Fled is that music: – do I wake or sleep?' though Hardy may not have remembered this questioning of romantic vision. If his is a debate with symbolism it is one Keats, a more conceptual thinker and a better critic than Hardy, had with himself.

'To Shakespeare' places human being with artist, reflexively if unsurprisingly alluding to the 'least capturable of themes' (*CPW*, 2:173). The specific and sacred place is Shakespeare's town:

And yet, at thy last breath, with mindless note
The borough clocks but samely tongued the hour,
The Avon just as always glassed the tower ...[8]

Hardy develops a lively historical drama like that of Time's Lulworth interview, with Stratford burgesses gossiping benignly about a neighbour they scarcely knew. Most distinctive in an everyday setting is the sustained fresh image:

So, like a strange bright bird we sometimes find
To mingle with the barn-door brood awhile,
Then vanish from their homely domicile –
Into man's poesy, we wot not whence,
   Flew thy strange mind,
Lodged there a radiant guest, and sped for ever thence.

It is a play with vehicle and tenor, repeating the poem's first word, 'Bright' of 'Bright baffling Soul,' which remembers Keats's star sonnet, as it starts off with a dead metaphor and later revives it in the simile of birds. The process is reversed with 'strange' which begins in the vehicle, 'like a strange bright bird,' but converts to tenor, 'thy strange mind' The poem keeps the figure of flight, blending metaphor with synecdoche not just to call the mind strange but to make it strange: 'Flew thy strange mind.' It is all Hardy, attentive to Shakespeare but not reaching for his language, telling about genius in common words like 'strange' and 'radiant,' showing it by developing and making them uncommon in the play with vehicle and tenor. His wit is not brilliant and assertive but it is not shown up by the wit which gets a mention, 'Witty, I've heard.' Praise is general not particular, an admiring reader's simple response but uttered in a poet's language.

'George Meredith: 1828–1909' praises the writer whose poetry may have influenced Hardy, and whose novels he seems not to have liked: when he said he could not read Meredith who had poetry, though he could read Henry James who lacked it, he must have meant the novels. Like the Keats and Shakespeare poems this elegy locates an artist in his own place, the 'green hill' right for Box Hill and Meredith's love of nature (*CPW*, 1:358). Hardy evokes Meredith's fresh-air early-morning energy and music in the 'morning horn ere men awake' and mimes his style in 'vaporous vitiate air.' Praise is specific for Meredith's bold register and cant-hating imagination, apt for the writer and the man who advised Hardy at the start of his career: 'His note was trenchant, turning kind.' Meredith was the candid poet of 'Modern Love,' which had been pruriently reviewed like *Jude*, one 'whose wit can shake / And riddle to the very core / The counterfeits that Time will break.' The pun on riddling makes the special image which blends a sly friendly joke about Meredith's obscurity with praise of his radicalism, and the poem is optimistic in a Meredithean way, hopeful that Time is on the iconoclast's side.

William Barnes was Dorset-dweller and mentor as well as fellow-poet, and Hardy praised him in obituary, essays, an edition, and 'The Last Signal,' which seizes one of those small random events poets can transform to marvel and keep particular. The shared sacred place came naturally as Hardy caught a flash from his old friend's coffin as he walked to his funeral over fields they both knew. Striking its spark from that bright accident the poem praises the scholar and tireless dialect poet, celebrating his diction in what he called 'common English' and his prosody in half-rhyme, internal rhyme, and consonant pattern, but not making them eccentric – they are less assertive than some of Hardy's own early idiosyncrasies of lexis and form. The imitation does not use Dorset dialect but has the quiet virtue of being allusively intricate enough to advertise its model and send a curious reader to Barnes:

Silently I footed by an uphill road
That led from my abode to a spot yew-boughed;
Yellowly the sun sloped low down to westward,
    And dark was the east with cloud.

Then, amid the shadow of that livid sad east,
    Where the light was least, and a gate stood wide,
Something flashed the fire of the sun that was facing it ...

Hardy's fine ear and care for Barnes's avoidance of latinate lexis can be seen in his revisions of line 7: he tried 'the fire,' 'a reflection,' then 'the fire' again, and Hynes tells us he put 'reflex,' never printed, in a list of proof corrections (*CPW*, 2:212, 499n).

There is a Dorset scene in *Jude the Obscure* where Hardy quotes his friend as his hero walks in Barnes country:

He descended from the town level by a steep road in a north-westerly direction, and continued to move downwards till the soil changed from its white dryness to a tough brown clay. He was now on the low alluvial beds

'Where Duncliffe is the traveller's mark,
And cloty Stour's a- rolling dark.'
More than once he looked back in the increasing obscurity of evening.
Against the sky was Shaston, dimly visible
'On the grey-topp'd height
Of Paladore, as pale day wore
Away ...'   (part IV, chapter 4, 243)

The first allusion blends happily with Hardy's description and place names, and the second is relevant enough, but they are joined by a third local view, a second poet, and an archaic diction, with Drayton's 'Polyolbion' (244): 'Where Stour receives her strength, / From six cleere fountains fed,' and Hardy's dictionary of quotations takes over Jude's journey.

The bad habit of piling up allusion goes back to *Desperate Remedies*, where in the chronicle of Manston's passion (chapter 10, 194) we might tolerate a relevant if not vital quotation from Crashaw's 'Wishes to his Supposed Mistress' if it were not followed at once and less relevantly by words from Keats's 'Ode to a Nightingale.' In chapter 6 of *Two on a*

Tower (71), Viviette's guilty inability to concentrate on prayer is acceptably compared with Angelo's similar problem in *Measure for Measure*. But three sentences later Macbeth's terror at Fleance's escape is pressed into superfluous service as her fancy for Swithin opens 'a new and unexpected channel for her cribbed and confined emotions.' In chapter 28 of *The Woodlanders*, a novel generously sprinkled with allusion, a reference to Tannhauser (224) is followed in the next sentence by a quotation from Shelley's 'Epipyschidion,' neither really right for Fitzpiers.

The multiple allusion can work. Sue Bridehead puts down her Gibbon, looks at a Calvary print hanging between pagan statuettes, and reads through 'the familiar' 'Hymn to Proserpine' – 'Thou hast conquered, O pale Galilean,' in a rich allusive passage wholly in character (book 2, chapter 3, 118). Swinburne articulates her Hellenism and makes a likely item in her modern agnostic reading list, though perhaps suggesting more than Hardy intended about her repressions and his own. He loved Swinburne, and 'A Singer Asleep: Algernon Charles Swinburne, 1837–1909' was written in quick response to Swinburne's death in 1909, to relive Hardy's first excitement when *Poems and Ballads* thrilled readers in 1866. The *tombeau* uses Sapphic allusion, flexible adapted sapphics, fluent dreamy smoothness, and Swinburne's luscious lexicon – passion, roses, sea, waves, time, foam, kisses, tears – as Hardy remembers his young rapture and gleefully flouts disapproval:

> – It was as though a garland of red roses
> Had fallen about the hood of some smug nun
> When irresponsibly dropped as from the sun,
> In fulth of numbers freaked with musical closes,
> Upon Victoria's formal middle time
>   His leaves of rhythm and rhyme.   (*CPW*, 2:31)

This is amusingly irreverent, and subtextual lubricious memories may lurk under the play of 'freaked,' roses associated with raptures of vice, and 'hot sighs,' 'love-anguished,' 'fitful fire of tongues' and 'burning' in other stanzas, though Sappho's gently gracious apparition is more like Hardy's sweet Muse (in 'Rome. The Vatican: Sala Delle Muse') than Dolores or Faustine. The grotesque conceit of a rose-garlanded nun is Hardy's illuminating image, like the strange bright fowl and the light flashing from Barnes's coffin, and makes it clear that sexual shock was part of the pleasure. Hardy knew Swinburne, found his religious and political radicalism congenial, and identified with his rejection by the reviewers of 'Victoria's formal middle time.' The contemporary was also responding to perverse 'passionate pages' and 'hot sighs.' There are desires, disgusts, and fears in Hardy with Swinburnean affinities: repressed fantasy and diseased Astarte in 'The Collector Cleans His Picture' (where links with Barnes must be innocent but reveal Hardy; *CPW*, 2:388), sadomasochism in the music of 'The Fiddler of the Reels' and *Desperate Remedies*, Troy's swordplay with Bathsheba, Tess on the threshing machine, and Sue Bridehead's self-immolation.

Hardy uses allusion successfully for the happy ending of *Far From the Madding Crowd*. Early in the novel there are routine allusions to Milton, Keats, and Shakespeare, but in the harvest-supper scene he has an easy natural way with socially placed ballad and folk song, as later on with Grandfather Cantle's cheerful wheezy songs in *The Return of the Native*. There is a good if obvious use of 'Lead Kindly Light' when Bathsheba and Gabriel meet outside the church (chapter 56, 389–90), and in the last two chapters married bliss is celebrated in sprightly mood and with operatic effects. After Bathsheba takes the initiative, she and Gabriel sit in awkward intimacy among his old furniture, warmly described not by Hardy but Barnes, 'all a-sheenen / Wi' long years o' handlen' (393). In the wedding chapter Gabriel steps to vigorous rhythms from R.H. Barham's *Ingoldsby Legends*, 'up the hillside / With that sort of stride / A man puts out when walking in search of a bride' (chapter 57, 398). His widow-bride's maidenly bloom is revived, 'as though a rose should shut and be a bud again' (399; Hardy drops a comma after 'shut') in imagery from 'The Eve of St Agnes,' Keats's joyful passionate night-piece. Allusion makes an epithalamion, unique in Hardy.

'Domicilium' is Hardy's first recorded poem, in which the sixteen-year-old writer cleverly imitates Wordsworth's narrative, diction, and form to relate a history of his home, through his grandmother's memories (*CPW*, 3:279–80). Like the first part of 'Lines written a few miles above Tintern Abbey' it begins by calmly registering visual sensations before developing emotional retrospect. Wordsworth has 'plots of cottage-ground, these orchard-tufts,' Hardy, 'garden-plots' and 'orchards'; each uses 'wild' twice; Wordsworth's narrator returns after five years, Hardy's inset narrator relates change over fifty years; Hardy's 'almost trees' echo Wordsworth's affectionate 'hardly hedgerows.' Hardy's poem is also Wordsworthian in conversational blank verse, plain style, precision, reserve, and imaginative caution: 'If we can fancy?' Hardy's narrative is more minimalist: Wordsworth wants readers to find a tale in everything, but his stoical soldiers, labourers, and beggars excite more pathos than Hardy's laconic grandmother:

> 'Yonder garden-plots
> And orchards were uncultivated slopes
> O'ergrown with bramble bushes, furze and thorn ...'

The ending is even quieter than Wordsworth's, closing with naturalistic abruptness a simple story where detail is less shaped than accumulated:

> 'Snakes and efts
> Swarmed in the summer days, and nightly bats
> Would fly about our bedrooms. Heathcroppers
> Lived on the hills, and were our only friends;
> So wild it was when we first settled here.'

Wordsworth proved philosophically unpalatable to Hardy and one of his strongest literary responses is a strident contempt in *Tess of the d'Urbervilles*: 'Some people would like to know whence the poet whose philosophy is in these days deemed as profound and trustworthy as his song is breezy and pure, gets his authority for speaking of "Nature's holy plan"' (Phase the First, chapter 3, 49). Towards the end, the narrator says that 'to Tess,' bitterly aware of being her siblings' only Providence, 'as to not a few millions of others, there was ghastly satire in the poet's lines – "Not in utter nakedness / But trailing clouds of glory do we come"' (Phase the Sixth, chapter 51, 380–1). When Jude does not know he is about to be thwarted, his happy hopeful appearance is said to be typical of the young, 'giving rise to the flattering fancy that heaven lies about them then' (book 1, chapter 4, 52). The Wordsworth celebrated in Hardy's early poem is not the thinker but the poet of lyrical narrative, pastoral teller and listener.

There are many allusions to Tennyson, whom Hardy knew and who returned his admiration.[9] 'An Ancient to Ancients' (*CPW*, 2:481-4) gloomily relishes cultural decline with what Hardy might call a 'humorous' imitation of Tennyson's 'Mariana,' adopting throughout its alliterative and assonantal octosyllabics, its refrain (the polite mock melancholy 'Gentlemen'), and its three rhymes in each stanza. The stanza devoted to Tennyson is affectionate parody: Mariana's grange makes a bower 'shrined to Tennyson,' its sympathetic decay becomes more decrepit, rusty nails off creepers not pears, weedy roof-wrecked, blue fly on the pane replaced by a spider, 'sole denizen,' Mariana granted the death she harped on: 'Even she who voiced those rhymes is dust.'

Tennyson liked *A Pair of Blue Eyes* and presides over it. It is full of conscious and perhaps unconscious Tennyson allusions, and its imagery and one big scene have Tennyson connections. The one novel in which Hardy used chapter epigraphs, it has five from 'In Memoriam,' one from 'Break, break, break,' one from 'The Two Voices' (another elegy for Arthur Hallam) and one 'In Memoriam' line in the text. 'To that last nothing under earth' prefaces the comically morbid crypt chapter (26), a mere title, tenuously attached to its source. Like *Hamlet*'s grave-digger, the workers crack jokes and tell sad stories about deaths of lords and ladies as they move old dead to bury new, providing useful information and preparing for the entry of Knight with Elfride, and the confounding of Stephen. Neither characters nor scene have anything to do with Tennyson's 'Two Voices,' a lyric desolately imagining bleak life annihilated by death, taking despair to extremity in order to defeat it.

The Tennyson allusions in the novel are magnetized by the conspicuously Tennysonian scene in chapter 20, its action and imagery presided over by the epigraph from 'Break, break, break': 'On thy cold grey stones, O sea!' Cold grey stones and sea are what threaten Henry Knight as he hangs suspended on 'the cliff without a name' before being saved by Elfride. Expecting death, he sees a trilobite in the cliff face and feels his small life dwarfed by geological time and indifferent evolution. As well as threatening stones and sea, there are echoes from 'In Memoriam' – 'scarped cliff and quarried stone,' its nature seeming 'So careful of the type ... So careless of the single life' but careless even of type, 'A thousand types are gone: / I care for nothing, all shall go' (LVI). The epigraph is a powerful allusion, explicitly and implicitly Tennysonian, dominating the best scene, backed by associations from 'In Memoriam.' In moving Tennyson's cold grey stones to this dangerous cliff and beach, Hardy remembers their purposes in two poems and finely adopts them.

Other Tennyson allusions in the novel are more weakly and distractingly snatched from context: since Hardy keeps to the highroad of literary allusion, Tennyson gets in the way rather than enriches Hardy's text. The epigraph to chapter 30, 'Vassal unto Love' (Hardy's capital 'V') emphasizes Elfride's submissive dependence, central in the novel but nothing to do with Section XLVIII of 'In Memoriam,' where

Tennyson meditates on the provisional nature of grief in poetry and beyond it. His 'vassal' is a personification of Doubt, temporarily made slave to Love by Sorrow, a continuing feminized presence in the poem: Hardy's use of the figure is less interesting, and raises a different subject. As a keen Tennyson reader Hardy must have known what he was ignoring, but there are times when he seems neither to remember context nor to imagine a reader's response, as in the routine quotations of some stories. The shallow-rootedness seems puzzling in a novel where there is so much Tennyson and so much 'In Memoriam.'

That poem's double preoccupation with the imagination's role in art, and in life – grief, love, and survivals of grief and love – is surprisingly ignored when Hardy is also analysing imagination, or fancy – he uses the terms indiscriminately – in Elfride, Stephen, and Knight. The Tennyson epigraph to chapter 16 is 'Then fancy shapes – as fancy can' (LXXX). Hardy's dash replaces Tennyson's comma. This introduces Elfride 's fantasy about Knight, Stephen's mentor, recently revealed as harsh reviewer of her romance and her new stepmother's relation, coincidences which keep her 'mind upon the stretch' (168). Hardy shows her mind-stretching, but only for a sentence or two in this chapter, which has nothing to do with Tennyson's meditation on imaginative memory and invention.

The theme of fantasy is developed in Knight's love for Elfride, initiated by physical attraction and constructed on conventional models rather than on a perception of an individual. (In section LII of 'In Memoriam' Tennyson rejects the egocentric words of elegy because 'love reflects the thing beloved'). Guilty fancy and forecast are traced in chapter 28 where the epigraph from 'In Memoriam' (LXV), 'I lull a fancy, trouble-tost' (with Hardy's comma) points to Elfride's suppressed guilt about emotional changeability. Once more, the quotation is not irrelevant but invites invidious comparison, in this case with the analysis that follows 'I lull a fancy' in 'In Memoriam,' in which Tennyson goes on contemplating survivals of memory and renewals of creativity (LXV). Hardy's lulled fancy simply calms the conscience, while Tennyson's generates new emotion and idea: 'And in that solace can I sing, / Till out of painful phrases wrought / There flutters up a happy thought ...' Hardy's fancy directs his people and plot but has nothing to do with Tennyson's passionate reasoning about imaginative resource. It is not till *Tess* and *Jude* that his imagining of imagination catches up with Tennyson's.

The last Tennyson allusion comes at the end of chapter 35, in which we follow Knight's reflections after rejecting Elfride, whose history and morality do not match his ideal. He realizes that his doubt and remorse will not last, and feels the prospect of feeling less as 'a superimposed sorrow': 'O last regret, regret can die.' But the poet of 'In Memoriam' (LXXVIII) imaginatively entertains and revises passionate thoughts in subtle reflexive coil and recoil:

> O last regret, regret can die!
> No – mixt with all this mystic frame,
> Her deep relations are the same,
> But with long use her tears are dry.

Tennyson's moving discriminations, his concept of teasing reconstructive grief, his compounded effort to imagine a role reversal in which he dies and his friend lives, his fine 'picture in the brain' (LXXX), show up Hardy's cruder colours.

The epigraph to chapter 20 is from an earlier passage of 'In Memoriam' (LXIV) : 'A distant dearness in the hill.' The poet imagines his dead friend's soul watching the sorrowing survivor from 'a higher height, a deeper deep'(LXIII) and develops an obsessive construction, reimaging Hallam's now angelic imaginative memory in the intricate story of a 'divinely gifted man' who recalls his humble origin as that 'distant dearness in the hill' where he played 'at counsellors and kings, / With one that was his earliest mate' (LXXIV). All we find in Hardy is unfocused narrative about the crystallization of Knight's love and Elfride's memory of Stephen.

Though he uses Tennyson quotations in other novels (*Desperate Remedies, The Hand of Ethelberta*, and *A Laodicean*) they are more frequent and more embedded in *A Pair of Blue Eyes*. Why did Hardy use so much Tennyson in this novel, and in ways going beyond routine reach-me-down reference but only once strongly resonant of Tennyson? There are some possible reasons. The novel draws on his courtship of Emma, with whom he read Tennyson on the 'wild and rugged' Cornish cliffs he associates with 'Break, break, break.' His later memories link love, 'the edge' of Beeny Cliff, and Tennyson's 'foot of thy crags, O Sea!' in the poem's last verse, not quoted in the novel but in his journal.[10] Letters from Moule 'who knew of the vague understanding between the pair,' Arthurian romance, and church restoration are neighbouring themes in *The Life and Work of Thomas Hardy*.[11] Tennyson and 'In Memoriam' may also have been suggested by the subject of death, so prominent in the novel, as in all Hardy's novels. This is not a tragic novel, but the plot, with its mixture of comedy and pathos, depends on the dying of Felix Jethway and Lady Luxellian, and Elfride's death offstage. Abruptly announced to reader and bereaved lovers, its pathetic end is insufficiently internalized and prepared for to be tragic, but significantly concludes the woman's passive restricted life and her abuse by powerful men. But Tennyson's elegy is most likely to have been suggested, perhaps unconsciously, by the subject which lies deeper below the novel's surface than its tragic feminist theme, the subject of male friendship.

After his friend and mentor Horace Moule killed himself in 1873, Hardy may have memorialized him in Henry Knight. Knight is a hard sententious reviewer, scholar, and a romantic, inhibited, conventional lover and survivor; Moule was a sensitive tolerant reviewer and stylist, a depressive, sexually oversusceptible, alcoholic suicide. Robert Gittings is convinced, almost convincingly, that Knight has nothing to do with Moule, and believes the shock of Moule's death caused Hardy's shift to tragic heroes who are markedly different from Knight.[12] But putting real people into art sometimes involves turning them inside out, and whether Hardy did so consciously or unconsciously, there is no doubt that the Tennyson references introduce the subject of death and almost always relate it to Knight, and the most powerful scene is one where Knight contemplates death with Tennysonian imagination and science, and nearly dies.

Tennyson's elegy for his friend was associated for Hardy with Moule. Hardy was fond of the poem, which turns up on the reading list he made when he was planning a career. About the same time he wrote an essay on Tennyson, never published. Moule first comes into the story by proposing for a debate at Marlborough College the motion, 'that Wordsworth, as a poet of thought and reflection, is superior to Tennyson.' When Hardy visited Moule's Cambridge rooms in 1880, seven years after his death, he wrote 'Cambridge HMM' in his 'In Memoriam' by the verse 'Another name was on the door,' which Tennyson wrote after revisiting Hallam's Cambridge rooms (LXXXVII). Hardy also marked the stanza beginning 'O last regret,' which he applies to Knight in the novel. If we see Knight as a version of Moule, which Michael Millgate plausibly invites us to do,[13] the Tennyson references taken as a whole look highly relevant, and their lack of relevance to local contexts in the novel looks significantly repressive (though we must remember that Hardy's literary allusions are often random).

Hardy plucks 'In Memoriam' quotations out of Tennyson's anguished self-analysis, which searches the meanings of bereavement to ruminate on his and his friend's imagination, setting Hallam's gifts, ambitions, success, and death, against his own past, present, and future in ways which may parallel Hardy's reflections on his own gifted friend, in memory and perhaps in the novel. Hardy is writing fiction not lyric poetry; his reflexiveness, if present, is oblique or subtextual; and his actual relation with Moule involved gratitude, jealousy, and guilt not present in Tennyson's feeling for Hallam. (They are present in the novel, as well as in one or two poems.) Hardy lamented a beloved talented dead friend like Hallam, a scholar and reviewer like Hallam and like Knight. In the novel he reflects like Tennyson on grief, in grief, and on imagination, but not about Knight, who does not die. Hardy does not plumb the imaginative or affective depths of Tennyson's poetry, but thirty years later he wrote his own tormented elegies, reflexively probing memory, imagination, art, and love. (Tennyson's long poem began as separate poems, often described as 'elegies' before the publication of 'In Memoriam.')

Hardy met Tennyson in March 1880 and was pleased by Tennyson's praise of *A Pair of Blue Eyes*, which Tennyson no doubt liked not only for its allusions to his poetry but for its tale of men's friendship. This is subdued or even disguised in Hardy's story of love rivalry, but it is important and keeps some features of his relationship with Moule, who was older, superior in education, helpful in some ways but not others, and a mentor about whose patronage, advice, and influence the younger man had ambivalent feelings. The 'In Memoriam' allusions suggest another subtext. They may reflect Hardy's guilt and jealousy about Moule or his desire to keep Moule's secrets; this would support Millgate's proposal that Moule may have had some sexual feeling for Hardy, unreturned or unperceived. Millgate reads an erotic element in the enigmatic poem 'Standing by the Mantelpiece,'[14] and it may be a subtext in *A Pair of Blue Eyes*, where allusions suggest and perhaps disguise deep relevance. Their puzzling concentration, directions and indirections, may result from deliberate suppression or unconscious repression of Hardy's feelings for Moule or his feelings about Moule's feelings.

The quotation from Corinthians 13: 4–7, used in 'The Blinded Bird' (*Moments of Vision, CPW*, 2:181) is not poetry but the eloquent prose of St Paul and the King James Bible, which Hardy incorporates in his last stanza, as he modulates the earlier pity and irony ('With God's consent') to anger. He is shocked, wants to shock us, and does :

> Who hath charity? This bird.
> Who suffereth long and is kind,
> Is not provoked, though blind
> And alive ensepulchured?
> Who hopeth, endureth all things?
> Who thinketh no evil, but sings?
> Who is divine? This bird.

'The Blinded Bird' wrests morality from the moral text to claim virtue for an animal and put down Christian anthropocentrism. It indicts human beings for a terrible failure of charity, in blinding and caging a bird for music. The poem's painful music most daringly revises St Paul, as after putting down humanity it goes on to propose that the singing bird suffers more than Christ, because 'blind and alive' in *its* sepulchre, equal to him in forgiveness, and – passionate thought in superb climax – in divinity. Hardy's most subtly didactic attack on Christianity, and his most subtly didactic plea for nonhuman animal life, the poem is also an apology for tragic art, though to say so is to abstract and generalize its passionate particulars.

He used a different part of the Epistle with the same wry hospitality for the poem 'Surview' in the next volume, *Late Lyrics and Earlier* (*CPW*, 2:485). It joins Corinthians 13:13 – the only Christian text admired by Jude in his agnostic prime – with folk or family superstition about the human voice in green firewood. Like 'The Blinded Bird' it is a dialogue between two texts, and sets side by side two passions, love (caritas or charity) and remorse. The form is appropriate: Sue Bridehead cut up the New Testament to make it new for herself, and Hardy cuts up Corinthians and puts it into his own text, interrupting and making his language new to subdue and rebuke self. In his appreciation of the poem, Gittings compares it to Yeats in old age,[15] and though Yeats gleefully casts off remorse and Hardy soberly takes it on, the poem is Yeatsian in the candour and passion with which it articulates a bitter state physically imaged in the Anglo-Saxon 'agenbite of inwit':

> A cry from the green-grained sticks of the fire
>   Made me gaze where it seemed to be;
> 'Twas my own voice talking therefrom to me
> On how I had walked when my sun was higher –
>   My heart in its arrogancy.

'You held not to whatsoever was true,'
   Said my own voice talking to me:
'Whatsoever was just you were slack to see;
Kept not things lovely and pure in view,'
   Said my own voice talking to me.

Refrain and repetition help to make the rigorous verse-by-verse examination. The self-spoken St Paul-quoting text shows self subdued, no longer arrogant, admitting guilt, giving way. As so often, Hardy's scrupulous 'seemed' places the act of imagination in a grave literal tone, especially striking in a fantasy.[16]

Hardy often treats sources as repositories to be rifled rather than texts to be respected, and this is particularly true of his classical allusions, for obvious linguistic reasons: their power depends not on manner but matter, subject not style. But some of them have considerable resonance. This is particularly true of an allusion to Horace in his last novel *Jude the Obscure*,[17] which, like the earlier *A Pair of Blue Eyes*, shows intricate traces of autobiography, though it is a much deeper and more complex tragedy. The classics are important in this story of frustrated scholarship, its tragic hero a poor man outside the walls of privileged Christminster or Oxbridge. A brief allusion links Jude with Antigone as he staggers drunkenly round the city with Arabella, in a scene which repeats his first visit when voices of the great thinkers and writers speak to him through the Christminster night, outside the college walls. Nearly at the end of his life and of the novel, he revisits the revered dead with drunken veneration, and memorably recalls Sophocles' Antigone, who says she belongs to the world of neither men nor ghosts. (This contrasts sharply with an obtrusive allusion in the last paragraph of the story 'For Conscience' Sake,' written about nine years earlier, when Millbourne's merely dutiful marriage is compared to Antigone's 'honourable observance of a rite' [430].) Jude's invocation of Antigone, so appropriate in genre and register, is desolately eloquent of his exile, solitude, and displacement. It is also typical of the novel, where three central characters are very well read, that most – though not all – allusions are socially and psychologically assimilated and motivated.

This culturally natural–seeming allusion begins, on some occasions, in the first published novel *Desperate Remedies* where Edward and Cytherea naturally exchange and cap poetic quotation, though in a narrative too heavily sprinkled with cultural allusion. But in the mature *Jude* the characterizing quotation is much better used, for instance when

Sue irritatingly and endearingly teases Jude to say she is like the ethe-real woman-image of 'Epipsychidion,' or offers comic-pathetic quota-tions from John Stuart Mill to back her request for separation, driving wretched Phillotson to complain, 'I don't care about John Stuart Mill,' or when Jude's reference to Antigone is justified by mind, feeling, and the tragic genre. Jude and Sue quote as pedantically as their author but their pedantry is placed and recognized in character and situation.

Hardy's great classical allusion is to Horace, in book I, chapter 5, of *Jude the Obscure*, making a moment in his work where classical and poetic influence is most sympathetic, structurally pointed, and locally effective. Jude reads Horace's 'Carmen Saeculare,' written to be sung by a chorus of young men and women in the Temple of Apollo at the Annual Games which Augustus revived, and for which Maecenas got Horace the commission:

> On a day when Fawley was getting quite advanced, being now about sixteen, and had been stumbling through the 'Carmen Saeculare' ... he found himself to be passing over the high edge of the plateau by the Brown House. The light had changed, and it was the sense of this which had caused him to look up. The sun was going down, and the full moon was rising simultaneously behind the woods in the opposite quarter. His mind had become so impregnated with the poem that, in a moment of the same impulsive emotion which years before had caused him to kneel on the ladder, he stopped the horse, alighted, and glancing round to see that nobody was in sight, knelt down on the roadside bank with open book. He turned first to the shiny goddess, who seemed to look so softly and critically at his doings, then to the disappearing luminary on the other hand, as he began:
>
> 'Phoebe silvarumque potens Diana!'
>
> The horse stood still till he had finished the hymn, which Jude repeated under the sway of a polytheistic fancy that he would never have thought of humouring in broad daylight. (58)

Jude is inspired by art and nature, teeming with passion for both. Neither has priority: he is arrested by a change in the light and his mind is ready, 'impregnated' by a poem. The consequence is a sacred mo-ment, pleasantly and pedantically glossed by the narrator, but only after he has presented a solemn drama, with the visionary student kneeling, in night and secrecy, gazing at the apotheosized heavenly bodies in turn, before reading aloud. Jude turns to the moon before the sun, reversing Horace's ordering in a nice nuance. This episode shows the writer writing about a reader, revering literature.

Of course the scene is structurally important, linked with one of the sacred places in the novel, the ridge by an old barn known as the Brown House, a place outside Marygreen from which in different lights – light is important to Hardy – the lights and buildings of Christminster are sometimes visible. It is recalled several times in childhood, as the place of Jude's first vision of Christminster, of his kneeling (on a ladder) in a later vision, for this salutation to a god of poetry and goddess of chastity, for a negation as Jude forgets its significance (along with learning and chastity) when he goes there with Arabella, for Sue's purchase of her Diana and Apollo, in another branch of narrative pattern, and as a fatal place where Jude catches his death on a blanket in rain and cold wind after the final parting from Sue. The place accumulates significance in a ritual proper to the novel but its roots go deeper than individual art.

The allusion links Hardy's novel with Horace's poem, for instance in its reference to youth and virginity – ironic, but unironic as well – in the metaphor 'impregnated,' so fertile compared with the actual impregnations in the story, and in its celebration of another older great seat of culture, Rome, in the site of Jude's real and fantastic Christminster visions. Horace was a poet Hardy presumably knew well, in translation and the original, quotes elsewhere, and surely found congenial in his metres (especially the Sapphics Hardy loved), as well as his humour, scepticism, poetic self-reference, cool acceptance of age and time, social and personal irony, and candid passion. Jude's reading comes from his author's love of the Roman poet, but it must be seen as an instance of the local strength of allusion, which is at least as important as its source-reference or its place in the pattern.

Jude's response to poetry is stimulated by his response to the natural world, as sunset and moonrise pull him out of his baker's cart to read the nineteen quatrains of the long poem, in privacy and solitude. Horace's ode is totally relevant to the thrilling natural scene of woods lit by sun and moon just when his learning is sufficiently assimilated to join love of art and nature with prompt recognition of the old gods. Hardy's choice of Latin line is tactful: the gods' names are fairly familiar, and probably only 'silvarumque' would be unintelligible to readers who knew no Latin, and he mentions woods, with sun and moon, before he quotes. Jude has to read the whole poem out loud, performing a ritual, but for the reader the one line is sufficient. (The whole would be impossible, too long, with too much Latin or too much translation.)

Jude's lonely classical study is paying off, not because it will get him into Oxbridge, but because it is real education, clarifying, enriching, and changing his personal life. This is one of Hardy's most powerful claims for education and also for his own art, and a highly successful allusion because it is so thoroughly internalized, so imaginatively placed in character. It is a good moment because Hardy is not only making Jude's reading part of character and plot – erotic, worshipful, secular, imaginative, resisted by super-ego, part of a young man's life process – but because it shows what happens when great books become part of the self, part of sexuality and mind, unifying sensibility, poetry, nature, beauty, and learning. Hardy has understood and internalized the poem and its archetypes, and through Jude's story he hands on poetry and myth to the reader, making a new archetype of secular prayer and worship.

Moreover, the novel's great social subject is all there, spelled out in the reading of the ode. The value of education is justified, classical learning and literature celebrated, but above all, Jude's extramural exile and rights are depicted with ease and beauty. It is the best defence of education in the humanities I know. It is a fine example of something rare and important, the use of literature to show a personal development in skill and learning. Hardy traces it from Jude's first sad funny disappointment, based on his own, when he finds no code for translating one language into another, to this episode where a studious neglected boy driving a cart reads a great dead foreign poet and knows why. He knows because his author knows that response to poetry should be a movement from learning to feeling, a rediscovery of the book in that life experience which is its origin. So he lets Jude join his passion and excitement with Horace's.

In the process he appreciates Horace. Like the best allusion – say Joyce reading Homer or Picasso mimicking Velasquez – this comes out of deep response to art. I do not want to exaggerate Hardy's sophistication: he was not a critic as Joyce was, and we cannot really know how good his Latin was, but he shows an understanding of Horace's poetry and his gods, renewing the secular sensual poet's response to Apollo and Diana in nature, in sun, moon, and youth. Hardy comments rather dryly that Jude repeated 'the hymn under the sway of a polytheistic fancy that he would never have thought of humouring in broad daylight' (part 1, chapter 5, 58). In this scene, however, Hardy opens his imagination, and ours, to ritual and its path to ecstasy. This is one reason why the scene is so moving.

There is a political reason too. Perhaps Hardy's experience of moving from the hard grind of learning to impassioned response and application to life explains why his best allusion is to a Roman not an English poet. It is an assimilated allusion because Hardy is thinking about assimilating poetry. And about assimilating knowledge. His last novel leaves us with Jude's deathbed yearning after academe. The reader's assent to this affirmation of a social need for educational equality – still unfulfilled – must draw on Jude stopping by woods at sunset and moonrise. The thoroughly motivated allusion ensures that the sensitive reader knows at the end what Jude's wasted powers have been. It is also of biographical interest, as Hardy's moving dramatized evidence of Jude's scholarship and ambition relives Hardy's scholarship and ambition, about which he was evasive. Perhaps he did once meet a boy reading Latin in a baker's cart as he claimed in *The Life and Work*, or perhaps he made up the story to strengthen his disclaimer of autobiography. What is certain is that he imagined Jude's ambition and achievement from intimate knowledge and feeling. The scene is fully responsive to the novel's subject of frustrated aptitude, responsible in no small measure for the feeling of waste Hegel thought essential to tragedy.

In 1895 Hardy was fifty-five, an experienced novelist and a poet recently restored to poetry, and in this late novel he could generalize and reparticularize a complex response to great poetry. His sympathy is active, is for a reader like his own young studious self, perhaps for the adolescent singers of Horace's 'Carmen Saeculorum.' Innocence and experience, as well as invention, make the allusion radiant and truthful. The episode reflects on Hardy's life with detached understanding, in maturity of art and life riper than his hero's, whose experience is tactfully kept spontaneous, intuitive, and short-lived. It looks like one of Sartre's privileged moments, but a backlash returns the hero to contingency, shocked into giving up poetry and Ionic dialect for 'the Gospels and Epistles in Griesbach's text': 'Ultimately he decided that in his sheer love of reading he had taken up a wrong emotion for a Christian young man' (chapter 5, 58). Like 'The Blinded Bird' this is a devastating critique of Christianity. It is also an appreciation of art's power and perils. The word 'impregnate' suggests inspiration, dangerous rapture, and strange gods, and the tragic ascetic recoil is a fine psychological touch which also controls romantic feeling, Jude's in one way, Hardy's and the reader's in another. There must be a return from ecstasy to contingency, though we regret Jude's self-chastening, and the life to which he returns.

The scene dramatizes and exemplifies Longinus's 'Sublime' in high art and nature, here coinciding to inspire thought and feeling. The lonely, reverent, and erotic reading of Horace's poetry in response to sublime nature is itself sublime, but placed historically, philosophically, and psychologically, not isolated but concentrated in a perfected imaginative moment, allusion at its best, a modern novelist's engagement with a classical poet, a dialogue crossing cultures and centuries, a participation in ritual.

NOTES

1 Paul Turner, *The Life of Thomas Hardy* (Oxford: Blackwell, 1998). Some proposed readings I find implausible; for example, couples caught in bad weather as versions of Dido and Aeneas.
2 Samuel Hynes, *The Pattern of Hardy's Poetry* (Chapel Hill: University of North Carolina Press, 1961); Kenneth Marsden, *The Poetry of Thomas Hardy* (London: Athlone, 1967).
3 Marsden, *Poetry*, 232.
4 Thomas Hardy, *Collected Short Stories*, New Wessex Edition, ed. F.B. Pinion, introduction by Desmond Hawkins (London: Macmillan 1988), 289. Hardy can fit style to teller but this detail is unlikely to be the idiolect of a rural dean telling the story. All references to the short stories are from this edition and hereafter cited parenthetically as *CSS*.
5 Shakespearean influence is present in comic-pathetic narrative like Mother Cuxsom's story of Susan Henchard's death in *The Mayor of Casterbridge*, which recalls the Hostess's narration of Falstaff's dying (*Henry V*).
6 All quotations from novels are from *The Novels of Thomas Hardy*, New Wessex Edition (London: Macmillan, 1974–5) and will be cited parenthetically.
7 *The Complete Poetical Works of Thomas Hardy*, ed. Samuel Hynes, 5 vols (Oxford: Clarendon, 1982–95), 1:133. All references to the poems are from this edition and hereafter cited parenthetically as *CPW*.
8 Hardy changes music and meaning of 'idled past the garth' in 'The Avon idled past the garth and tower' to 'just as always glassed,' the more precise 'glassed' replacing personification, rhyming with the deleted 'past' and making new internal rhyme, and the single 'a' assonance replaced by

alliterative 's'es (*CPW*, 2:173n). Hardy may allude obliquely to Shakespeare at 'The End of the Episode' (*CPW*, 1:277), which goes one better than 'the course of true love never did run smooth,' with 'The paths of love are rougher / Than thoroughfares of stone.'

9 The discussion of Tennyson that follows is a revision of material in *Tennyson and the Novelists* (Tennyson Society Occasional Paper 9, Lincoln: Tennyson Society, 1993). Tennyson quotations not in Hardy are from *Tennyson*, ed. Christopher Ricks (London: Longman Annotated English Poets, 1969).

10 See Robert Gittings, *Young Thomas Hardy* (London: Heinemann, 1975), 135.

11 *The Life and Work of Thomas Hardy*, ed. Michael Millgate (London: Macmillan, 1984), 81–2.

12 Gittings, *Young Thomas Hardy*, 166–8.

13 Michael Millgate, *Thomas Hardy: A Biography* (Oxford: Oxford University Press, 1982), 127. Unreferenced biographical information in this essay is from this book.

14 Millgate, *Biography*, 154–6.

15 Robert Gittings, *The Older Hardy* (London: Heinemann, 1978), 190.

16 See Barbara Hardy, 'Good Times in *Jude the Obscure*: Constructing Fictions,' in *Thomas Hardy: Imagining Imagination in Hardy's Poetry and Fiction* (London: Athlone, 2000), 57–82.

17 Ibid., 64–6.

5 Hardy's Subterranean Child

U.C. KNOEPFLMACHER

The recent speculation that Hardy may have authored or coauthored a group of child-poems previously attributed to Florence Hardy has re-kindled old questions about the nature of his engagement with child-hood.[1] Are the 'six helpless creatures' described as 'captives' of 'the two Durbeyfield adults'[2] and the wizened Father Time, an Ancient Mariner in a little boy's body, truly the quintessential figurations of the Hardy child they are often adduced to be? Does not the depiction of such 'little captives' conform with the insistence, in poems such as 'The Unborn,' 'In Childbed,' and 'To An Unborn Pauper Child,' that infants might fare better if 'unwombed'? Do verses like 'To A Motherless Child' and 'Midnight on the Great Western' thus merely ratify a steadfast belief that childhood cannot prepare us for the vicissitudes of adult life?

Hardy's Blakean tendency to view Innocence through the sobering eyes of Experience, I think, does not drastically depart from the dialectic that his nineteenth-century predecessors and contemporaries dramatized in works written for children as well as for adults. Hardy merely gives that dialogue some significant new twists of his own. For he is determined neither to deify living children nor to endow dead children with supernatural or transformative powers. Hardy's young are neither exemplary angel-children like George MacDonald's Diamond in *At the Back of the North Wind* nor inspirational ghost-children reabsorbed, like Lucy Gray, into 'Nature's holy plan.' Hardy's mockery of that Wordsworthian phrase at the end of his description of the Durbeyfield children (*Tess*, 28), signals his persistent scorn of the Romantic and Victorian tendency to exalt the pure, unclouded brow of virginal innocents as a foil to adult tribulations. In their steady subversion of a prevalent Romantic/Victorian typology, Hardy's constructions of childhood are not only antisentimental but also programmatically antiliterary and antiaesthetic.

Still, Hardy's subversive reliance on the typology of childhood is hardly limited to the shock tactics he introduces when he compels his readers to confront the 'triplet of little corpses'[3] he hangs in Jude's and Sue Bridehead's closet. There is a much broader range of roles that Hardy assigns to children who – in his poems as much as in his fictions – are always enlisted to correct faulty adult presuppositions. The 'journeying boy' whom a doleful speaker addresses in 'Midnight on the Great Western'[4] may well be as unsuited for life in the 'world unknown' towards which he travels as his fictional analogue, Father Time. But when Hardy deliberately creates another such child-pilgrim in 'At the Railway Station, Upway' (CPW, 2:377), he makes sure to reverse the earlier poem's emphasis.

Whereas the traveller of 'Midnight on the Great Western' becomes the mute and unknowing object of an adult speaker's apostrophes, the voice of a 'pitying child' dominates the opening of 'At the Railway Station, Upway.' The young fiddler promises to ease a handcuffed convict's cares, and, when he does, it is an adult 'captive' who can now be refreshed by a Song of Innocence. Stirred by the violin's music, the prisoner, infected by a 'grimful glee,' bursts into spontaneous song. Even the constable about to transport him to the prison house of Experience smiles benignly. The division between adult and child is briefly erased in something not unlike a lyrical Wordsworthian 'spot of time.' But the spell is broken as soon as movement resumes. The final couplet reinstates the temporal binaries of Blake's 'contrary' states of being. When 'the train came in –' we are left with a bare juxtaposition: 'The convict, and boy with the violin.'

I shall revisit Hardy's poetry with its wider array of childhood figurations in the last portion of this essay. But first I want to look at Hardy's reliance on fictional boy protagonists who perform subversive roles that markedly differ from the one he assigns to Father Time. Whereas Jude's son is belatedly introduced as a deus ex machina in Hardy's last novel, the boy who acts as his mother's agent in 'The Withered Arm' is given an ironic function from the very outset of that 1888 short story. And, unlike the bitterly ironic narrator who describes the Durbeyfield innocents from the distanced and disenchanted perspective of Experience, the untrustworthy adult narrator Hardy adopts for his 1892 novella, *Our Exploits at West Poley*, is a reminiscing grownup who tries to involve an audience of juvenile readers in a reconstruction of underground adventures he claims to have experienced at the age of thirteen.

1

Set in the 1820s, 'The Withered Arm' moves away from its opening focus on the bitterness of Rhoda Brook, a milkmaid who bore an illegitimate son to Farmer Lodge. As the story progresses, it moves from Experience to Innocence by depicting the increasing plight of the farmer's young wife, the well-meaning Gertrude Lodge, who knows nothing about her husband's liaison. Hardy quickly connects these two antipodal female figures through a child. Rhoda's boy, whose age and name are never given, allows himself to be drawn into a drama of sexual rivalry when his mother enlists him as her spy:

> 'They've just been saying down in barton that your father brings his young wife home from Anglebury to-morrow,' [she] observed. 'I shall want to send you for a few things to market, and you'll be pretty sure to meet 'em.'
> 'Yes, mother,' said the boy. 'Is father married, then?'
> 'Yes ... You can give her a look, and tell me what she's like, if you do see her.'
> 'Yes, mother.'
> 'If she's dark or fair, and if she's tall – as tall as I. And if she seems like a woman who has ever worked for a living, or one that has been always well off, and has never done anything, and shows marks of the lady on her, as I expect she do.'
> 'Yes.'
> They crept up the hill in the twilight, and entered the cottage. It was built of mud-walls, the surface of which had been washed by many rains into channels and depressions that left none of the original flat face visible; while here and there in the thatch above a rafter showed like a bone protruding through the skin. (I: 'A Lorn Milkmaid')[5]

Hardy here deftly prepares us for the melodrama he has yet to unfold. The resemblance between a rafter and a bone protruding through scarred skin anticipates the image of the horribly withered arm that Rhoda's jealousy will inflict on her female rival. Just as important, however, is Hardy's juggling of different levels of awareness. We expect the boy introduced here to be less knowing than his mother. But he is no

Wordsworthian innocent. Lucy Gray and Johnny Foy were wrongly
pressed into adult missions by their elders. Yet this boy, who is as
curious as his mother, is Rhoda's willing accomplice. Fully aware of his
father's identity – and hence of his own illegitimacy – he knows far
more than the newly wed Gertrude Lodge, who, in the story's next
segment, cannot fathom why she is being scrutinized 'through and
through' by a sharp-eyed young observer.

Trudging along on the road ahead of the gig in which Gertrude and
her husband are riding, the boy keeps looking back intently at Gertrude.
Although he is weighted down by a 'large bundle,' he takes note of her
every feature, 'from the curve of her little nostril to the colour of her
eyes' (60). The boy's anatomizing gaze resembles that of a male adult,
as mesmerized by the particulars of female beauty as the narrator of
Tess. His provocative behaviour almost makes him a precocious rival to
his 'annoyed' father. Yet Farmer Lodge is at a decided disadvantage.
Eager to hide his sexual history from his young bride, he must pretend
to take 'no outward notice of his son' (60). It is therefore Gertrude who,
unaware of the farmer's relation to Rhoda, is the sole innocent at this
point of the story. She is more childlike than the boy who acts as the
willing agent of the 'fallen' woman who is his mother:

'How that poor lad stared at me!' said the young wife.
'Yes, dear; I saw that he did.'
'He is one of the village, I suppose?'
'One of the neighbourhood. I think he lives with his mother a mile or
two off.'
'He knows who we are, no doubt?'
'Oh yes. You must expect to be stared at just at first, my pretty Gertrude.'
'I do, – though I think the poor boy may have looked at us in the hope
we might relieve him of his heavy load, rather than from curiosity.'
'Oh no,' said her husband, off-handedly. 'These country lads will carry
a hundredweight once they get it on their backs; besides, his pack had
more size than weight in it.' (II: 'The Young Wife,' 60)

Farmer Lodge's dismissal of the boy and of the weight he carries can
be applied to the slight part that we expect such a secondary character
to play in the narrative. But the reader's innocence will be disabused as
much as that of the naive Gertrude. After the boy reports to his mother
by declaring Gertrude to be a 'lady complete,' his function in the story
would appear to be over. Still, his meticulous listing of 'lightish' hair,

'bluish' eyes, 'red' mouth, and 'white' teeth only stings Rhoda into
hoping that her competitor might at least be shorter than she is (61).
When her child protests that he could hardly have been expected to
determine the height of a sitting woman, Rhoda again presses him into
service. Yet when a second inspection leads him to certify that Gertrude
is indeed 'rather short,' almost girlish in her tiny stature, the boy's role
as Hardy's surrogate narrator seems to have ended. There is no further
information he can provide:

> 'Ah!' said his mother, with satisfaction.
> 'But she's very pretty – very. In fact, she's lovely.' The youthful fresh-
> ness of the yeoman's wife had evidently made an impression even on the
> somewhat hard nature of the boy.
> 'That's all I want to know,' said his mother quickly. 'Now, spread the
> table-cloth. The hare you wired is very tender; but mind that nobody
> catches you. – You've never told me what sort of hands she had.'
> 'I have never seen 'em. She never took off her gloves.' (62)

Soon, however, Rhoda herself can inspect the 'uncovered' left hand
and arm of her sexual rival. For Gertrude visits her cottage after promising the boy that she would bring him 'better boots' (III: 'A Vision,' 64).
Having drawn this childless benefactress into his mother's orbit, the
boy can presumably be dropped from a tale that now shifts, unexpectedly, into a Gothic mode. As we move into the realm of the uncanny, we
depend on the guarded authority of Hardy's narrator. The account of
Rhoda's nightmare, of the terrifying mark that it leaves on Gertrude's
arm, and of the deformed arm's equally horrific antidote cannot be
rendered through the limited eyes of a child witness.[6]

But Hardy toys with the reader's innocence as relentlessly as he toys
with the innocence of Gertrude Lodge. We are almost as severely jarred
as she will be upon discovering that the boy who had apparently
dropped out of the narrative is, in fact, crucial to its climax when, as a
freshly hanged criminal, his broken neck supposedly cures Gertrude's
deformity. Only now, in retrospect, are we allowed to recall some of the
subtle forebodings that Hardy had implanted to suggest that this young
voyeur might well grow into a more deviant malefactor. The marginal
existence of Rhoda's illegitimate son has had unforeseen consequences.
Unchecked in childhood, his aberrant behaviour became excessively
punishable in adult life.

For the boy who caught the 'tender' hare that Rhoda prepared for dinner has in later youth declined further into criminality. Deprived of his patrimony, he cared as little about the property of others as Rhoda Brook cared about controlling her jealousy of the 'lady' who unwittingly usurped her rightful place. Obsessed by her desire to know more about her rival's physical appearance, Rhoda had earlier failed to notice that her son was busily 'cutting a notch with his pocket-knife' into one of the cottage chairs (59). The reader has been similarly inattentive. There seemed to be no good reason to put much weight on Hardy's seemingly casual allusion to the boy's 'somewhat hard nature' (62). Like the tender Gertrude, who had so genuinely pitied a destitute boy, we have ourselves been forced to harden our attitude towards all the story's characters. Our sentimentality has been undercut.

Innocence, then, is the satirical target of this pseudo-Gothic tale. 'The Withered Arm' is as merciless with poor Gertrude Lodge – repudiated because of her disfigured beauty and for bringing her husband 'no child' – as with unwary readers similarly disposed to overidentify with the plight of wronged dairymaids and unacknowledged children. The story's closure reinforces its hardened – and Hardyesque – satire of circumstance. Though healed, Gertrude dies of shock, and Rhoda disappears after she and Farmer Lodge bury their delinquent son. The Farmer soon bequeaths 'the whole of his not inconsiderable property to a reformatory for boys, subject to the payment of a small annuity to Rhoda Brook, if she could be found to claim it' (IX. 'A Rencounter,' 85). But Rhoda does not vanish or dissolve into Nature, as she might have done had she been cast as the desolate Margaret in Wordsworth's 'The Ruined Cottage.' When she returns to her native village, she rejects the annuity left by Farmer Lodge, preferring instead to resume the rhythms of her 'monotonous' milking at the dairy. She has become an icon of Experience. Outside observers cannot help but 'wonder what sombre thoughts were beating inside that impassive, wrinkled brow, to the rhythms of the alternating milk-streams' (85).

Unlike a youthful Tess, this withered milkmaid has survived a double subversion of Innocence. Not only her own innocence but also that of her naive sexual rival have been violated. Yet like Tess, she remains blameless. Rhoda cannot be held responsible for the vengeful fate that destroys the childish Gertrude as well as her unchildish son. She had no control over the nightmare that destroyed the woman who so kindly tried to provide the boy with better boots. And her imprudence in pressing her willing son into a mission triggered by sexual envy is hardly responsible for his early death. Like Father Time, this young coney-catcher has been Hardy's own agent rather than his mother's. We are not asked to bemoan his premature death with thoughts too deep for tears. Instead, his death – like that of Father Time – merely corrects our faulty post-Romantic overestimation of the redemptive power of Innocence.

2

Hardy wrote *Our Exploits at West Poley* as an 'experiment in first person-narration' five years before the 1888 'The Withered Arm.' But the novella he sold to the American *Youth's Companion* was not published until 1892–3.[7] His venture into the burgeoning market of children's literature allowed Hardy to view the clash between Innocence and Experience from a rather different vantage point. Whereas 'The Withered Arm' observes both children and childlike adults through the harsh lens of Experience, *Our Exploits at West Poley* supposedly adopts the perspective of a participant in youthful 'exploits' that were initiated without any inhibiting adult supervision or control. While on a visit to his permissive aunt, 'a farmer's widow,' the thirteen-year-old Leonard – whom the grownup narrator now remembers as having been 'rather small for my age' (though extremely 'robust and active') – is blissfully free from the authority of his 'schoolmaster' father.[8] He thus markedly differs from the boy who, controlled by the embittered Rhoda Brook, became an omniscient ironist's prime subversive agent.

In writing to the *Youth's Companion* to inquire about the delay in publication, Hardy seemed slightly self-conscious about having ventured into unfamiliar terrain. He worried that the American editors might possibly have found his story 'too juvenile for your side of the sea' and allowed that 'children here' were perhaps 'younger for their age than yours.' But he also hinted that it might be an error to read his narrative as overtly 'juvenile': 'I fancy you may be mistaken in that.'[9] He had earlier suggested that, for greater precision, *Our Exploits at West Poley* could be subtitled 'A Tale of the Mendips' or 'A Rural Tale of Adventure in the West of England.' Yet such extra geographical information might have diluted the impact of the word 'Exploits' in the title. Even without a reader's awareness of the story's outcome, the word seems hyperbolic, more reflective of teenage self-importance than of an implied author's emphasis. A narrative that opens with Leonard's recollections of boyish feats in an uncharted underworld will soon reflect his own insecurities as an adult story-teller.

'The Withered Arm' began with the uneasy alliance between an adult and her prematurely mature child. But the opening paragraphs of *Our Exploits at West Poley* introduce a harmonious partnership between two compatible boys. Leonard is warmly embraced by Aunt Draycot's 'son Stephen, or Steve, as he was invariably called by his friends ... He was two or three years my senior, tall, lithe, ruddy, and somewhat masterful withal. There was that force about him which was less suggestive of intellectual power than (as Carlyle said of Cromwell) "Doughtiness – the courage and faculty to do"' (114). Steve, the Cromwellian boy of action, and Leonard, the intellectual schoolmaster's son, complement each other extremely well. They descend into Nick's Pocket, a nearby cave, with the same zest that had led another such pair, the all-American Huckleberry Finn and Tom Sawyer, into subterranean recesses that harboured a treasure as well as a villainous adult.

But Hardy, who had already written 'The Thieves Who Could Not Help Sneezing,' is uninterested in any further updating of 'Ali Baba and the Forty Thieves,' the *Arabian Nights* story so dear to Victorian readers young and old. Nor is he interested in creating encounters with fantastic underground denizens such as goblin miners or timid White Rabbits. There are no infernal treasures to be mined in Nick's Pocket. And there are no devils. The figure who comes closest to a villain is an abusive miller readily foiled by his former apprentice, Job, the third member of Steve's and Leonard's juvenile partnership. The trio seems self-sufficient. The only foil to their energy and enthusiasm is an illusionless figure called the 'Man who had Failed.' Yet even this oracular adult who acts as the voice of Experience by recollecting the futility of his own youthful 'exploits' intervenes infrequently and without ever affecting the plot. Powerless, he cannot curb the actions of the impetuous young adventurers.[10]

Although an adult Leonard may resort to Carlyle's description of Cromwell in order to portray the 'doughtiness' of his partner, he also makes sure to inform his readers that the original adventures were uncluttered by any such bookish associations. Adult book-learning, he insists, dissolved as soon as the boys penetrated a primordial underworld: 'Had my thoughts been in my books, I might have supposed we had ... reached the Stygian shore; but it was out of sight, out of mind, with my classical studies then' (118). Even science, widely embraced as an 'ardent' pursuit by today's young, as Leonard tells the putative readers of the *Youth's Companion*, held no interest whatsoever for these earlier explorers. Leonard notes that skeletons of 'great extinct beasts, and the remains of prehistoric men' that would fascinate late-Victorian children failed to attract youngsters who, at that time, 'could only conjecture on subjects in which the boys of the present generation are well-informed' (117).

What *does* attract Steve and Leonard, however, is an 'arched nook' they reach on their first descent, a 'delightful recess in the crystallized stone work, like the apse of a Gothic church.' Their desire to reach this inner sanctum and to 'sit there,' in Steve's words, 'like kings on a crystal throne,' is thwarted by a deep and swiftly moving stream they do not dare cross. Yet, by using a spade to divert the waters into a mouth-like 'hole,' the boys manage to reach their goal (118). Stunned by his contact with 'the beautiful, glistening niche, that had tempted us to our engineering,' Leonard admits becoming 'child enough, at that time, to clap my hands' (119). His older partner prefers to express his joy by proclaiming a quasi-sexual possessiveness: '"That's the way to overcome obstructions!" said Steve, triumphantly. "I warrant nobody ever got so far as this before"' (120).

Yet it is the regressive nature of this quest that Hardy prefers to stress. Leonard's childish hand clapping and shedding of book lore is complemented by his suggestive description of the glistening nook the boys are so eager to enter: 'My attention was so much attracted by the beautiful natural ornaments of the niche ... These covered the greater part of the sides and roof; they were flesh-coloured, and assumed the form of frills, lace, coats of mail; in many places they quaintly resembled the skin of geese after plucking, and in others the wattles of turkeys. All were decorated with water crystals' (120). This wet, pink-skinned hollow – red in spots, sheathed in a shiny, placenta-like armour – resembles a giant womb or birth canal. Leonard's desire to remain there thus offers still another metaphorical sheathing for the retrogressive yearning that propels so many Romantic and Victorian escapes into exotic fantasylands. But the boys cannot linger in the seductive penumbra of this underground. After their fading candles prompt them to return to the daylight above, they discover that their thoughtless rerouting of the underground stream has had an unexpected effect. The adult world they tried to flee has been altered by their retrogressive action. They have unwittingly halted the forward progress of the brook that supplied West Poley. The waters they have diverted now flow in a reverse direction into the larger village of East Poley.

Hardy uses this bifurcation to signal a growing rift between himself and his narrator. As Pamela Dalziel astutely notes, our 'confidence' in

Leonard's control of the story's own narrative flow is now diminished by his uneasiness and his sudden tendency to blame Steve for 'exploits' that had been communal.[11] For a while, both boys still bask in the presumed omnipotence of their godlike power to control nature. They try to absolve unexpected ethical questions. Should they restore the water power that fuels Miller Groffin's West Poley mill? Or should they not punish the man who had so cruelly maltreated Job, their new ally? When Steve contends that by benefiting East Poley they would actually bestow happiness on a much larger segment of the population, Leonard suddenly recalls a snatch of the book learning he had chosen to forget. He pedantically informs his partner that such a felicity calculus might seem better 'suited to the genius of Jeremy Bentham than to me.' Intoxicated with the prospect of garnering an even greater 'glory,' however, Steve fails to listen (128). For his power over the underground river's course has led him to concoct a plan worthy of Tom Sawyer's most elaborate machinations.

Hardy now openly mocks the boys as would-be adults whose self-glorifying fiction making cannot match his own sobering appeal to an audience of young readers. Putting on men's clothing, caps, and long beards made out of horse hair, Steve and Leonard disguise themselves as powerful 'magicians' in order to impress a crowd of East Poley children. The incantations they chant appear to stop and start the flow of the newly formed river. Coordinating their efforts with Job, whom they instruct to redirect the waters at the proper moment, the two adult impersonators awe their puerile audience. But their fun is soon over. For Hardy wants his own juvenile audience to recognize the limits of power he also purveys in his adult fictions and poems. Steve's and Leonard's phoney magic show is a diversion that is bound to fail. They soon learn that the full and unremitting pressures of the forward flow of Experience can never be diverted. As pseudomagicians and pseudo-adults, the boys have allowed Hardy to have his own fun with those Victorian entertainers who offered the young of all ages the opportunity to find momentary relief from 'dull reality' in unsustainable dreamworlds and subterranean wonderlands.[12]

By their continued tampering with underground energies they cannot master, Leonard and Stephen inflict further damage on the world above. After an escalation of misfortunes that are exacerbated by the hostility of the villagers who have become privy to their secret, only a dynamite explosion that nearly kills Steve can halt the disturbances the boys have caused. The detonation ends any possibility for further 'exploits.' When the cave's entry is permanently sealed, the 'Man who had Failed' is granted a final word. His delivery of the story's presumed moral seems to parody Dr Johnson's most sententious utterances: 'Exceptionally smart actions, such as you delight in, should be carefully weighed with a view to their utility before they are begun. Quiet perseverance in clearly defined courses is, as a rule, better than the erratic exploits that may do much harm' (163).

Steve – though not Leonard, the schoolmaster's son – justifiably chafes at this ponderous summation. Still, when this 'exceptionally smart' boy-adventurer questions the authority of a man notorious for having been unsuccessful in managing his own life, his mother steps in to reinforce the dictates of Experience. The old man, she points out, did not fail in life for 'want of sense' but rather because he suffered a 'want of energy.' A messenger's own failings, she asserts, therefore should not detract from the validity of his message: 'people of that sort, when kindly, are better worth attending to than those successful ones, who have never seen the seamy side of things. I would advise you to listen to him' (163). Leonard informs us that Steve followed his mother's advice. Combining his youthful energies with a newly acquired sobriety, he can now grow up to become 'the largest gentleman-farmer of those parts, remarkable for his avoidance of anything like speculative exploits' (163).

Unlike 'The Withered Arm,' then, *Our Exploits at West Poley* rewards the follies of Innocence: the misdirected energies of youth, like a misdirected underground river, can still be rechannelled as good 'sense.' The failed child can become father of the successful man. Even Job, the abused apprentice, avoids future enslavements. By addressing himself to an audience of juvenile readers and by dispensing with the implied ironies of third-person narration, Hardy thus softens the emphasis of his adult fictions without compromising his insistence on the mandates of Experience. The fate of the boy in 'The Withered Arm' seemed as predetermined as the fates of the Durbeyfield children or of Father Time. Yet, even though the 'exploits' of Steve and Leonard are ironized from the very start of the narrative, the boys are allowed to mature. The narrator of *Tess of the d'Urbervilles* caustically challenges Roger Ascham's dictum that 'long wandering' can lead us to the wisdom of Experience, by noting that often such wandering only 'unfits us for further travel, and of what use is our experience to us then?' (*Tess*, 102). The boys in *Our Exploits at West Poley* do not have to wander for very long. Endowed with the 'energy' lacking in the 'Man who had Failed,' they can grow beyond this debilitated expositor.

It might be argued, however, that such concessions make *Our Exploits at West Poley* a rather uncharacteristic Hardy text. Does the novella's relaxation of Hardy's habitual adherence to the grimmer teachings of Experience make it an anomaly? That question is best answered, I think, if we turn from Hardy's fiction to his poetry, where children and childlike creatures are just as prominently featured as in his fictions. I began this essay by considering 'At the Railway Station, Upway' as a foil to its more lugubrious pendant, 'Midnight on the Great Western.' I now want to sample poems written for adult readers rather than for the young whom Bernard Jones assumes Hardy addressed in poems attributed to Florence Dugdale before she became the second Mrs Hardy. There is a major affinity between the lyrics I have chosen to highlight and *Our Exploits at West Poley*. For in them, Hardy also taps young energies as a subterranean counterforce to the ironizing perspective of Experience. The vitality of youthful imaginings, he seems to allow, can complement and even challenge the disenchantments of our adult constructions of meaning.

3

By pitting Innocence against Experience, all poems considered in this final section are dialogic in nature. That dialogue, however, does not necessarily rely on clashing voices such as those which Hardy had used in *Our Exploits at West Poley* when the pronouncements of 'the Man who had Failed' collided with young Stephen's impetuous credo. Although a poem such as 'The Child and the Sage' (*CPW* 2:380–1) also relies on conflicting speakers, Hardy just as frequently relies on a single speaker to dramatize conflicting outlooks. Yet these speakers are now significantly less rhetorical than those that he had employed as a voice for Experience in poems such as 'To A Motherless Child' (1898; *CPW*, 1:85–6) or 'To an Unborn Pauper Child' (1901; *CPW* 1:163–4). The apostrophes of such earlier verses are refreshingly absent in the later poems in which an older Hardy paradoxically appears to be more willing to entertain – and perhaps even endorse – a child's imaginative capacities.

Set into song by Benjamin Britten, the seemingly whimsical 'Wagtail and Baby'(1907, 1909; *CPW* 1:357) renders the education of a tiny child-observer whom Hardy places at a symbolic crossing. Instead of blending into an insentient nature, however, this shrewd little bird-watcher benefits from his spectatorship of an event that Hardy had jokingly aggrandized as 'An Incident of Civilization.'[13] The identification of child with bird is very different here from little Jude Fawley's sentimental self-projection on the 'poor' little birdies he refused to scare away:

> A baby watched a ford, whereto
>   A wagtail came for drinking;
> A blaring bull went wading through,
>   The wagtail showed no shrinking.   (ll. 1–4)

When, in the next two stanzas, the charging bull is replaced by a splashing 'stallion' and then by a 'mongrel slowly slinking' (ll. 5, 10), the wagtail remains as unfearing as before. But it is the approach of a 'perfect gentleman,' a human grownup, that causes the bird to rise in 'terror' (ll. 13, 14). At this very point, in the poem's last line, that 'baby fell a-thinking' (l. 16).

The 'ford' has acted not just as a crossing for animals but also as a door or portal[14] for the child whom Hardy situates at the very threshold between Innocence and Experience. What precisely has this no-longer-thoughtless baby learned from the instinctual flight of a bird more terrified by a 'perfect gentleman' than by the fiercer quadrupeds that have used the crossing? The poem's ambiguity is delicious. Will baby hereafter emulate the wagtail by sharing its distrust of seemingly civilized grownups? Or has this natural observer now grasped its own superiority by realizing, as the boy Mowgli does while still among the wolf pack, that a human child's power exceeds that of any creature of a lower order? Unlike the male bird, the baby pointedly remains ungendered throughout the poem. Will it, if a boy, evolve into a terror-inspiring 'gentleman'? Or will it, if a girl who must guard her innocence, learn to distrust such 'perfect' male creatures?

If Hardy toys here with the ambiguity of baby's Janus-like position betwixt Innocence and Experience, he surprisingly seems to tip the scales towards childhood in poems such as 'The Child and the Sage' and 'The Children and Sir Nameless' (CPW, 2:399–400). Both poems, which appeared in the 1922 volume Later Lyrics and Earlier, depict a sharp generational conflict. In the first, an old man's expostulation elicits an innocent's rather crafty reply; the point of view of the Sage is already encased in the speech of his child-antagonist. The child-speaker who repeats 'You say' in the first three stanzas of the poem, carefully recreates his counterpart's contention that unusual bliss will inevitably be followed by disenchantments: just as 'cloudless skies' should lead the child to expect 'rain or snow,' so may 'sickness' mar his uninterrupted health and loss forever alter 'Love's unbroken smile' (ll. 3, 4, 8, 10).

But whereas Stephen in *Our Exploits* was grudgingly compelled to accept the gloomy predictions of the 'Man who had Failed,' this optimistic child-speaker is allowed to challenge the validity of any formula that claims to be premised on the infallible predictability of disappointment. A belief in such infallibility may, in fact, depend on the same sort of wishfulness that the jaundiced Sage has tried to discredit. There are rare occasions, as the child cogently contends, in which a 'Continuance of joy' might well remain unimpeded; if so, there is no reason to expect that any protracted period of 'ease' must automatically be followed by a 'burden of annoy' (ll. 14–16). In its unusual freedom from pain, the child's projected universe almost seems naively Edenic: 'But, Sage – this Earth – why not a place / Where no reprisals reign, / Where never a spell of pleasantness / Makes reasonable a pain?' (ll. 17–20). Yet the poem gives the last words to the child-speaker, thus deliberately leaving its final question unanswered. It is the reader, Hardy seems to imply, who must determine the validity of this credo of Innocence.[15]

Wordsworth had apostrophized the child as 'best philosopher.' Hardy's philosopher-child, however, offers a reply that cannot refute or defuse the Sage's expostulation. Yet Hardy also seems to back up this little sophist by suggesting that pessimistic happiness-deniers may be as prone to the vanity of human wishes as the blindest of happiness-seeking optimists. As in 'At the Railway Station, Upway,' he has once again created a pendant to offset his own, more typical, Sage-like prognostications. There is a considerable amount of self-irony here; the stalemate between these two extremes amounts to an unresolved self-debate. There is, characteristically, no mediating, no compromising *tertium quid* as in earlier Victorian productions, such as Tennyson's 'Two Voices.'

'The Children and Sir Nameless' (originally called 'The Children *versus* Sir Nameless')[16] also attacks the vanity of self-projections on the future. But it is hindsight now, rather than a child's faith in an unbroken 'spell of pleasantness,' that allows Hardy to subvert the hopes of an ancient knight who not only hates the 'wretched children romping in my park' but also congratulates himself for having (like Hardy) no 'offspring' to carry on his name (ll. 2, 8). This Ozymandias-figure hopes to perpetuate himself by shaping a replica of himself, 'a figure stretching seven-odd feet / (For he was tall) in alabaster stone, / With shield, and crest, and casque, and sword complete' (ll. 13–15). Yet this barren aristocrat's pretentious 'mightiness' is undercut by oblivion, the total erasure of his ancient name. And his namelessness has, in fact, been ensured by children, his nemesis. An ever-replenishing stock of playful youngsters have progressively defaced – and will continue to deface – the monument through which the knight tried to perpetuate himself.

Sir Nameless has been unable to keep at bay the pesky antagonists who dared to 'trample' his park's 'herbage' (l. 3). Three hundred years later, his 'effigy so large in frame' acts as the flooring placed under 'the seats of schoolchildren' who depreciate him as much as he had depreciated them: 'And they / Kicked out his name, and hobnailed off his nose; / And, as they yawn through sermon-time, they say, / 'Who was this old stone man beneath our toes?" (ll. 21–4). The poem wittily reverses Blake's old binaries. Experience is not really represented by an adult but rather by the child-avengers who have contributed to the erosion of his name and face. The deformed and mutilated knight is actually as naive as Gertrude Lodge was in 'The Withered Arm.' His expectations are thwarted as much as those of the childless young woman who was unable to provide Farmer Lodge with an official heir.

In the grimly ironic conclusion to the earlier novella, the 'hard' child for whom a solicitous Gertrude felt such pity had to be sacrificed in order to provide her with the antidote for her withered arm. In the poem, however, hardy children exact the retribution that Rhoda Brook wished on Gertrude after her son took a close look at her rival. The children who once trampled out the herbage of a proud knight's park may have withered away. But their energies are kept alive by their successors. The schoolchildren who show such contempt for the stone man beneath their toes are as transgressive as the children who once disregarded the prohibitions of a living adult. Rhoda Brook's son, too, was a transgressor. The boy who defaced his mother's chairs had to harden into a corpse to cure Gertrude Lodge of her last illusions. But the children who deface a stone effigy have Experience on their side. They are as self-renovating as the new forms of life that Hardy placed in the hull of a skeletal Titanic.

In the three poems I have discussed, Hardy greatly complicates the opposition between Innocence and Experience he had dramatized in his fictions and his earlier verses. There are a good many other poems that illustrate his new attempts to find ways of transposing and inter-penetrating Blake's two 'contrary' states into more 'neutral-tinted' constructs. Thus, the perspectives of youth and age are also realigned in 1928 poems such as 'Boys Then and Now' (*CPW*, 3:226–7), 'Childhood

Among the Ferns' (*CPW* 3:199–200), and 'He Never Expected Much' (*CPW*, 3:225). And even 'The Calf,' an earlier production that seems to be accepted as his by those who may still question Hardy's authorship of all other verses in the 1911 *The Book of Baby Beasts*, can profitably be related to his undisputed text for child-readers, *Our Exploits at West Poley*.

Hardy's bovine speaker acknowledges that her future may be almost as much in doubt as that of Lewis Carroll's calf-headed Mock-Turtle. But she is no weeper. She claims that, if allowed to live 'in a dairy-home,' she, too, may become a quasi-fantastical hybrid. For she would become as 'contemplative' as any adult and yet remain as joyfully oblivious to time as any small child.[17] Hardy sets the calf's vision of a future in a watery crossing, much like the underground river that Leonard and Stephen managed to cross or the 'ford' in which a wagtail's responses to those who traversed the brook allowed baby to cross over into a new consciousness. The 'fair stream' in which the calf-turned-cow hopes to stand some day will continue to flow well beyond its stationary position. But the moving waters that lubricate its tongue allow it, for a very brief moment, to become as much of a fitfully joyous singer as any death-defying, darkling thrush:

> When grown up (if they let me live)
> And in a dairy-home,
> I may less wonder and misgive
> Than now, and get contemplative,
> And never wish to roam.
>
> And in some fair stream, taking sips,
> May stand through summer noons,
> With water dribbling from my lips
> And rising halfway to my hips,
> And babbling pleasant tunes.

NOTES

1 See Martin Ray's review of Bernard Jones, ed., *Fifty-Seven Poems by Thomas Hardy* in *Thomas Hardy Journal* 18.3 (October 2002): 123–6.

2 Thomas Hardy, *Tess of the d'Urbervilles*, ed. Juliet Grindle and Simon Gatrell (Oxford: Oxford University Press, 1988), 28. Future references to

this edition will be given in the text.

3   Thomas Hardy, *Jude the Obscure*, ed. Patricia Ingham (Oxford: Oxford University Press, 1985), 354.

4   *The Complete Poetical Works of Thomas Hardy*, ed. Samuel Hynes, 5 vols (Oxford: Clarendon, 1982–95), 2:262. Hereafter cited parenthetically as *CPW*.

5   *Wessex Tales*, ed. Kathryn R. King (Oxford: Oxford University Press, 1998), 58–9. Future references to this edition of 'The Withered Arm' will be given in the text.

6   In his 1919 preface to *Wessex Tales* (3), Hardy ironically depreciates his own reliability as a witness. An 'aged friend,' he claims, has reminded the author (himself now seventy-nine years old!) that he has misremembered the 'facts' about Rhoda Brook's dream. The 'incubus' that 'oppressed her' did not appear in a 'midnight dream' but rather while she was 'lying down on a hot afternoon.' Hardy's contention that 'my forgetfulness has weakened the facts out of which the tale grew' is relevant to what I shall have to say about his deliberate use of an unreliable narrator for *Our Exploits At West Poley*.

7   'Introduction,' *An Indiscretion in the Life of an Heiress and Other Stories*, ed. Pamela Dalziel (Oxford: Oxford University Press, 1994), xxii. Hereafter cited as *Indiscretion* The novella eventually appeared in *Household*, a short-lived magazine 'Devoted to the Interests of the American Housewife,' from November 1892 to April 1893. It was Hardy's second attempt to reach juvenile readers. But 'The Thieves Who Could Not Help Sneezing,' published in *Father Christmas* in December 1877 and reprinted by Dalziel (36–42) is a hastily written and anecdotal story that she rightly finds far too 'short and slight' (xxii).

8   Dalziel, *Indiscretion*, 114. All future page references given in the text will be to this edition.

9   Quoted by Richard L. Purdy in his introduction to *Our Exploits at West Poley* (Oxford: Oxford University Press, 1978), vii.

10 In 'The Withered Arm,' Conjuror Tremble, who first identifies the cause of Gertrude's malady and then informs her about the antidote she must seek, ostensibly affects the story's plot far more directly than the knowledgeable but impotent 'Man who had Failed.' But Hardy makes sure to stress that, for all his 'magical' knowledge, Tremble is similarly impaired: 'You think too much of my powers!' the conjuror tells Gertrude, protesting that he has become too 'old and weak' to intervene in her cure ('The Withered Arm,' 74). It is tempting to identify both Tremble and the 'Man who had Failed' as stand-ins for an author who is himself reluctant to assert his

own godlike powers over the actions of his invented characters. Even Hardy's narrators, as Linda Shires has argued, are always distanced from the implied author and hence are denied the omniscience other Victorian narrators often possess; see Linda Shires, 'The Unknowing Omniscience of Hardy's Narrators,' in Phillip Mallett, *Thomas Hardy: Texts and Contexts* (London: Palgrave, 2002), 41.

11 Dalziel, introduction, xxiv.

12 Lewis Carroll, *Alice in Wonderland*, ed. Donald J. Gray (New York: Norton, 1992), 98.

13 Upon placing the poem into the 1909 volume of *Time's Laughingstocks*, Hardy removed the subtitle he had used for the version published in the *Albany Review* in April 1907. See *CPW* 1:357.

14 The Latin *portus* is a root for both 'ford' and 'port.'

15 One such reader, J.O. Bailey, however, seems determined to allow no such ambiguity when he claims that the 'child's view suggests that of Little Father Time in *Jude the Obscure*.' See *The Poetry of Thomas Hardy: A Handbook and Commentary* (Chapel Hill: The University of North Carolina Press, 1970), 457.

16 See *CPW*, 2:309.

17 *Fifty-Seven Poems by Thomas Hardy*, ed. Bernard Jones (Gillingham, Dorset: Meldon House, 2002), 19.

6 Written in Stone:
Hardy's Grotesque Sublime

MARJORIE GARSON

Since Thomas Hardy is the son of a stonemason and an architect with a professional interest in Gothic design, it is not surprising that stone monuments, statues, and other objects figure in his writing, nor that among his characters are stonemasons who write upon stone and whose bodies are written upon by their labour.[1] Stone is also an inevitable motif for a writer interested in the temporal record and in the 'reading' of evidence of all kinds.[2] Hardy depicts ancient buildings and monuments as a kind of writing that must be preserved, urging for example that the government take responsibility for protecting 'any monument or relic which is of value to it as a page of history, even though the hieroglyphics of such monument or relic cannot be deciphered as yet.'[3] He demands that 'all tampering with chronicles in stone be forbidden by law,' lamenting the erasure of engraved records, and deploring the kind of institutionalized vandalism by which headstones in graveyards are 'removed from their positions ... and ... used for paving the church-yard walks, with the result that the inscriptions have been trodden out in a few years.'[4] With such monuments may also disintegrate the human bodies they were designed to memorialize. In the sketch of 'Shaston' (Shaftesbury) that introduces Jude and Sue's removal to that city, Hardy alludes to the demolition of the 'enormous abbey' and its poignant result: 'the whole place collapsed in a general ruin: the Martyr's bones met with the fate of the sacred pile that held them, and not a stone is now left to tell where they lie.'[5] More grotesquely, in the poem 'The Levelled Churchyard,' when the headstones are broken up and their inscriptions randomly redistributed, the corpses themselves, 'mixed to human jam,' mingle in carnivalesque yet anguished promiscuity:

'Where we are huddled none can trace,
     And if our names remain,
They pave some path or porch or place
     Where we have never lain!

'Here's not a modest maiden elf
     But dreads the final Trumpet,
Lest half of her should rise herself,
     And half some sturdy strumpet!   (*CPW*, 1:197)

This grisly re-membering is a burlesque version of a cluster of images that recurs in different ways in some of the most intense passages in Hardy's writing: the stone object, the fragmented body, and writing.[6]

The breaking up of the gravestones in 'The Levelled Churchyard' seems almost as outrageous an insult as the breaking up of the human remains. There is indeed a brief passage in the *Life and Work* that goes so far as to suggest that quarrying stone and using it as a building material is itself a kind of desecration – an imposition, if not an assault, on an integral and mystified body. Hardy was evidently much distressed at the gap between the age of a stone building and 'that of the marble hills from which it was drawn.'[7] Remarking on this passage, Hillis Miller observes that it is as if the carving on such a building has 'veiled' or 'traduced' the stone.[8] Miller's metaphors are suggestive, even more so in the light of Hardy's whole sentence, which goes on to compare such stone in its unworked form to 'Greek literature ... at the mercy of dialects.' It is as if both to cut stone and to modify 'standard' language were to contaminate something pure and whole. It is not clear precisely whether Hardy locates authentic 'Greek literature' in the original spoken word or in written texts. Nevertheless, what Derrida calls logocentric desire – the desire for the authenticity, the 'presence,' supposedly inhering in the voice as opposed to the written word – seems relevant to his feeling here, as does Derrida's association of writing with violence.

Critics who have read Hardy in the context of Darwin on the one hand and Derrida on the other have foregrounded complementary emphases in his writing. Darwin documents the continuity between human beings and the rest of the natural world, and Hardy has been seen as Darwinian in his blurring of the line between man and nature.[9] Derrida, on the other hand, who insists that 'writing' is already implicit in any form of social or symbolic organization, underlines the absolute break between man and nature – the constitution of the subject through language – and readers have also responded to what they see as Derridean elements in Hardy's work.[10] There is one particular passage in Derrida that seems to me oddly apposite to *The Return of the Native*, and, with both these critical approaches in mind, I want to juxtapose that passage – a single paragraph, near the beginning of the seminal essay 'The Violence of the Letter: From Lévi-Strauss to Rousseau'[11] – with the famous description of the heath at the beginning of that novel.

Contesting Lévi-Strauss's assumption that the Nambikwara Indians are illiterate, Derrida argues that it is based on an unexamined nature/culture binary. Lévi-Strauss, he says, represents the Indians as victims of the violent 'writing lesson' of Europeans, who penetrate their territory and violate their society by introducing the written word. Derrida insists, on the contrary, that it is a misunderstanding of what 'writing' means not to recognize that a society that has complex kinship relationships and taboos about naming already possesses what Derrida calls 'arche-writing': 'the difference ... that opens speech itself' (Derrida, 'Violence of the Letter,' 128). In passing – and this is the paragraph that invites comparison with Hardy – Derrida suggests that a people that travels back and forth over a network of footpaths must already possess 'writing' in the wider sense. Derrida's description of Nambikwara territory, striated both by the almost invisible paths the Indians make through the bush and by the route of an abandoned telegraph line cut into the forest by Europeans; the meditation that follows, on 'writing as the possibility of the road and of difference, the history of writing and the history of the road, of the rupture ... of the space of reversibility and of repetition traced by the opening, the divergence from, and the violent spacing, of nature'; his assertion that 'it is difficult to imagine that access to the possibility of a road-map is not at the same time access to writing' (107–8): all of these reflections would have resonated with Hardy, who supplements his novels with maps that allow the reader to trace the movements of his fictional characters and who is fascinated by the incising of both lines and letters. Indeed, the stony and somatic imagery that links human life to the heath in *The Return of the Native* can be read almost as a thought experiment designed to test Derrida's intuitions, while qualifying them with Hardy's own feelings about the body and its vulnerability to both nature and culture.

The Return of the Native invites a cartographic reading, in that much of its imaginative power derives from the motif of striation, of marking with lines. The heath is introduced in the famous opening chapter as a primal, unmarked expanse, a place vaguely personified, 'like man,

slighted and enduring,' with a 'lonely face, suggesting tragical possibilities'[12] – a face, however, without distinctive features. But by the
beginning of the second chapter, upon the first appearance of human
life, the 'old man' who turns out to be Captain Vye, the heath turns
more clearly into a metaphorical body, the road the captain follows
'bisect[ing] that vast dark surface like the parting-line on a head of
black hair' (37), and begins to be marked by human consciousness and
human activity – staked out in points and traversed by lines that will
map the motives of the romantic plot. Punctuated by the figures on the
top of Rainbarrow, first Eustacia and then the group of rustics with their
Guy Fawkes fire, and by 'the bonfires of other parishes and hamlets'
(43), '[p]erhaps as many as thirty' (44), the empty expanse is quickly
overwritten – inscribed with the pattern of furtive or abortive journeys
that lead individuals to their destiny or doom.[13] It is the contrast between the ephemerality of these points and lines, the passionate transience of the main characters' motives and movements, and the brooding
permanence of the heath on which they are traced that accounts as
much as the melodramatic plot events for the feeling of enervation and
anticlimax at the end of the novel, when the insubstantial net that has
been cast over the landscape by all this scurrying about suddenly
evaporates into the stasis of marriage and death.

If Hardy supplements Derrida's paradigm with the notion of fleeting
or even immaterial lines imposed upon and 'above' the landscape, he
also deepens it with the image of the stone 'below' the turf, scored and
incised by human travel. The road that Captain Vye follows 'overla[ys]
an old vicinal way, which branched from the great Western road of the
Romans, the Via Iceniana, or Ikenild Street' (36). The Roman roads
lasted because they were made of stone, and Miller, altering Hardy's
somatic metaphor, compares the road across the heath to carving on
stone: 'The imposition of a pattern on the stone,' he says, 'is only the
superficial laying on of an evanescent design, just as the old road is only
a slender white scar inscribed across the age-old monotony of Egdon
Heath.'[14] Evanescent indeed compared with the primeval heath; yet the
road's straight white line not only opens up a historical perspective in
the light of which the main characters' projects seem pathetically ephemeral but also testifies to the technological power of a sophisticated
civilization, in implicit contrast to the simpler lives of the modern
heath-dwellers, whose almost invisible pathways seem to offer a 'primitive' alternative to its aggressive imperial script.

Yet to Hardy, as to Derrida, it is by no means clear that all the sophistication rests with the invaders. Like the Nambikwara, the heath-dwellers travel along tracks so subtly inscribed that they can scarcely be seen at all. Indeed, the contrast between the non-natives' alienation from the landscape and the heath-dwellers' intimacy with it is developed partly by the motif of the invisible line. Mrs Yeobright and Olly follow a path invisible to a 'mere visitor' even by day but clear on the darkest night to 'the regular haunters of the heath,' for whom 'a difference between impact on maiden herbage, and on the crippled stalks of a slight footway, is perceptible through the thickest boot or shoe' (RN, 80). This is reading and writing of a highly developed kind, more refined and complex, one is invited to feel, than the Roman road's crude imperial text, while more 'grounded' than the romances dreamed up by Clym and Eustacia. The corporeality of the natives' responses is in contrast to the wilful, theoretical projects of the principal characters, whose enthusiasms are 'all in the mind' and who are thus doomed to disillusionment.

It is in the context of all of these cartographic and hermeneutic patterns that we respond to Clym's movements on the evening when he goes out to find his dying mother. Dusk is falling after a sultry day, and the colours of the heath have 'merged in a uniform dress without airiness or gradation, and broken only by touches of white where the little heaps of clean quartz sand showed the entrance to a rabbit-burrow, or where the white flints of a footpath lay like a thread over the slopes' (RN, 298–9). The thread of white flints is assimilated, by its colour, both to nature (the rabbit burrows) and to culture (the white highway), while in its linearity it is associated with the road but differentiated from the static, isolated 'touches' of sand where the rabbits dwell. The emergence of the spots and 'threads' of white in the half-light of dusk, when other visual distinctions have been erased, seems a revelation of the 'deep structure' of activity on the heath, a structure that links animals and human beings in an unexamined but ongoing relationship, just at the moment when the individual human animal, the super-conscious Mrs Yeobright, is about to succumb to exhaustion. After the sultry day, our imagination is cooled by the evening air and grounded in the white flint beneath the furze. The path Clym follows has been incised by feet of flesh through the skin of the heath, and the stone that is laid bare is its own enduring flesh.

Communal journeying across a supine stone body, then, is a kind of writing that, though it marks human beings off from nonhuman life, also connects them with it. But the more self-conscious 'writing' involved in erecting stone and carving it into human shape is a riskier activity, associated with rupture and extinction rather than vital continuity. Both Clym Yeobright and Eustacia Vye are compared to stone statues, out of harmony with their natural setting. Clym's face, described as the product of some modern Pheidias, is also enchased, scored by civilization, by the marks of fin-de-siècle consciousness, and Hardy's metaphors direct us to read these marks as writing and the protagonist's visage 'as a page' (*RN*, 185) that testifies to the angst of the historical moment. Eustacia, too, is a cultural text. While Clym's head represents the contemporary alternative to the kind of classical beauty that has become anachronistic in the context of the trauma of modern culture, Eustacia is a throwback, cobbled together from heterogeneous debris of the past, and as an anachronism she is anomalous, scandalous, and doomed. Like Clym's, Eustacia's face is also represented as damaged statuary, her voluptuous 'lip-curves' reminding the smitten narrator of stony lips 'lurking underground in the South as fragments of forgotten marbles' (*RN*, 90) – the allusion to burial and exhumation gives an unexpectedly 'deathy' note to her description. Though the image of stony lips may look back to Ozymandias, whose 'wrinkled lip' survives to testify to his passions, there is a more bathetic analogue for the slightly bizarre imagery here. Dalziel and Millgate point out that among the 'improbable stimuli' for some of Hardy's early phrase making in praise of female beauty was Thomas Rickman's description of architectural detail.[15] This fascinating intertext allows us to exhume a 'lurking,' 'underground' link between the nubile body of the heroine and the aged bodies of the rustic dancers in the third chapter, for the word 'mouldings' in Rickman's text, which leads in the notebook to a metaphor in praise of the female neck ('carved work, vein-work in thy *neck*'), turns up in the novel both in the image of Eustacia's lips and also in the 'sinews in old *necks*' that become 'gilt mouldings' in the light of the Guy Fawkes fire (*RN*, 45; *Studies, Specimens &c.*, 63; italics mine).

Hardy's somatic anxiety, complicated by peculiar stony imagery that associates sex with death, both enriches and qualifies Derrida's cartographic meditation, while endorsing the link between writing and violence on which Derrida also insists. In Hardy's texts, the idealized human body tends, like any stone structure erected and engraved, to invite profanation, disfigurement, and damage – damage that often, as here, is read within a story of sexual transgression and cultural collapse. Though this process is represented in a relatively decorous way in a major novel like *The Return of the Native*, in Hardy's less-regarded fictions, the fantasies both expressed and occluded by his stony imagery take more grotesque forms.

Hardy is fascinated by the uncanny moment when what is taken to be stone turns out to be human flesh. The effect can be frankly if rather trivially gothic, as when, 'passing near an altar-tomb ... on which was a recumbent figure,' Tess Durbeyfield has 'an odd fancy that the effigy moved'[16] and discovers that she has been tracked down by Alec d'Urberville. More gratuitous, more tactile, and decidedly odder, is a minor scene in *A Pair of Blue Eyes*. To touch what one takes to be stone and find it warm is a chilling experience, the narrator tells us, 'but a colder temperature than that of the body being rather the rule than the exception in common substances, it hardly conveys such a shock to the system as finding warmth where utter frigidity is anticipated.' This ponderous generalization is formulated to explain the reaction of Henry Knight when he touches the dead head of Mrs Jethway, recently killed and largely buried by the collapse of the church tower. Unable to see what he feels – the hair on her head – he ventures a series of improbable guesses – 'It is a tressy species of moss or lichen,' 'a tuft of grass,' 'a mason's whitewash-brush,' 'a thready silk fringe' – until finally 'He felt further in. It was somewhat warm. Knight instantly felt somewhat cold.'[17] This rather elaborate episode seems out of proportion, for Mrs Jethway's death makes nothing happen. Bringing together a dead head, a woman's metamorphic hair, and the image of stone introduces Medusa into the picture, though in a way that makes no particular sense in the wider context of the novel.[18] The oddly circumstantial response to the aged female body testifies to the uncanny suggestiveness of the stone/flesh interface for Hardy.

When this motif expands to structure an entire narrative, the result is more disturbing. In 'Barbara of the House of Grebe,' which is partly about the fear of ageing, the notion of a classical statue disfigured from *The Return of the Native* is developed in a gothically polarized way. As the name Willowes suggests, this tale of a prince who becomes a frog – this demonic parody of the Pygmalion myth – is also an elegy for doomed youth, in that Willowes's disfigurement by fire is a grotesque speeding up of the natural process of bodily decay.[19] Yet it is also a kind of murder: the ritual sacrifice of a beautiful youth at the hands of a father/priest figure and in the name of patriarchal values. Though T.S. Eliot loathed this story and identified it as an example of 'pure Evil,'[20] in fact the mythos of the piece revolves, as does *The Waste Land*, around the figure of the dying god: indeed, it can be read, in the manner of René Girard, as a myth about the origin of authoritarian religion. Like Clym Yeobright, Willowes becomes a statue disfigured by joyless modernity. The 'full-length figure, in the purest Carrara marble, representing Edmond Willowes in all his original beauty,' an erotically idealized 'specimen of manhood almost perfect in every line and contour,' is like the god of a sunnier religion, 'Phoebus-Apollo, sure.'[21] But when Barbara's jealous husband Lord Uplandtowers subjects the image to systematic and 'fiendish disfigurement,' so that it has neither 'nose nor ears, nor lips,' has it 'tinted to the hues of life, as life had been after the wreck' (GND, 85),[22] and sets it up in a shrine like a painted saint, 'with a wax candle burning on each side of it to throw the cropped and distorted features into relief,' the tension between stone and flesh becomes graphic, the 'grisly exhibition' (GND, 88) almost explicitly phallic, and the religion of male domination to which it testifies a new kind of barbarism. And when, in a development almost too neatly Lacanian, the lady who has worshipfully embraced the petrified phallus prostrates herself, like Sue Bridehead, before the Word of the Father, we get a weird sadistic fusion of fairy tale and Freud. Like Eliot in The Waste Land, Hardy is working in Golden Bough territory, where stony images are dismembered and living bodies are sacrificed.[23] In Hardy's writing, when patriarchal power is expressed in stone, nubile youths and maidens die – or live only to abase themselves before male 'angels.' To dismiss, as Hardy did in defending himself against an unfavourable review, this gruesome fable as 'a mere tale of a mutilated piece of marble'[24] seems all the more disingenuous if one senses how resonant and disturbing is the notion of disfigured stone for Hardy.

Somatic imagery of a stony kind also underpins The Well-Beloved, written at about the same time and also dealing with the loss of sexual attractiveness. Here the idealized stone form is not the male but the female body, the form of the Goddess as she exists in the imagination of the sculptor Jocelyn Pierston, and the protagonist is the sculptor himself, who falls in love sequentially with three real women, mother, daughter, and granddaughter. Projecting his ideal woman into stone – capable of referring to the mother of his current beloved as 'the pure and perfect quarry she was dug from,'[25] a metaphor with disturbing associations of assault and blasphemy[26] – Pierston attempts to reproduce his vision in 'marble images' in his studio (WB, 196). But flesh and stone, instead of fusing as they do in the Pygmalion story, painfully bifurcate, as Pierston, growing ever older – turning indeed (in the serial) into 'a strange fossilised relic in human form'[27] – finds the real female bodies that attract him increasingly inaccessible.

This disconcerting tale is set in the Isle of Slingers, an apparently gratuitous locale which, however, qualifies the story of masculine decline with the inscrutable image of a body whole and ever renewed. Against the splitting and proliferation of the female form is set the unified, resilient body of the island from which comes Pierston's raw material. A 'solid and single block of limestone four miles long' (WB, 28), a 'peninsula carved by Time out of a single stone' (WB, 26), the island is described as a body whose 'massive forehead' rises 'behind the houses' on its sides (WB, 110). This is a sleeping giant, warm, quiescent, apparently at peace, and Pierston's physical contact with its body is an untroubled and pleasurable, if barely erotic, communion. In a gesture almost identical to that of Stephen Knight when he touches the head of Mrs Jethway, Pierston 'stretche[s] out his hand upon the rock beside him' and discovers that 'It felt warm.' But what follows is entirely different in tone: 'That was the island's personal temperature when in its afternoon sleep as now. He listened and heard sounds: whirr-whirr, saw-saw-saw. Those were the island's snores – the noises of the quarrymen and stone-sawyers' (WB, 29). Although almost everything on the island is made of island stone, 'not only ... walls but ... window-frames, roof, chimneys, fence, stile, pigsty and stable' (WB, 29), the chipping away at this body does not seem to impair its massive unity and integrity. No mother rape here, no curse of Eve: male gestation is not painful, nor does it attenuate the father. The stone is quarried from the island as Eve is taken from Adam, sleeping. Like a complacent and undying god, the island serenely suffers its own fragmentation, offers its body to be consumed.

Resonant in the context of these mythical suggestions is Hardy's description of the pebbled beach, rhythmically dismembered and reformed by the waves that continually restore it. The incoming tide causes

a sudden breach in the bank; which, however, had something of a supernatural power in being able to close up and join itself together again after such disruption, like Satan's form when, cut in two by the sword of Michael,

'The ethereal substance closed,
Not long divisible' (WB, 45)

While the story, which focuses on three women, offers splitting, fragmentation, and replication, the physical setting, personified as male, speaks of bodily integrity, coming-together. That such unity is possible only for a mythologized rock-giant is, however, made clear by an earlier metaphor, describing the sound of the surf on the shingle. The narrator explains that, as the tide comes in, there arises 'a deep, hollow stroke like the single beat of a drum, the intervals being filled with a long-drawn rattling, as of bones between huge canine jaws. It came from the vast concave of Deadman's Bay, rising and falling against the pebble dyke' (*WB*, 35). The imagery here no doubt looks back to Arnold's 'Dover Beach,' but the focus is less on cultural and spiritual than on individual, bodily disintegration. On the bottom of the sea are the bones of all the men who have been drowned off the coast, and, like the pebbles, these many have become one:

> The evening and night winds ... brought ... a presence – an imaginary shape or essence from the human multitude lying below: those who had gone down in vessels of war, East Indiamen, barges, brigs, and ships of the Armada – select people, common, and debased, whose interests and hopes had been as wide asunder as the poles, but who had rolled each other to oneness on that restless sea-bed. There could almost be felt the brush of their huge composite ghost as it ran a shapeless figure over the isle ... (*WB*, 35)

Like the pebbles, the dead are 'rolled' into a single body. But apparently this is an oppressive unity, and the sound of the wind becomes the lament of an unquiet spirit, 'shrieking for some good god who would disunite it again' (*WB*, 35). The 'huge composite ghost' in this passage anticipates Eliot's 'familiar compound ghost';[28] Hardy's dead, who long for disconnection, are rather like the personified bones in *Ash Wednesday* that 'are glad to be scattered';[29] and, like the Isle of Slingers at the end of Hardy's novella, when Pierston orders the wells closed, Eliot's Waste Land of course is a land of 'empty cisterns and exhausted wells.'[30] I note the parallels not to argue that Eliot was influenced by Hardy, though I suspect he read this 'unwholesome' author more carefully and took more from him than he admits, but to suggest that the kind of material Hardy was working with can perhaps be successfully treated only in terms of metaphor and myth, and by excising as much as possible the 'personality' to which Eliot famously objects. The setting of *The Well-Beloved* is evocative and the metaphors are haunting and suggestive, but the 'realistic' story of Jocelyn Pierston's erotic attachments, however interesting the issues it raises, is ultimately rather grotesque.

Stony imagery associated with the male body, then, while it testifies to fear of emasculation, can offer compensatory fantasies of self-renewal. When associated with the female body, however, it is more consistently sinister. Hardy tends to equate female marmoreality with stupidity and stolidity, dismissing the 'wealthy Mrs. B.' at a Shakespeare reading, for example, as 'impassive and grand in her un-intelligence, like a Carthaginian statue,' and describing a young woman with 'absolutely perfect' features whom he saw in a railway carriage as '*too* statuesque': 'The repose of her face was such that when the train shook her it seemed painful' (*LW*, 157, 130). So cool a response to static perfection is not unexpected in a writer who responds intensely to not quite 'standard' female beauty and to the warmth and colour of human flesh.

But there is another set of stony imagery associated with the female body – a set of images at the other end of the associative spectrum, as it were – that verges on the bizarre. 'Apprehension is a great element in imagination,' Hardy asserts rather enigmatically in *Life and Work*: 'It is a semi-madness, which sees enemies, etc., in inanimate objects' (*LW*, 213). Nowhere is such 'apprehension' better exemplified than in the description of a number of objects that become associated with women and with female power. Consider the extended and quite gratuitous catalogue of Mrs Swancourt's rings in *A Pair of Blue Eyes*:

RIGHT HAND

1st. Plainly set oval onyx, representing a devil's head. 2nd. Green jasper intaglio, with red veins. 3rd. Entirely gold, bearing figure of a hideous griffin. 4th. A sea-green monster diamond, with small diamonds round it. 5th. Antique cornelian intaglio of dancing figure of a satyr. 6th. An angular band chased with dragons' heads. 7th. A faceted carbuncle accompanied by ten little twinkling emeralds. (*PBE*, 155)

Again there seems to be a lack of proportion: Mrs Swancourt, though worldly, is not actively malicious and does not seem to merit so elaborately sinister an introduction. The demonic heads here, devil and dragons, along with a 'monster' encircled by small stones, subliminally evoke the dragon-mouth of hell: an extravagant suggestion, perhaps, were the same image not to turn up again, more explicitly, not only in the notorious gurgoyle of *Far from the Madding Crowd* but also in the comic mask over the gateway in *The Mayor of Casterbridge*. The gurgoyle – the stone face that 'Mother' Nature, so benevolent to Gabriel Oak, shows to Frank Troy – is 'too human to be called like a dragon ... too animal to be like a fiend, and not enough like a bird to be called a griffin.' It is described, that is, in terms of three of the creatures listed on Mrs Swancourt's rings; but its mouth is also damaged as if by dental disease, the 'lower row of teeth ... quite washed away.'[31] This grotesque visage anticipates in turn the face on the keystone of the arch over the back entrance to High-Place Hall, the duplicitous Lucetta's two-faced house in *The Mayor of Casterbridge*: 'Originally the mask had exhibited a comic leer, as could still be discerned; but generations of Casterbridge boys had thrown stones at the mask, aiming at its open mouth; and the blows thereon had chipped off the lips and jaws as if they had been eaten away by disease.'[32] Here the idea of disease becomes explicit, and the image of the 'eaten-away' face will in turn be picked up in *The Well-Beloved* in the reference to 'the faces of [drowned] persons' with crabs clinging to and 'leisurely eating them' (*WB*, 53) – a prospect that discourages Jocelyn Pierston from soliciting death by water.

Hardy's description of these faces has an intriguing analogue in Ruskin's account of the gargoyle of Santa Maria Formosa in Venice: 'A head, – huge, inhuman, and monstrous, – leering in bestial degradation, too foul to be either pictured or described, or to be beheld for more than an instant'; indeed, the slight verbal echo here ('too foul' – 'too human ... too animal') might even suggest that this passage is a source for Troy's gurgoyle. For Ruskin, interestingly, the 'grossness' of what he calls 'the ignoble grotesque,' which is to be found 'manifested in every species of obscene conception and abominable detail,' is best exemplified by the fact that 'the *teeth* [of this particular gargoyle] are represented as *decayed*.'[33] The gratuitous energy behind all these very violent images demands an interpretative response. In the context of Hardy's plots, in which sexual self-indulgence leads to emasculation and death, these stony mouths are easy to read as nightmare metaphors for the female body, menacing, infected, and voracious.

I am arguing then that for Hardy the image of stone cut, carved, or quarried expresses, in a way that is often unexpected and sometimes grotesque, anxieties about mortality, fragmentation, and emasculation. Hardy, however, also responds intensely – it is the other side of the same coin – to the way stone has been used to transcend the body: to its power to evoke and embody spirit. A repeated trope in Hardy's writing is the personified statue, representing a past culture, which confronts an uncomprehending present. Sculptural fragments, listening to the alien Christmas bells, lament their eclipse and imprisonment in the gloomy Elgin Room; statues in St Paul's Cathedral, looking blindly down on frivolous visitors, remain deaf to the racket of commercial life outside.[34] Though Hardy himself is never a frivolous visitor, he cannot close the gap he observes. Witness his uncomfortable encounter with the 'faces of the Doges pictured on the frieze' in the Hall of the Great Council in Venice, faces that 'float out into the air of the room in front of me': '"We know nothing of you," say these spectres. "Who may you be, pray?" The draught brushing past seems like inquiring touches by their cold hands, feeling, feeling like blind people what you are' (*LW*, 200). Such statues function rather like the famous fossil in *A Pair of Blue Eyes*, another stony borderline figure that raises the issue of human consciousness in a particularly acute way. Hardy is always fascinated by nonhuman creatures – the fallow deer at the lonely house (*CPW*, 2:366–7), the heath-croppers in *The Return of the Native* – whose 'minds' are as mysterious as their gaze is impenetrable. In the famous scene where Henry Knight confronts the 'creature with eyes' that, 'dead and turned to stone, were even now regarding him,' no meeting of minds, however, can be imagined. When the creature is long extinct and eye of flesh meets eye of stone, the existential frisson is somewhat crudely amplified into a moment of intense self-consciousness. Without a gaze to meet, the human gaze is turned back upon its own gazing. The unforthcoming deadness of stone evokes in Hardy an intense awareness not only of the vulnerability of the human body but also of the mystery of human consciousness: a post-Darwinian mystery, a geological sublime.

The moment with the fossil is only the most striking example of a scenario that from time to time occurs in less elaborate ways elsewhere in Hardy's writing. Just as Knight, who knows something about geology, can recognize and place the fossil, so Faith Julian in *The Hand of Ethelberta*, having studied eastern iconography, can recognize the image of Sennacherib when she encounters it in the sculpture wing of the British Museum. But what fascinates Faith is less the identity of this image than what Benjamin would call its 'aura':[35] the fact that it is not a reproduction but the actual stone 'really carved at the time': 'Only just think that this is not imagined of Assyria, but done in Assyrian times by Assyrian hands. Don't you feel as if you were actually in Nineveh; that as we now walk between these slabs, so walked Ninevites between them once?'[36] It is not Sennacherib the historical personage who piques Faith's imagination, but the idea of the anonymous stone-carvers who made his image, and, more elusive still, all the anonymous passers-by who walked past it: individual human beings lost forever but for the shadows they cast in a museum-goer's mind.

Both the fossil and the ancient monarch had consciousness and a 'life to save,' but the sublime response does not depend upon the idea of an animate being. Stone from the past can evoke awe simply because it is from the past and because an awareness of its extreme age expands the mind. In *The Well-Beloved*, blocks of oolite that have 'just come to view after burial through unreckonable geologic years' (*WB*, 78) are worth looking at simply because, never seen before, they can offer themselves as virgin territory for the engendering of self via perception. Hardy reminds members of the Society of Dorset Men in London that the Dorset stone used in St Paul's Cathedral had another life before it was moved to London:

> its façade thrills to the street noises all day long, and has done so for three or four human lifetimes. But through what a stretch of time did it thrill all day and all night in Portland to the tides of the West Bay, particularly when they slammed against the island during south-west gales, and sent reverberations into the very bottom quarry there.[37]

The imaginative energy here is harnessed neither to Christian piety nor really to regional patriotism but to the notion of the noise that could not have been noise if only the stones 'heard' it – but that suddenly *is* noise, now, because Hardy's words, interposing a mind that registers it, have retroactively made it real.

In an important article, Gillian Beer has recently discussed two Hardy poems, 'In a Museum' and 'A Kiss,' that deal with sound waves and their transmission. Beer suggests that when Hardy muses that a bird's song or the sound of a kiss will never be completely extinguished – that they will blend with the ongoing pulse of the universe and go on forever, though 'in a space and time not capable of being tapped by us' – he is drawing on contemporary wave theory as developed by Helmholtz and popularized in England by Tyndall in the 1860s. [38] Her suggestion is convincing, but I would argue that the way Hardy develops the image of the wave of energy is not always as recuperative as in the two poems Beer cites.

In the poem 'In the British Museum' the sound in question, rather than simply travelling outward into the aether on its own, is propelled off a hard stony surface, and the emphasis is somewhat different. The poem depicts a working-class museum-goer, a 'labouring man,' who is thrilled to realize that the stone before his eyes, part of the wall of the Areopagus, stood in that wall at the very moment when St Paul spoke to the Athenians: not, fancifully, that it heard his voice, but rather that it diffused the sounds he produced:

'Words that in all their intimate accents
   Pattered upon
That marble front, and were wide reflected,
   And then were gone.   (*CPW*, 2:99)

The poem, which focuses neither on the survival of the sound nor on the survival of the message but rather on the vanishing of the voice, is suffused with logocentric wistfulness. The sounds of Paul's address have disappeared forever, 'gone' the poem does not attempt to say where, and the stone remains to testify not so much to the resilience of his message as to the evanescence of his voice as a material phenomenon. When sound waves bounce off stone, they can be saved from dissolution not (in this poem) by blending into the great vibration of universal energy but by impinging upon – being intercepted by – an awakened human mind: a mind, Hardy makes clear, as likely to be found among women and working people as among those who condescend to them.

The words, like the birdsong and the sound of the kiss, are sounds with personal or historical meaning, but Hardy will give the same kind of treatment to sounds like the waves beating on the oolite cliffs – sounds that carry no message at all, except the message of their own transience. The noise made by the Weatherbury church clock striking eleven as Bathsheba Everdene begins her journey to Budmouth is also described in terms of radiating sound waves: 'The notes flew forth with the usual blind obtuseness of inanimate things – flapping and rebounding among walls, undulating against the scattered clouds, spreading through their interstices into unexplored miles of space' (*FFMC*, 238). The emphasis here is on disintegration, flight, and atrophy rather than on persistence. Beer's linking of wave theory with Hardy's anxieties about mortality is illuminating but, particularly when the sound is deflected off stone, the emphasis may be on disappearance and loss rather than on continuity. The suggestion of death that becomes almost explicit in the description of the music Hardy heard at a party in Venice – 'the notes flapped back from the dilapidated palaces behind with a hollow and almost sepulchral echo, as from a vault' (*LW*, 202) – is often implicit in such conceits. Stone shatters and disperses waves of energy, animates these 'inanimate things' so that they 'flap' away out of human perception, and there is death in their flight, at least for human beings whose experience is composed of such transient and intrinsically meaningless impressions.

Like sound, light strikes stone without marking it – without writing on it. One of Hardy's favourite images is the shadow that cannot imprint itself where it falls. To register the passing of time on the Isle of Slingers in *The Well-Beloved*, the narrator rather elaborately observes that 'many who had formerly projected their daily shadows upon its unrelieved summer whiteness ceased now to disturb the colourless sunlight there' (*WB*, 145). A similar point is made about the group at Talbothays dairy, milking the cows at the end of the day 'while the sun ... threw their shadows accurately inwards upon the wall':

> Thus it threw shadows of these obscure and homely figures every evening with as much care over each contour as if it had been the profile of a Court beauty on a palace wall; copied them as diligently as it had copied Olympian shapes on marble *façades* long ago, or the outline of Alexander, Caesar, and the Pharaohs. (*Tess*, 142)

Would that the shadow of Cleopatra, we reflect, could have been fixed where it fell, burned by the mindless sun into the marble as the shadows of passers-by were in fact burned into the walls of Hiroshima in a monstrous photography, for then we would have had a material trace of her individual presence.[39] But unlike film or wax or sand, stone resists such writing.

As this comparison suggests, I suspect that Hardy's response to the virginal, resistant aspect of stone may be shaped by his awareness of film, a material that can be so written upon.[40] The photographic process was described by a contemporary, Lady Eastlake, as 'availing itself of the eye of the sun,'[41] and Oliver Wendell Holmes emphasizes the miraculous nature of the camera: 'Under the action of light ... a body makes its superficial aspect potentially present at a distance, becoming appreciable as a shadow [on a surface] or as a picture [i.e., a reflection in a mirror]. But remove the cause – the body itself – and the effect is removed.'[42] What is so poignant about a photograph, which Holmes calls 'a mirror with a memory,' is that the effect is not removed. The aura of the photograph derives from its direct connection with material reality, from 'the ontological fact [that] its image is both chemically and optically caused by the things in the world it represents':[43] that it is inscribed on the film in a particular moment by real living human bodies. Stone cannot capture such phenomena. Its dense materiality, the very quality that seems to make it useful for monuments, makes sure that the actual events it witnesses, it cannot directly record. Too brittle to preserve human meaning as expressed in carving, inscriptions, and architecture, it is also too impermeable to take a copy directly from nature. The phenomena of everyday life continuously disperse into waves of light and sound, and the harder and deader the substance they collide with, the faster they go.

As characteristic as Hardy's sense of the great web of nature or of the never-ending energy pulse of the universe that both absorbs and somehow preserves the human trace is the colder vision of the impregnability, the permanent unscathedness, of the material on which we try to imprint our memories, our ideals, and our desires. Though human subjectivity is nothing but writing, it has evolved, as Hardy lamented, in a universe that cannot be written upon. Hardy's romanticizing of the human imprint is grounded upon his power to imagine a substance that cannot be so imprinted. Though he values human 'writing' on stone and laments its erasure, he nevertheless depends, for the sublime response he equally values, upon the notion of a substance that resists such writing – a substance on which the first human footprint must be a kind of desecration. Indeed, Hardy's 'pessimistic' view of the universe as a place that has no use for man is the necessary condition of his intense response to material phenomena, for such a universe – a stonily blank entity with no use for minds or messages – while it renders the human situation ironic, renders the poet's apprehension of that situation sublime. That this sublimity is informed by Hardy's 'apprehension' of somatic damage, of fragmentation, of bodily harm, helps to constitute the 'idiosyncratic mode of regard' that makes his writing so compelling and essential a record of the human condition.

NOTES

1 I am thinking, for example, of 'The Old Workman' whose body is 'crookt' and 'ruined' by his work on a mansion whose owners, he says, 'don't

know me, or even know my name' (*The Complete Poetical Works of Thomas Hardy*, ed. Samuel Hynes, 5 vols [Oxford: Clarendon, 1982–95], 2:442; hereafter cited parenthetically as *CPW*), and of Jude Fawley, who is rendered invisible to the Christminster students by the stone dust on his clothing.

2 Discussions of Hardy's treatment of stone include Phillip Mallett, 'Noticing Things: Hardy and the Nature of "Nature,"' in *The Achievement of Thomas Hardy*, ed. Phillip Mallett (London: Macmillan, 2000), 155–70; Sophie Gilmartin, *Ancestry and Narrative in Nineteenth-Century British Literature* (Cambridge: Cambridge University Press, 1998); Timothy Hands, 'Hardy's Architecture: A General Perspective and a Personal View,' in *Achievement*, ed. Mallett, 95–104; and Michael Irwin, *Reading Hardy's Landscapes* (Basingstoke: Macmillan, 2000).

3 See 'Shall Stonehenge Go,' *Daily Chronicle*, 24 August 1899, 3; collected in *Thomas Hardy's Personal Writings*, ed. Harold Orel (Wichita: University of Kansas Press, 1966), 196–201.

4 Thomas Hardy, 'Memories of Church Restoration,' *The Society for the Protection of Ancient Buildings ... Twenty-Ninth Annual Report* (London, 1906), 59–80; collected in *Thomas Hardy's Public Voice: The Essays, Speeches, and Miscellaneous Prose*, ed. Michael Millgate (Oxford: Clarendon, 2001), 239–53 (quoted passages 241, 245).

5 Thomas Hardy, *Jude the Obscure* (London: Macmillan, 1974), 220.

6 As I have suggested in a previous study, the link that Lacan makes between the fantasies of the *corps morcelé* and that of the building (e.g., fortress, stadium, castle) that symbolizes 'the formation of the *I*' illuminates certain patterns in Hardy's writing, particularly those that seem to express anxieties about emasculation and death. See Jacques Lacan, *Écrits*, selected and trans. Alan Sheridan (New York: Norton, 1977), 4–5.

7 Thomas Hardy, *The Life and Work of Thomas Hardy*, ed. Michael Millgate (London: Macmillan, 1984), 96. Hereafter cited parenthetically as *LW*.

8 J. Hillis Miller, *Thomas Hardy: Distance and Desire* (Cambridge, MA: Harvard University Press, 1970), 95.

9 See Gillian Beer, *Darwin's Plots: Evolutionary Narrative in Darwin, George Eliot and Nineteenth-Century Fiction*, 2nd ed. (Cambridge: Cambridge University Press, 2000), 232-6, and George Levine, *Darwin and the Novelists: Patterns of Science in Victorian Fiction* (Cambridge, MA: Harvard University Press, 1988), 231–2.

10 See, for example, J. Hillis Miller, 'Thomas Hardy, Jacques Derrida, and the "Dislocation of Souls,"' in *Taking Chances: Derrida, Psychoanalysis and Literature*, ed. William Kerrigan and Joseph H. Smith (Baltimore: Johns

Hopkins University Press, 1984); Marjorie Garson, *Hardy's Fables of Integrity: Woman, Body, Text* (Oxford: Clarendon, 1991), 153; Beer, *Darwin's Plots*, 231; and Tim Armstrong, *Haunted Hardy: Poetry, History, Memory* (Basingstoke: Palgrave, 2000), passim.

11 Jacques Derrida, 'The Violence of the Letter: From Lévi-Strauss to Rousseau,' in his *Of Grammatology*, trans. Gayatri Chakravorty Spivak (Baltimore: Johns Hopkins University Press, 1976), 101–40.

12 Thomas Hardy, *The Return of the Native* (London: Macmillan, 1974), 35. Hereafter cited parenthetically as *RN*.

13 Although the metaphor of writing is not overt at the beginning of *The Return of the Native*, Hardy is always ready to see even purely ideal trajectories as 'writing' upon the land, as in the poems '"Sacred to the Memory"' (*CPW*, 2:452–3) and 'On an Invitation to the United States' (*CPW*, 1:142–3). Sophie Gilmartin discusses both 'The Levelled Churchyard' and 'On an Invitation to the United States' in connection with Hardy's interest in genealogical records (Gilmartin, 'Geology, Genealogy and Church Restoration in Hardy's Writing,' in Mallett, *Achievement*, 22–40).

14 Miller, *Distance and Desire*, 95.

15 In his *An Attempt to Discriminate the Styles of Architecture in England*. Rickman's 'fine hollow mouldings' inspires Hardy's 'fine-drawn kisses'; 'sweep of mouldings' becomes 'sweep of lip' (*Thomas Hardy's 'Studies, Specimens &c.' Notebook*, ed. Pamela Dalziel and Michael Millgate [Oxford: Clarendon, 1994], xix–xx). In the context of an argument about somatic fragmentation, it is also fascinating to find Hardy quoting Spenser's *Faerie Queene* 1.7.35.67 on the powers of Arthur's magic shield: 'Men into stone therewith he cd transmew / And stone to dust, & dust to nought at all' (*Studies, Specimens &c.*, 4). This unexpected selection makes the glamorous and generous Arthur sound like Talus the Iron Man of *Faerie Queene*, Book V.

16 Thomas Hardy, *Tess of the d'Urbervilles* (London: Macmillan, 1974), 413. Hereafter cited parenthetically as *Tess*.

17 Thomas Hardy, *A Pair of Blue Eyes* (London: Macmillan, 1975), 346–7. Hereafter cited parenthetically as *PBE*.

18 Hardy would no doubt have known Shelley's 'On the Medusa of Leonardo da Vinci in the Florentine Gallery,' first published in *Posthumous Poems* (1824), which contains the lines: 'And from its head as from one body grow, / As grass out of a watery rock, / Hairs which are vipers' (Percy Bysshe Shelley, *Poetical Works* [Oxford: Oxford University Press, 1970], 582). See also note 34.

19 Kristin Brady notes the funereal associations of 'Willowes' (see Brady, *The Short Stories of Thomas Hardy* [New York: St Martin's Press, 1982], 59–60).

20 T.S. Eliot, *After Strange Gods: A Primer of Modern Heresy* (London: Faber and Faber, 1934), 58.

21 Thomas Hardy, *A Group of Noble Dames* (London: Macmillan, 1968), 81. Hereafter cited parenthetically as *GND*.

22 On the painting of statues, Hardy might have been familiar with the opinions of Coleridge – 'If there be likeness to nature without any check of difference, the result is disgusting, and the more complete the delusion, the more loathsome the effect' (S.T. Coleridge, *Biographia Literaria, with his Aesthetical Essays*, ed. J. Shawcross, 2 vols [London: Oxford University Press, 1962], 2:256) – and of Ruskin, who criticizes hawthorn moulding painted green (*The Works of John Ruskin*, ed. E.T. Cook and Alexander Wedderburn, 39 vols [London: George Allen, 1903–11], 10, part 6, section 49:220).

23 The story, published in 1890, anticipates the first edition of Frazer's famous work by six years.

24 Thomas Hardy, 'The Merry Wives of Wessex,' *Pall Mall Gazette*, 10 July 1891, 2; collected in *Thomas Hardy's Public Voice*, 111.

25 Thomas Hardy, *The Well-Beloved* (London: Macmillan, 1975), 112. Hereafter cited parenthetically as *WB*.

26 See for analogies Ovid, *Metamorphoses*, 1. 138–40, and John Milton, *Paradise Lost* 1.684–90.

27 Thomas Hardy, 'The Pursuit of the Well-Beloved,' *Illustrated London News* 101, 1 October–17 December 1892: 711.

28 T.S. Eliot, 'Little Gidding,' *Four Quartets*, in *The Complete Poems and Plays 1909-1950* (New York: Harcourt, Brace & World, 1962), 140.

29 Eliot, *Ash Wednesday*, in *Complete Poems*, 62. Gilmartin (*Ancestry and Narrative*, 196–7) draws attention to Hardy's allusion, in *A Group of Noble Dames*, to the 'dry bones' passage in Ezekiel.

30 Eliot, *The Waste Land*, in *Complete Poems*, 48. At the end of the one-volume version, Pierston has the 'natural fountains' of the island closed 'because of their possible contamination' and a system of pipes installed instead (193).

31 Thomas Hardy, *Far From the Madding Crowd* (London: Macmillan, 1974), 350. Hereafter cited parenthetically as *FFMC*.

32 Thomas Hardy, *The Life and Death of the Mayor of Casterbridge* (London: Macmillan, 1974), 168.

33 Ruskin, *Works*, 11, part 3, section 15:145, and section 39:162 (italics Ruskin's). Associated with such faces for Ruskin was the head of Medusa: he says that the artist who conceives such images 'is stone ... and needs no Medusa head to change him to stone' (2, part 3, section 47:169). Freud

identifies the Medusa as symbolizing the female genitals and connects the figure with castration anxiety, though he does not comment on the analogous fantasy of the *vagina dentata*, by which both Ruskin's and Hardy's images seem also to be informed. See Sigmund Freud, *The Standard Edition of the Complete Psychological Works of Sigmund Freud*, gen. ed. James Strachey, 24 vols (London: Hogarth Press and the Institute of Psycho-Analysis, 1953–74), 19:144n3; 22:24.

34 See 'Christmas in the Elgin Room' and 'In St Paul's a While Ago' (*CPW*, 3:272–3; 3:23–4).

35 Walter Benjamin, 'The Work of Art in an Age of Mechanical Reproduction,' in *Illuminations*, ed. and intro. Hannah Arendt, trans. Harry Zohn (New York: Harcourt, Brace, and World, 1968), 219–53 (223), 219–44 (215).

36 Thomas Hardy, *The Hand of Ethelberta* (London: Macmillan, 1975), 183.

37 Thomas Hardy, 'Dorset in London,' *Society of Dorset Men in London* (Year-Book 1908–9), [3]–7; collected in *Thomas Hardy's Public Voice*, 276–83 (279).

38 Gillian Beer, 'Hardy and Decadence,' in *Celebrating Thomas Hardy: Insights and Appreciations*, ed. Charles Pettit (London: Macmillan, 1996), 97. The currency of wave theory by the 1860s is demonstrated by an allusion in Dickens's 'Night Walks' (1860), where he observes that 'the spreading circles of vibration' made by the striking of a church clock 'go opening out, for ever and ever afterwards widening perhaps (as the philosopher has suggested) in eternal space' (Charles Dickens, *Selected Journalism 1850–70*, ed. David Pascoe [London: Penguin, 1997], 78).

39 Documenting a similar kind of traumatic photography, Oliver Wendell Holmes observes that 'The lightning from heaven does actually photograph natural objects on the bodies of those it has just blasted' ('The Stereoscope and the Stereograph,' *Atlantic Monthly* 3, June 1859, 748).

40 Critics who have discussed photography in relation to Hardy's work include Arlene M. Jackson, 'Photography as Style and Metaphor in the Art of Thomas Hardy,' *Thomas Hardy Annual* 2 (1984): 91–109; Mark Durden, 'Ritual and Deception: Photography and Thomas Hardy,' *Journal of European Studies* 30 (2000): 57–69; Ronald Schleifer and Nancy M. West, 'The Poetry of What Lies Close at Hand: Photography, Commodities, and Postromantic Discourses in Hardy and Stevens,' *Modern Language Quarterly* 60 (1999): 33–57; and Armstrong, *Haunted Hardy*, 59–61.

41 Lady Elizabeth Eastlake, 'Photography,' *Quarterly Review* 10 (March 1857): 442–68. She refers to photographers as 'the sun's votaries' (443) and 'Pilgrims of the Sun' (451).

42 Holmes, 'The Stereoscope,' 738. Did Hardy ever read this essay? When he met Holmes at the Gosses' and Holmes 'said markedly that he did not

read novels; I did not say I had never read his essays, though it would have been true, I am ashamed to think' (*LW*, 187). Yet Hardy's description of the faces of the dancers around the fire in the third chapter of *The Return of the Native* has so much in common with Holmes's description of the photographic negative – the demonic ambience, the emphasis on depth, the image of gilt, the dark/bright eye – that one feels it could have been in the back of Hardy's mind when he was writing this passage. Hardy's description runs as follows: 'Shadowy eye-sockets, deep as those of a death's head, suddenly turned into pits of lustre: a lantern-jaw was cavernous, then it was shining; wrinkles were emphasized to ravines, or obliterated entirely by a changed ray. Nostrils were dark wells; sinews in old necks were gilt mouldings ...' (45). Compare this to Holmes: 'out of the perverse and totally depraved negative – where it might almost seem as if some magic and diabolic power had wrenched all things from their properties, where the light of the eye was darkness, and the deepest blackness was gilded with the brightest glare – is to come the true end of all this series of operations, a copy of Nature in all her sweet gradations and harmonies and contrasts' (741).

43 Durden, 'Ritual and Deception,' 67.

7 The Erotics of Dress in *A Pair of Blue Eyes*

SIMON GATRELL

The action of *A Pair of Blue Eyes* takes place during 1864–7; thus there are six or eight years between the setting of the novel and its first publication in 1872–3 as a serial in *Tinsley's Magazine*. The eleven monthly episodes were accompanied by illustrations, which provided for the earliest readers the most direct evidence of the appearance of Hardy's characters.[1] One detail not often noticed is that the artist clothed the heroine Elfride in the fashion of 1872 rather than 1864, something that alert contemporary readers must have noticed, as hooped dresses, essential in 1864, had disappeared eight years later – indeed, in the novel's chronology Elfride would not have lived long enough to wear the bustle of the seventies, as she does in this detail from the drawing for the fifth episode.

This small anachronism suggests a thought about a relationship between fashion as a system and Hardy's understanding of the way the world functions. To a large degree the dress that Elfride is shown wearing was imposed upon her by fashion. Of course the details would have been her choice – colour, depth of ruffle, decoration of hat, size of earrings; but she (had she still been alive) could no more have worn a hoop in 1873 than she could have flown, and it would have been still more impossible for her to have worn, say, a skirt baring her thighs, or a bodice that revealed the true shape of her breasts. The subject of fashion has been much theorized in the last quarter of a century, but most commentators agree that though the forces driving the system are complex, they are primarily social or cultural. Most critics of Hardy would also agree that he attempts to reveal in his writing the way in which individuals have a bare margin of free will, and that most of their actions, thoughts, beliefs are constrained by social or cultural systems,

Elfride on Endelstow Tower

to transgress which is to court disaster in one way or another. Success (however measured) in this world is to accept that bare minimum of free will and work with it to shape your individuality, to choose your fabric, your lace, your feather, as it best suits your understanding of yourself and others, even if you have to wear a corset and a bustle and skirts brushing the dirt.

It is also well understood that Hardy was forced by conventions directing the judgment of magazine editors and publishers to find indirect ways of indicating, to readers who shared his view, what he saw as the inescapable sexual element in love relationships. Hardy recognized that there is always somewhere a sexual component in dress and its relation to the body and to the viewer, and thus it seems a good idea to investigate more fully than heretofore what Hardy does with what people wear. Every writer on the topic agrees that dress is ambiguous. It is part concealment, part revelation; it is invitation and repulsion; it is a boundary between the self and the rest of the world, to cross which is fraught with risk; it has designs upon the observer, though how the observer will receive those designs is uncertain; it structures the self-awareness as well as the body. All these implications are active for Hardy.[2] His reputation does not conventionally include a fascination with dress or an awareness of its power in shaping or representing individual identity or personal relationships – but it should; and this very limited exploration of dress and the body in *A Pair of Blue Eyes* is a beginning.

Since *A Pair of Blue Eyes* is not Hardy's most frequently read text, here is a brief outline of the context for what follows. Elfride Swancourt is the daughter of the rector of Endelstow, on the northwest coast of Hardy's version of Cornwall, passing from her late teens to her early twenties in the course of the narrative. She is the possessor, among other things, of the blue eyes, of a luxuriant head of hair, and of a passionate love of earrings. She first loves an architect's assistant of about her own age, Stephen Smith; her father objects to their relationship, and they decide to elope and to marry secretly, which attempt fails; but they consider themselves as good as wed. Smith goes to India in the hope of making his fortune and thereby sufficiently impressing her father. While he is away Elfride meets Henry Knight, coincidentally young Smith's mentor, and some ten or twelve years their elder. Where she had the pleasure of feeling superior in most ways to Stephen, she tells herself how far above her Knight is, and falls more profoundly in love with him, while feeling intensely guilty about her emotional abandonment of Stephen. She keeps her previous relationship from Knight for as long as she can. The sexually fastidious Knight thinks himself in love with her in return, but rejects her when he learns about Stephen. In the end Elfride, emotionally and physically exhausted, marries a third man, and dies in childbirth. Hardy's crowning irony has Smith and Knight, unaware of her death, travelling down to Endelstow together to compete face-to-face for her hand, in the train that also carries her coffin.

The whole story is shaped by Hardy's powerful sense that life would be comic if it were not so sad, and to embody this perception in *A Pair of Blue Eyes* he uses for the first time a structuring pattern that later becomes particularly effective in his poetry. It is impossible, for instance, to miss the fact that Elfride defeats Stephen at chess, and is herself defeated by Knight, or that Stephen searches for a lost earring and Knight finds it. The pattern is one of repetition with variation, and what Hardy is out to show is that while for Elfride the process of attraction and falling in love is similar each time it happens, there can be but one master-passion. His understanding of the social, psychological, and symbolic implications of dress provides one dimension of this pattern of repetition.

When Stephen first sees Elfride, she appears 'in the prettiest of all feminine guises, that is to say, in demi-toilette, with plenty of loose curly hair tumbling down about her shoulders'(15).[3] After the appropriately in-between meal of high tea she sings to him, and he falls in love with her. Hardy writes one of his trade-mark epoch-making moments in the emotional lives of his characters:

> Miss Elfride's image chose the form in which she was beheld during these minutes of singing, for her permanent attitude of visitation to Stephen's eyes during his sleeping and waking hours in after days. The profile is seen of a young woman in a pale gray silk dress with trimmings of swan's-down, and opening up from a point in front, like a waistcoat without a shirt; the cool colour contrasting admirably with the warm bloom of her neck and face. The furthermost candle on the piano comes immediately in a line with her head, and half invisible itself, forms the accidentally frizzled hair into a nebulous haze of light, surrounding her crown like an aureola. Her hands are in their place on the keys, her lips parted, and trilling forth, in a tender *diminuendo*, the closing words of the sad apostrophe:
>
> 'O Love, who bewailest
>   The frailty of all things here,
> Why choose you the frailest
>   For your cradle, your home, and your bier!'
>
> Her head is forward a little, and her eyes directed keenly upward to the top of the page of music confronting her. (22–3)

Elfride has been nervous about meeting the professional gentleman alone. Thus her choice of pale grey silk is neutral, unassertive; but it is also appropriate to her character at this phase of her life – misty, unformed, indeterminate. The fabric is rich enough to mark her class, and she has had the dress trimmed in swan's down as a conceit on her last name. The down is also an early allusion to her unlooked-for death – the mute swan that sings once before it dies (it is the only time we hear her sing), an allusion reinforced by the words of her song.

Hardy's description of the shape of the dress's neckline is interesting; we are shown it in terms of male clothing, and though waistcoats in the 1860s or 1870s buttoned fairly high up on the chest, nonetheless Hardy quite deliberately offers male readers a momentary frisson, encouraging them to feel in imagination the unusual texture of rough cloth next their skin – more sharply aware for a moment of the woman's sensation of dress. And his account moves seamlessly from this evocation of the body to a direct description of it. The first detail is what Amy King in her admirable study *Bloom* has shown us is a master image of post Linnaean fiction: Hardy describes how the cool grey of Elfride's dress contrasts with 'the warm bloom' on her neck and face.[4] King describes the trajectory of the floral metaphor – and in particular the sexual element at the basis of Linnaean taxonomy – from its fresh and living employment in Austen's novels to represent the sexually interesting girl at the centre of her marriage plots, to James's recognition of the blooming girl as a literary stereotype. Hardy's variation on the theme is in the attendant adjective: the warmth of the bloom might initially be a matter of colour values, but the implied warmth of her skin also revitalizes the sexual element in 'bloom,' which, King suggests, had become ossified by the 1870s.

And then we are directed to Elfride's hair. What accident can have made it so tightly curled? Did she get it wet in an earlier manuscript version, and now it has dried that way? But there is no doubt of the vitality of the hair; it has a life of its own, and in the context of Stephen's gaze it is interesting that the *OED* offers 'aureola' as a variant of 'areola,' the area of dark skin surrounding a nipple. This sense is active if the image is seen as in a photographic negative: Elfride's head as the dark erogenous zone, her back-lit hair as the brilliant surround.

From hair our attention is transferred to other visible body parts, themselves charged with erotic potential: hands 'in their place' pressing the piano keyboard (not Stephen's hand), lips apart (with singing, not yet from erotic stimulation). Hardy shows the dress and the body all working together to attract Stephen, who moves so that he can see her not in profile, but full face. He stares at her with such evident intent that the bloom on her face turns brighter red, in the full blush of sexual awareness.

The next stage in the development of love between the two is marked with a characteristic moment of sexual contact transmuted through clothing, and linked to the previous scene through a deliberate though indirect allusion:

> Elfride did not make her appearance inside the building till late in the afternoon, and came then by special invitation from Stephen during dinner. She looked so intensely *living* and full of movement as she came into the old silent place that young Smith's world began to be lit by 'the purple light' in all its definiteness. Worm was got rid of by sending him to measure the height of the tower.
>
> What could she do but come close – so close that a minute arc of her skirt touched his foot – and ask him how he was getting on with his sketches ... ? (30)

The primary source for the narrator's quotation is Thomas Gray's 'The Progress of Poesy':

> O'er her warm cheek and rising bosom move
> The bloom of young Desire and purple light of Love.

The couplet enforces the connection with Elfride through Hardy's earlier use of 'bloom.' At the same time, the representation of the flush on the girl's bosom as well as her cheek indicates the degree to which fashion in the mid-eighteenth century permitted a more expansive inspection of the female body for evidence of emotional excitation, and allows the reader more clearly to imagine the behaviour of Elfride's blood in surfaces concealed beneath her dress.

When the narrator then demands 'What could she do but ...' the reader responds with other questions: is she driven to her action by an awareness of the flood of purple light in the church, or is she driven by her inner desire for the excitement of flirtation, or is she drawn by the animal magnetism of sex? What she does embodies a characteristic of Hardy's early writing, always attempting to find substitutes acceptable to his audience for the direct statement of sexual arousal. Elsewhere he notes that women are as aware of their clothing as they are of their skin, and it is important that it is Stephen's foot, rather than his boot or shoe, that Elfride's skirt touches. We do not seriously imagine that Stephen has come out unshod but the word is there and as with the shirtless waistcoat, we are encouraged to feel her hem on the bare foot, and to experience the shiver of excitement transmitted by the contact through Elfride's nervous system.

When Stephen is rejected out of hand by Parson Swancourt as a suitor for his daughter's hand, the two lovers meet late at night to discuss the situation. Elfride has 'partly undressed'; hearing Stephen packing, she flings her dressing gown round her and taps on his door. They decide to go downstairs to talk:

> She preceded him down the staircase with the taper light in her hand, looking unnaturally tall and thin in the long dove-coloured dressing-gown she wore. She did not stop to think of the propriety or otherwise of this midnight interview under such circumstances. She thought that the tragedy of her life was beginning, and, for the first time almost, felt that her existence might have a grave side ... (94)

Grey is Elfride's colour at this stage in her life; but where earlier it was a cool grey, here it is the warmer dove-grey – not just warmer as a shade, but warmer in emotional tone and symbolic reference. And here she is in her underwear beneath the gown, 'looking unnaturally tall and thin.' This phrase registers the alteration to the proportions of a woman's shape made by the several layers, the bustle and petticoats or hoop that fill out the costumes of the period, by the corseting that pinches the body in. But the really telling word is 'unnaturally.' Hardy's narrator has been seduced by long experience of the artificial form produced by the framework of dress to think of a woman without it as appearing unnatural. But what the reader sees in imagining Elfride at this moment is something much closer to her natural form than at any other time in the novel so far.

Under most circumstances Elfride would have been horrified at the thought of appearing before a young man so late at night in such undress, but she feels this as a crisis. The narrator, from his privileged viewpoint, may not quite see the situation as tragic, but asserts clearly that she does, and such dishevelment is after all appropriate to the tragic heroine.[5] It is perhaps surprising that the narrator does not allow Stephen to comment in some way on her slenderness or her softness, since at one point she hides her face on his shoulder. On the other hand, Stephen's proposition that they marry secretly again produces in Elfride's body the evidence of sexual excitement in 'quick breathings, hectic flush, and unnaturally bright eyes' (98).

Their attempt to marry fails, a failure of nerve on the part of both man and woman; Stephen goes to India and Henry Knight turns up to take his place with Elfride. In this text compounded of parallelisms, Hardy provides Knight and Elfride with moments that repeat each of those she experienced with Stephen, but with significant incremental variations. This is the first time that Knight really sees Elfride:

> Knight could not help looking at her. The sun was within ten degrees of the horizon, and its warm light flooded her face and heightened the bright rose colour of her cheeks to a vermillion red, their moderate pink hue being only seen in its natural tone where the cheek curved round into shadow. The ends of her hanging hair softly dragged themselves backwards and forwards upon her shoulder as each faint breeze thrust against or relinquished it. Fringes and ribbons of her dress, moved by the same breeze, licked like tongues upon the parts around them, and fluttering forward from shady folds caught likewise their share of the lustrous orange glow. (158)

For Knight, as for Stephen beside the piano, the relationship among Elfride's dress, her body, and his senses is intimate and powerful. The weight and texture of her hair are caught up for him in the phrase 'softly dragged,' and the passionate colouring he sees in her face is matched by that on straying decorations of her costume, fragments of fabric he figures with desire as tasting and feeling with the sensitivity of tongues the texture of her dress, touching her as intimately as such dress will allow, much more intimately than he can, save with his eyes. This is the archetypal male gaze, mediated through Victorian convention, so that for Knight her dress and her hair act as he wishes (subconsciously) to act.[6] For Stephen she had been an angel in grey, though not without touches of sensuality; for Knight she is vermillion and a stimulant for all the senses.

Elfride's emotional entanglement with the two men comes to a crisis on the day when Stephen returns to Off-Wessex from India. She goes armed with a telescope to watch his steamer pass the high cliffs north of the port of his disembarkation, but as she walks she encounters Knight and they go onward together, though of course she does not tell him the purpose of her outing. Stephen is in her mind, Knight by her side, and soon the two are superimposed, for it is Knight who looks through the glass, and sees Stephen on the boat. Again Elfride's blood reveals her feelings. Knight tells her of the 'slim young fellow' watching them watching him, and she 'grew pale.' He notices her pallor, and innocently comments that the air on the cliff ought to 'make [cheeks] rosy that were never so before,' whereupon 'Elfride's colour returned again' (201).

There follows the novel's best-known episode, in which Knight slips in the rain on the lip of the cliff, and hangs on a steep slope over the Atlantic by a tenuous handhold. He famously contemplates death in the face of fossils embedded in ancient geological strata, but the point of attention here is Elfride's rescue of him. In preparation for this she makes a 'woollen and cotton rope' of her underclothing, torn into strips.[7] The narrator tells us explicitly that in order to get at the materials she had taken off everything she was wearing, and had replaced only her outer bodice and skirt. He thus invites us to imagine her naked on the cliff top in the rain, pale or blushing as we choose. The rescue accomplished, what Knight sees in his survey of her 'from crown to toe' after they have embraced passionately for the first time, is that she seemed 'small as an infant.'[8] Through this perception Hardy reminds us of the similarly attenuated shape Elfride had presented to Stephen at midnight as they decide to elope – though in recognizing the parallel we also note the difference between Elfride in her dressing gown and underclothes, and Elfride (in later editions at least) in her single thin layer of muslin and silk rendered diaphanous by the rain. The difference marks the deeper erotic and sexual passion Elfride feels for Knight. This is the closest we come to the complete elimination of the barrier of dress between the observer and the observed: Elfride, pushed to the last resort, content to open her body to her beloved. And though they embrace, 'every nerve of [Elfride's] will ... now in entire subjection to her feeling' he (fully clothed) still does not offer her the kiss she craves, and Hardy allows him (as also Stephen) to register nothing of the feel of her natural, unencumbered body in his arms. It is only when she finally breaks free and he uses his eyes that he understands some of what she has done for him.

It is another carefully placed hint at Elfride's imminent death that Knight then remarks 'the rain and wind pierce you through' – through the material certainly, but also, the phrase momentarily implies, through the skin that is all but visible to him, and the solid flesh, as if she were, at what is for her a moment of supreme ecstasy, a spirit, a ghost.

The next chapter opens with Stephen, having landed at Castle Boterel and walked part of the way home, watching from a remote height, first one, then another figure hurrying from the cliffs to Endelstow rectory. He finds out soon enough that he has lost Elfride; the three come face to face in the crypt of Endelstow church, when Knight tells Stephen that he and Elfride are engaged:

> Low as the words had been spoken, Elfride had heard them, and awaited Stephen's reply in breathless silence, if that could be called silence where Elfride's dress, at each throb of her heart, shook and indicated it like a pulse-glass, rustling also against the wall in reply to the same throbbing.[9] The ray of daylight which reached her face lent it a blue pallor in comparison with those of the other two. (258)

It was in the same church that Elfride had first approached Stephen by touching his foot with the hem of her skirt. As everything in these paralleled repetitions, the intensity of the emotion felt is much stronger, and her dress, tight against her body, communicates the feeling much more clearly. And she is at this moment far from bloom or blush.

I have so far deliberately avoided discussion of the single dress-element to which Hardy gives the greatest significance in the novel, and it is now necessary to return to Stephen's courtship of Elfride:

> 'Now, Mr. Smith,' said the lady imperatively, coming downstairs, and appearing in her riding-habit, as she always did in a change of dress, like a new edition of a delightful volume, 'you have a task to perform to-day. These ear-rings are my very favourite darling ones; but the worst of it is that they have such short hooks that they are liable to be dropped if I toss my head about much, and when I am riding I can't give my mind to them. It would be doing me knight service if you keep your eyes fixed upon them, and remember them every minute of the day, and tell me directly I drop one. They have had such hairbreadth escapes, haven't they, Unity?' she continued to the parlour-maid who was standing at the door.
>
> 'Yes, Miss, that they have!' said Unity with round-eyed commiseration.
>
> 'Once 'twas in the lane that I found one of them,' pursued Elfride reflectively.
>
> 'And then 'twas by the gate into Eighteen Acres,' Unity chimed in.
>
> 'And then 'twas on the carpet in my own room,' rejoined Elfride merrily.

'And then 'twas dangling on the embroidery of your petticoat, Miss; and then 'twas down your back, Miss, wasn't it? And O, what a way you was in, Miss, wasn't you? my! until you found it!' (56)

There are certain complications in the playful publishing simile that opens this passage, in that, if you look very far, you might first of all wonder how many editions of any particular book you might desire to possess – as many as the changes a mid-Victorian young lady, even a provincial one, might be expected to make to her costume in a day or two? And then you might consider that the author of the book (presumably Elfride in this instance) could not improbably have taken the opportunity of a new edition to make changes to the text within (as, of course, Hardy did when offered the slightest opportunity), perhaps even radical changes, that might not be so pleasing as the new appearance. At least this is what Stephen will ultimately discover.

However, it is earrings that need to be attended to. Elfride's tone in talking about this particular pair, 'my very favourite darling ones,' suggests that, in so far as is conceivable, she is in love with them, perhaps as one might be in love with a pet – a rather wayward pet, as the sequel indicates. It might be supposed that a provident guardian of such favourites would, in the face of such a harrowing history of close shaves, have tried to safeguard them by having longer hooks fitted. Unity it is, though, who brings the narrative of the errant earrings to the point that Hardy wishes to make. Each is (mostly) attached to a part of Elfride's body which is mostly visible, unless her hair takes precedence, and is designed to draw attention to it – to its shape, its texture, and its relation to the rest of her head and her neck; and though when one falls off it is for the most part innocently to the ground, from time to time it is held suspended elsewhere, in an undergarment, against the flesh of her back. Elfride would never have given Stephen these intimate moments in their history, which surely prompt him to follow in his imagination their fortunate fall. But she does not protest.

Inevitably, one of the earrings is lost, falling from Elfride's ear at a moment of high intensity – her first kiss, shared with Stephen in a natural alcove on a cliff path, at the furthest extension of their ramble. It is important in this context to note that the earring is not dislodged in struggle or resistance. Stephen takes her by surprise, but she is, if anything, too eager in responding, 'so awkward and unused ... full of striving – no relenting.' The ambiguity of 'unused' is potent in the long view of the novel – Elfride was utterly unused to kissing, but also she was utterly unused in a physical way by any other man. After the embrace, Hardy has Stephen reinforce the importance of 'unused.' He asks Elfride: 'And no lover has ever kissed you before?' When she replies 'Never,' he says, 'I knew that; you were so unused. You ride well, but you don't kiss nicely at all' (61). The relationship thus established between the accidental loss of Elfride's earring and the deliberate loss of erotic innocence that the kiss symbolizes is significantly developed later.[10]

It is Unity who notices, after they return, that one of the earrings is missing, and Elfride says, 'I know now where I dropped it, Stephen. It was on the cliff. I remember a faint sensation of some change about me, but I was too absent to think of it then.' The irony in 'change' and 'absent' is carefully placed, and the lost earring again stands in for what will come to seem to her the much greater loss. She sends Stephen off to retrieve it, and it is not surprising that he fails – since the untouched quality it has been brought to represent cannot be retrieved. To take this undertext a little further, Elfride's distress at the loss of the earring, and her passionate upbraiding of Stephen for neglecting to safeguard it, suggest that she has also suddenly, on her return to domestic familiarity, been made aware of what she has done, and that Stephen has not only failed in his role as ideal romance-knight, but has also become the seducer – all this despite the fact that they have fully declared their love to each other. And of course, on a second reading of the novel, it is hard to miss the allusion to a more specific Knight, whose obsessions lend a weight of significance to this lost earring, and what it symbolizes.

The subject of earrings is raised between Elfride and the older man when Elfride, who longs to be taken seriously by Knight, asks: 'How would you draw the line between women with something and women with nothing in them?' Knight responds with a counterquestion:

> 'Which will you have of these two things of about equal value – the well-chosen little library of the best music you spoke of – bound in morocco, walnut case, lock and key – or a pair of the very prettiest earrings in Bond Street windows?'
> 'Of course the music,' Elfride replied with forced earnestness.
> 'You are quite certain?' he said emphatically.
> 'Quite,' she faltered; 'if I could for certain buy the ear-rings afterwards.' (179)

It can be no coincidence that Knight's test for vanity poses music against earrings (remember Stephen falls in love with her as she sings).

When Elfride says that music 'doesn't do any real good,' Knight exclaims with astonishment, 'what conceivable use is there in jimcrack jewellery?' Of course to Knight's mind Elfride condemns herself out of her own mouth, but his hostility to what have already become for the reader markers of erotic intensity also anticipates his ultimate erotic failure.

It is with a strong sense of irony that within a week Hardy has Knight in great anxiety himself over the purchase of earrings for Elfride. He has gone to Ireland in continuation of his holiday and, separated from Elfride, he rapidly understands that he has fallen in love with her. He equally rapidly alters his opinion of her vanity: 'how natural to womankind was a love of adornment, and how necessary became a mild infusion of personal vanity to complete the delicate and fascinating dye of the feminine mind' (186).

The subsequent history of the pair finally selected is intimately connected with Elfride's complicated feelings about Stephen and Knight. Knight rushes back from Ireland to give them to her, and though she desires both the earrings and the man, she refuses the ornaments and by implication him: her engagement to Stephen is at the forefront of her mind. She is embarrassed of course, and perhaps ashamed, and Hardy uses a striking phrase to describe the flush that comes with the feeling – he writes of her 'turning to a lively red.' It is only marginally fanciful to imagine the energetic blood, stimulated by the sight of the wonderful earrings and the complex of her contrary emotions, rushing to the surface of her skin, not just in her face but all over her body. In writing 'turning to' rather than simply 'turning' Hardy invites the thought that Elfride turns towards, embraces, the vermillion her body again produces for Knight. The narrator enhances these tentative impressions in further describing Elfride's response to the earrings:

> 'They are beautiful – more beautiful than any I have ever seen,' she answered earnestly, looking half-wishfully at the temptation, as Eve may have looked at the apple. (190)

And though the comparison with Eden is conventional enough, it is hard not to think of Milton as well as the Bible, and not just to anticipate the eventual acceptance of the tempting gift, but to consider also the power with which the poet represents the contrast between prelapsarian sexual innocence and the subsequent fig leaves of knowledge.

That evening Knight gives Elfride another chance to accept his gift:

she finds them on her dressing-table. She blushes 'hot' as she lifts them up beside her ear; they are Knight's own presence in her room (though she does not actually push the hooks through her ear lobes). Then she puts them by, thinking of Stephen, whose absence is symbolized still by the one earring lost on the cliff seat while the other rests at home in Elfride's jewel case. By the end of the evening she has returned the earrings to Knight's room and written to Stephen to reaffirm her intention to marry him (though she cannot bring herself to post the letter). Knight remains with the Swancourts and a few days bring another note from Stephen announcing his imminent arrival at Castle Boterel, by coaster from Bristol.

As we have seen, the day of his arrival is also the day Elfride finally rejects Stephen for the man whose life she has saved. Eventually, after what seems a remarkable delay, Knight offers his earrings a third time, and this time she accepts them, and by now even Knight can sense the erotic charge they represent. He wants more:

> 'Elfie, I should like to touch that seductive ear of yours. Those are my gifts; so let me dress you in them.'

After some sparring she gives in:

> Elfride inclined herself towards him, thrust back her hair, and poised her head sideways. In doing this her arm and shoulder necessarily rested against his breast.
>
> At the touch, the sensation of both seemed to be concentrated at the point of contact. All the time he was performing the delicate manoeuvre Knight trembled like a young surgeon in his first operation. (270)

Hardy does not distinguish Elfride's feeling as the thin metal shaft guided by a lover's finger penetrates the flesh of her ear, nor what Knight experiences through his fingers' ends, but it would be difficult, even as it is written, to ignore the sexual undertone. Having felt it once Knight wants it again, and again Elfride holds out, because 'it agitates me so,' but Knight is now master. So she turns, and now, at last, they kiss for the first time, and then a second. When Knight tries for a third kiss she flings away her face, and then 'hardly thinking of what she said' (not quite involuntarily, therefore), exclaims: 'Ah, we must be careful! I lost the other ear-ring doing like this.' And at once Stephen and his kiss are present in the scene. But when Knight asks her 'Doing like what?' she responds 'Oh, sitting down out of doors,' and the chapter ends (272).

Nevertheless, in the logic of Hardy's plot, it is not very long before Knight finds out the whole truth behind her unguarded exclamation. The lovers repeat the earlier outing of Stephen and Elfride to the seat in the alcove on Windy Beak. Hardy attempts to render naturalistic the inevitable retrieval of the earring lost on the earlier occasion by suggesting that only for a few minutes on any day did the sun shine directly into the cracks and niches about the seat. As Knight has to 'probe and scrape' with a penknife to get the earring out of its crack, so he has to drag its story out of Elfride. He questions her about the kisses and caresses she had shared with Stephen; each detail reluctantly wrung from her is torture to him, though he affects not to care. As they ride home there is another allusion to Milton's account of the Fall: '"Fool'd and beguiled: by him thou, I by thee!"' (304). And they see the tower of Endelstow Church, on the top of which Knight had first held Elfride in his arms, crumble in the name of church restoration. Knight's illusions about Elfride crumble likewise, and he abandons the woman who loves him so passionately, who has saved his life, because he cares much more for his self-image than he does for her. The lost earring restored to its partner marks the circle events have taken for her; she is alone as she was at the beginning of the novel, but the incremental intensity with which she has experienced life in the interim has left her drained.

But that is not the end. There comes, offstage, in the last chapter, a third proposal. The ironies of the last episode of the novel have been commented on from the first reviews – often adversely. Smith and Knight are both made to look ridiculous and sad, excluded even from Elfride's body in the Luxellian vault by the man, a vague figure, who has superseded them both and who (we are forced to see) must have loved her deeply, more deeply than they, if the profound grief he feels at her death is an accurate measure.

All we know of this final movement in the fantasia of Elfride's life is given to Smith and Knight (that composite failure) by Unity, her erstwhile maid, the same young woman who told us intimate details of the errant earrings. Inevitably, in this novel of symmetries, it is the Luxellian girls (defined here as at the beginning of the novel by their clothes), who are instrumental in delivering Elfride to their father.[11] But what is particularly striking in Unity's narrative in the present context is an image she uses in her account of the courtship. Elfride has asked her to guess to whom she is to be married; Unity, unaware of events, answered 'Mr. Knight, I suppose' (369). '"Oh!" she cried, and turned off so white, and afore I could get to her she had sunk down like a heap of clothes, and fainted away.' On being reminded of her misery at Knight's desertion, Elfride becomes a pile of discarded clothes, waiting for the maid to pick them up, waiting for the wash, clothes without their shaping body, not even possessing the disturbing potential of dresses hanging in a wardrobe waiting to be filled, but crumpled, tossed aside (or even waiting to be torn into strips). And thus Elfride's body is reduced from its public presence shaped by her fashionable clothes not just to the intimate slight form seen in outline by Smith and wholly by Knight, but to nothing at all. She becomes, for the space of Unity's simile, once again a ghost, a spirit, a disembodied soul.

The climax of Unity's narrative is another symbolic gift of jewellery:

> So he made her the beautifullest presents; ah, one I can mind – a lovely bracelet, with diamonds and emeralds. O, how red her face came when she saw it! The old roses came back to her cheeks for a minute or two then. I helped dress her the day we both were married – it was the last service I did her, poor child! (370)

The bracelet revives her delight in lovely adornments for her body, and her blood responds – for a minute or two. It is all the passion that remains to Elfride, and we imagine a bride as pale as the dress Unity puts upon her.

NOTES

1 The illustrations, drawn by J. Pasquier, are all reproduced in the Penguin Classics edition of *A Pair of Blue Eyes*, ed. Pamela Dalziel (London: Penguin, 1998). This edition also reproduces the text of the 1873 first edition.

2 This is an almost trivial summary of a profoundly complex issue. Three books that have particularly helped to shape my ideas about dress are Elizabeth Wilson, *Adorned in Dreams: Fashion and Modernity* (Berkeley and Los Angeles: University of California Press, 1987); Susan Kaiser, *The Social Psychology of Clothing: Symbolic Appearances in Context*, 2nd ed. (New York: Macmillan, 1990); and Alexandra Warwick and Dani Cavallaro, *Fashioning the Frame: Boundaries, Dress and the Body* (Oxford: Berg, 1998).

3 Page references are to the World's Classics edition of *A Pair of Blue Eyes*, ed. Alan Manford (Oxford: Oxford University Press, 1985).

4 Amy King, *Bloom* (New York: Oxford University Press, 2003).

5 There is more obvious irony in her idea that until this moment there has been nothing 'grave' in her life – for we may think of the grave of young Jethway, whose death will later be held against her to devastating effect.

6 A page or so earlier Hardy described Elfride's gaze:

> She had, unconsciously to herself, a way of seizing any point in the remarks of an interlocutor which interested her, and dwelling upon it, and thinking thoughts of her own thereupon, totally oblivious of all that he might say in continuation. On such occasions she artlessly surveyed the person speaking; and then there was a time for a painter. Her eyes seemed to look at you, and past you, as you were then, into your future; and past your future into your eternity – not reading it, but gazing in an unused [MS1 (first MS reading): in a rapt], unconscious way – her mind still clinging to its original thought [MS1: way – as a kitten might look upon a page of Holy Writ].
>
> This is how she was looking at Knight. (157–8)

It is particularly interesting that Hardy chose to replace 'rapt' by the 'unused' that is significant in the scene of Elfride's first kiss (see 128–9).

7 Elfride's first attempt to rescue Knight by reaching out her hand to him, the one illustrated in *Tinsley's Magazine*, results in her slipping alongside him; she escapes from the predicament by climbing up his body. John Sutherland, in a chapter of his *Can Jane Eyre Be Happy* (Oxford: Oxford University Press, 1997), 160–80, imagines Knight looking directly up her skirt as she springs from his shoulder to safety, and doubtless it would have been possible for him to have done so; but it is much more likely that he would have shut his eyes, and in any case his head would most probably have been turned to one side, rather than with his chin into the rock looking up the slope. Hardy also designs matters so that the telescope through which it had been possible to see Stephen flies off into the Atlantic the moment before Elfride flings her arms round Knight's neck to save herself.

8 Sutherland (*Jane Eyre*, 160–80) thoroughly and amusingly investigates the episode, though he neglects to consider the corset which Elfride would almost certainly, given her class and the date of the action, have been wearing. Irving Howe pointed out in his *Thomas Hardy* that had such a situation occurred in the 1960s when he was writing, Knight would have hurtled to his doom without recourse; see Irving Howe, *Thomas Hardy* (London: Weidenfeld and Nicolson, 1968), 38.

9 A pulse-glass is 'a glass tube with a bulb at each end, or at one end only,

containing spirits of wine and rarified air, which when grasped by the hand exhibits a momentary ebullition, which is repeated at each beat of the pulse' (*OED*).

10 Stephen asks for a kiss 'lips on lips' earlier on their outing, but from her superior position on horseback, Elfride flings down a hand effectively shielded from even remotely erotic contact by a riding glove. Stephen looks his disappointment, and Elfride peels back the glove (in itself a much more erotically charged action in the nineteenth century than in the present) and examines what is revealed: 'Isn't it a pretty white hand' she says, in the first of several moments of frank public self-admiration she has in the course of the novel. Then she withdraws the hand after all, Stephen tries to grab it and there 'ensued a mild form of tussle for absolute possession of the much-coveted hand, in which the boisterousness of boy and girl was far more prominent than the dignity of man and woman.' The earring might well have become unhooked then, but it did not.

11 At the beginning of the novel the girls had begged Elfride to be their little mother while their big mamma was away in London (41).

8 Hardy's Rural Painting of the Dutch School

RUTH BERNARD YEAZELL

Thomas Hardy first published a sensation novel; then, by his own account, he published a painting. Though his works are famous for their visual effects, only *Under the Greenwood Tree* (1872) – subtitled 'A Rural Painting of the Dutch School' – is explicitly characterized as a picture. By identifying his second published novel with the art of the Dutch, Hardy sought to capitalize on strengths that his earliest critics had identified in his work, even as he self-consciously called upon a well-established tradition of associating such painting with the realistic novel. Indeed, long before there was novelistic 'realism' there was 'Dutch painting': seventeenth-century painters had anticipated in visual form many of the features later identified with the rise of the novel; and writers had been registering the connection for at least half a century before 'realism' in a literary sense came into currency. The detailed rendering of material particulars, the representation of ordinary people and events rather than heroic and mythical ones, the close attention to the habits and rituals of daily life, especially the domestic life of the middle classes: all these familiar characteristics of novelistic realism had visual precedents in the so-called Golden Age of Dutch painting, and however they conjured with this comparison, nineteenth-century writers were well aware of the fact. From 1804, when Anna Barbauld observed that Samuel Richardson had 'the accuracy and finish of a Dutch painter,' to 1863, when Hippolyte Taine suggested that the proliferation of novels which represent 'contemporary life, as it is' resembled 'the great age of Dutch painting,' the analogy had been used to characterize, often with considerable ambivalence, both the manner and the matter of countless works of fiction.[1] Walter Scott's contention in his review of *Emma* (1815) that Jane Austen's art had 'something of the merits of the Flemish school of painting' is only one of the better known examples.[2] (For the purposes of this topos, the Flemish and the Dutch were virtually interchangeable.) Trollope was compared to a Dutch painter, and so were Harriet Martineau, Thackeray, Dickens, Gaskell, and Margaret Oliphant – not to mention Scott himself – while the comparison of Balzac to Dutch and Flemish painters quickly became commonplace on both sides of the Channel. Hardy's contemporaries would not have been surprised to learn that 'réalisme' in an aesthetic sense first came into circulation with an 1846 study of Dutch and Flemish painters,[3] and that its earliest migration into English seems to have been an essay on Balzac in the *Westminster Review* of 1853 – an essay that also evoked 'the well-known comparison of Balzac to Dutch painters.'[4]

Hardy's own Dutch painting was partly a creation of his readers. Like his first published novel – but more successfully – *Under the Greenwood Tree* reflected the beginning author's acute responsiveness to criticism. When George Meredith, acting as a reader for Chapman and Hall, advised him to withdraw the manuscript of his first novel and attempt something with 'a more complicated "plot,"' the result was the sensational narrative of *Desperate Remedies* (1871);[5] when critics faulted the latter while praising its pictures of rustic life, Hardy responded with his novelistic version of a Dutch painting. (The review that most seems to have wounded him specifically compared the 'redeeming' bits to the paintings of Teniers.)[6] Of course, matters were not quite so simple, if only because the evidence suggests that some of the scenes in *Under the Greenwood Tree* most reminiscent of Dutch painting were closely based on childhood memories, and that certain of these, at least, were already present in the unpublished manuscript of his first effort, *The Poor Man and the Lady*.[7] On the other hand, the fact that they too had been singled out by a reader who rejected the rest – *The Poor Man* having been shipped to Macmillan before being submitted to Chapman – confirms that Hardy was more than willing to let his artistic instincts be guided by the preference of his critics. When *Under the Greenwood Tree* appeared, the *Athenaeum* duly commended the still anonymous author for confining himself to the 'graphic pictures of rustic life' it had praised in its earlier remarks on *Desperate Remedies*.[8] Though Hardy later claimed that his second novel should really have been titled *The Mellstock Quire*, he never seems to have questioned his decision to label it a Dutch painting.

The literary profession had not always been so ready to encourage

'Dutch painting' in narrative. For much of the nineteenth century, in fact, the phrase and its variants had served as shorthand for kinds of realism that many reviewers found distinctly limiting. That Hardy's Dutch painting was nonetheless welcomed may owe something to the increasing dominance of photography, which eventually supplanted such painting as a paradigm for the faithful mimesis of the visible world. Where once critics routinely identified the art of the seventeenth-century Netherlands with 'mere' copying, they now had recourse to the photograph instead – a change that may have gradually enabled them to recognize the artful selection of the painters. But the relative warmth with which Hardy's rural pictures were greeted surely owes still more to the immediate precedent of George Eliot. Even if he did not model his early work on her example – he himself vehemently disclaimed any influence – there is no question that she had helped to create the taste by which that work was judged.[9] Her famous defence of Dutch painting in the seventeenth chapter of *Adam Bede* (1859) lent moral and intellectual weight to an art long ranked low in the generic hierarchy precisely because it was thought lacking in such significance. Defiantly responding to those 'lofty-minded people' who had hitherto kept Dutch painting in its place, she simultaneously instructed her readers how to approach her literary versions of the art.[10] By the 1870s George Eliot's own novels may have no longer borne any obvious resemblance to Dutch pictures, but the very fact that many of her contemporaries regretted the change is one measure of her initial success. At a time when readers were increasingly nostalgic for her early fiction, it is not surprising that one reviewer should have fondly associated the anonymous serial of *Far from the Madding Crowd* (1874) with her pen, or that another should have characterized *Under the Greenwood Tree* as 'Dutch paintings of English country scenes after the manner of *Silas Marner*.'[11]

Hardy's connection to pictures of all sorts was, of course, far more immediate than George Eliot's. He came to novel writing from architecture, not reviewing and philosophy; and his repeated insistence that his novels were 'impressions' rather than arguments could hardly be further from what she memorably called 'the severe effort of trying to make certain ideas thoroughly incarnate.'[12] Indeed, by his own account, Hardy's literary ideas often presented themselves to him first in the guise of pictures – a number of which he himself sketched and painted.[13] At one time he had thought of becoming an art critic, and he briefly kept to this end a 'Schools of Painting' notebook (1863) that included entries for both the Flemish and the Dutch. (In a rare characterization of a school as a whole, the notebook records that the Dutch School 'owes none of its fame to dignity of subject.')[14] But unlike George Eliot, who characteristically set out to mount an explicit defence of Dutch painting, Hardy was more engaged in looking at pictures than in theorizing about them. While he was working for a London architect in the 1860s, he began the practice of devoting twenty minutes every day to the National Gallery, 'confining his attention to a single master on each visit': 'He went there from sheer liking, and not with any practical object; but he used to recommend the plan to young people, telling them that they would insensibly acquire a greater insight into schools and styles by this means than from any guide books to the painters' works and manners' (LW, 53). The Gallery already had substantial holdings in Dutch and Flemish art when Hardy visited it in the 1860s, but its strength in this area was vastly increased with the acquisition of Sir Robert Peel's celebrated collection in 1871 – an event that coincided, as J.B. Bullen has noted, with the writing of Under the Greenwood Tree. Among the Peel Collection were a number of works by Teniers and Hobbema, both of whom were explicitly named by reviewers in connection with the rural scenes of Desperate Remedies.[15] Though Hardy appears to have been in the country when the Peel Collection was first put on display that June, one is tempted to imagine that he had it in mind when he completed his own 'Dutch painting' later that summer.

But what did it mean to identify a novel with Dutch painting? For modern commentators who have considered the question, it has primarily meant looking at how specific scenes in Under the Greenwood Tree appear to compose themselves like Dutch pictures.[16] And there is no doubt that the visual cues of many passages in this and other Hardy novels – as well, of course, as their subject matter – conjure up analogues from Dutch and Flemish art. Like Adam Bede, which returns repeatedly to the image of a woman posed in a doorway, Under the Greenwood Tree adopts the Dutch practice of framing the female figure in the spaces of domestic architecture. Our first glimpse of the heroine, for example, is that of 'a young girl framed as a picture by the window architrave' – a motif made familiar in numerous paintings by Gerrit Dou, among others.[17] (One of the most popular Dutch painters in the first half of the nineteenth century, Dou virtually invented the so-called niche format in the 1640s.)[18] Though Dou himself painted many candlelit scenes, the fact that Fancy Day is 'unconsciously illuminating her countenance to a vivid brightness by a candle she held in her left hand, close to her face' (34) may also suggest the work of his pupil, Godfried Schalcken, who specialized in such scenes – one of which later made its way into Hardy's own small collection.[19] A few chapters later, Fancy appears to her would-be lover, Dick Dewy, in another characteristic format: 'the door opened and three-quarters of the blooming young schoolmistress's face and figure stood revealed before him – a slice on her left-hand side being cut off by the edge of the door' (64). As Bullen has noted, Hardy's pictorial vocabulary in such instances is more self-conscious than George Eliot's: when we first see the hero's mother in *Adam Bede*, for example, we are told that 'the door of the house is open, and an elderly woman is looking out' (38), but there is nothing like the allusion to Fancy 'framed as a picture,' or the effect of spatial relations on a flat surface conveyed by that truncated 'slice' of her form.[20]

A similar self-consciousness about picture making characterizes the group portrait of the choir on its visit to the vicar, when the accidental fall of his pen arouses the curiosity of those waiting in the hall to learn the outcome of the interview:

Thus when Mr Maybold raised his eyes after the stooping he beheld glaring through the door Mr Penny in full-length portraiture, Mail's face and shoulders above Mr Penny's head, Spinks's forehead and eyes over Mail's crown, and a fractional part of Bowman's countenance under Spinks's arm – crescent-shaped portions of other heads and faces being visible behind these – the whole dozen and odd eyes bristling with eager Enquiry. (87)

This passage has sometimes evoked comparisons to a nineteenth-century British picture, *A Village Choir* (1847) by Thomas Webster;[21] but the motif of the curious onlookers crowded in a doorway or window appears with some frequency in Dutch genre painting, while the comically reductive effect of the 'fractional' body parts seems closer to the work of artists like Steen or Ostade than it does to Webster's more thoroughgoing illusionism. In another often cited case, the depiction of the choir members grouped by the open window of Mr Penny's workshop, Hardy combines a typical subject and format from Dutch genre with an explicit allusion to a sixteenth-century Italian painter – 'Mr Penny himself being invariably seen working inside like a framed portrait of a shoemaker by some modern Moroni' (70). A belated addition to the manuscript, the reference was presumably inspired by Moroni's famous *Portrait of a Tailor* (c. 1570) in the National Gallery.[22]

Yet apart from the fact that he too sports the tools of his trade, that distinguished-looking gentleman, standing erect in his elegant jacket, bears little resemblance to the rustic shoemaker seated near the window, 'with a boot on his knees and the awl in his hand' (70). Even when the author of *Under the Greenwood Tree* is evoking the Italian painter – or his modern equivalent – his own picture more nearly recalls the arrangements and subjects of the Dutch.

These are not the only moments in Hardy, needless to say, that resemble Dutch pictures. As Joan Grundy has remarked, 'most of his later novels have passages in which he recognisably "goes Dutch"'[23] – whether openly, as when he compares Liddy Smallbury's complexion in *Far From the Madding Crowd* to 'the softened ruddiness on a surface of high rotundity that we meet with in a Terburg or a Gerard Douw,'[24] or more obliquely, as in the 'dozen' such pictures that the reviewer for the *Athenaeum* professed to find in *The Trumpet Major* (1880).[25] But for the nineteenth century, I should like to argue, 'Dutch painting' was an idea (or set of ideas) as much as a model for local description; and rather than multiply such examples, I propose to take seriously Hardy's decision to identify his entire novel with a rural picture of the Dutch school.

Of course, Hardy knew that his subtitle was only a figure of speech. A novel is not a painting, though it may aspire to evoke visual images; and while paintings may imply narratives and even contain texts, they have at most a limited capacity for storytelling. But the perceived limitations of painting – especially painting of a certain kind – are very much to the point. Although there are a number of reasons why Hardy would have associated *Under the Greenwood Tree* with a painting of the Dutch school, one of them has to do with its comparative absence of plot. The manuscript of Hardy's first novel, *The Poor Man and the Lady* was originally subtitled, somewhat paradoxically, 'A Story with no plot' (*LW*, 58); and having perhaps taken too literally Meredith's advice that he attempt something more elaborately plotted in *Desperate Remedies*, he responded to the criticisms of that work by writing a novel with as little plot as possible. According to his own testimony, parts of *Under the Greenwood Tree* were directly lifted from the unpublished *Poor Man*[26] – among them, presumably, 'the opening pictures of the Christmas Eve in the tranter's house' that John Morley had praised when he read the manuscript for Macmillan's. 'What *Under the Greenwood Tree* owed to its unpublished predecessor,' Michael Millgate has suggested, was 'the evocation of a particular setting and a particular community, not a story.' On the evidence of the manuscript, Millgate speculates that

Hardy began writing the novel without having fully worked out its plot;[27] and the impulse to postpone narrative for picture making is still apparent in the dilatory pace of the opening chapters. While *Under the Greenwood Tree* does finally have a plot of sorts, even two plots – that of the conflict over the choir and that of the courtship of Fancy Day – both of these are so managed, I shall argue, as to keep their disruptive effects to a minimum.

From one perspective, all painting is essentially static, at least by comparison to the temporal art of 'poetry' – a position articulated most influentially by Lessing's celebrated essay on the *Laocoon* (1766).[28] But it is no accident, I think, that Hardy identified his least plotted novel with a Dutch painting, just as it is no accident that Scott associated Austen's 'Flemish' art with a novel that had, by his account, 'even less story' than usual.[29] Because Victorian genre painters were more inclined to storytelling than their seventeenth-century predecessors, modern critics have sometimes suggested that Hardy's contemporaries offer the more relevant comparison;[30] but it is the very tendency to picture rather than story, I believe, that would have principally associated *Under the Greenwood Tree* with the Dutch. Unlike the history painting of the Italians, which told a story, or at least alluded to one, and thereby appealed to the more intellectual capacities of the spectator, the 'low' genres of the North had long been associated with the absence of narrative. For classical theorists, who sought to dignify painting as a labour of the mind rather than the hands, the highest art was that which approximated to the status of language: while the Italians sought to abstract and generalize, according to this paradigm, the Dutch attended too closely to the visible surface of things – producing an art of 'mere' images and nothing more. What Roland Barthes has called the appearance of 'an entirely self-sufficient nominalism' in Dutch painting – 'an art of the catalogue ... of the concrete itself' – continued to haunt nineteenth-century commentary[31] – even, ironically, when critics adopted the analogy to talk about the verbal art of the novel. In an essay that appeared in *Blackwood's* in 1845, for example, Archibald Alison explicitly invoked the authority of Joshua Reynolds as he set out to attack the vogue for realism by mapping the generic hierarchy of classical art theory onto literary distinctions between the romance and the novel. In Alison's telling formulation, 'descriptions of still life – pictures of scenery, manners, buildings, and dresses – are the body, as it were, of romance; they are not its soul.' While they have their place in a narrative, 'the skillful artist' is 'to regard them as an inferior part only of his art,' duly subordinated to the grand passions that move the plot. Elsewhere in the essay Alison makes quite clear that such descriptions are the verbal equivalent of Dutch and Flemish painting – the novels associated with them bearing 'the same relation to the lofty romances of which our literature can boast,' in his phrase, 'that the Boors of Ostade, or the Village Wakes of Teniers, do to the Madonnas of Guido, or the Holy Families of Raphael.'[32] Ten years later R.H. Hutton would advance a similar argument against what he chose to call, among various other labels, 'the realistic,' 'the statical,' and 'the quiet, chatty school of novelists' – a school of which Austen, significantly, was 'by far the most distinguished representative.' Contending that 'a plot of some rapid movement is of the very essence of art,' Hutton also managed to suggest that only such rapid movement could reveal the 'deeper' aspects of human nature. 'As Dutch paintings of the highest imitative perfection soon weary because the mind cannot rest long on a mere lesson in accurate details,' so Austen and her school 'soon weary us, because what we naturally seek after is wanting.'[33]

Something of Hardy's own later impatience with the novel of manners, as well as with realism both in fiction and painting, can already be heard in these mid-century critics. But in *Under the Greenwood Tree*, at least, he was still prepared to identify his work with that of the Dutch. This is not to say that he would have classed himself with Austen and her followers: like most critical terms, including such notorious examples as 'realism' itself, 'Dutch painting' named a set of family resemblances rather than a clearly defined essence – a set of overlapping and related characteristics, not all of which were necessarily invoked in any single use of the phrase.[34] While Balzac's fame as a 'Dutch painter in prose' seems principally to have rested upon his descriptions of material objects, for example,[35] George Eliot seems to have thought first of the unidealized human figure when she associated her own art with that of the Dutch. At once a term for certain kinds of subject – Balzac's bourgeois interiors, George Eliot's peasants – and for certain kinds of treatment – primarily a close attention to material detail and to local matters of costume and custom – 'Dutch painting' signified above all an art of the ordinary and the commonplace, both in the class of persons depicted and in the familiarity of their activities. 'Everybody has sympathy for the concerns of every-day existence,' Anna Jameson had remarked in explaining the popularity of the school in 1844.[36] Of course, Dutch painting no more represented the whole of life in seventeenth-century Holland than Victorian fiction did that of nineteenth-century

Britain: what counts as the 'every-day,' in pictures and novels alike, is the product of artful construction, and *Under the Greenwood Tree* is no exception. But Hardy's version of such painting is still worth examining – if only to recognize how much his subsequent novels depart from its measure of reality.

As 'a rural painting of the Dutch school,' *Under the Greenwood Tree* occupies an ambiguous place between landscape and the type of picture we would now usually categorize as genre. Until well into the nineteenth century, in fact, that distinction would itself have been a blurry one. Once used as a catch-all category for everything other than the historical or religious subjects traditionally classified as history painting, the French word *genre* only gradually began to acquire its present sense as the representation of everyday life. When Diderot referred to *peinture de genre* in an essay of 1765, the term included landscape and still life as well as pictures of anonymous persons engaged in daily activities.[37] Though the process by which a word that originally meant 'kind' or 'manner' came to mean one kind in particular is somewhat obscure, the evidence suggests that it was not until the 1860s and 1870s – the very years when Hardy first began writing fiction – that the term finally settled into its current meaning.[38] Even today, it is not always clear what distinguishes a landscape with human figures from a genre painting set outdoors – except, presumably, the relative prominence of the people depicted. Unlike history painting or portraiture, on the other hand – both of which depend on the viewer's knowledge that a specific person, whether real or fictional, is intentionally represented – genre only exists as a category so long as its people are anonymous.[39] The moment an individual picture is recognized as the Holy Family, for example, it ceases to be classified as a genre painting of a carpenter's household. While there is no evidence that the nineteenth century explicitly registered this distinction, the very anonymity of the figures in Dutch genre painting – an anonymity nonetheless rendered with detailed attention to the particular – clearly encouraged the impulse to associate them with the daily and the familiar. Like the elements of a landscape (or, for that matter, the objects in a still life), the people in Dutch genre painting acquire their reality effect because they are at once individualized and typical. And any action in which they engage – a lady playing a musical instrument, say, or some peasants dancing beneath a tree – registers not as a unique event but as ongoing and repeatable.

Hardy's own rural picture creates its reality effects by analogous methods. 'To dwellers in a wood,' the novel begins, 'almost every species of tree has its voice as well as its feature. At the passing of the breeze the fir-trees sob and moan no less distinctly than they rock: the holly whistles as it battles with itself: the ash hisses amid its quivering: the beech rustles while its flat boughs rise and fall. And winter, which modifies the note of such trees as shed their leaves, does not destroy its individuality' (11). Attention will soon shift from this chorus of trees to a chorus of people, but in both cases the narrative proceeds by simultaneously typing and individualizing. After a brief portrait of the novel's hero, whose only distinctiveness here is the utter ordinariness of his profile ('an ordinary-shaped nose, an ordinary chin, an ordinary neck and ordinary shoulders'), we are introduced to the other principal members of the choir:

> Scuffling halting irregular footsteps of various kinds were now heard coming up the hill, and presently there emerged from the shade severally five men of different ages and gaits – all of them working villagers of the parish of Mellstock ...
>
> The first was a bowed and bent man, who carried a fiddle under his arm, and walked as if engaged in studying some subject connected with the surface of the road. He was Michael Mail – the man who had hollaed to Dick.
>
> The next was Mr Robert Penny, boot- and shoe-maker – a little man who, though rather round-shouldered, walked as if that fact had not come to his own knowledge, moving on with his back very hollow and his face fixed on the north-east quarter of the heavens before him, so that his lower waist-coat-buttons came first – and then the remainder of his figure. His features were invisible, yet when he occasionally looked round two faint moons of light gleamed for an instant from the precincts of his eyes, denoting that he wore spectacles of a circular form.
>
> The third was Elias Spinks who walked perpendicularly and dramatically. The fourth outline was Joseph Bowman's, who had now no distinctive appearance beyond that of a human being. Finally came a weak lath-like form trotting and stumbling along with one shoulder forward and his head inclined to the left, his arms dangling nervelessly in the wind as if they were empty sleeves. This was Thomas Leaf. (12–13)

Just as the trees have their characteristic notes, so the human beings have their characteristic gaits; yet even as Hardy takes care to distinguish one member of the group from another, he also continues to represent them as a collective. From the comparatively detailed sketch of Robert Penny to Joseph Bowman's wholly indistinctive outline is a difference of degree rather than of kind. What begins with a collective noun that is nonetheless said to be differentiated – those 'shuffling halting irregular footsteps of various kinds' – ends with more collective nouns, as humans and trees alike are assimilated to the group: 'they all advanced between the varying hedges and the trees dotting them here and there – kicking their toes occasionally among the crumpled leaves' (14).

Rather than a chorus in the Greek sense, which simply comments on the action, this chorus (or choir) nearly doubles as the protagonist. Though the courtship plot seems to have gained in prominence as Hardy revised,[40] almost half the published novel still concentrates on the musicians and their activities. Only in the ninth chapter do the two lovers first separate themselves from the others; and even after the courtship plot – such as it is – gets under way, the novel persists in its habit of identifying the individual with the group. 'Ay, ay, my sonny: every lad has said that in his time,' the tranter tells young Jimmy, when the latter protests that his brother said he would never marry (37); and something like this law of the typical and the repeatable governs the ordinary hero's surrender to love as well. As Dick's father sums up his condition:

> There's too many o' them looks out of the winder without noticing any-thing: too much shining of boots: too much peeping round corners – too much looking at the clock: telling about clever things She did till you be sick of it, and then upon a hint to that effect a horrible silence about her. I've walked the path once in my life and know the country, neighbours; and Dick's a lost man! (75)

Even without his final remark, the tranter's gerunds make clear that action in such a case is both generalizable and continuing.

As for the heroine of this story, the double set of furniture with which her father's house is stocked – the late Mrs Day having provided for Fancy's eventual marriage by acquiring two of everything – clearly trumps her vague aspirations after 'surroundings more elegant and pleasing than those which have been customary' (176). The 'most no-ticeable instance' of this arrangement is 'a pair of green-faced eight-day clocks, ticking alternately' in the Day front room (93) – a detail that Hardy's friend and mentor, Horace Moule, particularly remarked when he cited the 'picture' of this interior as 'entirely justifying the author's mention of the Dutch school upon his title-page.'[41] Like the Day boots, whose common last the shoemaker adapts, with small variations for bunions and such, from father to son, the two clocks offer inanimate versions of the individual as type: produced by rival clockmakers and marked with distinctive signatures, they keep slightly different times, while nonetheless signalling the fundamental repetition of history from mother to daughter. At the wedding itself, Fancy twice attempts to alter local custom in the direction of greater refinement, only to acquiesce and do just like her mother. 'Why we did when we were married, didn't we Ann?' says the tranter of one such custom; 'and so do everybody, my sonnies.'

> 'And so did we,' said Fancy's father.
> 'And so did Penny and I,' said Mrs Penny. 'I wore my best Bath clogs I remember, and Penny was cross because it made me look so tall.'
> 'And so did father and mother,' said Miss Mercy Onmey.
> 'And I mean to, come next Christmas!' said Nat the groomsman, vigorously and looking towards the person of Miss Vashti Sniff.
> 'Respectable people don't nowadays,' said Fancy. 'Still, since poor mother did, I will.' (188–9)

From the dominance of the chorus – its individual voices at once mildly idiosyncratic and repetitive – to Fancy's brief protest and swift assimilation to the pattern, the sequence neatly sums up the action of the courtship plot as a whole.

When Hardy looked back on *Under the Greenwood Tree* more than a quarter century later, it was only the choir that he saw: the prefaces of 1896 and 1912 make no mention of the courtship plot at all. 'This story of the Mellstock Quire and its old established west-gallery musicians,' the 1896 preface begins, 'is intended to be a fairly true picture ... of the personages, ways, and customs which were common among such orchestral bodies in the villages of fifty or sixty years ago. One is inclined to regret the displacement of these ecclesiastical bandsmen by an isolated organist ...' (3). To the extent that the novel focuses on those 'personages, ways, and customs' – rather than on that conflict with the 'isolated organist' – it does in fact approximate to 'picture.' Though the story of the choir is finally one in which the group yields to the individual, *Under the Greenwood Tree* prefers to keep its eye on the group. 'I never in my life seed a quire go into a study to have it out about the playing and singing! ... And I should like to see it, just once,' pleads the half-witted Leaf, when the musicians undertake their interview with the vicar in the hope of persuading him to postpone their displacement (81). The innocent Leaf speaks as if such a meeting were a customary practice, like carolling at Christmas or a wedding, rather than a singular episode in history; and despite the gentle joke at his expense, the novel almost manages to share his vision. The very ease with which the musicians give way to the vicar – not to mention the physical comedy of the scene – tends to mute any impression that something significant has occurred. And so, too, does the way the courtship plot reinstates the choir at the end, both by marrying the intrusive organist to one of their own and by bringing the musicians themselves back to perform at the ceremony.

Yet even in this most static of novels, picture inevitably gives way to history. Like George Eliot before him, Hardy associated Dutch painting with his own rural past; and however nostalgically he might view the image of reality it presented, he could hardly write fiction without plotting against it. Maybold himself is a recent arrival in Mellstock, and his decision to replace the choir with Fancy's organ playing is not so different, after all, from the more momentous signs of historical change that Hardy would register in works like *The Mayor of Casterbridge* (1886) or *Tess of the d'Urbervilles* (1891). By the measure of such novels, Fancy's short-lived acceptance of the vicar's marriage proposal scarcely qualifies as an event, yet her momentary surrender to 'ambition and vanity' (177) anticipates the restlessness that drives so many of Hardy's protagonists; while her decision to conceal her lapse hints, if ever so faintly, at betrayals to come. Only *Far from the Madding Crowd* perhaps approaches the 'Dutch' painting of *Under the Greenwood Tree*; and that novel retains its investment in the ordinary only by arranging for subordinate figures to act out the more restive impulses of its hero and heroine.[42] 'And at home by the fire, whenever you look up there I shall be – and whenever I look up there will be you,' Oak proposes to Bathsheba at the novel's opening; but not until Boldwood is locked up and both Fanny and Troy are dead will the novel reward its 'everyday sort of man' and settle into something like his picture of quotidian domesticity (34, 32).

Both in fiction and in painting, Hardy himself would not long rest content with certain kinds of realism. Though he would never fully abandon the Dutch masters, his taste in landscape would increasingly incline towards Turner and the Impressionists, while his theoretical statements about art would repeatedly emphasize the subjective distortion of material appearances.[43] A notebook entry for 1887 dismisses the 'simply natural' as no longer interesting: 'I don't want to see landscapes, i.e., scenic paintings of them, because I don't want to see the original realities – as optical effects, that is. I want to see the deeper reality underlying the scenic, the expression of what are sometimes called abstract imaginings ... The exact truth as to material fact ceases to be of importance in art' (LW, 192). An essay published the following year would similarly strive to distinguish 'the accidental from the essential' in fiction – citing in support the very passage in which Taine had disparagingly compared the painstaking detail of contemporary novels to the work of Dutch painters.[44] 'Art is a disproportioning – (i.e. distorting, throwing out of proportion) – of realities, to show more clearly the features that matter in those realities,' he announced in an often-quoted notebook entry of 1890. 'Hence "realism" is not Art' (LW, 239).

When the art in question was that of the novelist, Hardy's rejection of realism was inseparable, I think, from his allegiance to plot. He immediately followed *Under the Greenwood Tree* with a novel whose 'essence' was plot, as he told his publisher;[45] and plotting, as he conceived it, necessarily arose from resistance to the commonplace and the repetitive. The 'purpose of fiction,' he wrote in 1881, 'is to give pleasure by gratifying the love of the uncommon in human experience ... The writer's problem is, how to strike the balance between the uncommon and the ordinary so as on the one hand to give interest, on the other to give reality.' By 1893 he was even more emphatic: 'A story must be exceptional enough to justify its telling. We tale-tellers are all Ancient Mariners, and none of us is warranted in stopping Wedding Guests (in other words, the hurrying public) unless he has something more unusual to relate than the ordinary experience of every average man and woman.'[46] Throughout Hardy's career, 'ordinary experience' would continue to be the province of his rustics, but only his rural painting of the Dutch school would make such experience the principal subject of the work. Rather than Dutch painting, he would return more consistently to the model of Shakespeare, as he once more relegated his low mimetic figures to their traditional choral function. *A Pair of Blue Eyes* (1873) has a grave-digging scene almost worthy of *Hamlet* – not to mention some lively talk of pig killing – but like most of the novels to follow, *Under the Greenwood Tree*'s successor directs its principal attention to those who aspire to something more than the ordinary rhythms of life and death.

150   Ruth Bernard Yeazell

NOTES

1 Mrs [Anna] Barbauld, 'The Life of Mr. Richardson,' in *Correspondence of Samuel Richardson*, 6 vols (London: Richard Phillips, 1804), 1:cxxxvii; H[ippoylte] Taine, *Histoire de la littérature anglaise*, 4 vols (Paris: Hachette, 1863–4), 3:494, 495.
2 [Walter Scott], Review of *Emma*, in *Quarterly Review* 14 (1815); repr. in *Sir Walter Scott on Novelists and Fiction*, ed. Ioan Williams (London: Routledge & Kegan Paul, 1968), 235.
3 According to Bernard Weinberg, it was Arsène Houssaye's *Histoire de la peinture flamande et hollandaise* of 1846 that first gave the word 'réalisme' in this sense 'any real prominence,' although he finds isolated uses of the term for art and literature in the previous decade. Among the earliest of the latter is an article by Gustave Planche in the *Revue des deux mondes* for 1835, where 'réalisme' is used to characterize the 'vérité humaine' (as opposed to 'idéalité poétique') of Rembrandt. See Weinberg, *French Realism: The Critical Reaction, 1830–1870* (Chicago: Modern Language Association of America, 1937) 118–19, 114n.
4 [Henry Sutherland Edwards], 'Balzac and his Writings,' *Westminster Review* 60 (1853): 208. This use of 'realism' in an aesthetic sense antedates the first citation given in the *OED*, which is to the fourth volume of Ruskin's *Modern Painters* (1856). I owe its identification to Richard Stang, *The Theory of the Novel in England, 1850–1870* (New York: Columbia University Press, 1961), 148. Stang in turn credits Robert Gorham Davis, 'The Sense of the Real in English Fiction,' *Comparative Literature* 3 (1951): 214. A well-known piece on Dickens and Thackeray by David Masson in the *North British Review* for 1851 had already compared the styles of the two novelists by way of an extended analogy to the 'Ideal' and the 'Real' in painting.
5 See Thomas Hardy, *The Life and Work of Thomas Hardy*, ed. Michael Millgate (London: Macmillan, 1984), 63–4. Hereafter cited parenthetically as *LW*.
6 *Spectator* 44 (1871): 482.
7 See Michael Millgate, *Thomas Hardy: His Career as a Novelist* (New York: Random House, 1971), 57–61, 19. Cf. also Millgate, *Thomas Hardy: A Biography* (New York: Random House, 1982), 137–8.
8 *Athenaeum*, 15 June 1872, 748.
9 See his protest to Samuel Chew, who had posited such influence in his *Thomas Hardy: Poet and Novelist* (1921): 'It was Shakespeare's delineation of his Warwickshire clowns (who much resemble the Wessex peasantry) that influenced Hardy most. He found no clowns i.e. farm-labourers or rustics,

anywhere in G. Eliot's books, and considered her country characters more like small townspeople than peasantry.' See to Samuel Chew, 17 September 1922, *The Collected Letters of Thomas Hardy*, ed. Richard Little Purdy and Michael Millgate, 7 vols (Oxford: Clarendon, 1978–88), 6:155. For related evidence, see also *The Literary Notebooks of Thomas Hardy*, ed. Lennart A. Björk, 2 vols (London: Macmillan, 1985), 1:381. For this novel's debt to Shakespeare, see Millgate, *Thomas Hardy: His Career*, 44–9. The title of *Under the Greenwood Tree*, of course, comes from *As You Like It*.

10 George Eliot, *Adam Bede*, ed. Carol A. Martin (Oxford: Clarendon, 2001), 166. Further references to this edition will be given by page number in the text.

11 *Spectator* 47 (1874): 22; *Saturday Review* 39 (1875): 57.

12 For Hardy, see, e.g., his 1892 preface to *Tess of the d'Urbervilles* and his 1895 preface to *Jude the Obscure* in the Wessex Edition. The quotation from George Eliot is from a letter to Frederic Harrison, 15 August [1866], in *The George Eliot Letters*, ed. Gordon S. Haight, 9 vols (New Haven: Yale University Press, 1954–78), 4:300.

13 J.B. Bullen, *The Expressive Eye: Fiction and Perception in the Work of Thomas Hardy* (Oxford: Clarendon, 1986), 2, 15–19.

14 *The Personal Notebooks of Thomas Hardy*, ed. Richard H. Taylor (New York: Columbia University Press, 1979), 112.

15 Bullen, *Expressive Eye*, 43–4. According to Bullen, the *Catalogue of Furniture and Paintings ... from Max Gate* (1938) suggests that Hardy's 'most prized possessions ... were several pictures of the Dutch school,' including a wooded landscape with a Holy Family and figures engaged in an archery contest, two merry-making scenes, and a candlelit interior attributed to Godfried Schalcken (28). Though it is not clear when Hardy acquired these, it seems highly unlikely that any of them belonged to the struggling author of *Under the Greenwood Tree*.

16 See especially Norman Page, *Thomas Hardy* (London: Routledge & Kegan Paul, 1977), 68–9; Joan Grundy, *Hardy and the Sister Arts* (London: Macmillan, 1979), 26–31; and Bullen, *Expressive Eye*, 42–53.

17 Thomas Hardy, *Under the Greenwood Tree*, ed. Simon Gatrell (Oxford: Oxford University Press, 1999), 34. All further references to this edition will be given parenthetically by page number in the text.

18 Martha Hollander, *An Entrance for the Eyes: Space and Meaning in Seventeenth-Century Dutch Art* (Berkeley: University of California Press, 2002), 48.

19 See note 15 above.

20 Bullen, *Expressive Eye*, 46–7.

21 Page, *Thomas Hardy*, 68; Bullen, *Expressive Eye*, 46.
22 For the manuscript information, see Gatrell's note to the Oxford edition, 210. For an elaboration of the Moroni comparison, see Bullen, *Expressive Eye*, 49.
23 Grundy, *Hardy and the Sister Arts*, 29.
24 Thomas Hardy, *Far from the Madding Crowd*, ed. Suzanne B. Falck-Yi (Oxford: Oxford University Press, 2002), 74. Further references will be given by page number in the text.
25 *Athenaeum*, 20 November 1880, 672.
26 See *Thomas Hardy's Public Voice: The Essays, Speeches, and Miscellaneous Prose*, ed. Michael Millgate (Oxford: Clarendon, 2001), where these are characterized (in an article published by Florence Dugdale but 'edited' by Hardy) as 'delightful pictures of rural life' (314).
27 Millgate, *Thomas Hardy: His Career*, 43.
28 Cf. Lloyd Fernando, 'Thomas Hardy's Rhetoric of Painting,' *Review of English Studies* 6 (1965): 62–73, which argues that Hardy's visual rhetoric in *The Return of the Native* tends to freeze the narrative into static tableaux, modelled on the paintings of the pre-Raphaelites.
29 [Scott], Review of *Emma*, 232.
30 See especially Page, *Thomas Hardy*, 70–8, and Grundy, *Hardy and the Sister Arts*, 30–40.
31 Roland Barthes, 'The World as Object,' in *Critical Essays*, trans. Richard Howard (Evanston: Northwestern University Press, 1972), 7.
32 [Archibald Alison], 'The Historical Romance,' *Blackwood's Edinburgh Magazine* 58 (1845): 354, 342.
33 [R.H. Hutton], 'A Novel or Two,' *National Review* 1 (1855): 337, 339–40.
34 Nor did every work produced in the Dutch Republic, paradoxically, count as 'Dutch painting': when nineteenth-century writers conjured with the phrase, they primarily had in mind genre, landscape, still life and portraiture – the types of picture at which northern artists were thought to excel – rather than the historical and mythological subjects that recent scholarship has reminded us were also produced by artists in seventeenth-century Holland. For a useful summary of that scholarship, see Eric J. Sluijter, 'New Approaches in Art History and the Changing Image of Seventeenth-Century Dutch Art between 1960 and 1990,' in *The Golden Age of Dutch Painting in Historical Perspective*, ed. Frans Grijzenhout and Henk van Veen, trans. Andrew McCormick (Cambridge: Cambridge University Press, 1999), 247–76.
35 [George Henry Lewes], 'Recent Novels: French and English,' *Fraser's Magazine* 36 (1847): 695.

36 Mrs [Anna] Jameson, *Companion to the Most Celebrated Private Galleries of Art in London* (London: Saunders and Otley, 1844), 342.

37 Denis Diderot, *Essai sur la peinture*, in *Oeuvres*, ed. André Billy, Bibliothèque de la Pléiade (Paris: Gallimard, 1951), 1189. Though the *Essai* was written in 1765, it was not published until 1795.

38 Wolfgang Stechow and Christopher Comer, 'The History of the Term *Genre*,' *Allen Memorial Art Museum Bulletin* 33 (1975–6): 89–94. While the Dutch themselves classified pictures by subject – a merry company, a barrack-room scene, etc. – they had no term for the category as a whole.

39 I owe this crucial point to Albert Blankert, 'What Is Dutch Seventeenth Century Genre Painting? A Definition and Its Limitations,' in *Holländische Genremalerei im 17. Jahrhundert: Symposium Berlin 1984*, ed. Henning Bock and Thomas W. Gaehtgens (Berlin: Mann, 1987), 9–32.

40 See Simon Gatrell's introduction to his Oxford edition, xi–xiii.

41 [Horace Moule], Review of *Under the Greenwood Tree*, in *Saturday Review* 34 (1872): 418.

42 For evidence that Boldwood partly took over Oak's original role in the novel, especially by acting out what was once the latter's violence against Troy, see Millgate, *Hardy: His Career*, 84–5.

43 See Grundy, *Hardy and the Sister Arts*, 50–64; Shelagh Hunter, *Victorian Idyllic Fiction: Pastoral Strategies* (Atlantic Highlands, NJ: Humanities Press, 1984), 186–94; and Bullen, *Expressive Eye*, esp. 169–222.

44 Hardy, 'The Profitable Reading of Fiction' (1888); repr. in Millgate, ed., *Thomas Hardy's Public Voice*, 82.

45 Millgate, *Thomas Hardy: His Career*, 66.

46 Hardy, *LW*, 154, 268. Cf. another variant on these remarks, which dates from 1891: 'Howells and those of his school forget that a story *must* be striking enough to be worth telling. Therein lies the problem – to reconcile the average with that uncommonness which alone makes it natural that a tale or experience would dwell in the memory and induce repetition' (251).

9 Individual and Community in *The Return of the Native*: A Reappraisal

J. HILLIS MILLER

Michael Millgate's magisterial *Thomas Hardy: His Career as a Novelist* places *The Return of the Native* in the context of Hardy's admiration for William Barnes's work, especially Barnes's poems in Dorsetshire dialect. Hardy admired the linguistic accuracy of those poems, as well as Barnes's deep understanding of local Dorset customs. As is proper for a biographical study, Millgate also places *The Return of the Native* in the context of Hardy's life, for example, his nomad existence with his wife at the time he was writing the novel. Hardy and his wife moved from temporary dwelling to temporary dwelling. They had not yet settled at Max Gate, the house Hardy built for himself not far from his birthplace. Building Max Gate, one might say, made him an example of the return of the native. Millgate is right, however, to end his chapter on *The Return of the Native* by echoing Thomas Wolfe. Clym Yeobright in the novel discovers, as did Thomas Hardy in his own life, that 'you can't go home again.'[1] Why not? What would it mean to go home again, that is, to return to your native soil after a period away?

This essay will investigate these and several related questions. What is the relation of individual to community in *The Return of the Native*? Do the events of the novel take place within what can be legitimately called a 'community,' that is, a 'home' for those who dwell within it? Just what is a 'community'? Why is it that 'you' can't go home again? What conception of the 'you,' that is, of the separable individual, would be necessary in order to make plausible the claim that once uprooted from your native soil you cannot be planted there again? Hardy says in the *Poems of 1912–13* that his first wife was in a way made homeless by being moved to Dorset from her native Cornwall and then ultimately being buried far from the sea she so loved: 'She will never be stirred / In her loamy cell / By the waves long heard / And loved so well.'[2] Is living rooted and eventually buried in some native soil the normal and proper condition for humankind? Must uprooting be called 'alienation' or some such bad thing?

An understanding of what is at stake in answering these questions may be approached indirectly. I shall do so by a detour through a juxtaposition of Raymond Williams and Martin Heidegger, unlikely bedfellows, to be sure. I have in mind Williams's *The Country and the City* and Heidegger's *Being and Time*.[3] It is impossible in a short essay to discuss Williams and Heidegger in detail. The results of a careful reading would show that no two positions could be in starker contrast. What is good for Williams, belonging to an egalitarian community, is bad for Heidegger. It is given the dyslogistic name of being lost in the 'they.' What is bad for Williams, alienation from any organic community, is good for Heidegger, since only by such detachment can Dasein ('Being there' in German: Heidegger's term for 'selfhood') become an authentic self. Which authority has it right? It is not all that easy to decide, though much is at stake in making a decision. It is somewhat easier to focus on an example that will at least permit understanding further just what is at stake.

What is the relation between individual and community in *The Return of the Native*? In earlier discussions of the novel, I noticed Hardy's attention to the material presence of centuries and centuries of history in the setting of *The Return of the Native*.[4] The layers of ashes on the top of Rainbarrow, as described in the opening scenes, form a series of embodied time coulisses. Nevertheless, I paid too little attention to the presence in the novel of an ongoing action, in the now of the novel. The heath men and women perform this action as they live there and change the landscape even further, bit by bit. The narrator, for example, mentions quite recent and often unsuccessful attempts to clear and cultivate bits of the heath. The heath folk form a community that intervenes between the protagonists and the heath. This community constitutes the immediate milieu within which or, rather, above which they can act, can live, love, and die.

Should we say that this group of heath folk constitutes a genuine community or is it a spurious one? I think it does fit Williams's definition of an organic community of neighbourly mutuality. It is also sequestered, for the most part, from the evils of agrarian capitalism that, in Williams's view, gradually destroys any possibility of true rural communities.

What are the distinctive characteristics of the community above which, as one might say, rather than within which, the main events take place? The community of *The Return of the Native* is introduced in the initial scene of the Fifth of November bonfire that all the natives gather to make and light on the top of Rainbarrow, as their forefathers have done for generations. They work cooperatively together. No one is in charge or gives orders. This community is made up of the working men and women who live on or adjacent to the heath. It does not include, as I shall specify, the main protagonists of the story. The members of this native community make their living from the heath or work as servants to the genteel folk who live nearby. Hardy mentions one man who lives by digging turf for fuel, another who cuts furze, and a woman who lives by making 'besoms,' or brooms, from plants that grow on the heath. These people have been born and bred there. They have never left Egdon Heath. An exception is Grandfer Cantle. Cantle was in the 'Bang-up Locals' in 1804, that is, he was a member of a local militia organized to resist the expected invasion by Napoleon. As a local militiaman, he made it all the way to Budmouth, on the neighbouring seacoast a few miles away. The chief act of the 'Locals' seems to have been to march away when an actual invasion was (falsely) reported in Budmouth.

All the members of this community speak in the local dialect, or in Hardy's rendition of it. Early reviewers criticized this rendition for inaccuracy and for being too 'intellectual.' Hardy defended himself in an essay by saying that an exact reproduction of the way Dorset rustics talk would be too hard to read. He just wanted to convey a sense of that dialect to his educated, metropolitan readers.[5] Hardy's heath men and women are relatively undifferentiated from one another, though they have distinctive names: Humphrey, Timothy Fairway, Susan Nunsuch, Olly Dowden. Grandfer Cantle is individualized, as is his son Christian Cantle. Christian is a weedy man scared of his own shadow. He is a man whom no woman will marry because he is not masculine enough. This is because he was born at the new moon and fulfils the folk adage, 'No moon, no man.' Christian is said to be like a wether, that is, like a castrated sheep: "Tis said I be only the rames [dialect for 'skeleton' or 'carcass'] of a man, and no good for my race at all,' says Christian, upon which Fairway observes, to the company generally, 'Well, there's many just as bad as he ... Wethers must live their time as well as other sheep, poor soul.'[6] All these characters reveal themselves by their talk. That talk certainly resembles the idle talk of the 'they,' as described by

Heidegger. It is desultory, gossipy, and wandering. It is made up of received opinions and well-known stories, for the most part. The heath folk tell one another what they all already know.

Hardy's rustics seem to have little in the way of separate interiorities. At least those subjectivities are rarely and sparsely presented directly. The reader is told what the heath folk say, what clothes they wear, something of what they look like, what their gestures and behaviours are. They make comments on one another and on their 'betters.' Their talk, or 'chatter,' is a mixture of folk wisdom, superstition, ideological biases, and shrewd insight. An example of the latter is Timothy Fairway's comment on his own marriage. This is a prophetic anticipation of the miserable marriages of the protagonists later in the novel:

> 'all the time I was as hot as dog-days, what with the marrying, and what with the woman a-hanging to me, and what with Jack Changley and a lot more chaps grinning at me through church window. But the next moment a strawmote would have knocked me down, for I called to mind that if thy [Humphrey's] father and mother had had high words once, they'd been at it twenty times since they'd been man and wife, and I zid myself as the next poor stunpoll to get into the same mess. ... Ah – well, what a day 'twas!' (51)

The heath folk go through life in a way like sleepwalkers. The mind of the community speaks through them. They light Fawkes Fires, or perform the mummers' play of St George and the Saracens at Christmas, or put up a maypole on the first of May in the same somnambulistic way. These things are what you do and have always done as long as anyone can remember, at set times of the year. Hardy's narrator comments that you can always tell a true folk performance from a reproduction by the unimpassioned way it is run through:

> A traditional pastime is to be distinguished from a mere revival in no more striking feature than in this, that while in the revival all is excitement and fervour, the survival is carried on with a stolidity and absence of stir which sets one wondering why a thing that is done so perfunctorily should be kept up at all. Like Balaam and other unwilling prophets, the agents seem moved by an inner compulsion to say and do their allotted parts whether they will or no. This unweeting manner of performance is the true ring by which, in this refurbishing age, a fossilized survival may be known from a spurious reproduction. (147)

The reference to Balaam is a characteristic Hardyan learned allusion dragged in by the narrator. The rustic characters would never have thought of such a parallel. The narrator is inside. He (or it) is an expert on the ways of this community. At the same time the narrative voice speaks as an outsider who sees those ways from an ironic distance. The narrator's task is to explain that community to middle-class urban literate readers. How many of my readers today have ever witnessed or participated in a genuine 'fossilized survival'? In my own life only certain things done at Christmas time come even close: trimming the tree, singing carols whether you want to or not, eating certain foods, because it is what you do at Christmas, what your parents and grand-parents did.

One curious feature of the Egdon community is that for the most part they do not go to church. The church is too far away to be easily reached, even on Christmas. This has some importance. It means that the church does not often function as a social gathering place for all classes and levels of this community. Church in some communities is a place to see and be seen, a place where courtships may be surrepti-tiously begun and carried on. The lack of church going also means, perhaps, that the heath folk's Christianity is to some degree merely nominal. As the narrator comments, apropos of the erection of a may-pole outside Thomasin's bedroom window: 'Indeed, the impulses of all such outlandish hamlets are pagan still: in these spots homage to na-ture, self-adoration, frantic gaieties, fragments of Teutonic rites to di-vinities whose names are forgotten, seem in some way or other to have survived mediaeval doctrine' (401). The lack of church going also means that no conspicuous community gathering externalizes class distinc-tions, with the squire and his family in a special pew, lesser folk in lesser pews, and the minister above them all. Here is the narrator's quasi-ethnographical comment on this:

The customary expedient of provincial girls and men in such circum-stances [when they want to see their neighbours or be seen by them] is churchgoing ... But these tender schemes were not feasible among the scattered inhabitants of Egdon Heath. In name they were parishioners, but virtually they belonged to no parish at all. People who came to these few isolated houses to keep Christmas with their friends remained in their friends' chimney-corners drinking mead and other comforting liquors till they left again for good and all. Rain, snow, ice, mud everywhere around, they did not care to trudge two or three miles to sit wet-footed and splashed to the nape of their necks among those who, though in some measure neighbours, lived close to the church, and entered it clean and dry. (146)

The role in courtship sometimes played in rural communities by church going is to a considerable degree replaced in the Egdon community by country dancing. Examples are the improvised community dance atop Rainbarrow in the embers of the Fifth of November bonfire, or the dances that precede the mummers' play at Mrs Yeobright's Christmas party, or the outdoor public dance that Eustacia goes to alone when her marriage to Clym has turned sour. She dances there with Wildeve, who just happens to have come there too: 'The dance had come like an irresistible attack upon whatever sense of social order there was in their minds, to drive them back into old paths which were now doubly irregular' (284). They are doubly irregular because each is married to someone else. It is a double infidelity. The passage is also an example of Hardy's figurative use of the paths that the characters literally traverse across the heath in their interactions with one another. Hardy's narrator comments, apropos of Mrs Yeobright's Christmas party dance, on the social function of dancing in this community. The passage expresses, in indirect discourse, Eustacia's awareness of the seductive power of dancing: 'To dance with a man is to concentrate a twelvemonth's regulation fire upon him in the fragment of an hour. To pass to courtship without acquaintance, to pass to marriage without courtship, is a skipping of terms reserved for those alone who tread this royal road' (156).

The world of *The Return of the Native* is an imaginary world, a virtual reality. It is hard to resist believing, however, that Hardy is speaking through the narrator as a kind of anthropological expert reporting on a vanishing way of life. The novel's action is supposed to have taken place, according to Hardy, between 1840 and 1850, thirty or more years before the novel was published, in 1878. C.J. Weber has narrowed this to 1842–3.[7] Hardy is no doubt basing what he says on his own childhood experience in the village of Upper Bockhampton, near the 'original' of Egdon Heath. There is no reason to doubt that this particular virtual reality is closely based on real landscapes, real ways of living, and even real houses. *The Return of the Native* in the Anniversary Edition (1920) of Hardy's works contains photographs of the originals of Blooms-End, of the Yeobrights' house, and of Alderworth Cottage, where Clym Yeobright lives with Eustacia after their marriage, as well as photographs of what Hardy calls, in the novel, 'Egdon Heath' and 'Shadwater Weir.'

The narrator's knowledge of this community is detailed and circumstantial. He records that the behaviour and judgments of the heath folk reveal all sorts of prejudices and superstitions. They take a dim view of education. They think Clym Yeobright's scheme to educate the rural population is foolish and ill conceived. 'But, for my part,' says one of the rustics, 'I think he had better mind his business' (195). All the heath folk know folk songs, as well as the text of the mummers' play. Grandfer Cantle sings by the bonfire a ballad that was recorded in the seventeenth century and that has an ironic parallel to the main action. It was called, variously, according to the notes in the New Wessex Edition, 'Queen Eleanor's Confession,' 'Earl Marshal,' or 'The Jovial Crew' (428). Queen Eleanor, like Eustacia Vye, was not altogether a good and faithful wife. The novel is full of other folk customs and folk beliefs. These include the custom of singing a song at the bridegroom's house when he has taken his bride home on the wedding night, the belief that only the fat of a fried adder will cure an adder bite, and Susan Nunsuch's belief, shared by some of her neighbours, that Eustacia is a witch. Susan believes Eustacia has hexed her children and made them ill. She pricks Eustacia's arm in church, drawing blood. This was supposed to cure her of witch's powers. At the end of the novel, on the stormy, rainy night when Eustacia drowns herself, Susan sticks pins in a wax effigy of Eustacia and then melts the effigy in the fire in an attempt to perform a little malign magic of her own. It seems to work.

The members of this community are good at telling stories about themselves or about their neighbours. They have a long collective memory, for example Humphrey's memory, by way of his mother's memory, of the beheading of Louis the Fourteenth (133), or, closer by in the past, Timothy Fairway's memory and circumstantial account of the scene in the church when Mrs Yeobright 'forbad the banns' between Wildeve and her niece Thomasin (48–9), or the wonderful memorial celebration, by Timothy Fairway again, of what a great musician Thomasin Yeobright's father, now long dead, was: 'Whenever a club walked [an annual parade of some local community organization] he'd play the clarinet in the band that marched before 'em as if he'd never touched anything but a clarinet all his life. And then, when they got to church-door he'd throw down the clarinet, mount the gallery, snatch up the bass-viol, and rozum away as if he'd never played anything but a bass-viol' (75). All these highly specific details of local life go to make the collection of heath folk a genuine community. They have in common a whole set of assumptions and ways of living. They thereby fulfil the conditions for a genuine community as defined by Raymond Williams.[8]

The members of the Egdon community have, for the most part, no separate individualized lives and no interiorities worth investigating. Nothing dramatic ever happens to them. They are born, marry, quarrel with their wives, work, have children. They do all the quasi-ritualistic things Hardy's narrator tells us they do during the round of the seasons. Then they die and are buried in the local churchyard. Their separate individualities are lost in the 'they.' They are representatives, however, of a more or less positive version of Heidegger's 'das Man.' They do not, even so, have enough consciousness of themselves as separate individualities to be anything like Heideggerian authentic Daseins. Therefore they do not have life stories worth telling. Hardy's narrator is not particularly condescending to them for that lack, as Heidegger certainly is in his description of newspaper-reading, public-transportation-taking members of the 'they,' who think and judge not for themselves but just as those around them do.[9] Hardy, on the contrary, admires and warmly sympathizes with the heath folk. *The Return of the Native* celebrates and commemorates the true natives of the heath as a vanishing species. Hardy's double attitude toward the Egdon Heath community is neatly expressed in a sentence from his essay of 1883, 'The Dorsetshire Labourer': 'it is among such communities as these that happiness will find her last refuge on earth, since it is among them that a perfect insight into the conditions of existence will be longest postponed.'[10] Hardy's essay is a detailed and eloquent account of the gradual passing away of this happiness. This happens through manifold social and material changes in rural working-class life, as the 'natives' become more educated, more mobile, more open to the outside world, and more directly subjected to capitalist agrarian practices.

All the main protagonists of *The Return of the Native* differ from those in the community of heath folk in already beginning to approach a perfect insight into the conditions of existence, to their sorrow. This means that, unlike the heath folk, they do have separate subjectivities. They are aware of themselves as different and as having unique destinies. They therefore have life stories that the narrator can tell. They might therefore be considered to have what Heidegger calls authentic Daseins. They have wrested themselves, or have been wrested, from the 'they' of the local community. Their lives are lived not only against the background of the heath, as they criss-cross it in their transactions with one another, but also against the background of the local community that to some degree intervenes in their lives, as the heath does. It is a community, however, of which they are not really members. The crucial difference between Heidegger and Hardy, however, is that Heidegger sees authentic Dasein in highly positive terms, even though it means having a conscience, feeling guilty, and living 'towards death,' whereas self-consciousness is a more or less unmitigated disaster for Hardy's protagonists.

The stories Hardy's narrator tells, moreover, involve exclusively characters that are not really members of the Egdon community in another sense. In Deer Isle, Maine, where I now live most of the year, a sharp distinction is made between those who are 'from here' and those who are 'from away.' If you are 'from away' you have no hope of ever becoming a native, 'from here,' nor do your children or grandchildren. It will take generations and generations of local inhabitation before people might forget that your family is from away. All Hardy's characters are in one way or another 'from away.' They have not been born in Egdon into a family that has lived and died there for many generations, as long as anyone can remember. Even if they have been born there, like Clym, Thomasin, and Diggory Venn, they have not, except for Thomasin, lived all their lives there. They have not always lived absorbed into the life and prejudices of the community. To go away even for a short time is to cease forever to be a real 'native.'

The narrator is quite specific for each of the protagonists about just how this is the case. Eustacia is the granddaughter of a ship captain in the Royal Navy who, invalided out, has come 'from away' to live in a house, 'Mistover,' next to Egdon Heath. Eustacia's father was a bandmaster from Corfu. She is definitely from away. Mrs Yeobright is a curate's daughter who has married a now deceased local farmer. Nevertheless, she has 'a standing which can only be expressed by the word genteel,' and had 'once dreamt of doing better things' (59–60). She too is from away. Her detachment, as well as her gentility, has rubbed off on the orphan niece she has brought up, Thomasin. Wildeve was trained as a civil engineer and has worked in an office in Budmouth, the neighbouring fashionable seaside resort, just as Eustacia lived there as a child. Wildeve has failed as an engineer and has come to Egdon 'from away' to take over the local tavern, the Quiet Woman Inn. Diggory Venn is the son of a dairy farmer nearby, but he has taken up the wandering trade of 'reddleman,' that is, someone who goes from sheep farm to sheep farm over a wide area selling reddle for dipping sheep. He is only a periodic and temporary resident in Egdon, as he travels from place to place in his gypsy cart mobile home. Clym Yeobright has been well educated and has worked as a diamond merchant in Paris. His experience detaches him permanently from his beloved natal heath, however hard he tries to return to it and to immerse himself in the local trade of furze cutting.

All these characters are also detached from the community by several other characteristics they all have, in a different form for each. Each is of a higher class than the heath folk and recognized as 'genteel' by them. Each is more highly educated than they. Each is, finally, in one way or another an 'intellectual.' Each is thoughtful and reflective, someone who sees himself or herself and the surrounding world from a detached perspective. Each, unfortunately for him or her, unlike 'the Dorsetshire labourer,' does have something approaching 'perfect insight into the conditions of existence.' The introductory presentation of each or some later moment of crisis gives the narrator an opportunity to specify the particular self-awareness and awareness of the grim universal human condition a given protagonist has. This self-awareness might be called that taking possession of one's 'ownmost possibilities of Being' which Heidegger calls 'authentic Dasein.' Each has detached himself or herself from the 'they' of the Egdon community. Each lives an independent inner life that is to a considerable degree secret and silent. Each inner life is not only kept hidden from the others, but is also in any case incommunicable to them. This secrecy manifests a universal failure of any one character in this novel to understand the others or to be understood by them. Nevertheless, the narrator betrays the secret life of each to the reader, according to a conventional practice in novels.

It is a peculiarity of Hardy's presentation of his protagonist's 'Daseins' that notations of what they are actually thinking and feeling at a given moment are relatively brief and laconic. Relatively little use (as opposed, say, to Trollope's practice) is made of that basic convention of Victorian fiction, free indirect discourse. Free indirect discourse presents the intimate here and now of a character's thoughts and feelings, transposed from first-person present tense to third-person past tense. An example of the latter is a brief passage about Diggory Venn:

He sat in his van and considered. From Thomasin's words and manner he had plainly gathered that Wildeve neglected her. For whom could he neglect her if not for Eustacia? Yet it was scarcely credible that things had come to such a head as to indicate that Eustacia systematically encouraged him. Venn resolved to reconnoitre somewhat carefully the lonely road which led along the vale from Wildeve's dwelling to Clym's house at Alderworth. (289).

Direct notations of subjectivity in *The Return of the Native* tend, unlike the one just cited, to move rapidly out into generalizations about the constant qualities of that person's mind. A passage describing Wildeve's yearning for Eustacia just because she is marrying Clym exemplifies several features of the presentation of character in *The Return of the Native*, as well as this one. It exemplifies the law of mediated desire, formulated earlier for Eustacia. This is a given person's desire only for those who are desired by others. The passage also exemplifies the way Hardy's narrator tends to move rapidly from sparse notations about the subjective here and now of the characters' subjectivities to generalizations, and then to literary or historical allusions. The narrator dilates further and further away from direct, intimate notation of a subjectivity's actual texture and contents. The passage also exemplifies the way subjectivity tends to be registered in this novel in terms of the body, as it affects the body, or in terms of the characters' habitual ways of seeing the outside world in which they find themselves, that is, in a particular situation. Such notations stand by metonymy for their characteristic subjectivities. They tend to see the world as if from a distance, as an antagonist, or as something within which they do not fit. The passage also exemplifies the way the local community functions as the means by which the main protagonists learn about one another. Since they are often estranged from one another and have little direct contact, they often communicate or get information about one another through the Egdon rustics. The passage I shall cite describes Wildeve's reaction to learning from the driver of a cart coming down from Mistover, who has stopped for a drink at the Quiet Woman Inn, that Eustacia is going to marry Clym. Such passages are characteristic of Hardy's narrative tactics. They are more a comment by the narrator about the character's constant quality of mind than a direct, intimate representation of it at a particular moment:

The old longing for Eustacia had reappeared in his soul: and it was mainly because he had discovered that it was another man's intention to possess her.

To be yearning for the difficult, to be weary of that offered; to care for the remote, to dislike the near; it was Wildeve's nature always. This is the true mark of the man of sentiment. Though Wildeve's fevered feeling had not been elaborated to real poetical compass, it was of the standard sort. He might have been called the Rousseau of Egdon. (237)

The narrator begins with the here and now of Wildeve's state of mind but withdraws rapidly to a wider compass, moving through a general definition of Wildeve's temperament to end with a comparison to Rousseau. The latter functions in the same complex and multiple way the multitude of such literary, historical, and biblical allusions operate in the novel. They are meant, one guesses, to establish the narrator's credentials to be respected by his metropolitan, literate readers, and by the reviewers. They also establish the narrator as someone with a wide comprehensive vision. The narrator may notice little things like grass-hoppers and rabbits' ears in the sunlight, but he also sees all particulars in the context of an all-embracing insight into the ephemerality and ultimate pointlessness of any individual human existence. This is that insight into humanity's true 'conditions of existence' that Hardy says would destroy the happiness of the Dorsetshire labourer. He sees such insight as more and more characterizing all mankind in this late age of the world. Hardy's narrator ascribes some version of this devastating insight to all the main protagonists of the novel, except Thomasin. Since, as we know, innocence is bliss, this might possibly justify the happy ending for her. About that happy ending there will be more to say.

The main characters echo the narrator's wide vision, though each is isolated in his or her special version of it. This awareness of the futility of human existence and of the way 'I' in particular exemplify that is Hardy's dark version of Heideggerian benign withdrawal from the 'they' into autonomous and authentic Dasein.

Mrs Yeobright, for example, the narrator tells the reader, sees human things as though from a vast distance and as a pointless swirling of ephemeral creatures. This figure anticipates the more highly developed version of this in the choruses of *The Dynasts*. The passage also exemplifies the way Hardy often presents subjectivity in terms of special ways of perceiving the external world as opposed to reporting introspection as such:

She had a singular insight into life, considering that she had never mixed with it ... What was the great world to Mrs Yeobright? A multitude whose tendencies could be perceived, though not its essences. Communities were seen by her as from a distance; she saw them as we see the throngs which cover the canvases of Sallaert, Van Alsloot, and others of that school – vast masses of beings, jostling, zigzagging, and processioning in definite directions, but whose features are indistinguishable by the very comprehensiveness of the view.

One could see that, as far as it had gone, her life was very complete on its reflective side. (212)

Diggory Venn lurks here and there on the heath as what the narrator calls a 'Mephistophelian visitant' (104). He spies on the other characters as a detached and unseen seer who objectifies the narrator's invisible clairvoyance. The reflective reader may note that Thomasin's name is a feminine version of Hardy's own name. This suggests that in some way, conscious or unconscious, Hardy identified himself with Thomasin, or idealized himself in her passivity and more or less unreflective goodness. The narrator of *Tess of the d'Urbervilles* characterizes himself by way of the novel's epigraph, from Shakespeare's *Two Gentlemen of Verona*, as a protective enclosure for Tess, or at least for her 'name': 'Poor wounded name! My bosom as a bed / Shall lodge thee.' Diggory Venn, as an objectification of the narrator's watching distance, plays somewhat the same role in *The Return of the Native* as that of the narrator in *Tess*. Diggory, however, often intervenes actively, often with disastrous consequences, whatever his loving good intentions towards Thomasin may be. An example is his manipulation of Eustacia, Mrs Yeobright, and Wildeve so that Wildeve decides to marry Thomasin after all. Venn, the reader might conclude, should have kept his distance.

Wildeve, as the passage cited above indicates, is a Rousseau-like man of sentiment. He cares only for the remote and unattainable. This is a sure recipe for unhappiness and perpetually unsatisfied desire. It ultimately leads Wildeve to his death when his love for Eustacia returns in intensified form just because she is unattainable.

A full chapter is devoted to a description of Eustacia's character. She is presented as a narcissistic, melancholic 'Queen of Night' (93), 'the raw material of a divinity' (93). 'Her high gods were William the Conqueror, Strafford, and Napoleon Buonaparte, as they had appeared in the Lady's History used at the establishment in which she was educated' (97). Eustacia wants only to exercise power over men by way of her beauty. She is incapable, as she knows well enough, of loving anyone for long. For her, as for Hardy's characters generally, possession rapidly destroys love, but she differs from most of them in knowing this beforehand. 'To be loved to madness – such was her great desire' (96). She knows, however, 'that any love she might win would sink simultaneously with the sand in the glass ... Fidelity in love for fidelity's sake had less attraction for her than for most women: fidelity because of love's grip had much. A blaze of love, and extinction, was better than a lantern glimmer of the same which should last long years' (96). Eustacia does actually carry an hourglass in her wanderings on the heath. She is obsessed with a foolish and unfulfillable desire to be somewhere else, somewhere different, especially Paris, though if she ever got there she would soon find it as unsatisfactory and boring as Egdon Heath. She believes that 'certain creatures of her mind, the chief of these being Destiny' (96), not particular human beings, have it in for her. When she wanders up to the top of Rainbarrow in the rainstorm, before she throws herself into Shadwater Weir, she does not blame herself or those around her, in her self-pitying suicidal despair, but large abstractions, 'destiny' and 'Heaven,' in which the narrator evidently does not believe:

> 'How I have tried and tried to be a splendid woman, and how destiny has been against me! ... I do not deserve my lot!' she cried in a frenzy of bitter revolt. 'O, the cruelty of putting me into this ill-conceived world! I was capable of much; but I have been injured and blighted and crushed by things beyond my control! O, how hard it is of Heaven to devise such tortures for me, who have done no harm to Heaven at all!' (372)

Eustacia might almost be seen as an ironic parody of Heidegger's 'authentic Dasein.' She is certainly withdrawn from the 'they,' and she certainly thinks of herself as a unique singularity with a special destiny of her own that does lead straight to death, but all these Heideggerian elements are presented in a dyslogistic and self-deceptive form. They are not presented as the heroic heeding of the conscience's call in a resolute being towards death that Heidegger praises. Rather than taking possession of her selfhood and special situation, her suffering leads her to detach herself from herself, and to see herself as if from a great distance, in a way rather like the detached vision of the narrator: 'Eustacia could now, like other people at such a stage, take a standing-point outside herself, observe herself as a disinterested spectator, and think what a sport for Heaven this woman Eustacia was' (357–8).

Clym Yeobright is presented explicitly as the man who already is what mankind as a whole is rapidly becoming. He is someone who already sees clearly the sad conditions of existence. Clym, like Hardy himself, is a thoughtful intellectual. His bodily beauty is being consumed and gradually destroyed by thought. As in the case of Eustacia, a long generalizing characterization of Clym prepares for his behaviour in the novel. Like so many others of the main protagonists, he sees things from a distance. The narrator defines him by this detached disillusioned vision rather than by his interior thoughts or feelings at any one moment of his life. His disillusionment is the exact opposite of the naive faith, the 'old-fashioned revelling in the general situation,' the Egdon rustics have:

> In Clym Yeobright's face could be dimly seen the typical countenance of the future ... The truth seems to be that a long line of disillusive centuries has permanently displaced the Hellenic idea of life, or whatever it may be called. What the Greeks only suspected we know well; what their Aeschylus imagined our nursery children feel. That old-fashioned revelling in the general situation grows less and less possible as we uncover the defects of natural laws, and see the quandary that man is in by their operation. (191)

Hardy, in short, ascribes to Clym Yeobright his own 'disillusive' insights into the way the mismatch between what men and women want and what natural laws allow makes happiness and the satisfaction of desire impossible. The heath folk may think they are at home on Egdon Heath, but humankind and the world they find themselves in do not fit. Men and women can never be at home in the world. They are permanently 'unheimlich,' whether they know it or not.

One might say that the narrator has distributed among the main characters different facets of himself, though in each case in a different, idiosyncratic combination. Each of the characters is imprisoned within his or her own version of what Hardy in *Jude the Obscure* calls the 'coming universal wish not to live.' None can ever communicate his or her secret interiority to others. The actions of the novel are therefore made up of the doomed contretemps of the characters as they interact fatefully. These interactions are dramatized in their criss-cross movements over the heath. They are always at cross-purposes with one another, never able to achieve happiness for themselves or for others. Their intentions, however well meant, tend to misfire, just as do the speech acts they perform, such as promises to love one another forever, or marriage vows, or attempts to stop bad marriages, such as Mrs Yeobright's forbidding of the banns between Thomasin and Wildeve.

The latter is a striking and little-used performative utterance. The minister of the church announces on successive Sundays the 'banns,' that is, the intention to wed of two of his parishioners. Each time he asks if anyone in the congregation knows of any impediment to the marriage, Mrs Yeobright, to everyone's consternation, stands up in church and 'forbids the banns.' This event takes place before the action begins. All the heath community know about it as a local scandal (48–9). In three cases – Mrs Yeobright, Wildeve, and Eustacia – the characters' intersecting trajectories lead to deaths that are ignominious rather than tragic. The bringing to the surface of the barely alive Clym, whose legs are clasped tightly by the dead Wildeve's arms, emblematizes the destructive relation among the main characters in this novel.

Clym is left alive to vibrate between a Hardyan pessimism and a returning idealism that makes him end in a faintly ridiculous role as an itinerant preacher of a secular ethics: 'Yeobright had, in fact, found his vocation in the career of an itinerant open-air preacher and lecturer on morally unimpeachable subjects' (423). Much irony is present in that phrase 'morally unimpeachable subjects,' since Hardy was often accused of being far from morally unimpeachable. He gave up novel writing for good after the uproar over the supposed immorality and blasphemy of *Jude the Obscure*.

My rereading of *The Return of the Native* has been motivated by investigations I have been making of Victorian and modernist multiplotted novels as models of community. That formulation does not really fit this novel. Though the heath folk form a community, the main actions of the novel focus on a noncommunity of distinctive individuals who interact with one another destructively and without mutual understanding. Nor is *The Return of the Native* really 'multiplotted.' Each of the main characters, rather, has his or her own separate, and to a considerable degree private, plot. Each has a life story that intersects fatefully with those of the others, but the whole does not form an integrated plot of the sort that Aristotle had in mind and that he saw as exemplified by *Oedipus the King*.

What then should the reader make of the happy ending? Thomasin marries Diggory Venn, who has loved her from afar so faithfully, and for the most part secretly, after she refuses him twice. A footnote at the end of the next to the last chapter is an intrusion on the narrator's discourse by Hardy himself. Hardy speaks in his own voice as a ghostly intruder who has not been heard from before, except in the 'Preface' and in the 'Postscript,' printed, for some reason, at the beginning, in the

New Wessex Edition. Hardy speaks in the footnote as the 'writer' who
has made up the whole fiction. That footnote passes implacable judgment on the meretricious and inconsistent happy ending. Hardy wrote
the new ending because the editor of *Belgravia*, the popular magazine in
which *The Return of the Native* was first published in instalments, had
insisted that Hardy write a happy ending.[11] He did that against his
original intention, against consistency, and against the laws prohibiting
human happiness that govern so sternly the virtual reality of *The Return
of the Native*. Here is the footnote:

> The writer may state here that the original conception of the story did not
> design a marriage between Thomasin and Venn. He was to have retained
> his isolated and weird character to the last, and to have disappeared
> mysteriously from the heath, nobody knowing whither – Thomasin re-
> maining a widow. But certain circumstances of serial publication led to a
> change of intent.
>
> Readers can therefore choose between the endings, and those with an
> austere artistic code can assume the more consistent conclusion to be the
> true one. (413)

So much for the happy ending! Who would not want to have 'an
austere artistic code' rather than a banal one, the one shared with the
'they'? And who would admire a novel whose ending is inconsistent
with all that has gone before? The only problem is that Hardy did not
ever write that consistent ending.

Where, I ask in conclusion, should we put Hardy in relation to Williams and Heidegger? Somewhere in between, I think, or, rather, in an
anomalous position that does not fit exactly what either says about the
nature of community, about the nature of the individual, and about the
proper or desirable relation between them. The relation between Williams and Heidegger on these points, the reader will remember, is a
chiasmus. What seems good to Williams, living immersed in an organic
community, seems bad to Heidegger. It is defined as being lost in 'das
Man.' What seems good to Heidegger, the detached self-possession of
authentic Dasein, seems bad to Williams. It is defined as alienation from
belonging to a community. Hardy's *The Return of the Native* does not fit
either of these paradigms. An organic, traditional, egalitarian community, to a considerable degree sequestered from capitalism, forms the
background of the main action of the novel, superimposed as an active,
present-day way of living on the landscape of Egdon Heath. That

community, however, is presented as happy because it is blissfully ignorant. It is lost in illusions. It does not understand humankind's true conditions of existence. The main characters live in detachment from that circumambient community. They live in self-conscious awareness of their specific situations and of the general conditions of human existence, as Hardy sees them. They might therefore be taken as examples of Heideggerian authentic Dasein.

The crucial difference, however, is the judgment passed by the two authors on that state. For all his dark rigour and talk of a primordial 'being guilty,' Heidegger sees authentic Dasein as on the whole a positive and desirable state. It is the state of someone who is rooted in Being, who has resolutely taken possession of his or her 'ownmost possibilities of Being,' who has answered the call of conscience, and who is living authentically oriented towards his or her own death. Heidegger, moreover, explicitly sees authentic Daseins as able to live together in a new kind of community in which each Dasein helps the others to be their authentic selves.[12] What Heidegger says is somewhat surprising because it modifies his general stress on the privacy, secrecy, and silence of authentic Dasein.

Heidegger's description of a utopian community of authentic Daseins, each helping the others to activate resolutely their ownmost (belonging intimately to Dasein, that is, the self) potentialities for Being is wonderfully optimistic and positive. Nothing of the sort seems possible in Hardy's imagined world. For one thing, Hardy's characters are not shown as resolutely choosing to be what they are. Their distinctive natures are imposed on them, willy-nilly. They cannot help being what they are and behaving accordingly. For Hardy, detaching oneself from the community, or never having belonged to one, and living as not a 'native' anywhere, is a more or less unmitigated disaster. It leads to deaths that are, as I have said, ignominious or melodramatic rather than tragic. Those deaths hardly correspond to the sort of thing Heidegger appears to have had in mind in his talk about each person dying his or her own death. The deaths in *The Return of the Native* are often the result of bad luck and misunderstanding, including self-misunderstanding, or they are the result of basic character flaws that the characters cannot help. Nor can Hardy's thoughtful and self-conscious characters help one another be themselves. They work continually against one another. They have no true understanding of one another. They cause one another much grief. They even contribute, as Clym Yeobright conspicuously does, and in spite of his best intentions, to the deaths of others. Clym is partly responsible for his mother's death, for Eustacia's death, and for Wildeve's death. He blames himself bitterly for the first two of these.

Nothing in Hardy, finally, corresponds to Heidegger's conviction that authentic Dasein is rooted in Being. The characters may believe that they must be the sport of some malign deity or fate, but the narrator presents this as an illusion, a fantasy. Hardy is more correct than Heidegger, I believe, in his prophetic insight into the rootless conditions of existence, as more men and women within Western modernity endure those conditions. Clym's Oedipal anguish in no way testifies to some inscrutable wish of God to punish him. It is evidence rather of the vast and total indifference of nature to human suffering or joy. At the climax of his despair, Clym sees 'only the imperturbable countenance of the heath, which, having defied the cataclysmal onsets of centuries, reduced to insignificance by its seamed and antique features the wildest turmoil of a single man' (342). He achieves at that moment 'a consciousness of a vast impassivity in all which lay around him' (343). Clym's consciousness here coincides closely with the narrator's, and with what the evidence of his writing in fiction and in poetry suggests was Hardy's own habitual consciousness. Hardy would probably have seen the appeal, all over our 'globalizing' world today, to extreme forms of traditional religions as one response to this painful sense of rootlessness.

NOTES

1 Michael Millgate, *Thomas Hardy: His Career as a Novelist* (New York: Random House, 1971), 144.
2 'I Found Her Out There,' in *The Complete Poetical Works of Thomas Hardy*, ed. Samuel Hynes, 5 vols (Oxford: Clarendon, 1982–95), 2:52.
3 Raymond Williams, *The Country and the City* (New York: Oxford University Press, 1975); Martin Heidegger, *Being and Time*, trans. John Macquarrie and Edward Robinson (London: SCM Press, 1962).
4 See J. Hillis Miller, *Thomas Hardy: Distance and Desire* (Cambridge, MA: Belknap Press of Harvard University Press, 1970); and Miller, *Topographies* (Stanford: Stanford University Press, 1995).
5 See Thomas Hardy, 'Dialect in Novels,' in *Thomas Hardy's Public Voice: The Essays, Speeches, and Miscellaneous Prose*, ed. Michael Millgate (Oxford: Clarendon, 2001), 14.

6 Thomas Hardy, *The Return of the Native* (London: Macmillan [New Wessex Ed.], 1974), 54. Hereafter cited parenthetically.

7 See Carl J. Weber, 'Chronology in Hardy's Novels,' *PMLA* 53 (1938): 314–20. For a corrective to Weber's dating, see John Emery, 'Chronology in Hardy's *Return of the Native*,' *PMLA* 54 (1939): 618–20.

8 See Raymond Williams, 'Enclosures, Commons and Communities,' and 'Wessex and the Border,' in Williams, *The Country and the City*, 96–107, 197–214. In 'Wessex and the Border' Williams claims Hardy had experienced a 'local community' (197) as a child and that the slow vanishing of such communities is the main topic of his fiction.

9 See Martin Heidegger, *Sein und Zeit* (Tübingen: Max Niemeyer, 1967), 126–7; and *Being and Time* 164–5.

10 Millgate, *Thomas Hardy's Public Voice*, 39.

11 Timothy O'Sullivan, *Thomas Hardy: An Illustrated Biography* (London: Macmillan, 1975), 85.

12 Heidegger, *Sein und Zeit*, 298; *Being and Time*, 344–5.

10 *The Woodlanders* and the Darwinian Grotesque

GEORGE LEVINE

1

Thinking about *The Woodlanders*, it is hard to shake from the mind certain recurring images, and the pervasive sense that the citizens of Little Hintock (well, most of them) are deeply and significantly involved in nature – green thoughts in a green shade – except that Little Hintock has its nonwoodland strangers, or returned natives, who know, it seems, very little greenness. The unmistakable corporeality of the book's characters does not keep them from seeming as well embodiments of ideas – not in any traditional allegorical sense, but as very much creations of an imagination imbued with the sentiment of reality and a pervasive belief that the corporeal and the ideal are in constant tension, often in opposition, each threatening to slip away from the other, each utterly dependent on the other. The very intensity of material reality virtually forces a kind of idealism on the characters (who imagine each other, often incorrectly) and on the narrator, who dramatizes repeatedly the way meaningless events become, for himself, his readers, and his characters, invested with meaning.

Giles Winterborne, the native, moves through the fourth and fifth chapters, on his gig, holding a tree 'like an ensign,'[1] meant to advertise his work and his wares, 'the twigs nodding with each step of the horse' (33), and so the returning Grace Melbury first sees him, and we remember him. We remember him too climbing and disappearing into the top of the tree that terrifies John South, 'shrouding' the branches away, 'cutting himself off more and more from all intercourse with the sublunary world' (93). Only the noise of his work, as his bill hook lops the branches and they crash to the ground, marks his terrestrial reality.[2] Such images are clearly the stuff of poetry, straining towards a meaning that can be contained or gathered only in image itself. There are narrative meanings as well, of course, but these too tend to be bound up in the images. So it is with Hardyesque irony that Giles indirectly kills John South and thus loses his own home, for Giles, though he is in certain respects one with the woods, understands no better than any of the others that John South's life is entirely inwoven with the life of that frighteningly swaying tree – South too is a part of nature. Nature and its images are as much humanly projected idea and feeling as they are wood and sap and morning dew and the light that emanates from Marty South's open door as she works deep into the night.

The ironies that play through *The Woodlanders* drift from image to image, with a lyrical seriousness that makes the book at times meltingly beautiful, and that justifies the almost tragic conclusion, in which we hear Marty's extraordinary elegy for Giles, and her determination not to forget him as all others do. But of course, these images constitute only one part – if the most powerful and memorable – of that extraordinary book, and while at no point does Hardy lose his virtually instinctive commitment to attend to the minutiae of nature, with resonating significance, the book notoriously slides away quite frequently into social comedy, into sexual play, into farce, into melodrama, into scenes that might be thought invented to parallel the low-life moments of comic relief that mark Shakespeare's comedies. A drunken and bruised Fitzpiers is 'flung' from the mare he rides, unknowingly, with Melbury, having lamented to his angry father-in-law that he would rather be with the superior Mrs Charmond – a moment from eighteenth-century farce (256). The jealous Grace notices that Suke Damson's teeth are excellent and easily infers her husband's casual infidelities; Grace and Mrs Charmond stumble into each other in the woods and warm each other into life as Grace learns that Fitzpiers has 'had' the older woman, whose hair (we remember vividly from the extraordinary opening scene that is both Hardyesque poetry and a bit of 'Rape of the Lock') was really Marty South's. The three women unselfconsciously cluster around the bed of the possibly dying philosophical roué, in a moment that has the ritual and comic shape of restoration comedy, unsentimentally representing a fundamental natural sexual energy.

All of this might seem a long way from the poetry of Giles's and Marty's relations to work and woods. It seems out of harmony with Hardy's almost neurasthenic sensitivity to the life (and death) of the woods as, for example, Marty hears 'the creaking sound of two overcrowded branches in the neighbouring wood, which were rubbing each other into wounds' (16). But there is another famous passage that needs attending to if we are to make sense of the generic chaos of the book, of its shifting from elegiac poetry to bedroom comedy and to the banalities of unhappy marriages. Right at the start, the narrator reminds us, as Giles and Marty talk:

> Hardly anything could be more isolated or more self-contained than the lives of these two walking here in the lonely hour before day, when grey shades, material and mental, are so very grey. And yet, looked at in a certain way, their lonely courses formed no detached design at all, but were part of the pattern in the great web of human doings then weaving in both hemispheres, from the White Sea to Cape Horn. (21–2)

There are echoes here of the romantic and highly moralized organicism that we recognize as central to classic early Victorian thought – Carlyle's *Sartor Resartus*, or yet more familiarly, virtually any high Victorian novel, like *Bleak House* or *Middlemarch*. Everything, the argument goes, is connected to everything else, and there are deep moral consequences to this cosmic fact.

Connectedness, which has been allied traditionally to a kind of moral-determinist reading of experience, in Hardy is always made to feel like sheer chance, most particularly when the book's aesthetic design – the sometimes even mathematical ordering of the narrative – is most clear. For connections are there regardless of the interests and knowledge of the characters in an impersonal and unintentional, quite Darwinian, way; connections are not moral but, in a certain sense, aesthetic: they are the overlaying of the ideal work of human consciousness on the regardlessness and mindlessness of nature. It is the 'artist' who perceives the design in events and movements that must feel and be mere 'Hap' to the people who are seen as part of that design. For the characters, the felt gratuitousness of these inescapable connections intensifies not so much the moral, as the social significance of connections. Hardy's characters, in virtually all of the novels, but certainly in *The Woodlanders*, worry not so much about the moral worth of their actions as about the respectability. Will they be *seen* breaking the canons of community respectability. The answer in Hardy is usually, yes.

Contemporaries, who by and large admired *The Woodlanders* and who certainly were moved by the green interweavings of the premodern citizens with the loveliness (and distortions) of the woods, found something disturbing about the book. As well they might have. From the perspective of previous novelists, R.H. Hutton had it about right:

This is a very powerful book, and as disagreeable as it is powerful. It is a picture of shameless falsehood, levity and infidelity, followed by no true repentance, and yet crowned at the end with perfect success; nor does Mr. Hardy seem to paint his picture in any spirit of indignation that redeems the moral drift of the book.[3]

But it was even more than the moral irresponsibility of the characters (and the author, in not meting out appropriate punishments or manifesting appropriate indignation). Hardy's contemporary critics noted the strange unevenness (as they saw it) of the book, the generic leaps that a modern critic like Penny Boumelha sees as making it 'unsettling to read.' Boumelha begins her chapter on the novel this way: 'It is difficult to say what kind of novel *The Woodlanders* is; it draws on genres so widely disparate as to be at times incompatible.'[4] Early critics register what they take to be the difference in quality between the representation of the woodland characters and that of the unpleasant modern ones, most particularly Fitzpiers and Mrs Charmond, who, as Coventry Patmore wrote, 'give an ill-flavour to the whole book.'[5]

The Woodlanders' strange conjunction of Hardyesque motifs – the splendid and memorable detailed images of the natural world; the material traces (marked so well by Elaine Scarry)[6] of the past that are visible on fence posts and in their materiality register a form of consciousness, or memory; the pains in the aching bones of Mr Melbury; the imposition of the ideal on a universally material world; and finally the extraordinary casual juxtaposition of ostensibly incompatible genres – all of these, I want to argue, make sense if they are seen in the light of the pervasive presence of Darwin in Hardy's imagination.

2

It is hard to write about *The Woodlanders* without invoking Darwin somewhere along the line. Everyone, rightly, does it. As Michael Millgate indicated many years ago, the novel's world is a 'microcosm ... in which the struggle for existence is everywhere the chief condition of existence,' and its story 'transplants exotic growths' and 'takes one promising plant from its natural soil.'[7] Such a view of *The Woodlanders* is by now something of a commonplace; the presence of Darwin in Hardy's work is unmistakable, and Hardy himself was apparently pleased to make that plain. According to Carl Weber, in a letter Hardy included Darwin among those with whom his thought was in 'harmony' – along with Huxley, Spencer, Comte, Hume, Mill.[8] And in preparing the 'biography' whose protective strategies he hoped would allow him to be remembered as he wanted to be remembered, he noted how, on 26 April 1882, he 'attended ... the funeral of Darwin in Westminster Abbey. As a young man he had been among the earliest acclaimers of *The Origin of Species.*'[9]

This self-advertisement has done a great deal of work in the history of Hardy scholarship, critic after critic noting, often without footnote or reference, that, as Carl Weber wrote twice in his well-known study of Hardy, 'the young Hardy was among the first to read and to acclaim Darwin's *Origin of Species.*'[10] While the sentence has had wide acceptance because so much of Hardy's narrative really does echo aspects of Darwin's vision, there is little direct evidence of that first enthusiastic reading, or of where he might have done the 'acclaiming.' Millgate, registering that useful sentence, goes on to say, however, that 'it is possible to document for these years only his reading of such thinkers as Fourier, Comte, Newman, and Mill.'[11] It seems clear from Millgate's study of the available materials that through the 1860s Hardy was not particularly Darwinian, and that his religious convictions eroded through 'a gradual process.' Millgate is particularly and usefully emphatic in pointing out that Hardy's approach to life was 'essentially emotional and non-intellectual' (132). Hardy simply does not write much *about* Darwin. Surprisingly, his published *Personal Writings* contain only one very indirect allusion to him.[12] And it is not unreasonable to argue, as does Martin Seymour-Smith, that Hardy's notion of 'Hap,' of those 'purblind Doomsters' who replace an all-caring God in his sense of the world, predated his reading of Darwin (presumably in 1859 or 1860) and can be linked back to the time of his first reading Aeschylus.[13] But the biography's single sentence has allowed scholars to attribute to Hardy precisely what he wanted: evidence that he was ahead of his time in reading and understanding Darwin.

Thus despite his declared affinity for Darwin, Hardy typically descended from the theory to its working at the level of the individual, and registered with an intensely sympathetic imagination the sad effect of the materialism Darwin espoused. Where Darwin speculated about species, Hardy worried about people – and the way their stories were to be told. Where Darwin contented himself with attributing fundamental human qualities – the moral and the aesthetic – to the material world, Hardy turned the materialism into a kind of idealism. The great Victorian mystery was how material conditions turned into spiritual and intellectual ones.[14] Although Darwin, and Tyndall, and Huxley, and Hardy, too, tended to believe that the world is entirely 'material,' the very intensity of materialism led Hardy to an equally intense focus on the mystery of the ideal, the disparity between the world that consciousness conceived and the crude unthinking material conditions of nature and natural processes. Surely, if inexplicably, the mind did work, the characters in novels imagined conditions (often incorrectly), and the artist constructed meaningful patterns out of observed mindlessness.

The most familiar view of Hardy's relation to this problem is that he read the worst cultural consequences into the new science and Darwinian theory – something, of course, that Darwin himself did not do. Millgate is obviously correct when he argues that Hardy 'found little difficulty in ranging ideas newly derived from Darwin and Huxley alongside the necessitarian views already instilled in him by both the peasant fatalism of his upbringing and the tragic patterns of the Greek dramatists.'[15] But *The Woodlanders* complicates this view because it not only evokes and in certain respects reembodies the tragic patterns of those Greek dramatists; it at the same time refuses tragedy. And the refusal is as much an aspect of Hardy's Darwinism as the affirmation. Certainly, as early as the end of the first chapter of *The Woodlanders*, the narrator makes a move already familiar in the tradition of Victorian realism, suggesting that the quotidian places and details of ordinary life are as latent with epic and tragic significance as the more heroic details of other genres. Mock epic similes in eighteenth-century novels, and morally solemn parallels in the novels of George Eliot anticipate the move. The narrator, creating the details of the place, Little Hintock, notes how 'from time to time, no less than in other places, dramas of grandeur and unity truly Sophoclean are enacted in the real, by virtue of the concentrated passions and closely-knit interdependence of the lives therein' (8). To be sure, certain lines of the narrative move toward Sophoclean moments, but the novel notoriously rejects the Sophoclean for a farcical anticlimax. Although, as we have noted, it famously closes with Marty South's gorgeous and powerfully elegiac celebration of Giles Winterborne, the central narrative ending is the comedy of an at least momentarily henpecked Fitzpiers, with Grace 'queening it' so as to 'freeze yer blood' (365). It is the latter, the more surprising (and for contemporary audiences the more shocking) aspect of the narrative that is truly Darwinian, if distinctly unSophoclean, as well.

Victorians concerned with the arts lamented – as did Darwin himself in his autobiography – Darwin's loss of aesthetic sensibility. Yet the world that Darwin evoked (and the language with which he evoked it) had powerful aesthetic implications. Many years ago, A. Dwight Culler argued that the form of Darwin's argument is, in the long run, more important for our understanding of the relation of his work to the art that followed it than the apparent substance. As he put it, 'to trace the way in which ... writers derive from Darwin their views of nature, man, God, and society does not seem to me quite to get at the heart of the problem.'[16] The clear connection between Hardy's bleak vision of a competitive and indifferent natural world in *The Woodlanders* and Darwin's 'Struggle for Existence,' does not, I would say, in following out Culler's argument, get one far enough.

Certainly the tragic can be taken as implicit in the fundamental arguments of Darwin's discussion of the way nature works, but Culler goes on to assert something quite different: that the essential *form* of Darwin's argument is comic (this formulation itself has something of the Darwinian method, something of the paradox about it). Darwin's fundamental rhetorical strategy is to take the arguments of his predecessors, most particularly of natural theologians like Paley, and invert them, to show, most obviously, that devices that seem only attributable to an intelligent creator are the product of mindless and chancy operations of nature. Culler does not claim that Darwin single-handedly invented this mode of argument; he traces a modern tradition, particularly through Malthus (so influential in triggering Darwin's theory) and Bentham, and even Hume, which methodically inverts dominant assumptions and expectations and produces a vision of the world that, in its constant violation of expectations, is comic in form. The model literary text – in Culler's argument – for this way of imagining the world is Samuel Butler's *Erewhon*. That is, even a satire on Darwinian theory takes a Darwinian form, essentially satirical (as Darwin's arguments might be taken as a satire on Paley's). In respect to England, Culler says, the protagonist of *Erewhon* is 'upside down.'[17]

The Darwinian method is to turn things upside down. Where most taxonomists studied species by focusing on the similarities, Darwin found that the exception, the anomaly, was most telling and important. 'Darwin,' claims Paul Barrett, 'was always looking out for natural phenomena that would be imperfect or pointless from the point of view of an all-knowing Designer.'[18] The Darwinian aesthetic, then, leans towards parody and paradox, repeating the traditional forms and reversing the meaning. Surely Culler is right in thinking that the essential strategy of Darwin's argument is to look intensely at things, but, as it were, look backwards, reversing classic explanations of adaptation like Paley's. Darwin, without deliberate irony, anticipates late Victorian parody, and even the paradoxes of Oscar Wilde.

It is, as Boumelha says, hard to categorize *The Woodlanders*. But formally, the ending is as distinctly comic as anything in high Victorian literature, while Marty South in the book's last two paragraphs speaks a distinctly tragic elegy. This mixture of comic and tragic is distinctly within the range of the Darwinian aesthetic. Culler does not quite attend to other aspects of the Darwinian method (again, not related so much to the substance of Darwin's argument, but to the way the argument is conducted) that clearly had a strong impact on the aesthetic culture that followed. Darwin's world is notoriously a mixed world, one in which categories normally viewed as radically distinct are demonstrated to be intimately connected. Hardy seems temperamentally disposed to see Darwin's questioning of species categorization as demonstrating that categories are fictions – ideal human constructions – rather than fully representative of what really goes on in nature.

Jonathan Smith, in a new book dealing with Darwin's use of illustrations and his relation to visual culture (where, again, Darwin had lamented his loss of feeling), argues that

> Darwinism, with its blurring of boundaries and blending categories, its focus on variation, eccentricity, and irregularity, and its interest in bodies and their functions, especially sexual reproduction, digestion, defecation, and death ... had many of the hallmarks of the grotesque. While Darwin and his allies clearly reveled in nature's grotesqueness, and took delight in their celebration of them, those who regarded nature as complete, ordered, stable, and hierarchical looked upon Darwin's vision with horror.[19]

The comic elements that Culler detected reemerge in Smith's description, but with a difference. It is not only that the Darwinian method leads to inversions and paradox, but that it points to a generically mixed mode, in a world where, indeed, values are turned upside down (since Darwin was to argue for the material basis of both art and morality) and where conventional proprieties about the body, and expectations of unified identity, consistent behaviour and feeling, are constantly disappointed.

Darwin, of course, wanted, almost above all things, to avoid controversy and retain respectability. Smith shows, for example, how, in the illustrations for his books, Darwin remained fairly conservative, stay-

ing close to the conventions of figurative representation that had domi-
nated scientific and even natural theological illustrations in pre-
evolutionary days. But his aim was anything but conservative, and his
problem was to take images, often designed within arguments to confirm evidences of the creator, and turn them into evidence for natural
selection. This required what Smith, borrowing from J.T. Mitchell, calls
imagetexts, illustrations that were completed by verbal commentary,
word and image fully dependent on each other. The imagetexts of
Darwin tend to reverse traditional perceptions so that an illustration
from a book on natural theology might well serve Darwin as perfect
evidence for natural selection. But with all his extraordinary attention
to the details, to the 'facts,' with which he was so persistently and
meticulously engaged, Darwin seems inattentive to the aesthetic vir-
tues of the illustrations he uses.

Of particular interest and I believe of distinct relevance to the way
The Woodlanders works, Darwin's very popular books on earth worms
(and vegetable mould) had, as Smith points out, only minimal illustrations, the primary one being 'a diagram of a worm's alimentary canal.'
Much of the success of the 'worm' book, which ostensibly was not
aimed at arguing for natural selection but at returning to the sorts of
geological work Darwin did at the start of his career, had to do with its
quite human interest. Human, first, in that Darwin's astonishing attention to worms, his sense that they were indeed sensible, living organisms, had the immediate appeal of strangeness and curiosity; but second,
in that the argument of the book leads to an almost romantic vision of
the way in which great things grow from small. The book's last paragraph moves us away from the technical workings inside a scientist's
experimentations to a recognizably picturesque and romantic poem:

When we behold a wide, turf-covered expanse, we should remember that
its smoothness, on which so much of its beauty depends, is mainly due to
all the inequalities having been slowly leveled by worms. It is a marvelous
reflection that the whole of the superficial mould over any such expanse
has passed, and will again pass, every few years through the bodies of
worms. The plough is one of the most ancient and most valuable of man's
inventions but long before he existed the land was in fact regularly
ploughed, and still continues to be thus ploughed by earth-worms. It may
be doubted whether there are many other animals which have played so
important a part in the history of the world, as have these lowly organized
creatures. Some other animals, however, still more lowly organized, namely

corals, have done far more conspicuous work in having constructed innumerable reefs and islands in the great oceans; but these are almost confined to the tropical zones.[20]

There is much to be said about this paragraph as a piece of popular prose. Of course, by his insistence on the large scale and visible effects of the work of these small and unattractive organisms, Darwin is reinforcing his career-long argument for Charles Lyell's uniformitarian and actualist notion of the way geological phenomena, no matter how grand, are the result of causes now in operation. And, of course, this fundamental assumption was a condition of Darwin's theory of evolution by natural selection. In addition, it reasserts the counterintuitive nature of Darwinian thought, the sort of reversal that Culler talks about in another context: grand phenomena are produced by minuscule forces; the ostensible peace of a scene in springtime disguises the determining struggle for survival that sustains it. And a notion that could easily be received as disgusting, the notion that the pleasures of the landscape are the product of what Smith appropriately calls 'worm shit,' edges the passage over into the grotesque and the comic.

The emphasis here, on the beautiful and visible surface of things, is characteristically Darwinian in forcing us to consider the grotesque realities that persistently work to make the world as we see it. Not divine reason, but worms, shape the beautiful landscape. Darwin had claimed, in the famous passage in his autobiography lamenting his loss of feeling for poetry, that he had lost as well his feeling for landscape, a feeling that, early in his life, had helped prompt him to visit the tropics in the first place. Here the landscape is held out temptingly to the nonspecialist audience that was in fact buying the book in unprecedented numbers.

Much of Darwin's work, claims, Smith, 'can be characterized as grotesque.' And he lists, along with the fascination with worm castings and their work, 'the bizarre sexual arrangements of barnacles and orchids; the outré forms of fancy pigeons; the extravagant plumage, ornament, and weaponry of male birds; the hideous facial expression [in illustrations for *The Expression of Emotions*] of Duchenne's galvanized old man; the elaborate traps of insectivorous plants.' Moreover, throughout his career, Darwin's commitment to explode easy and pretty explanations of natural phenomena tended to have an aesthetic component. Early in *The Voyage of the Beagle*, discussing the emergence of life on a recent volcanic island, Darwin concludes: 'I fear it destroys the poetry of the story to find, that these little vile insects [e.g., dung covered wood lice and spiders], should thus take possession before the cocoa-nut tree and other noble plants have appeared.'[21] But whatever his aesthetic intentions, Darwin – Smith conclusively shows – saw the world in a mode almost instinctively 'grotesque,' and, among other things, along with his emphasis on bodily functions, 'blurring ... boundaries and blending ... categories.'[22]

Darwin is, moreover, a master of bathos – the 'art of sinking.' It is as though all of his instincts about the world refused Ruskinian purple passages, denied great climaxes and dramatic changes. His prose refuses to claim attention and applause. Such qualities are evident even in this passage, which echoes strategically the famous ending of *The Origin of Species*, summing up in an attractive and popular and even somewhat romantic way the conclusions of the book as a whole and pointing to a larger than scientific significance. But the conclusion to *The Origin of Species*, with its metaphor of the 'tangled bank,' and its movement towards an ever-changing world is not characteristic of Darwin or his work. Bathos triumphs in the book on worms: in a passage that is rich with ironies and, potentially, with the tragic implications of a vision of the world developed through millennia by the working of earthworms, Darwin does not allow his reader to end with a celebration of earthworms, and he certainly does not offer allusions to traditional invocations of the way the human body is food for worms. Instead, Darwin once again backs off from the poetry of his own paragraph, and even leaves his worms behind, minimizing their work in relation to 'other animals.' These other animals, the corals, are 'still more lowly organized' yet 'have done far more conspicuous work in having constructed innumerable reefs and islands in the great oceans.' On the edge of the sublime, Darwin backs off not once, but twice, and the book ends with an anticlimactic clause, leaving both worms and corals behind: 'but these are almost confined to the tropical zones.' The work here, whatever the potent context of traditional significances, is to reinforce an idea rather than the poetry: the moral of the story is neither moral nor poetic; it is that Lyell's actualism governs the way the world works.

No wonder Ruskin was, as Smith argues, so insistent on Darwin's failure to understand or appreciate art. Darwin's writing resists romantic elevation, points persistently downward, flirts always with bathos. This is not to argue that those who learned from him followed scrupulously his stylistic manners or modes of argument. On the whole, Hardy is not given to bathos, and yet the distinctive conclusion of *The Woodlanders* makes an excellent analogy to the rhetoric of the worm passage, and plays out in a mixed narrative the art of bathos. Certainly, a writer saturated with Darwin's thought and ways of arguing would have recognized a world flirting always with the grotesque, hovering among tragedy, comedy, and bathos, refusing to allow transcendence. What emerged in much late Victorian writing as satire or parody, emerges – in the great reversals that mark most of Hardy's fiction – as something more than 'Life's Little Ironies.' The irony is there, sometimes a satire that tastes of bitterness, but always strategies of reversals – human ideas and aspirations do not match with the movements of material reality. In Hardy's novels, this fundamental Darwinian mode tends rather towards tragedy than comedy; but it is always on the edge of comedy, and in *The Woodlanders* it in fact becomes comedy formally.

3

It is worth, then, looking at *The Woodlanders* from the point of view that Culler announced many years ago, bearing in mind that 'to trace the way in which ... writers derive from Darwin their views of nature, man, God, and society does not ... get at the heart of the problem.' The overt Darwinian motifs are certainly there, and they are invoked when critics quote a passage virtually obligatory in any analysis of the book: 'Here, as everywhere, the Unfulfilled Intention, which makes life what it is, was as obvious as it could be among the depraved crowds of a city slum. The leaf was deformed, the curve was crippled, the taper was interrupted; the lichen ate the vigour of the stalk, and the ivy slowly strangled to death the promising sapling' (52).

This is Hardy's Darwin, clearly announced. But it is important to note the formal twist by which Hardy replicates the tendency of Darwin's prose to leap taxonomic boundaries. It is not so much the overt meaning of struggle, suffering, overcrowding, and consequent distortion, but it is the double and (bitterly) ironic vision. Hardy is not merely looking at the woods but seeing them against an ideal – the very strategy of satire and irony. There are, indeed, the material woods, meticulously, painfully described, but there is too the human dream of their fullest fruition – akin, one might say, to the vision of natural theology. In the ideal woods, each organism comes to full growth without encroaching on its neighbours. 'The Unfulfilled Intention' implies again the Darwinian mode of reversal, irony, and grotesquerie. It suggests a radical juxtaposition of ostensibly incompatible things – woods and city – while it indulges the grotesque emphasis on distorted corporeality about which Smith writes. The pastoral woods become an urban slum and the Wordsworthian romantic ideal slides into the method of late nineteenth century urban realism.[23]

The shocking juxtaposition is just one of many that mark *The Woodlanders'* narrative. The grotesque, as Smith locates it in Darwin, is absolutely central to the method of the novel, which plays itself out in different, one might almost say contradictory, modalities. Its insistence on strange and unpredictable juxtapositions distinguishes it from its more consistently tragic successors. There are, of course, sudden eruptions of generic differences even in *Tess* and *Jude*, the suicide of Old Father Time in *Jude* taking the novel to a level of extravagant melodrama that is so extreme that one might almost need Oscar Wilde to mock it. But in these later novels there is a consistent movement, and the occasionally clashing elements do not push the narrative in new directions. There is, that is to say, a *predictable* chanciness in the narrative flow. The reader knows and is not surprised by the way in which bad fortune follows the protagonists at the moments of their greatest hopes. One knows in *Tess*, for example, that the letter will slip under the rug and Angel will not read it; one knows that if Tess 'confesses' to Angel as he has done to her, she will be doomed; one knows that Angel will return to save her too late and that the police will catch up with them in the end. And in *Jude*, of course, one watches with mathematical but unsurprised horror Jude and Sue's descent into their perfect hells. Moreover, however resistant the novels might seem to dominant assumptions of Victorian morality, each of the books invests its protagonists with moral value (even, and especially, if those values seem to controvert those of respectable middle class Victorian life) and clearly makes tragedy out of their defeats, while at the same time punishing to the letter of the law their various sexual sins and thus escaping the worst of Grundyism.

But in *The Woodlanders*, this Hardyesque pattern of reversing the real, evident already in such a novel as *The Mayor of Casterbridge*, is never completed. There are sad intimations of it, of course, most obviously in the sequence of events leading Giles to his doom – his encounter on the road with Mrs Charmond, the fatal preparations for a party to which he invites the Melburys, the false hopes about a possible divorce, and then his ultimate death. But the major turn in the book's narrative – Grace's escape from the mantrap, and her return to Fitzpiers, following upon the melodramatic offstage murder of Mrs Charmond – is not self-evidently predictable and, interestingly, was precisely the turn that appalled even those readers most favourably disposed to Hardy.

The most morally disturbing element of *The Woodlanders* is not the affirmation of the Darwinian struggle for existence, the revelation that in the beautiful world of the woods there are distorted and suffering organisms. It is, rather, the juxtaposition of supposedly distinct categories; in Darwin, of course, there is the implicit juxtaposition, without moral judgment, of human and animal (spelled out at last in *The Descent of Man*); in *The Woodlanders* there is the juxtaposition of a traditionally virtuous and innocent protagonist (Giles) to a traditionally wicked rake (Fitzpiers) – and with no moral judgment. *The Woodlanders* is a moving and disturbing novel not so much (though of course this matters a great deal) because it makes Darwinian thematics the centre of its narrative meanings, but because it enacts in its method the startling juxtapositions, the comic grotesqueries, and the stunning, detailed, and amoral registration of the particulars of nature.

The novel's first two chapters brilliantly open the world of contradictory genres and disturbing juxtapositions, most forcefully because that world is so precisely described and so imaginatively embodied in the deeply pastoral place, Little Hintock. The opening is a quietly spectacular tour de force of Hardyesque perceptions, locating Little Hintock in the deep isolation of the woods, bringing into it a stranger utterly incapable of finding his bearings without help, suggesting in virtually every line the mysteries of perception and the pervasiveness of human vulnerability in nature. The narrator's focus on perceiving and being perceived registers with a virtually trembling sensibility the way no world is self-contained, every world and every act inside that world is likely to be perceived – and intruded upon – by another. When Percomb enters Marty's cottage while, unawares, she works at cutting spars, she exclaims, 'Oh, Mr. Percomb, how you frightened me!' His quick reply reverberates throughout the novel: 'You should shut your door – then you'd hear folk open it' (11). Every world is vulnerable to intrusion of that sort, and it becomes only a matter of whether one is going to be surprised by it. Here, in the first of the many juxtapositions in the novel of fundamentally opposed genres, the sophisticated comedy of the city rubs against the solemn, romantic pastoral of the woods.

We observe the mysteries of Little Hintock, at first, with the eyes of a 'rambler,' embodied immediately in those of Barber Percomb. Even the juxtaposed names (never literally juxtaposed on the page but implicit in the opening scene) suggest generic muddling. Percomb belongs to the coxcomb world of 'The Rape of the Lock,' that is, to sophisticated urban comedy. Marty South (a girl with a boy's name) belongs to the provinces. Yet their coming together in an act that so clearly if indirectly alludes to Pope's poem, does not jar dramatically: such juxtaposition of urban stranger with country provincial makes the substance of the book itself. At the centre of the book is the figure of Grace, who belongs to both worlds, whose fate is worked out by a struggle between lovers representing the different worlds, and who, from chapter to chapter, can be seen to occupy either of those worlds. She will, as it were, rescue Mrs Charmond from the woods, as only a native could do; she duels with Mrs Charmond over Fitzpiers; she allows herself to fall in love with the socially clumsy and inept Giles.

Like the juxtapositions in the earliest scene, the other generic disturbances in *The Woodlanders* seem, for the most part very 'natural.'[24] John Bayley correctly notes that 'no one ... is troubled at a first reading by the mixture of modes in the novel.'[25] Part of the power of the novel (and then of its ultimately disturbing ramifications) is that the very generic disturbances do, indeed, feel natural. Hardy incorporates the Darwinian grotesque vision into the natural flow of his narrative, which is so richly and precisely filled with the texture of the woodlands that it creates a feeling of authenticity that is not disrupted by the various generic dances the characters living inside that world perform. Michael Irwin has very usefully attended to these kinds of textured 'backgrounds' to the human dramas in Hardy, and argues that they are not, indeed, backgrounds, but utterly central to the narratives' conception. 'Story,' he claims, 'is not to be read in isolation from context.'[26] As Irwin argues, Hardy sees an absolute continuity between the 'natural' world, and the human – just, I would add, as Darwin did. The grotesque and the comic, the blurring of distinction between human and animal is in the book's texture, as Irwin insists. As Darwin eradicated the divide between the human and the animal (and beyond that, between the animal and the vegetable), for Hardy, humans are not – in the cosmic scheme of things, that is – more important than the bugs, horses, and birds that seem constant companions to the humans, whether the humans are always aware of them or not. Human failure to note them is often thick with moral implications. And it need not be an easy moral matter, for those who do not attend are as often the protagonists as the villains. Tess, the 'pure woman,' moves along the grass in gauzy skirts like those of the other dairymaids, as 'the innumerable flies and butterflies' are brushed up by the 'gauzy skirts' of the dairymaids; and 'unable to escape,' the insects 'remained caged in the transparent tissues as in an aviary.'[27] The full drama of Hardy's novels, Irwin claims, is not confined to the fates of the protagonists but is involved in the same natural processes. Nature, in Hardy's novels 'is not background but subject-matter,'[28] and nowhere is this more true than in *The Woodlanders*.

In virtually every way, the novel does indeed perform the kind of comic and grotesque inversions that Culler and Smith identify as characteristic of the Darwinian method. The ultimate form of *The Woodlanders* is comic, both in the sense that it concludes with something that (in other circumstances, at least) would be taken as a happy ending, the reuniting of lovers, and in the sense that it is filled with absurd and grotesque details, some of which are recognizably comic – and funny – although in Hardy, laughter is almost always associated also with sadness and loss. It is not only the usual country bumpkin choral comedy, to which Hardy frequently resorts, but it is associated with virtually every class represented in the book – the aspiring Melbury, indignant on the horse with his drunken son-in-law, the terrified Grammer Oliver, worrying about her brain, the awkward Giles preparing the house for Grace and Mr Melbury's visit, the absurdly philosophical Fitzpiers speculating in bad German philosophy while longing to be back in civilization, the pathetic Mrs Charmond pursued by the gentleman from South Carolina.

The pastoral hero, Giles, is as vulnerable to grotesque comedy as those who work for and with him. The party he gives to impress Grace is of course full of pathos and scenes from stage comedy: the chairs are over-oiled so that Grace's dress is stained (it is 'not a new one' [73] she reassures the mortified Giles); Creedle splashes Grace's face with grease from the dish he brings in on a three-legged pot; Giles was in a 'half-unconscious state' and 'did not know that he was eating mouthfuls of bread and nothing else' (74). Throughout, the other guests talk in a dialect with a vulgarity that Mr Melbury takes as offensive to his newly returned daughter, and as beneath her.

The grotesque comedy, built for the most part on contrasting modes, is perhaps most striking in the representation of Fitzpiers, who in some respects is a parody of the bohemian intellectual. Interestingly, the parody takes us into the heart of Hardy's own deepest concerns, for Fitzpiers, one remembers, enters the novel as a young Lydgatian man (and the contrast with the way George Eliot represents the cosmopolitan doctor in the provinces is striking, for she – while also suggesting the deep flaws in his character – treats his ideas with the greatest of seriousness) speculating on the unbridgeable gulf between mind and body. The episode with Grammer Oliver has its own folk-comic resonances, and of course becomes the occasion for the coming together of Fitzpiers and Grace, but the comic, satiric grotesquerie of the situation emerges most fully when Grammer Oliver tries to explain to Grace what Fitzpiers has said to her: the unlikelihood that Grammer Oliver, realistically speaking, could drop from her own dialect and be able to quote Fitzpiers's pretentious narcissistic philosophy is itself an indication of the post-Darwinian extravagance of the reversals here. But she does quote him as telling her: 'Ah Grammer ... Let me tell you that Everything is Nothing. There's only Me and Not Me in the whole world' (49). All of this watered down German romantic philosophy, coming from the mouth of a lazy and hedonistic child of the aristocracy and addressed to a superstitious old woman whose brain he offers to buy, is clearly a cause for laughter. If Grammer Oliver takes it all seriously, Hardy's sense here of the absurdity of the contrasts and contradictions is primary – it is very distinctly a clash of distinct cultures turned into something like burlesque.

However much we (and presumably the narrator) may want to dismiss Fitzpiers's philosophizing, it is to the point that his ideas are not far from those that might fairly be attributed to Hardy himself and are implicit even in the 'Unfulfilled Intention' passage. Fitzpiers is clearly right about himself, for example, when he puts it abstractly to precisely the wrong person (Giles), that isolated people 'get charged with emotive fluid like a Leyden jar with electric. Human love is a subjective thing ... it is joy accompanied by an idea which we project against any suitable object in the line of our vision ... I am in love with something in my own head and no thing-in-itself outside it' (115). This essentially Feuerbachian understanding of the relation of idea (and ideal) to the material world is fundamental to Hardy's work here and everywhere, culminating in *The Well-Beloved* (it applies, for example, to Mr Knight in *A Pair of Blue Eyes* and Angel Clare in *Tess*, and it is the source there of catastrophes). The absurdity emerges not from the ideas but from the way they are formulated, the context in which they emerge, and the narrative ease with which philosophy here can be read as lazy self-justification. The grotesque comedy emerges from the form more than from the substance of the ideas. Hardy's own scepticism about philosophical thought is enacted by embodiment, by recognizing the context in which the ideas are articulated, and the range of corporeal matters that tincture the ideas. Narrative allows Hardy just that ironic detachment that turns his serious ideas into comedy, and subjects them to the hard force of the material world, whose pervasive secular presence is part of the endowment of post-Darwinian consciousness.

The comedy is extended in Fitzpiers's actual courtship of Grace. When Grace comes to ask him to release Grammer Oliver from her promise, Fitzpiers is quick to seduce her with his ideas. He leads her to his microscope, in which she comes to see some 'cellular tissue' which turns out to be from John South's brain. Grace's shock is the occasion for another bit of philosophy: 'Here am I,' he said, 'endeavouring to carry on simultaneously the study of physiology and transcendental philosophy, the material world and the ideal, so as to discover if possible a point of contact between them; and your finer sense is offended' (133). The enterprise is the same as Lydgate's, who, in his search for the primitive tissue, seeks also to 'pierce the obscurity of those minute processes which prepare human misery and joy.'[29] The coincidence of objectives and situation is so close that it is hard not to think of this as something of a parody of George Eliot, herself; but in any case, it is a parody of ideas that Hardy takes with the greatest of seriousness and that are central to the novel. The post-Darwinian sensibility of the narrator (as well as of Fitzpiers, one can presume) is imbued with a sense that all of life can be traced out into the material world. That is the fundamental 'trope' of Darwinian argument. How then to account for, how to deal with, consciousness, art, love, morality? *The Woodlanders* is thick with the ironies of the incompatibility between consciousness and matter, between the social and the natural.

The body affirms itself everywhere, and as it does (as with the fragment of John South's brain) the grotesque is at work virtually everywhere; human and tree, human and pigeon, human and mere matter are confused. The woods themselves are fundamentally inhuman, not the Wordsworthian pastoral space for contemplation and calm. The contrast between material and ideal is strikingly present in even the smallest of details. The narrator notes, for example, that the 'green shades' of the trees in spring 'disagreed with the complexion of the girls who walked there' (144). Those Marvellian green shades turn out not to be ideal, although the point of view that judges girls' beauty lives in the ideal.

But there are many more extended moments, as, for example, the scene in which, some time after the barking, Grace returns to the site looking for her purse and Fitzpiers, dreamily abstracted from the physical context in which he sits alone by the fire and contemplates settling down in the 'quiet domesticity' of this rural world, surprises her. The awkward movements of incipient lovers begin, interrupted by this detail: 'A diversion was created by the accident of two birds, that had either been roosting above their heads or nesting there, tumbling one over the other into the hot ashes at their feet, apparently engrossed in a desperate quarrel that prevented the use of their wings' (143).

This easy and absurd juxtaposition of bird and human is preceded by an even more exaggerated moment. Beyond the passage about the 'Unfulfilled Intention,' the woods emerge not in pastoral calm but as a place where violence and grotesquerie dominate. Take this fine description of the 'barking season':

> Each tree doomed to the flaying process was first attacked by Upjohn. With a small bill-hook he carefully freed the collar of the tree from twigs and patches of moss which encrusted it to a height of a foot or two above the ground, an operation comparable to the 'little toilette' of the executioner's victim. After this it was barked in its erect position to a point as high as a man could reach. If a fine product of vegetable nature could ever be said to look ridiculous it was the case now, when the oak stood naked-legged, as if ashamed, till the axe-man came and cut a ring round it, and the two Timothys finished the work with the cross-cut saw.
>
> As soon as it had fallen the barkers attacked it like locusts ... (136)

Readers might take this as quaint and delightful, but the metaphorical language is clear that this is a ruthlessly cruel (and Darwinian) activity. This is how the woods people make their living: they flay, they execute, they descend like locusts. And the trees are given a kind of conscious-ness for a moment to extend the violence and the comedy – they are 'ashamed' of their stripped condition (a line, of course, that comments more than indirectly on the anomaly of human consciousness and aspirations to respectability). The passage may be quaint but it is also grotesque – the juxtapositions are extravagant and at the same time comic.

4

But, again, the most striking part of the novel, the part that inspired the most surprise and distaste, is the ending – or the two endings: the coming together of Grace and Fitzpiers again, and Marty's elegy for

Giles. I want to look at these now, in conclusion, as most distinctly, in form and content, post-Darwinian.

Hardy was himself uneasy about the way he ended the book. Writing to various of his friends and acquaintances, he warns: 'It is rather a failure at the end.'[30] As the characters inside the narrative are surprised by Grace's return to Fitzpiers, Hardy's first audience tended to be positively offended. It may be that Hardy believed that the whole narrative, from Giles's death, to the working of the mantrap (yet another bit of melodrama turned to comedy), to Grace's renewed acceptance of Fitzpiers, failed to live up to the idea of the book with which he had begun. He may indeed have been made uneasy by the mixture of modes. Bayley suggests that Hardy's criticism of the book's ending was defensive and disingenuous, and that its refusal (Grace's refusal in particular) of a more straightforwardly daring and potentially tragic ending was the rejection of an ideal inconsistent with the generic mix of the novel.[31] It is characteristic of Hardy as writer and as narrator that he deeply admires the heroic (and inevitably catastrophic)[32] actions of his protagonists, but that he fears such actions and represents figures – like Farfrae, in *The Mayor of Casterbridge* – who survive in sometimes attractive but always compromised ways precisely by being incapable of excess, or heroic aspiration. Grace's nature as she is imagined in the novel, is fully consistent with the novel's generic mixture, and makes the heroic – except in the passive form – an impossibility. Again, it seems to me that Bayley is right in arguing, first, that Hardy's was essentially *not* a heroic nature, and, second, that the ending is the only right one in a novel characterized by such mixed modes. In the long run, however, the refusal of a heroic and daring ending turns out to have been the most daring aspect of the book.

The Darwinian aspect of the book probably should begin with a recognition of what it is that constitutes success in Darwin's nature. The answer is simple: survival and, more important, reproductive success. But there is virtually no reproductive success in *The Woodlanders*. Or rather, it would be better to say, the protagonists have virtually no reproductive success. Although the traditional reading of the book emphasizes its preoccupation with the death of the ancient woodland culture before the thrust of modernity, it is important to note that even Grace and Fitzpiers, and certainly Mrs Charmond, produce no offspring, and it is they who are largely responsible for the decline of woodland culture. The woods, it would seem, continue to propagate, but for a novel so richly engaged in the life of the woods, it offers a peculiarly barren landscape. One notes the curious failure of the garden plots of Little Hintock, plots that 'were planted year after year with that curious mechanical regularity of country people in the face of hopelessness,' but 'no vegetables would grow for the dripping' of the trees (123).

Precisely the sort of behaviour that led Little Hintock gardeners to keep planting in impossible spots, that led Giles to in effect kill himself by disguising from Grace his illness and discomfort and keeping her respectable, and that leads Marty South to her dogged loyalty to Giles, will shortly wipe out the whole woodland culture. Reading the novel from this perspective, one would find that the effect, and the moral force of the endings become exactly the reverse of what they seem directed to be – that is, moral and heroic. The moral value of the Fitzpiers/Grace world is, from this perspective, greater than the moral value of the woodland protagonists. Virtue would seem to be on the side of the dogged and persistent, but survival is on the side of transient visitors to the woodlands. So, on the one hand, Giles sacrifices his life for the woman he loves (but rather for a social ideal that she herself will betray), and Marty's elegy is by far the most moving and powerful moment in the book; on the other hand, Fitzpiers, the adulterer, and Grace, the indecisive, succeed.

It is difficult in any reading of the novel not to feel something other than virtuous heroism in Marty's barren loyalty. The very power of the speech lies in its latent paradox, and there is even something of 'Porphyria's Lover' in Marty's elegy: '"Now, my own love," she whispered, "you are mine, and on'y mine; for she has forgot 'ee at last, although for her you died"' (367). Marty, whose only sexual characteristic is her luxuriant hair, will die barren. Her lyrical invocation of her own and Giles's remarkable power to plant things and to make them grow is both moving and an idealization of Giles, a projection of her frustrated desire on a man who, as he moves through the novel, is often bumbling and mistaken and ideal only at the moment when he sacrifices himself for Grace. Marty's love is for a dead man, for only when he is dead can she possess him.

Against Marty's marvellous absence of plasticity, Grace's capacity to 'change her mind' is played out in a scene out of another sort of romance. There is the comic/melodramatic setting of the mantrap for Fitzpiers (and the introduction of a characteristic Hardyesque chance that draws Grace towards the machine), but most of this is played out offstage. What we see onstage is the reaffirmation of the powerful sexual attraction between Fitzpiers and Grace (the reverse of the totally asexual relation between Giles and Marty and the virtually asexual relation – with one illegitimate kiss – between Giles and Grace). The reconciliation takes place outside of consciousness, choice, or even respectability. When Fitzpiers discovers that Grace has not been caught in the trap, he springs to his feet 'and his next act was no less unpremeditated by him than it was irresistible by her, and would have been so by any woman not of Amazonian strength. He clasped his arms completely round, pressed her to his breast, and kissed her passionately' (356).

Grace and Fitzpiers, unselfconsciously united again, find themselves once more in a green shade. Hardy's instinct for the image that speaks emerges again as the two 'noticed they were in an encircled glade in the densest part of the wood,' at a moment in that 'transient period' of May – 'an exceptionally ... balmy evening' – 'when beech trees have suddenly unfolded large limp young leaves of the softness of butterflies' wings' and the boughs hung low so 'that it was as if they were in a great green vase' (358). The rich sensuousness and fertility of that green moment also suggest something about the sensuous and impermanent relations to come between Fitzpiers and Grace, something about how tightly the relationship is tied to material rather than conventionally romantic or moral conditions.

Although the novel moves to a close with the comic and cynical interpretations of the woodland chorus, it ends with Marty's elegy. That juxtaposition, however, further emphasizes the generic instability of the book. Grace and Fitzpiers do escape the rigidities of Little Hintock and move, with a plasticity about which, surely, Hardy was ambivalent, into a modernity that bears the lines of life after all. The reversals are complete, and Grace's father, deeply disillusioned by Grace's choice, sullenly understates the novel's and the reader's understanding of the reuniting of Grace and Fitzpiers. 'I have been a little misled in this,' he says, as he hastens away from the daughter in whom he had invested the deepest feelings of his life.

Darwin lurks behind all of these elements of the novel. The radical materialism implicit in the Darwinian way of viewing the world, the reversals and boundary blurrings that mark his representation of nature; the emphasis on the corporeal – as in the unequivocal sexual power that pulls Grace and Fitzpiers together, the frustration of intention and consciousness; the disparity between human conceptions and material reality – all of this plays through the novel.

Hardy, like Darwin, preferred not to violate the conventions although he knew, with Darwin, that only violation of those conventions made life possible. The remarriage of Grace and Fitzpiers is a means of survival and plasticity, even if it violates the moral norms. It is the ultimate joke of a novel that refuses the tragedy that the 'Unfulfilled Intention' would seem elsewhere to have demanded. He took the mind-less fusions of Darwinian processes not only to register the grinding competitiveness and tragic fatalism of all forms of life, but to set in motion a narrative that refuses to stand still for genre, that breaks the boundaries between tragic and comic, farce and melodrama, and that repudiates the tragic even as it enacts it.

NOTES

1 Thomas Hardy, *The Woodlanders* (London: Penguin, 1998), 36. Subse-quently cited parenthetically.
2 It is much to the point of the book's tension between material and ideal reality that the narrator makes plain that while up in the tree, if Giles had responded aggressively to Grace's call, slipped down from his detachment from the sublunary world, he might well have won her – and, of course, short-circuited the entire narrative.
3 R.H. Hutton, review from the *Spectator*, in *Thomas Hardy: The Critical Heritage*, ed. R.G. Cox (London: Routledge & Kegan Paul, 1970), 142.
4 Penny Boumelha, *Thomas Hardy and Women: Sexual Ideology and Narrative Form* (Madison: University of Wisconsin Press, 1982), 98.
5 Coventry Patmore, review from the *St. James's Gazette*, in *Critical Heritage*, 148.
6 Elaine Scarry, *The Body in Pain: The Making and Unmaking of the World* (Oxford: Oxford University Press, 1985).
7 Michael Millgate, *Thomas Hardy: His Career as a Novelist* (New York: Random House, 1971), 250.
8 Carl Weber, *Hardy of Wessex* (New York: Columbia University Press 1940), 203.
9 Thomas Hardy, *The Life and Work of Thomas Hardy*, ed. Michael Millgate (London: Macmillan, 1984), 158.
10 This quotation comes from p. 15, but on p. 96, Weber asserts once more, 'He had been one of the first to read and appreciate (*The Origin of Species*) in all its epochal significance.'
11 Michael Millgate, *Thomas Hardy: A Biography* (New York: Random House, 1982), 90.
12 See *Thomas Hardy's Personal Writings*, ed., Harold Orel (London: Macmillan,

1967). The allusion is brief and marginal, appearing in some reminiscences of George Meredith, published in February 1928: '*The Ordeal of Richard Feverel* was finished before Darwin settled the question of the Origin of Species' (151). In a late preface to his lyrical poems, he sardonically comments on the way men's minds appear to be moving backwards, and says that 'belief in the witches of Endor is displacing the Darwinian theory' (57). These comments and the absence of others do not mean, of course, that Hardy wasn't much concerned about Darwin, but rather that he took Darwinian thought as an incontestable fact of life, and did not have to write about it much.

13 Martin Seymour-Smith, *Hardy* (London: Bloomsbury, 1994), 77.
14 John Tyndall famously conceded the impossibility of resolving the mind/body problem. In his essay 'Scientific Materialism,' he argues that 'thought has its correlative in the physics of the brain,' but that the utmost the scientist can say is that there is an 'association of two classes of phenomena, of whose real bond of union he is in absolute ignorance. The problem of the connection of body and soul is as insoluble, in its modern form, as it was in the prescientific ages.' See *Fragments of Science*, vol. 2 (New York: D. Appleton, 1898), 58.
15 Millgate, *Biography*, 132.
16 A. Dwight Culler, 'The Darwinian Revolution and Literary Form,' in *The Art of Victorian Prose*, ed. George Levine and William A. Madden (New York: Oxford University Press, 1968), 225.
17 Ibid., 234.
18 Charles Darwin, *Metaphysics, Materialism, and the Evolution of Mind*, transcribed and annotated by Paul H. Barrett (Chicago: University of Chicago Press, 1974), 66.
19 Jonathan Smith, *Seeing Things: Charles Darwin, John Ruskin, and Victorian Visual Culture* (Cambridge: Cambridge University Press, forthcoming).
20 Charles Darwin, *The Formation of Vegetable Mould through the Action of Worms, with Observations on their Habits* (London: John Murray, 1883), 316.
21 Charles Darwin, *Voyage of the Beagle*, ed. Janet Browne and Michael Neve (London: Penguin, 1989), 49.
22 Smith, *Seeing Things*.
23 Discussing a Hardy poem ('In a Wood') that works out some of the details that were so significant in *The Woodlanders*, Roger Ebbatson notes what would be an appropriate description of the novel: 'The poem rejects what Hardy took to be the Wordsworthian position and states his own Darwinism, with its insistence upon combat as a valid metaphor for life. The poem concludes: "But having entered in, / Great growths and small /

Show them to men akin – /Combatants all! / Sycamore shoulders oak, / Bines the slim sapling yoke, / Ivy-spun halters choke / Elms stout and tall."' See Roger Ebbatson, *The Evolutionary Self: Hardy, Forster, Lawrence* (Brighton: Harvester Press, 1982), 5.

24 One would have to except the forced narrative of the stranger from South Carolina, an element so oddly intruded into the text that it always remains offstage. In one of the very finest essays on the novel, John Bayley points out that 'Hardy himself seems neither to know nor to care that comic, pastoral, pathetic and tragic modes – to name only the most obvious ones – are all collectively at work' (John Bayley, 'A Social Comedy? On re-reading *The Woodlanders*,' reprinted in *Critical Essays on Thomas Hardy: The Novels*, ed. Dale Kramer [Boston: G.K. Hall, 1990], 191).

25 Ibid.

26 Michael Irwin, *Reading Hardy's Landscapes* (New York: St Martin's Press, 2000), 6.

27 Thomas Hardy, *Tess of the d'Urbervilles* (London: Penguin, 1983), 146.

28 Irwin, *Reading Hardy's Landscapes*, 20. Irwin's comments on the formal work of the details is to the point of my overall argument: 'What in the work of many a "traditional" novelist is merely enabling matter, casual amplification, or "corroborative detail," can be central to his purpose ... the incorporated poetry modifies the meaning of the story he tells. To read the novels in their fullness we must read even the detail attentively: the small things become the big things' (24).

29 George Eliot, *Middlemarch: A Study of Provincial Life* (Oxford: Oxford University Press, 1996), 162.

30 Thomas Hardy, *Thomas Hardy: Selected Letters*, ed. Michael Millgate (Oxford: Clarendon, 1990), 54.

31 Bayley, 'A Social Comedy?' 193–4.

32 See George Levine, *The Realistic Imagination: English Fiction from Franken-stein to Lady Chatterley* (Chicago: University of Chicago Press, 1981) for a discussion of Hardy's relation to the heroic ideal.

11 Plato and the Love Goddess: Paganism in Two Versions of *The Well-Beloved*

JEREMY V. STEELE

'I am not of those vicious Amorists, but of your chaste Platonicks.'
> Cervantes, *Don Quixote* (trans. Thomas Shelton)

1997, the centenary of the publication of Hardy's 'last' novel, *The Well-Beloved*, saw the appearance of a new edition, prepared for Penguin Classics by Patricia Ingham. It was notable because it was the first to couple the accustomed book version of the story with its serial predecessor, *The Pursuit of the Well-Beloved*, which had been issued in weekly instalments in the *Illustrated London News* over the last three months of 1892. Although it has been possible to compare the two versions at any time since 1897, for most of us that has entailed access to a major library. So it is a large and instructive convenience to have both texts available between the same covers – not least because the protracted interval between them is unique in the history of Hardy's novel writing.

The serial had been promised to Tillotson's in February 1890, five months after the cancellation of Hardy's contract with them for another serial more than twice as long, which would finally emerge elsewhere as *Tess of the d'Urbervilles*. Hardy appreciated the generous spirit in which the cancellation had been effected and seems to have felt some obligation to make up for the miscarriage. However, largely because of work on *Tess*, he put off writing the agreed 60,000-word replacement until the winter of 1891–2, about eighteen months later.[1] His ambitions for this debt of honour were, he claimed, limited: early in 1892 he told Harper and Brothers, who held the American serial rights and were interested in a book version, that the story was 'short and slight and written entirely with a view to serial publication'; a book edition might be 'inadvisable in the interest of future novels' and he reserved his right to withhold one indefinitely.[2] Four years later, however, his reputation as a novelist no longer mattered to his livelihood as it had: with the commercial success of *Tess, Jude the Obscure*, and the first collected edition of his fiction, he could at last afford to devote himself to his preferred medium, verse. This more relaxed attitude – and perhaps the promise of further sales for relatively little effort – encouraged him to return to the neglected serial towards the end of 1896, and the revised book version was published the following March as *The Well-Beloved: A Sketch of a Temperament*, in series with Osgood McIlvaine's collected edition.

The book had a gentler reception than *Tess* or *Jude*, as Hardy expected. Nevertheless he was upset by a venomous review printed in the *World* (24 March), and besides expressing his anger and dismay to some of his friends, he defended himself publicly in the *Academy* (3 April). In his preface to the book he had suggested that the main character might be seen as a realization, albeit imperfect, of 'a delicate dream which in a vaguer form is more or less common to all men, and is by no means new to Platonic philosophers.'[3] Now, countering the *World's* charge of 'sex-mania,' he stated that he had returned to a sketch made many years before the serial, when he was 'a comparatively young man, and interested in the Platonic Idea, which, considering its charm and its poetry, one could well wish to be interested in always.'[4] Of course the word 'Platonic' carries in itself a denial of carnality, but there is more at issue here: for instance, how long ago had the sketch been made? Although Hardy's phrasing is imprecise, the invocation of Plato points towards the happiest years of his first marriage, spent at Sturminster Newton. There, in the early summer of 1876, he had made nineteen brief notes on two of Plato's shorter dialogues, the *Charmides* and *Lysis*,[5] and an allusion to the former was soon absorbed into *The Return of the Native*.[6]

These notes were taken from the beginning of the first volume of Benjamin Jowett's translation of Plato, published in 1871. Although there is no record of a copy from Hardy's library – or of any other text or translation of Plato[7] – that does not necessarily mean the one he used in 1876 was borrowed. Indeed, his 1889 reading of the *Cratylus*, placed last in the same volume, suggests that it was his own. A free-wheeling discussion about the nature and origins of language, the *Cratylus* prompted this note, dated 6 February: 'A very good way of looking at things would be to regard everything as having an actual or false name, and an intrinsic or true name, to ascertain which all endeavour should be made. ... The fact is that nearly all things are falsely, or rather inadequately, named.'[8] The idea was a linguistic version of Hardy's concern (variously noted about this time) to reach past the appearance of things or experiences to their essence. In turn, this shaded into another preoccupation, noted two years earlier, on 13 February 1887: 'I was thinking a night or two ago that people are somnambulists – that the material is not the real – only the visible, the real being invisible optically. That it is because we are in a somnambulistic hallucination that we think the real to be what we see as real' (*LW*, 192). Whether aware of it or not, Hardy was here moving close to Plato's theory of ideal forms, existing beyond known dimensions. Was that what he had in mind when he invoked 'the Platonic Idea'? Well, only in part it seems; Plato, of course, had more than one idea.

Among the fourteen dialogues translated in Jowett's first volume were the *Ion, Symposium,* and *Phaedrus.* Early in 1876 Hardy had noted that the final dictum of the *Ion* was 'inspiration, not art,' but his source was J.A. Symonds, writing about Aeschylus in the January issue of the *Cornhill.*[9] However, his surviving notebooks do not define the extent of his reading (offering instead almost accidental confirmation), and he may well have read Jowett's version of the *Ion* later in the year. It is an unusually short dialogue which explores topics that would have engaged him: Ion is a self-important performer of Homer whom Socrates questions about the nature of poetry and the creative imagination. It is equally likely that he was drawn to look at the *Symposium* and *Phaedrus,* for in Jowett's words, 'together [they] contain the whole philosophy of Plato on the nature of love.'[10]

The *Symposium* dramatizes a private party at which the guests – all male in classical Athens – agree to take turns in praising Eros, the god of love. The result is a spread of views, often irreconcilable. The third speaker, Pausanias, postulates two kinds of love, heavenly and common, on the ground that they are the offspring of two different Aphrodites, whom he distinguishes thus: 'The elder one, having no mother, who is called the heavenly Aphrodite – she is the daughter of Uranus; the younger, who is the daughter of Zeus and Dione, whom we call common.' Common love 'has no discrimination, being such as the meaner sort of men feel, and is apt to be of women as well as of youths, and is of the body rather than of the soul.'[11] By contrast, heavenly love is noble; it is the feeling of a man for a youth with his first beard, whom he will guide in the pursuit of virtue. Plato's assumption that love relationships between males were the only ones worth taking seriously (entailing frank and easy discussion of 'nameless crimes') was a distinct embarrassment to the High Victorian mind, and Jowett's commentaries show him wriggling on the point of this moral disjunction. His later solution was to assume that a contemporary Plato would have seen the error of his ways, and so what he said could be applied to heterosexual relationships. Hardy did the same, and in *Jude* Sue Bridehead invokes Venus Urania as the patron of 'strong attachment where desire plays, at least, only a secondary part.'[12]

When Aristophanes (whose comedy *Clouds* had lampooned Socrates) takes his turn, he offers his fellow guests a fantastic tale – at once ingenious, funny, and spiced with sharp observation. Originally, he says, humans were round and double (like Siamese twins), with four hands, four feet, two faces, and so on. And there were three sexes – male, female, and an androgynous combination – which turns out to be the reason for current differences in human sexual preference. However, these prototypical humans became obstreperous and threatened Olympus, and so Zeus split each pair down the middle like apples, telling Apollo to patch them up. Afterwards they wandered about looking for the twins from whom they had been sundered, and that is why people now feel incomplete unless reunited with their 'other half.' This notion is reflected in *Jude* when Phillotson is telling his friend Gillingham about Sue and Jude: he says that he has been struck by '"the extraordinary sympathy, or similarity, between the pair. (He is her cousin, which perhaps accounts for some of it. They seem to be one person split in two!)"' (*JO*, 229). The narrative voice echoes Phillotson's impression in describing the couple at the Great Wessex Agricultural Show: 'That complete mutual understanding ... made them almost the two parts of a single whole' (*JO*, 292).

Plato made another attempt to distinguish different qualities of love in the *Phaedrus*, where Socrates spins an extended parable combining ideas about the Olympian gods, the transmigration and purgation of souls, and the timeless existence of absolutes in a remote upper realm. The key image is of the soul as a charioteer drawn by a pair of winged horses – one noble and aspiring, the other ignoble and dragging the chariot down. Souls have one mortal life every thousand years and are then judged. The love of a beautiful soul, which is allied to philosophy, is a passport to redemption, and it is kindled when human beauty recalls to a virtuous soul the visions of absolute beauty experienced before birth. Yet love also releases conflicting impulses, embodied in the opposed qualities of the horses: the white one is 'erect and well-formed ... guided by word and admonition only,' while his dark fellow is 'put together anyhow ... hardly yielding to blow or spur.'[13] The wanton one must be quelled and controlled, and ideally the lovers will achieve a union of souls. Those who also yield to physical desire are not dishonoured, but their love is less fine.

The supreme value accorded to love that transcends the physical is even more apparent when Socrates finally speaks in the *Symposium*. He recalls a series of conversations he once had with Diotima, a wise woman with mysterious powers, who showed him that love is necessarily love of the beautiful (an aspect of the good), while creativity is the desire to use beauty to produce offspring and so bypass mortality. For most people this is limited to sexual reproduction, but a few, such as poets, artists, and statesmen, have souls that produce much more distinctive and lasting issue. The elusive goal Diotima proposed was an almost mystical contemplation of absolute beauty, which is reached by a long ascent – from one fair form to two, 'and from two to all fair forms, and from fair forms to fair actions, and from fair actions to fair notions, until from fair notions [one] arrives at the notion of absolute beauty, and at last knows what the essence of beauty is.'[14]

More than twenty years after *The Well-Beloved* was published, Hardy prepared an account of it for *Life and Work*, claiming that 'The theory on which this fantastic tale of a subjective idea was constructed is explained in the Preface to the novel, and again exemplified in a poem bearing the same name, written about this time.' The theory was 'the transmigration of the ideal beloved one, who only exists in the lover, from material woman to material woman' (*LW*, 303). One may search the preface in vain for corroboration; moreover, if this was what lay behind his references to Platonism in 1897, it was a parody of Plato's ideas. The moral dimensions of love and beauty have been silently removed, leaving an image of the beloved with no warrant beyond the lover's consciousness. Transmigration has become a metaphor for the erratic track of one person's desires. However, Hardy's working copy of the *Life and Work* typescript preserves a more open-ended reading, somewhat closer to Plato: 'the theory that the real is not the ideal beloved one, who only exists in the lover' (*LW*, 538). This is the shaping idea of his spectral poem 'The Well-Beloved,' and also connects with his notes about the essence beyond appearances mentioned earlier.

In this confusion of mixed messages, it is useful to recall the terms in which Hardy had characterized his Platonic Idea in 1897: a delicate dream, youth, charm, and poetry. They strongly suggest that he was also thinking of Shelley (a devoted student of Plato, who had translated the *Symposium*), and in particular of 'Epipsychidion,' a poem celebrating Shelley's discovery of the twin soul he had encountered in youthful dreams and imaginings (arguably an equivalent of the Platonic memory of an existence before birth). His long quest for her has been painful and frustrating (and his mistakes along the way may have contributed to Hardy's version of transmigration in *Life and Work*). Now he invites her to escape with him to an idyllic union on a remote Aegean island, somehow preserved from the golden age (an equivalent of Plato's heaven). Shelley, still under thirty, transfused ideas from the *Phaedrus* and *Symposium* with an urgency of feeling which the middle-aged Hardy could scarcely emulate; characteristically his 1897 *Academy* apologia placed his earlier interest in Plato at a hazy distance, coloured by wistful regret for its passing. The Well-Beloved story may have been germinating in his mind for many years, but neither published version is the work of a young man, as he himself acknowleged.[15]

He had come nearer Plato (and Shelley) when in March 1897 he wrote to Lewis Hind, the *Academy* editor, declining an invitation to reply to the *World* review: 'I can defy any sane person to see immorality or impropriety in an applied Platonic Idea – a phantasmal narrative of the adventures of a Visionary Artist in pursuit of the unattainable Perfect in female form – a man repeatedly stated to be singularly free from animalism.'[16] The novel poises this 'unattainable Perfect' between aesthetic beauty and the union of twin souls, the alternatives being realized in a sculptor's attempts to capture the ideal feminine in his work and in his life. The choice of a sculptor as protagonist was perhaps intended to tilt the balance towards aesthetic beauty, but Jocelyn Pearston's artistic career never acquires enough textual prominence to challenge his emotional gyrations, and it is symptomatic of the imbalance that the serial version introduces him at the age of twenty, not in his London workshop, but vainly trying to burn packets of love letters in his rooms.

These redundant letters, the relics of Pearston's precocious dalliance with nine girls, are then taken to his family home on the isle of Portland, where he makes a bonfire of them in his father's garden. Their destruction is interrupted by Avice Caro, his childhood companion, who has become a young woman in his absence. Her dismay on recognizing the letters for what they are prompts him to an impetuous proposal of marriage, to which she replies:

> 'Ah! – I am only one of many!'
> 'You are not, dear. You knew me when I was young, and they didn't – at least, not many of them. Still, what does it matter? We must gain experience.'[17]

In the book (where Pearston is respelt Pierston) the letters are entirely suppressed – though their absence rather undermines the ground for the sudden proposal. Avice's objection becomes her mother's and the cavalier attitude to women implicit in Jocelyn's earlier reply almost disappears:

'Ah! – mother says I am only one of many!'
'You are not, dear. You knew me when I was young, and others didn't.'
(183)

Such changes, ranging in effect from a phrase to the deletion of the whole of the serial's first chapter, are typical of Hardy's effort in revision to deflate Jocelyn's sexual curiosity. Besides, the love letters came too close to suggesting heartlessness – an aspect of his behaviour which, though diminished in the book, never entirely disappears.

Jocelyn's misgivings following his proposal are grounded in what he knows of his 'Well-Beloved,' whom he has so far followed faithfully through her numerous migrations from one body to another. She is like the sea-god Proteus in her ability to change shape at will, but attempts to capture her essence – 'a spirit, a dream, a frenzy, a conception, an aroma, an epitomized sex, a light of the eye, a parting of the lips' (17, 184) – tend to cancel each other out. 'She was indescribable,' the serial concludes, 'unless by saying she was a mood of himself.' In the book, however, Jocelyn is said to never much consider 'that she was a subjective phenomenon vivified by the weird influences of his descent and birthplace' – the influences, that is, of a community isolated on a virtual island, enfolding countless generations of intermarriage. The book also introduces a note of menace, the first of an important series: 'Sometimes at night he dreamt that she was "the wile-weaving Daughter of high Zeus" in person, bent on tormenting him for his sins against her beauty in his art – the implacable Aphrodite herself indeed' (184–5). The recurrent dream crystalizes Jocelyn's continuing doubts of his ability as a sculptor, while the Well-Beloved as goddess promises to be not only beyond his reach or control, but capricious and vengeful too.

The source of the inserted quotation was Sappho's 'Hymn to Aphrodite' (really an urgent appeal for her help) in a version by J.A. Symonds which Hardy had read in Wharton's 1895 edition of Sappho.[18] He had bought himself a copy that year, and writing to Florence Henniker on 4 August, he told her it was 'a delightful book. How I love her – how many men have loved her! – more than they have Christ I fear.'[19] That love blossomed from fragments more or less tantalizing; the 'Hymn to

Aphrodite' was the only complete poem Wharton could print. A fervid admirer like Swinburne (or, with less rapture, Hardy) was thus free to fill out the fragments and the scant certainties about Sappho's life with his own imagination.

One of Hardy's aims in revision was to amplify the peculiar qualities of Jocelyn's birthplace and to particularize its pagan past. So on the first page of the book it is named as 'the ancient Vindilia Island, and the Home of the Slingers,' and a few pages later the main thoroughfare becomes 'the long straight Roman street' (185). Hope Churchyard, long ago cast into a ravine by a landslip, is now given an overtly symbolic role: 'It seemed to say that in this last local stronghold of the Pagan divinities, where Pagan customs lingered yet, Christianity had established itself precariously at best' (186). In the book this 'solemn spot' is where Jocelyn first kisses Avice; in the serial he chooses it to sound her feeling about the most pertinent of these pagan survivals – the island custom of marrying only when the proposed union has been proved fertile. Hardy would have found the practice generously detailed in one of his favourite sources, John Hutchins's *History of Dorset*,[20] but he could not afford to be nearly so explicit about premarital intercourse. Nevertheless the serial contrives to show that Jocelyn is by no means averse to putting his and Avice's fertility to the test, although he leaves the choice to her. His covert desire was written out of the book, however, because Hardy was revising in sometimes contradictory directions. On the one hand, he wanted to downplay the sexual element in Jocelyn's pursuit of women; on the other, he wanted to suggest an environment that would help excuse a life conducted well outside the conventions of Christian marriage and fidelity. The pagan emphasis added to the book is in part a substitute for the more candid treatment of Jocelyn's sexuality in the serial.

Walking from the island to the railway at Budmouth, Jocelyn falls in with Marcia, another native islander of a very different stamp. Her profile is the most classical he has ever seen – 'dignified, arresting, that of a very Juno' – and consonantly her face emerges from the darkness as 'handsome, commanding, imperious ... quite of a piece with the proud tones of her voice' (22, 190).[21] The challenge presented by this latter-day Olympian queen, reinforced by a storm which presses her body to his, stimulates Jocelyn to thinking that she may be a true embodiment of his Well-Beloved (he has remained doubtful about Avice). By the time he is drying Marcia's clothes at a small temperance inn, he is convinced and adores her. This episode is elaborated in the serial, where the lace and embroidery on her underclothes are lovingly described, the fabrics seem 'almost part and parcel of her queenly person' (28) and Jocelyn kisses each garment. But such erotic suggestiveness had no place in the book and it was cut.

Next morning the pair travel together to London, where Jocelyn makes another sudden proposal of marriage. Going out alone to get a licence, he turns aside to visit his friend Somers, to whom he relates the history of his obsession with the Well-Beloved. His account is substantially the same in both versions, but the book incorporates two insertions that pick up earlier ones. By way of preface Jocelyn explains awkwardly: '"I am under a curious curse, or influence. I am posed, puzzled and perplexed by the legerdemain of a creature – a deity rather; by Aphrodite, as a poet would put it, as I should put it myself in marble ..."' (199). And shortly he mentions his birthplace as a factor: '"We are a strange, visionary race down where I come from, and perhaps that accounts for it"' (200). When he has finished, Somers tells him he shouldn't marry anyone, even Avice: '"You are like other men, only rather worse. Essentially, all men are fickle, like you; but not with such perceptiveness"' (203). Thus the book; the serial had ended more critically: '"but not with such activity, such open-eyed perceptiveness"' (35). The deletions are symptomatic of the revision's tendency to deprive Pierston of volition and agency and present him rather as the victim of an external power.

At this point the two texts diverge. In the serial the couple marry and live together for four years before separating; in the book they remain unmarried and part within a week or so. The marriage became undesirable not only because it implied a sustained sexual intimacy, but because the serial had here rehearsed in crude form Hardy's criticisms of conventional marriage that were to become well known, even notorious, with the publication of *Jude* in 1895. Yet Marcia's unusual endowment of Juno-like qualities seems excessive for a brief affair; it looks more like preparation for the erosion of a marriage. So in the serial, when the couple quarrel about the business rivalry of their fathers, Jocelyn can pause to gaze

> at the fine picture of scorn that his Juno-wife's face and dark eyes presented.
> 'I ought to have known it,' he murmured.
> 'What?'
> 'That such a face as that meant temper.' (38)

In the book (207) the allusion is necessarily weaker ('his Juno's classical face') and the ensuing dialogue has disappeared.

In the years following his parting from Marcia, Jocelyn enjoys unexpected success as a sculptor in London. He devotes himself to the female form in various guises, mostly classically inspired, and the summary narrative links his quest for perfection in carving or modelling with his pursuit of living examples of feminine beauty. The weakness of the link is that his work as a sculptor scarcely emerges from the plane of background reference. Unlike the stone quarrying trade on the island, with its distinctive sounds of hammer and saw, it achieves no life or energy of its own. Jocelyn is never shown at work in his studio; sculpture is simply what he 'does.' The most animated of the few occasions when a piece of his earns a place in the narrative is confined to the serial, where the married couple's final argument ends with Marcia throwing a statuette at his head. It smashes against a wall, and infuriated by the loss of 'his darling little work,' he shakes her and goes off to his club (41).

The Well-Beloved duly reappears in Jocelyn's life, and over a decade or so he worships from a distance a disparate variety of her manifestations. About the time of his fortieth birthday his father dies, leaving him a handsome sum, and the detailed narrative resumes with his arrival at a fashionable party (an occasion for Hardy's heaviest satire). Surveying the ladies present for a promising quarry, he singles out a young widow, Nichola Pine-Avon, and leaves the gathering with an impression that the Beloved has reemerged in her. Here the book first registers a division in his understanding of the Beloved that confirms the menace of his earlier dreams of 'the implacable Aphrodite': he now sees her as a puppet manipulated by 'the Goddess' (a change of reference marking the potential – soon exploited – for expanding her identity). The split might be compared with Plato's two-stage version of 'reality,' but it is much closer to mainstream Greek ideas about the Olympians' unpredictable exercise of their supernatural power. The inserted paragraph continues: 'He had lately been trying his artist hand again on the Dea's form in every conceivable phase and mood. He had become a one-part man – a presenter of her only. But his efforts had resulted in failures. In her implacable vanity she might be punishing him anew for presenting her so deplorably' (224). His obsessive concentration on the love goddess in his work, rewarded by recurrent failure, points to a self-defeating circularity in his art that will be repeated in his life.

Within a fortnight, at a dinner party where Nichola is a fellow guest, Jocelyn covertly reads a letter telling him of Avice's death. He has long known of her marriage to a cousin (though the narrative has passed over any explanation or apology for his own desertion of her), and he has seldom thought of her during the intervening years. Yet by the end of the evening his memories of their youthful friendship have 'flamed up into a yearning and passionate attachment, embittered by regret beyond words.' There is a new purity in his emotion: 'The flesh was absent altogether; it was love rarefied and refined to its highest attar. He had felt nothing like it before' (58, 231). Poor Nichola is extinguished; now that the unattainable Avice lives only in his memory, he can idealize without fear of any external check. If this is Platonic love, it is certainly of an eccentric sort.

Looking out from his bedroom window the following night, Jocelyn finds that 'the young pale moon' is positioned above the island and Avice's corpse: 'The symbol signified well. The divinity of the silver bow was not more excellently pure than she, the lost, had been' (59, 231). The divinity is Artemis/Diana, the virgin huntress, who became associated with the moon, while the phrase 'more excellently pure' plays on 'Goddess excellently bright,' the refrain of Ben Jonson's 'Hymn to Diana.' The image of purity is common to both versions, but in the book Jocelyn's visions of 'the island of Ancient Slingers' lead him to fresh insights. Avice's family and his have been 'islanders for centuries – from Norman, Anglian, Roman, Balearic-British times. Hence in her nature, as in his, was some mysterious ingredient sucked from the isle; otherwise a racial instinct necessary to the absolute unison of a pair' (232). So, even if he may feel inhibited by an islander's lack of refinement, he believes he cannot love any non-islander for long (nor of course has he). The 'absolute unison of a pair' returns us with a musical twist to Aristophanes' fable in the *Symposium*; it also suggests that the pressure of loneliness is beginning to alter the balance of Pierston's ideal.

A second inserted paragraph explores the island's past and genetic heritage. Jocelyn fancies that Avice's family, the Caros, whose features remind him of Italian peasants, share the blood of the Romans and their predecessors, the Slingers. He knows of

> evidences that the Roman colonists had been populous and long-abiding in and near this corner of Britain. Tradition urged that a temple to Venus once stood at the top of the Roman road leading up into the isle; and possibly one to the love-goddess of the Slingers antedated this. What so natural as that the true star of his soul would be found nowhere but in one of the old island breed? (232)

Such a temple reappears as erotic symbol in Hardy's contemporaneous poem 'The Well-Beloved,' which inhabits the same malign fairy world as Keats's 'La Belle Dame sans Merci.' Hardy's speaker, walking overnight to his wedding, thinks that the sprite who appears by his side has come from the site of a pagan temple. She tells him that she is his only love, the dream he has projected onto his betrothed (whom he will find wasted at his journey's end). It is not until the penultimate stanza, when the sprite vanishes, that the temple's dedication to Venus is revealed.[22]

Whether or not the sudden accretion of pagan references is felt as an ill omen, it signals a change in the story's direction. Jocelyn decides to leave London for the island the following morning, characteristically preferring the dead Avice over his expected attendance at the opening of the annual Academy exhibition. He arrives in time to watch her funeral from a distance and visits her grave at nightfall. (This marks the end of Part First in the serial; in the book the break comes three chapters earlier, with the death of Pierston senior.) Drowsing near the grave, he seems to see Avice herself bending over it, but soon discovers he has been deluded by the close resemblance between her and a previously unmentioned daughter. He loses no time in calling on Avice II, and though she is 'more matter-of-fact, unreflecting, less cultivated than her mother' (67, 237), he is immediately attracted to her. He is also uncomfortably aware that while she is about the same age as her mother had been during their courtship, he is now twice as old.

Jocelyn's return to the island marks a crucial turn in his life and in the novel's focus: no longer will he expect scattered epiphanies of his Beloved, but will devote himself to Avice II and, twenty years later, to her daughter, Avice III. The change of focus can be directly linked to a note which Hardy placed in *Life and Work* immediately after the one prompted by Plato's *Cratylus*: 'Feb. 19. The story of a face which goes through three generations or more, would make a fine novel or poem of the passage of Time. The differences in personality to be ignored' (*LW*, 226). As he recognized in a bracketed addition, he had 'to some extent' carried out this idea in *The Well-Beloved* and his poem, 'Heredity.' Only 'to some extent,' however, because nothing in the novel before the emergence of Avice II foreshadows the generational theme sketched in the note, nor are differences in personality between the three Avices ignored.

Back in London, Jocelyn cannot escape the change in himself: 'He thought of nothing but the isle, and Avice the Second dwelling therein.' Thus the serial (68), but the book continues the sentence: '– inhaling its salt breath, stroked by its singing rains and by the haunted atmosphere of Roman Venus about and around the site of her perished temple there' (238). Evocative in itself, the added imagery testifies to Jocelyn's gift for erotic fantasy – especially 'stroked by its singing rains.' His aroused imagination draws him regularly to the wharves where the island's stone is unloaded, and a chance encounter there with Avice II (who has sailed up for the trip) intensifies his feeling for her and his qualms about its incongruity. As the serial has it: 'He began to have misgivings as to some queer trick that his migratory Well-Beloved was about to play him' (70). Again the book extends – 'or rather the capricious Divinity behind that ideal lady' (240). The addition reflects Jocelyn's revised aetiology of the Beloved, but it also throws an accidental emphasis on his distance from any form of Platonism. Given this, it is no surprise that he finds it 'recklessly pleasant' to ignore his apprehensions and 'follow the lead' (70, 241) by taking a summer lease on the island's largest house to begin his pursuit.

Once installed there, he is confronted by differences. While his infatuation grows, Avice remains impervious to his presence. She is confusingly like her mother in appearance, but inferior in culture and understanding. Socially he stands far above her. She is about nineteen and he is forty – though his emotions are as turbulent as when he was twenty. He has good reason to feel apprehensive: 'A sudden Sapphic terror of love would ever and anon come upon the sculptor ... It threw him into a sweat. What if now, at last, he were doomed to do penance for his past emotional wanderings (in a material sense), by being chained in fatal fidelity to an object that his intellect despised?' (75, 246). Here the serial continues with the note of divine menace sounded much earlier in the book: 'Sometimes he thought he saw dimly visioned in that young face "the white, implacable Aphrodite."' The quotation was drawn from Swinburne's 'Sapphics' (l. 9), included in the scandalous *Poems and Ballads* of 1866, which probably introduced Hardy to Sappho.[23] But of course by the time he came to revise the serial text he was familiar with Wharton's edition, and that is duly reflected in his substitutions: 'One night he dreamt that he saw dimly masking behind that young countenance "the Weaver of Wiles" herself, "with all her subtle face laughing aloud."' The first quotation is common to Wharton's prose version of the 'Hymn to Aphrodite' and a verse rendering by M.J. Walhouse (where Hardy underlined it); the second is Swinburne's paraphrase of a line from the 'Hymn' which he worked into 'Anactoria' (l. 72; conveniently reprinted by Wharton). Jocelyn still believes he has kept faith with his 'Protean dream-creature' (72, 242) – he has only wandered 'in a material sense' – but now he fears suffering precisely on that account. The love goddess is a figure onto whom he can project the anxieties dominant at any particular time – in this instance, a humiliating loss of his emotional freedom. In the revised text the irony of his position finds expression in the goddess's delight over the entrapment she has devised.

Nevertheless Jocelyn is soon so overwhelmed by his feeling for Avice, or rather his idea of her, that only marriage will satisfy him. Her advent has led him to focus on the Caro family as the most promising source for an island partner, even though it may never produce 'an individual nature which would exactly, ideally, supplement his own imperfect one and round with it the perfect whole' (251). Like his previous idea that an islander must pair with another islander for the chance of 'absolute unison,' this addition in the book derives from the *Symposium*, but its phrasing reflects some of the detail of Aristophanes' fable much more closely. It also marks a further tilt away from Jocelyn's unfettered pursuit of 'beauty' – notwithstanding his connoisseur's eye for Avice's contours.

One evening when he hopes to intercept her, the serial has him walking up and down 'till his legs ached' (82). The book amplifies his anxiety by loosing his imagination on the island's pagan heritage: 'He walked the wild summit till his legs ached, and his heart ached – till he seemed to hear on the upper wind the stones of the slingers whizzing past, and the voices of the invaders [Romans] who annihilated them, and married their wives and daughters, and produced Avice as the ultimate flower of the combined stocks' (252). That he has surveyed the deficiencies of this 'ultimate flower' only a page earlier is a measure of his capacity to interpose an idealizing lens between himself and external realities – and of the emotional agility asked of the reader.

Shortly his idealizing vision is brought to the forefront in a startling moment of projection. He watches Avice toiling up a steep road with a basket of washing, 'for the moment an irradiated being, the epitome of a whole sex: by the beams of his own infatuation

... robed in such exceeding glory
That he beheld her not;

not, that is, as she really was, even to himself sometimes' (86; the book version [256] is substantially the same). Hardy took the quotation, altering 'I' to 'he,' from Shelley's youthful dreams of his twin soul in 'Epipsychidion' (ll. 199–200), and the extravagance of the combined images is at once marvellous and absurd. They prepare the way for the only mention of Plato in either version – prompted by the fortuitous appearance of Somers, who has noticed Jocelyn staring at '"a pretty little washerwoman."' Jocelyn corrects him: '"Yes; it was that to you, but not to me. Behind the mere pretty island-girl (to the world) is, in my eye, the Idea, in Platonic phraseology – the essence and epitome of all that is desirable in this existence"' (86, 257). The duality implied in 'Behind ...' corresponds with Plato's theory of ideal forms, to which earthly forms approximate as shadows. But Plato would never have endorsed a single idea representing 'all that is desirable in this existence,' and it is doubtful that Jocelyn would long have survived a Socratic enquiry about what he means. How do we decide what is desirable? And by what standards? In terms of this existence only? Jocelyn's 'Idea' is enclosed within himself; he is the arbiter of what is desirable. And yet his desires have now escaped his control – he tells Somers that he is under a curse or doom because the errant phantom (the image of the Beloved) which he expected to vanish on close approach to Avice will not leave her. Moreover he knows it is a phantom: '"That girl holds me, *though* my eyes are open and I see that I am a fool!"' (87; the book [257] repeats *though* before 'I see'). Plato's theory has become a metaphor for the unsatisfied longings which Jocelyn can no longer regulate.

When Avice becomes anxious to get away from the island, Jocelyn offers to take her to London, where she can clean up his studio and dust all his 'Venus failures' (264) – an acid touch added to the book. Living in his flat, she remains quite oblivious of his feelings until he embraces her and proposes, forcing her to confess she is already married (and, it will emerge, pregnant). Her response to him on their journey back to the island is just warm enough to tantalize him further and prompts another fantasy of divine retribution – this time not for his 'emotional wanderings' but for his fidelity to Avice. As the serial has it: 'Aphrodite was punishing him sharply, as she knew but too well how to punish her votaries when they reverted from the ephemeral to the stable mood' (106). The book opens out the goddess's identity with a final, inclusive flourish: 'Aphrodite, Ashtaroth, Freyja, or whoever the love-queen of his isle might have been, was punishing ...' (276). Jocelyn's indistinct fears are well grounded; mortals do not escape contests with goddesses (or the forces they represent) unscathed. Now, baffled of marriage himself, Jocelyn arranges the reunion of Avice and her husband, and later attends the birth of their daughter, Avice III, at the end of Part Second.

Nineteen or twenty fallow years elapse before the opening of Part Third, which finds Jocelyn in Rome. The quality of light reflected from the stone ruins reminds him of his native island, and shortly he returns there for the first time since Avice III's birth. Her enticing appearance fully grown stifles at once any revival of his former feeling for her widowed mother. Yet he is now three times as old as this new Avice, and there is a mixture of pathos and absurdity in his anxiety to prevent her seeing him in too strong a light. The unequal erosions of time, already a handicap in his pursuit of Avice II, become dominant in his courtship of her daughter: despite his physical decay and a growing tendency to depression, his capacities for obsessive emotion and self-delusion are little diminished. Both versions of the story agree on his eventual surrender of Avice III to her young lover, Leverre, but they differ sharply in their accounts of the circumstances. The serial narrative is more hectic; Jocelyn marries Avice and makes an unsuccessful attempt to drown himself. Finally Marcia, still his wife, reappears as 'a wrinkled crone ... The Juno of that day was the Witch of Endor of this' (168). The book allows him a slower, more measured decline into sharing old age with a rheumatic Marcia.

Part Third sees little extension of the pagan images and associations already clustered around the Well-Beloved and her island origins: the sense of varied repetition in Jocelyn's concentration on a single woman encourages echoes of their established resonance rather than further development. Thus his first vision of Avice III (through a window) is enough to make him feel that his doom or curse has returned: 'Aphrodite was not yet propitiated for that original sin against her image in the person of Avice the First' (120; the book [290] changes Aphrodite to 'His divinity'). He is now using his desertion of Avice I to legitimize his feelings for her daughter and granddaughter. Consequently, in the serial, when he discovers that Avice III has a young lover and realizes that as her husband he is the 'kill-joy' of her life, his 'gloom of responsibility' is doubled or trebled, 'for this life was the quintessence of his own past life, the crowning evolution of the idea expressed by the word "Avice", typifying the purest affection it had ever been his lot to experience' (153). Ageing has moved him closer to the territory of Plato's Venus Urania, for there is a distinct generosity in his treatment of Avice II and III once his own failure with each is apparent.

An image that *is* extended turns on the new moon, earlier viewed by

Jocelyn as a symbol of Avice I's purity. On the evening that succeeds his first glimpse of Avice III, it emerges that he has long cherished a special kinship with the moon, matching 'her so-called inconstancy' to 'his own idea of a migratory Well-Beloved' (122, 292). In the serial she is 'his chosen tutelary goddess' and her rising on this occasion makes him 'start as if his sweetheart in the flesh had suddenly looked over the horizon at him.' The book brings her closer still: she becomes 'this sisterly divinity' and her appearance makes him 'feel as if his wraith in a changed sex had suddenly looked over the horizon at him.' While this revision inevitably suggests a narcissistic closed circuit, it also plays on the moon's borrowed light to suggest Jocelyn's *taedium vitae* (162), the depleted confidence and appetite he brings to his last attempt to win an Avice.

The same elegaic tendency colours his vigil beside the dead body of Avice II after her daughter's elopement with Leverre, found only in the book: 'As he sat darkling here the ghostly outlines of former shapes taken by his Love came round their sister the unconscious corpse, confronting him from the wall in sad array, like the pictured Trojan women beheld by Aeneas on the walls of Carthage' (324). The allusion is to Book I of the *Aeneid* (which Hardy had studied in his youth), where frescoes in the temple of Juno at Carthage confront Aeneas with episodes from the war that destroyed his city; this one shows a procession of Trojan women carrying an offering to Athena, their city's enemy. It is the retrospective contemplation of devastating loss that draws the two disparate situations together. However, Jocelyn's imagination does not reanimate his women in idealized form (as he has portrayed many of them in his sculpture), but rather 'in all their natural circumstances, weaknesses, and stains.' Too late he has come to understand what Hardy noted in 1891, while working on the serial: 'October 28. It is the incompleteness that is loved, when love is sterling and true. This is what differentiates the real one from the imaginary, the practicable from the impossible, the Love who returns the kiss from the Vision that melts away. A man sees the Diana or the Venus in his beloved, but what he loves is the difference' (*LW*, 251).

Appropriately enough, the curious reader may well find Hardy's Well-Beloved story elusive – for several reasons. For a start there is its prolonged gestation: first, it seems to have been an idea displaced by others that either required development more urgently or seemed more suited to the prospective audience; then, many years later, it was written up as an evanescent serial to discharge a perceived obligation;

finally, a more considered version (but still 'a Sketch of a Tempera-ment') was produced by way of teasing postscript to the author's career as novelist. Furthermore, although the serial is less inhibited in its invention of incident and the book richer in allusion and texture, it is difficult to hold in the mind a clear separation between the two, differ-ing as they do in countless details as well as in their narrative lines, and some seepage appears unavoidable. Even within each version Hardy never quite settled his stance: the authorial point of view sways be-tween cool, sometimes sharply critical detachment and empathetic in-sight, and the degrees of Jocelyn's responsibility and agency are blurred. Jocelyn himself is another source of instability, with little capacity to check emotions that issue in abrupt changes of attitude and behaviour. Then there is the major shift in the story's direction, away from Jocelyn's wide-ranging quest for his ideal Beloved to his exclusive focus on the Caro family under the increasing handicaps of age. With all this, it is not surprising that the original Platonic idea remains elusive too – certainly less graspable than the imagery that flourishes around the Well-Be-loved and the island's pagan past. Ironically the most purely Platonic echo is aroused not by Jocelyn but by Avice II, who regards the models and casts in his studio 'with the wistful interest of a soul struggling to receive ideas of the beautiful, vaguely discerned yet ever eluding her' (102; the book [272] reads 'beauty' with no comma following). Both alternative endings suggest that the sketch Hardy made when 'com-paratively a young man' had led him into a cul-de-sac. In the book Jocelyn's libido and aesthetic sense are cancelled by a severe illness; he is effectively neutralized. In the serial he explodes into prolonged laugh-ter to cover his despair: '"it is too, too droll – this ending to my would-be romantic history!" Ho-ho-ho!' (168). It sounds as though his creator could not wait to escape.

NOTES

 1 Richard Little Purdy, *Thomas Hardy: A Bibliographical Study* (London: Oxford University Press, 1954), 94–5.
 2 Anne C. Pilgrim, 'Hardy's Retroactive Self-Censorship,' in *Victorian Authors and Their Works: Revision Motivations and Modes*, ed. Judith Kennedy (Athens: Ohio University Press, 1991), 127.
 3 Thomas Hardy, *The Well-Beloved: A Sketch of a Temperament* (London: Osgood McIlvaine, 1897), v.

4 *Thomas Hardy's Public Voice: The Essays, Speeches and Miscellaneous Prose*, ed. Michael Millgate (Oxford: Clarendon, 2001), 143.
5 *The Literary Notebooks of Thomas Hardy*, ed. Lennart A. Björk, 2 vols (London: Macmillan, 1985), nos. 442–60.
6 Thomas Hardy, *The Return of the Native*, ed. Tony Slade (London: Penguin, 1999), 175.
7 See Michael Millgate, 'Thomas Hardy's Library at Max Gate: Catalogue of an Attempted Reconstruction' (www.library.utoronto.ca/fisher/hardy).
8 Thomas Hardy, *The Life and Work of Thomas Hardy*, ed. Michael Millgate (London: Macmillan, 1984), 226. Hereafter cited parenthetically as *LW*.
9 *Literary Notebooks*, no. 167n.
10 *The Dialogues of Plato*, trans. B. Jowett, 4 vols (Oxford: Clarendon, 1871), 1:543.
11 Ibid. 1:498.
12 Thomas Hardy, *Jude the Obscure*, ed. Dennis Taylor (London: Penguin, 1998), 167–8. Hereafter cited parenthetically as *JO*.
13 *Dialogues of Plato*, 1:587–8.
14 Ibid. 1:527.
15 *Thomas Hardy's Public Voice*, 144.
16 *The Collected Letters of Thomas Hardy*, ed. Richard Little Purdy and Michael Millgate, 7 vols (Oxford: Clarendon, 1978–88), 2:155.
17 Thomas Hardy, *The Pursuit of the Well-Beloved and The Well-Beloved*, ed. Patricia Ingham (London: Penguin, 1997), 15. Quotations will be taken from this edition, and will be followed by bracketed page references. Those from 1 to 168 denote the serial version, while those from 169 to 336 denote the book version. A simple double reference indicates that both versions concur in a particular reading.
18 Henry Thornton Wharton, *Sappho: Memoir, Text, Selected Renderings and a Literal Translation*, 3rd ed. (London: John Lane, 1895). Hardy's copy is now in the Dorset County Museum.
19 *Collected Letters*, 2:84.
20 John Hutchins, *The History and Antiquities of the County of Dorset*, 3rd ed. by W. Shipp and J.W. Hodson, 4 vols (London: J.B. Nichols, 1861–70), 2:809, 811, 820. Hardy's copy is in the Dorset County Museum. He certainly drew on Hutchins's coverage of 'The Island and Liberty of Portland' (2:808–32), but since it virtually ignores human settlement before Danish incursions began at the end of the eighth century, it was not his source for the island's pagan past.
21 Hardy's image of Juno was shaped by his reading of Virgil's *Aeneid*; his

mother's gift to him of a copy of Dryden's translation c.1848 was the
overture to a lifetime's devotion.

22 Though the temple was always pagan, its dedication to Venus was an
afterthought incorporated in the Wessex Edition of 1912; see *The Complete
Poetical Works of Thomas Hardy*, ed. Samuel Hynes, 5 vols (Oxford:
Clarendon, 1982–95), 1:168–70, 372–3.

23 *Collected Letters*, 2:158. Ingham's note that 'the reference is unclear but may
allude to a passage in *The Iliad* III. 412 ...' is sadly mistaken.

12 Aesthetics and Thematics in Hardy's Volumes of Verse: The Example of *Time's Laughingstocks*

WILLIAM W. MORGAN

1 Introductory

I would imagine that few readers of this essay will have sat down to the pleasure of reading straight through one of Hardy's volumes of verse as a book. Likewise I would imagine that rather fewer of the teachers and professors who may read this piece will have assigned a book of Hardy's poems to be read by a class of students. We do not commonly encounter or even think about Hardy's poems as literary texts available to be read as constituents of an authored book that has a title, an individual history, often an authorial preface, and an organizational logic of its own – a logic chosen by the poet. Instead, we think about Hardy's poems singly, and we read and assign them in anthologies, or we read them according to some plan of choice in *The Complete Poems* or in an edited selection. We might read the work of our favourite living poets in books of their verse – as Hardy's contemporaries often read his work. But it is a curious fact of literary reputation that once a poet has achieved sufficient status, he or she is almost universally read in a context not of the poet's own making.

And it would be folly to claim that even a very strong and familiar poem will be the same no matter the context in which it is read, since the medium and company in which a poem appears go a long way towards shaping the dynamics of a reading experience and even the available meaning of the poem. Imagine Hardy's 'Hap,' for instance, as you might read it – or may perhaps have read it – in contexts such as the following:

- as the first poem in the twentieth-century section of a major historical anthology of English literature (where it has in fact appeared numbers of times, despite its 1866 date)

- in a collection devoted to English-language sonnets (it is an irregular English sonnet)
- as an instance of the young Hardy's favourite themes and forms in an essay about his poetry from the 1860s (I have treated the poem thus in one of my essays)[1]
- more fancifully, as the epigraph to a book of theology (where it might serve as a statement of the problem that theology sets out to overcome)
- as an example in a logic textbook (it is, after all, a hypothetical syllogism – if, then, therefore)
- as an item in an imaginary collection that might be called something like *Poems by Frustrated and Disillusioned Young Men* (where it would have pride of place)

I take it as self-evident that even though 'Hap' never ceases to be itself in any of these proposed contexts, nevertheless, each context would tug at the poem in different ways, and thus would shift its grain and texture so as to foreground different features of it, and would call upon us to exercise different strategies in reading it.

And so did the context Hardy himself provided for the poem when he placed it in third position in *Wessex Poems*, his first volume of verse, within a group of four poems about Time's ravages – or the effects of 'dicing Time,' as he calls it in the poem – and when he then placed that subgroup early within another group of fifteen pieces dated mostly from the 1860s and concerned largely with the trials of heterosexual love. There is no reason to think that Hardy wrote 'Hap' in 1866 with a view to nestling it some day within such a subtle chronological and thematic context; but when he was faced in 1898 with the challenge of creating not a poem but a book of poems, he did thus place it, and we are missing an engaging and rewarding feature of his creative activity if we do not give ourselves the opportunity to encounter the shapes and shadings that Hardy worked into his volumes of verse – to encounter, that is, Hardy as the maker not only of poems but also the maker of groupings of poems and finally of books of poems. I propose in this essay to open up the subject of Hardy the maker of books of poems and to suggest some reading strategies for those who may be interested in encountering this almost totally neglected dimension of Hardy's work in poetry. In particular, I hope to convince you that it is worth your time to devote a long evening to reading *Time's Laughingstocks*, Hardy's third volume of verse, published in 1909.[2]

2 The Idea of the Book of Poetry

Although there are some scholarly books and essays that show an awareness of Hardy's volumes of verse as important in themselves, the main body of critical work on the idea of The Book of Poetry addresses the work of other poets, and the great bulk of it has been either written or solicited and edited by one scholar: Neil Fraistat. His two books on the subject – *The Poem and the Book* and *Poems in Their Place* – would be important works even if they did not stand virtually alone in the field.[3] But their importance is magnified by their singularity. There is little else to turn to if one is looking for exemplary commentary on how poets have organized their collections and how readers may engage knowledgeably with the structure and sequence of those collections. But unluckily neither Fraistat nor any of the other scholars whose work he has edited makes mention of Hardy or his several ventures into creating what Fraistat calls 'the larger poem that is the book of poems.' Nevertheless, because Fraistat's work is so central to the task I have set for this essay, I want to begin by summarizing his main ideas

Fraistat's underlying claim is that poems published in the company of other poems will inevitably be read as related to one another in some way. He states this position simply as follows: 'poems published within the same volume inevitably interact. A poet can either attempt to control the chemistry of that reaction or passively accept the results.'[4] Most poets try to control the results, at least to the extent of finding a way to create unity in the volume of verse. Readers, Fraistat believes, are usually prepared to collaborate with the poet in this project, since when we read a volume of poems by a single author, we will ourselves create a rudimentary kind of unity for the poet:

> No doubt the very fact that a poet gathers certain of his works into a single book or collection grants them unity of a sort, implying that the poems share common ground (if only because they are his creations) and that they ought to be read together.[5]

Thus even the poet who passively accepts the effects of collecting poems together in a volume can expect readers to go some way towards creating a unified effect for the volume. But poets typically are not passive about the organization of their volumes. They manage that organization in a variety of ways, exploiting the provisional unity afforded by the poet's perceived presence and adding other structural effects:

> As we read a volume by a single poet, part of the outer structural energy of each poem will be directed toward fashioning and reflecting an image of the poet.
>
>   By placing his poems in a book united primarily by his own presence, then, a poet may create a coherent perceptual field ... [in which] miscellaneous poems, written on several occasions ... can nonetheless present a coherent ... [reading experience], unified by a distinct persona, resonant effects, and structural symmetries.[6]

Here Fraistat comes very close to a description of Hardy's usual practice – that of organizing into a single volume poems written over the course of a number of years and treating many different kinds of subjects. Fraistat is claiming that by the simple act of collecting the poems, any poet gains the unity of the 'image of the poet' thus created and the 'coherent perceptual field' within which he or she can exploit other more specifically organizational strategies – what he calls here 'resonant effects, and structural symmetries.' I hope to show something more of Hardy's practice in this regard below when I turn to an overview of Hardy's volumes of verse and then to some specific comments on *Time's Laughingstocks*.

    'The outer structural energy of each poem' is an important concept in Freistat's thinking about collections, as is its opposite, the 'inside meaning' of a single poem:

> each object in an aggregate [has] both an 'inside meaning,' comprised of its own internal 'object character,' and an 'outside meaning,' created when the object is 'structured in' as part of a more inclusive order.[7]

The 'inside meaning' or 'object character' of a given Hardy poem is the meaning we usually encounter or construct when we read a poem in isolation; but in a collection, that meaning shares significance with the meanings associated with the place that the poem holds within the larger poem that is the book. In any given case, the inner and outer meanings may be in a tug-of-war, but when they balance one another out, there is a desirable aesthetic harmony. Fraistat observes:

> Since outer meaning can be increased only at the expense of inner meaning, the poems in a weakly unified collection are likely to seem disparate as well as discrete. In most sonnet sequences and in collections such as Whitman's *Leaves of Grass* or Herbert's *The Temple*, the inner and outer

structural energies approach equilibrium: we are aware of the poems both as discrete units and as members of the larger set they collectively shape.[8]

Poems within well-unified collections, in other words, come to have less rigid individual boundaries than poems read alone or in anthologies: they do not necessarily start at their first line or end at their last, for example, because that first line may have been artfully anticipated by the placement of an earlier poem, and the last line may lead in some important way to something that follows in a subsequent poem. They yield some of their individuality to their function within the larger whole. But reading poems in collections is not purely a matter of subtracting significance from individual poems in order to give greater weight to the collection; such reading, Fraistat holds, may also enrich the individual poem:

> Because reading is a process of patterning, to read an individual poem in isolation or outside of its original volume is not only to lose the large retroactive sweep of the book as a whole ... but also to risk losing the meanings within the poem itself that are foregrounded or activated by the context of the book.[9]

Fraistat wants to argue, in other words, that both the individual poem and the larger poem-that-is-the-book will be enriched by reading poems in their original volumes.

Sequence, it will be evident, is of major importance in poetic collections, and even if the beginning and ending of an individual poem may be blurred by the experience of reading a collection, the position of first and last poem in the collection remains critically important:

> Like the opening poem, which generates our initial expectations, the concluding poem will have special significance in our understanding of the whole, because (as [Barbara Herrnstein] Smith says about the ending of a poem) 'it is only at that point that the total pattern – the structural principles which we have been testing – is revealed.'[10]

3 Hardy's Volumes of Verse

This last observation offers a good opportunity to return to Hardy. In all of his volumes of verse, he is keenly alert to this principle of the first and last poem, especially attending to the question of how to end his volumes. Consider these examples of Hardy's ending poems:

'I Look Into My Glass'	*Wessex Poems*
'A Young Man's Epigram on Existence'	*Time's Laughingstocks*
'Afterwards'	*Moments of Vision*
'Surview'	*Late Lyrics and Earlier*
'He Resolves to Say No More'	*Winter Words*

In each of these cases, Hardy has placed in the final position a poem that makes a particularly strong and clear claim; and in so doing he has provided not only a sense of closure but also an opportunity for retrospection – an occasion, however brief, for allowing our minds to range backward over the experience of the entire volume we have just finished, asking ourselves, perhaps: does that last poem offer a just and adequate summary of what I have been reading? The experience of reaching the last line of, say, 'Afterwards' at the end of *Moments of Vision* is not unlike the experience that comes at the end of a symphony; it marks the end of anticipation and the beginning of retrospection.

Hardy is not always sure of touch with his opening poems – at least in his early volumes. *Wessex Poems* and *Poems of the Past and the Present* in particular begin awkwardly (with 'The Temporary the All' and 'V.R. 1819–1901: A Reverie'). But starting with *Satires of Circumstance* in 1914, Hardy seems consistently to open his volumes with an impressive poem that both forecasts much of the thematic material of the volume it introduces and is notably resistant to the strong sense of interpretive closure that characterizes his most effective closing poems. Examples include 'In Front of the Landscape' (*Satires of Circumstance*), 'Moments of Vision' (*Moments of Vision*), 'Waiting Both' (*Human Shows*), and 'The New Dawn's Business' (*Winter Words*). These are poems more of question than of statement, poems in which the speaker is groping for understanding or passively observing the unfolding of things. As such, they invite readers to enter the experience of reading the volumes they introduce with a sense of open expectancy. And in every case, Hardy's volumes of verse take their readers on an intriguing journey before presenting them with a finishing poem offering closure and retrospective meditation.

Before moving specifically to *Time's Laughingstocks*, I would like to offer thanks to those Hardy scholars who *have* paid attention to Hardy's books of poems. Notable among these are Alan Shelston and Trevor Johnson who began a very promising series of Hardy editions. Sadly, the series survived through only two handsome volumes, *Moments of Vision and Miscellaneous Verses* and *Wessex Poems and Other Verses*.[11] According to the 'General Editors' Preface,' the series proposed to

> reproduce ... [Hardy's volumes of verse] in a form as close to the originals as can be achieved. In particular the text of each volume will be reproduced exactly. Readers will thus be able to read the poems as Hardy first gathered them and as his publishers first produced them, spaciously laid out and boldly and elegantly printed. Such an approach not only allows the opportunity of seeing the poems on the page as their first readers saw them, it imposes at once a more coherent and a more measured perusal, inviting consideration of the inter-connectedness of the poems as they were originally grouped together. (8)

The editors also note that although the various collected and complete editions of Hardy's verse 'do indeed publish the poems in their original volume sequence ... the overall effect of presenting the reader with nearly one thousand poems in such an edition is inevitably overpowering' (7). They might have added that Hardy's modern editors, for very good reasons in each case, have chosen to offer not the texts of Hardy's first edition volumes but other, later texts; hence, when we read, say, *Moments of Vision* in a collected edition, we are not reading the same book that Hardy's first readers would have encountered in 1917 or that we would be reading if we read the Keele/Ryburn reprint.[12] Before these reprints, the main awareness of and commentary on Hardy's books of verse is to be found in reference works such as Richard L. Purdy's magisterial *Thomas Hardy: A Bibliographical Study* (Oxford: Clarendon, 1954) and in the two principal guides to Hardy's work in verse, J.O. Bailey's *The Poetry of Thomas Hardy: A Handbook and Commentary* (Chapel Hill: University of North Carolina Press, 1970) and F.B. Pinion's *A Commentary on the Poems of Thomas Hardy* (London: Macmillan, 1976). More recently, the *Oxford Reader's Companion to Hardy*, ed. Norman Page (Oxford: Oxford University Press, 2000) offers a substantial short essay about each of Hardy's eight volumes. Likewise, Sarah Bird Wright's *Thomas Hardy: A to Z* (New York: Facts on File, 2002) offers an entry for each volume of verse. Virtually all these treatments of Hardy's books of poetry are descriptive, historical, and biographical rather than analytical and interpretive. What is still lacking is an overview of how Hardy assembled his books of verse, and an aesthetic analysis of a Hardy volume as a book.

What are some of the features of the journey along the way from opening to closing poem in a volume of Hardy's poems? What are his books of poetry like? To begin with, it is helpful to separate his books into two kinds: those that feature sets, suites, or sequences of poems, each with its own title and internal logic, as constituents of their organizational scheme, and those that are continuous or seamless – without such subdivisions. Hardy produced four of each kind of book. Neither his first book, *Wessex Poems* (1898), nor any of the last three (*Late Lyrics* [1922], *Human Shows* [1925], or *Winter Words* [1928]), includes such subsections; they are all continuous. On the other hand, there are five titled subdivisions in *Poems of the Past and the Present* (1901), four in *Time's Laughingstocks* (1909), four in *Satires of Circumstance* (1914), and two in *Moments of Vision* (1917) – a total of fifteen. The books with titled sequences occur in a cluster between 1901 and 1917, and those with a continuous, undifferentiated structure were published early, in 1898 (*Wessex Poems*), and then in a late cluster: 1922 (*Late Lyrics*), 1925 (*Human Shows*), and posthumously in 1928 (*Winter Words*).

That there are so many titled sequences in Hardy's *Complete Poems* will perhaps come as a surprise to the readers of this essay, since, just as we do not usually read his work in books of poetry, likewise we do not commonly read his sequences as sequences, or the poems within them as parts of those sequences: have you thought about 'The Sick Battle-God' as part of the sequence called 'War Poems' – or have you read the sequence? How about 'Shelley's Skylark' as part of the 'Poems of Pilgrimage' or that sequence itself? 'The Dark-Eyed Gentleman' as part of 'A Set of Country Songs' or 'A Set of Country Songs' as an extended, multipoem work? And so forth. We are probably all aware of the 'Poems of 1912–13' and 'Satires of Circumstance' as sequences, but generally speaking we are probably not aware of the others: 'Finale' and 'Poems of War and Patriotism' (both in *Moments of Vision*); 'Lyrics and Reveries' (in *Satires of Circumstance*); 'Imitations, etc.' (in *Poems of the Past and the Present*) – these are not familiar contexts for reading Hardy's poems or for thinking about the ways in which he arranged his volumes of verse. But the rewards of reading Hardy within the contexts he himself created are real and substantial. Each of his titled sequences is a little work in itself and will reward thoughtful reading. And of course the volumes that are divided into separate groupings derive a goodly part of their overall organization from the juxtaposition of those sequences.

For the other half of his work, those volumes that present themselves as one continuous reading experience, I recommend the practices we will have developed if we have read his sequences carefully: attention to narrative and thematic movement and awareness of the little verbal linkages that Hardy provides to move us from poem to poem with a sense not of the separateness of each lyric but of the continuity between – and finally among – them. In the 'Poems of 1912–13,' for example, Hardy has arranged the point of view in the various poems so that as we read them in sequence, we are brought into awareness of the major time frames of the relationship and of the meta-narrator's struggle (that is to say, the struggle of the author who has arranged the poems) to come to terms with the disharmonies among the distant past, the recent past, and the present in that relationship. How can the tormented present be reconciled with the joys of the distant past or the estrangements of the more recent past? The point of view in the sequence also moves between two speakers (the dead woman and the mourner) and two forms of address on the part of the mourner who speaks sometimes to and sometimes of the dead lover – sometimes she is 'you' and sometimes she is 'she.' These two features of point of view in the sequence control the reader's movement through the eighteen (later twenty-one) poems and lead us to the resolution, in 'The Phantom Horsewoman,' in which 'she' lives on in the golden and joyful distant past and where she still 'Draws rein and sings to the swing of the tide.' And alongside this overarching structural control, the sequence has little textural touches as well that remind us as readers that we are engaging in something larger than one poem at any given moment.[13] Repeated images of eyes, mist, flowers, and rain, for example, serve to remind us of the unity of the sequence, and verbal echoes, such as these in 'The Haunter' and 'The Voice,' add to the linked associations between poems:

> Yes, I companion him to places
> > Only dreamers know,
> Where the shy hares print long paces,
> > Where the night rooks go;
> Into old aisles where the past is *all to him,*
> > Close as his shade can do,
> Always lacking the power to *call to him,*
> > Near as I reach thereto!   ('The Haunter,' 17–24; italics mine)

Then the next poem opens:

> Woman much missed, how you *call to me, call to me,*
> Saying that now you are not as you were
> When you had changed from the one who was *all to me,*
> But as at first, when our day was fair.   ('The Voice,' 1–4; italics mine)

The juxtaposition of 'all to him,' 'call to him' in the first poem with 'call to me,' 'all to me' in the second reassures us that we are reading not only poems but also linked groupings of poems under the sure management of a metanarrator whose 'voice' is to be found in the artful silence of aesthetic control. I would suggest that Hardy's four continuous volumes of verse should be read, rather simply, as long Hardy sequences in which a metanarrator is at work guiding and enriching our experience in these and other ways.

4   *Time's Laughingstocks*

When we turn to a subdivided volume such as *Time's Laughingstocks*, we enter a different kind of structural complexity, one in which the various sequences will all have their own aesthetic logic, and in which the interrelation among those sequences will constitute the aesthetic logic of the book as a whole. The chart that accompanies this essay will, I hope, help readers to visualize the larger thematic patterns that I detect in *Time's Laughingstocks* (see 238–44); it offers a copy of the table of contents of the volume as it appears in *Complete Poems*[14] (since I judged that contemporary readers would be most likely to read the volume there) and a guide to my analysis of the themes of the book as they are organized into and by the four sequences. It is important to note that there are other organizational features at work in *Time's Laughingstocks*, features such as formal symmetries (duple and triple metres; two, three, and four-line stanza forms, etc.) and dated groupings. A few of the poems have different titles in *Time's Laughingstocks* as it was published in 1909 from those in *Complete Poems*; I have noted the alternate titles on the chart. There are of course also numbers of textual variants between the first edition and the text of *Complete Poems*, but these will not be considered here. My main concern is to present a reading of the book as a whole, a reading I hope to achieve by focusing, in order, on the leading themes of the four sequences that comprise it.

   After its authorial 'Preface,' in which Hardy emphasizes the miscellaneous nature of the volume and the dramatic or impersonal nature of many of its poems, *Time's Laughingstocks* opens with a series of fifteen poems that bears the same title as the volume itself and that, not surprisingly, gives great weight to the surprises, losses, punishments, and occasional epiphanies that Time enforces as it moves relentlessly on. Twelve of these first fifteen poems turn on this theme. And clustered around this major theme are three others that appear at intervals: women's loss of beauty through ageing, the potential tragedies that lie about like pitfalls in the area of time-bound experience we call love, and an attitude of welcoming on the part of some of the poems' characters towards death – which is here imaged as relief from the burdens imposed by time. The thematic 'line' running through these fifteen poems is that of 'Time's transforming chisel,' as the narrator calls it in the first poem; it is the main idea to which a reader will be likely to attach attention. The other themes are supplementary to it: the effects of time on women's beauty in 'The Revisitation,' 'The Two Rosalinds,' and 'Reminiscences of a Dancing Man'; the sorrows attendant upon mistiming in 'A Trampwoman's Tragedy,' 'A Sunday Morning Tragedy,' and 'The Curate's Kindness'; and the idea of death as a release from time's impositions in 'John and Jane,' 'Bereft,' 'The Curate's Kindness,' and the final poem in the group, 'The Dead Man Walking.' These fifteen poems offer a highly unified reading experience, and I would suspect that most readers would finish 'The Dead Man Walking' with a clear sense that there is an author in charge of this sequence, pointing them towards larger patterns of meaning to be found in the aggregate of the fifteen poems. Hardy twice uses the kind of verbal linking I pointed out earlier between poems in the 'Poems of 1912–13': 'Thereaft I walked the world alone,' line 81 of 'A Trampwoman's Tragedy,' towards the end of the ballad, is echoed in the next poem's second line by 'And I walked the Town alone ...' ('The Two Rosalinds,' l. 2). And later on, line 12 of 'Shut Out That Moon,' 'When faded ones were fair' is echoed early in the next poem, 'Reminiscences of a Dancing Man,' with 'For faded ones so famed' (l. 4). Thematic unity – and complexity – coupled with this kind of verbal linking is enough to suggest that Hardy is working towards a particular kind of somber aesthetic argument in this sequence, an argument that goes something like this: time brings mostly losses, and neither beauty nor love is much of a palliative against those losses; only death can bring any real relief from the exigencies of time.

But surely I am being too dark here, you may say; my interpretation reads like a parody of the popular idea of Hardy the gloomy pessimist.

There are in fact two poems in the sequence that suggest the possibility of redemptive moments capable of being salvaged from the largely destructive movement of time. The first is in 'The Rejected Member's Wife,' the tenth poem in the sequence, in which we are encouraged to join the narrator in holding on to the beauty of the moment when the defeated politician's wife stands

> In the sunshine there,
> With that wave of her white-gloved hand,
>   And that chestnut hair.   (ll. 22–4)

The poem encourages us to salvage this one moment of beauty from the ongoingness of time – time that sweeps (male) politicians out of office (and their wives with them) but that leaves moments of epiphany in its wake. Likewise, the contented narrator, raking up leaves in 'Autumn in King's Hintock Park,' stands above the wasting work of time when she steps outside the egoism of considering her own loss of youth and declares:

> New leaves will dance on high –
>   Earth never grieves! –
> Will not, when missed am I
>   Raking up leaves.   (ll. 21–4)

So within the grim, deterministic argument of the sequence at large, Hardy has proposed that sympathetic engagement with others and an ego-less recognition that the world goes on in spite of us can give comfort, even joy.

The next grouping, 'More Love Lyrics' is even more tightly unified; every poem in it clings to the theme of love – and loss. Broadly speaking, the twenty-six poems in this sequence are concerned with the ways in which love seems to promise complete fulfilment but never really fulfils its promise. A beautiful memory is superseded by something more mundane, as in 'On the Departure Platform'; the richest love does not guarantee that one of the partners will not marry someone else, as in 'Four Footprints'; time changes lovers' bliss into suffering, as in 'The End of the Episode':

> Though fervent was our vow,
> Though ruddily ran our pleasure,

Bliss has fulfilled its measure,
   And sees its sentence now.

   Ache deep; but make no moans:
Smile out; but stilly suffer:
The paths of love are rougher
   Than thoroughfares of stones.   (ll. 13–20)

This is the thematic 'line' that runs through all of the poems: love offers bliss but always takes it away and substitutes something lower down the scale of human fulfilment – sometimes outright misery. That Hardy is grouping these twenty-six poems by theme rather than, say, by date, is evident from the fact that he has included seven poems from the 1860s, one from the 1870s, one from the 1880s, and one from the 1890s alongside the sixteen undated poems, presumably written between 1901 and 1909. The dates suggest that such has been his conviction for many decades.

But why should this be so? Why can love in Hardy's world not sustain the promise with which it begins? The poems here do not answer that question, but they probe at its edges by offering little moments that examine the psychology of love, as in 'In the Vaulted Way':

In the vaulted way, where the passage turned
To the shadowy corner that none could see,
You paused for our parting, – plaintively;
Though overnight had come words that burned
My fond frail happiness out of me.

And then I kissed you, – despite my thought
That our spell must end when reflection came
On what you had deemed me, whose one long aim
Had been to serve you; that what I sought
Lay not in a heart that could breathe such blame.

But yet I kissed you; whereon you again
As of old kissed me. Why, why was it so?
Do you cleave to me after that light-tongued blow?
If you scorned me at eventide, how love then?
The thing is dark, Dear. I do not know.

The jarring disjunction between the couple's feelings and their behaviour is 'dark' to the narrator – a 'shadowy corner that none could see' – and his urge to understand is left frustrated. Likewise, in 'The Sigh,' the narrator notes that even as his lover yielded to his importunity and granted the momentous first kiss, she sighed; and although she has loved him 'staunchly, truly' for many years since that kiss, he wonders still what 'sad thought' lay behind that sigh. The female narrator of 'Her Confession' explains herself, as does the presumably male narrator of 'The Minute Before Meeting,' and each of them tells a story of conscious thought interfering with love's pleasures: the former tells of turning away from her lover's kiss in hopes of making him want the kiss even more, then being chagrined when he seemed to lose interest; the latter confesses that the nearer he and his beloved come to meeting, after months of separation, the more concerned he becomes not with the fulfilment of the meeting itself but with the emptiness that will succeed it when they are apart again: his anticipated joy is undercut by his awareness of its transience. There is a suggestion in these poems that love arouses some primal, childlike needs for comfort, assurance, and protection but that the mind, with its rapacious will to understanding, can only hobble along after, looking in vain for explanations and destroying the feeling of primal comfort in the process.

'More Love Lyrics' ends with a particularly strong poem – and one that is especially suited to its work as the final piece in the sequence. 'He Abjures Love' offers us a lover's autobiography and builds to a ringing promise that he will learn his lesson and give up on love's illusions; but then, in a wonderful moment of self-correction in the last stanza, the narrator turns back on himself with

> – I speak as one who plumbs
>   Life's dim profound,
> One who at length can sound
>   Clear views and certain.
> But – after love what comes?
>   A scene that lours,
> A few sad vacant hours,
>   And then, the Curtain.   (ll. 41–8)

Life without love, the poem seems to say, is empty. Thus the sequence ends with an acceptance of love, with all its pains and puzzlements. Love is not a salvation, according to 'More Love Lyrics,' but it is the only experience life offers that even resembles one.

The eighteen poems of 'A Set of Country Songs,' not surprisingly, hover around the ideas of music and dance, though they also take up a group of other themes associated with love and sexuality – the psychology of love (again), illegitimate children, and marriage. Hardy uses the theme of music and dance as a central body of subject matter and weaves around it a group of other themes that begin, early in the sequence, as inquiries into the psyches of lovers and make their way through discussions of bastard children and finally into a five-poem meditation on marriage. 'A Set of Country Songs' encloses within itself another, smaller sequence called 'At Casterbridge Fair,' which touches on all the themes of the larger sequences except that of illegitimacy. And what of this theme of illegitimacy? In 'The Dark-Eyed Gentleman,' the female narrator has outlived her grief and shame and now celebrates her 'fine, lissom lad' and declares herself 'thankful' that 'his daddy once tied up my garter for me.' Julie-Jane, in the poem by that name, is full of laughter, song, and dance, and the poem suggests that her having a 'baby-boy' before she became a wife is simply an extension of her ebullience and spirit:

> 'I suppose,' with a laugh, she said,
> 'I should blush that I'm not a wife;
> But how can it matter, so soon to be dead,
>   What one does in life!'   (ll. 21–4)

The strength and spirit of these two women sustain them in the face of social disapproval, and Hardy seems to associate their spirit with music, dance – and probably erotic energy. More stolid is the newly-wed husband in 'The Husband's View,' who says of his wife's pregnancy by a previous lover,

> 'I am not a particular man;
> Misfortunes are no crime:
>
> 'And what with our serious need
> Of sons for soldiering,
> That accident, indeed,
> To maids, is a useful thing!'   (ll. 31–6)

On the whole, marriage fares less well in this sequence than love, eroticism, music, dance, and even illegitimacy. Here it figures as an economic and civic responsibility that makes a virtue of necessity. In

'News for Her Mother,' the coming of marriage creates in the daughter an anxiety lest she lose the close love she has known with her mother. In 'Rose-Ann,' the naive male narrator is angered to learn that the woman he has been counting on 'was promised' already and had not told him; the marriage market, his beloved's one chance for success in life, has apparently made her less candid with him than he thinks she should have been. The ill-sorted couple in 'The Homecoming' are shown as improbable honeymooners, much less life partners, since he and his house are rough and coarse while she is timid, fragile, and sensitive. And perhaps most telling, the fiddler, in the poem by that name, sees a tragic connection between music, dance, and the doom of eternal conflict in marriage:

> The fiddler knows what's brewing
>   To the lilt of his lyric wiles:
> The fiddler knows what rueing
>   Will come of this night's smiles!
>
> He sees couples join them for dancing,
>   And afterwards joining for life,
> He sees them pay high for their prancing
>   By a welter of wedded strife.   (ll. 1–8)

'A Set of Country Songs,' then, tests the question of whether human energy and desire, most fully expressed in music, dance, and sexuality, can be adequately housed within the institutions that human society has devised for containing it – namely marriage and the family. The answer seems to be a sometimes sarcastic, sometimes wistful, sometimes humorous *No*.

The last grouping in the volume, called simply 'Pieces Occasional and Various,' is, despite its diffident title, likewise a coherent grouping of poems on some of the themes taken up in the earlier sequences and on two additional ones: (1) the value of the local and the familial, and (2) the ultimate failure of either the natural or social order to satisfy human needs for comfort, certainty, and love. The dominant theme early in this sequence is all that is sacred to the family and the local culture of one's birth. No fewer than eleven of the thirty-five poems in the group are dedicated to stories, memories, and traditions of the Hardy family and the Stinsford and Bockhampton area. Such tender poems as 'A Church Romance,' 'The Roman Road,' 'Night in the Old Home,' and 'After the Last Breath' are among them. But 'Pieces Occasional and Various' also looks backward into earlier parts of the volume to comment on marriage (four poems) and illegitimacy (one poem), and most importantly, it gradually – perhaps I should say relentlessly – moves forward into direct and unflinching critiques of the natural and social order of the world as an inadequate structure for nurturing human feelings. And it is on this theme that the volume unequivocally closes. Two poems appearing early in the sequence introduce the theme – 'A Dream Question,' with its petulant god-figure who refuses to answer the questions put to him by an inquiring human character, and 'The Reminder,' in which the struggle of a starving blackbird interrupts the narrator's Christmas contentment and brings him back to awareness of suffering in the natural world. The theme all but takes over the sequence, however, beginning with 'Before Life and After,' which regrets 'the birth of consciousness' (l. 3) when 'the disease of feeling' (l. 13) entered the world. This poem is followed by 'New Year's Eve' and 'God's Education,' two more lyrics arguing that the cosmic order is inhospitable to living things with feelings and then by 'To Sincerity' and 'Panthera,' both of which suggest that the social order, both secular and sacred, likewise, is somehow awry. With two exceptions, the rest of the sequence (eleven poems) stays with one of these two critiques: either the natural order of the world or the social order created by humans is over and over again tested and found wanting. There are two short looks back to earlier themes in 'Geographical Knowledge,' a tribute to one of the Hardy family's neighbours in Lower Bockhampton,[15] and 'The Noble Lady's Tale,' another consideration of marriage. But the main direction of the remainder of the book is established, and it moves on forward to its final claim in 'Yell'ham-Wood's Story' and 'A Young Man's Epigram on Existence.' The former poem interprets the woodland as saying

> ... that Life would signify
> A thwarted purposing:
> That we come to live, and are called to die.
> Yes, that's the thing
> In fall, in spring,
> That Yell'ham says: –
> 'Life offers – to deny!'   (ll. 8–14)

And the concluding poem in *Time's Laughingstocks*, just four lines long, indicts that vast abstraction, 'Existence,' for insisting on a temporal logic that does not, indeed *cannot* by its very nature, give honour to joy. Existence, the poem says, is

A senseless school, where we must give
Our lives that we may learn to live!
A dolt is he who memorizes
Lessons that leave no time for prizes.

Time teaches us how to live but leaves us with no time to live; Life teases us with joy and beauty but then withholds them. Our lives show us 'prizes' and then cruelly say, 'Sorry: time's up.'

Time's Laughingstocks offers a stern assessment of the possibilities for joy in human life – not only here in its cluster of closing poems, but throughout. It looks at the very groundwork of our lives – the passing of time – and judges that Time is at best indifferent to our happiness. It looks at love and finds it to be always something less than it seemed at first. It looks at the allure of music, dance, desire, and all the erotic impulses that run through our lives and judges them to be hemmed in by social structures in such a way that they cannot bring real fulfilment. It looks at marriage and finds it dull and inadequate if not downright demeaning. It looks at the sacred texture of family and the culture of the local that nurtured our childhoods and finds them beautiful but necessarily of – and limited to – the past and a world of memory. And it ends by judging both the cosmic and the social order to be unworthy of the best that is in us. Is this not the tragic vision we know from *Tess, Jude*, and the *Mayor*? – the vision that Hardy summarized in a notebook entry of October 1892 as 'the WORTHY encompassed by the INEVITABLE.'[16] Why is it that when we finish those great novels we do not leave them with a sense of defeat? I think it is because Hardy's ultimate concern is never with the forces arrayed against human dignity and love but instead with 'the best that is in us.' In *Time's Laughingstocks* as in others of his works, his is a tragic vision of life, but he allows us to leave this book as we leave, say, *Tess of the d'Urbervilles*, with a sense that there is something truly worthy about being human, even if the world at large does not seem to recognize it.

NOTES

1 See 'Thomas Hardy's Apprenticeship to the Craft of English Verse,' *Victorians Institute Journal* 13 (1985): 1–10.
2 An earlier version of this essay was delivered as a lecture on 29 July 2003 as part of the 'Thomas Hardy in Cambridge' conference sponsored by the

Thomas Hardy Society and the Thomas Hardy Association. The holograph of *Time's Laughingstocks* is housed at the Fitzwilliam Museum, Cambridge.

3 Neil Fraistat, *The Poem and the Book: Interpreting Collections of Romantic Poetry* (Chapel Hill: University of North Carolina Press, 1985), and *Poems in Their Place: The Intertextuality and Order of Poetic Collections* (Chapel Hill: University of North Carolina Press, 1986).

4 Fraistat, *The Poem and the Book*, 4.

5 Ibid., 11.

6 Ibid., 16–17.

7 Ibid., 11.

8 Ibid., 12.

9 Fraistat, *Poems in Their Place*, 8.

10 Fraistat, *The Poem and the Book*, 13–14.

11 Alan Shelston and Trevor Johnson, *Moments of Vision and Miscellaneous Verses*, introduction by Alan Shelston (Keele: Ryburn/Keele University Press, 1994), and *Wessex Poems and Other Verses*, introduction by Trevor Johnson (Keele: Ryburn/Keele University Press, 1995).

12 At the same time as the first of the Keele/Ryburn editions, there appeared another reprint edition of *Wessex Poems*, a facsimile published by Woodstock Books (1994). Unless otherwise indicated, all quotations from Hardy's poems in this essay are from the Variorum edition of *The Complete Poems of Thomas Hardy*, ed. James Gibson (London: Macmillan, 1979).

13 I have argued this case in more detail in my 'Form, Tradition, and Consolation in Hardy's "Poems of 1912–13,"' *PMLA* 89 (May, 1974): 496–505.

14 *Thomas Hardy, The Complete Poems*, ed. James Gibson (London: Palgrave, 2001).

15 The poem is a tribute to Christiana Coward, a neighbour of the Hardys and postmistress for many years at Lower Bockhampton; see J.O. Bailey, *The Poetry of Thomas Hardy: A Handbook and Commentary* (Chapel Hill: University of North Carolina Press, 1970), 255.

16 Thomas Hardy, *The Life and Work of Thomas Hardy*, ed. Michael Millgate (London: Macmillan, 1984), 265.

Time's Laughingstocks and Other Verses
Preface
Time's Laughingstocks

	Female Aging and Loss of Beauty	Love's Tragic Turns	Time's Onward March	Death as Relief	The Psychology of Love	Love's Promise, Love's In-adequacy	Music and Dance	Illegiti-macy	Marriage	The Local and Familial	The Failure of the Natural and Social Orders	Linking Language
The Revisitation	x											
A Trampwoman's Tragedy		x										I walked the world alone
The Two Rosalinds	x		x									I walked the town alone
A Sunday Morning Tragedy		x										
The House of Hospitalities			x									
Bereft			x	x								
John and Jane			x	x								
The Curate's Kindness		x		x								
The Flirt's Tragedy			x									
The Rejected Member's Wife			x									
The Farm-Woman's Winter			x									

When faded
ones
were fair

For faded
ones so
famed

Time's Laughingstocks and Other Verses (continued)

	Female Aging and Loss of Beauty	Love's Tragic Turns	Time's Onward March	Death as Relief	The Psychology of Love	Love's Promise, Love's Inadequacy	Music and Dance	Illegitimacy	Marriage	The Local and Familial	The Failure of the Natural and Social Orders	Linking Language
The End of the Episode						x						
The Sigh					x	x						
In the Night She Came	x					x						
The Conformers						x						frigid tone of household speech
The Dawn after the Dance						x						household life's mechanic gear
The Sun on the Letter						x						
The Night of the Dance						x	x					
Misconception						x						
The Voice of the Thorn						x						
From Her in the Country						x						

Her Confession

To an Impersonator
of Rosalind

To an Actress

The Minute Before
Meeting

He Abjures Love

A Set of Country Songs

Let Me Enjoy

At Casterbridge Fair:
I. The Ballad Singer

II. Former
Beauties

III. After the
Club-Dance

IV. The Market-Girl

V. The Inquiry

VI. A Wife Waits

VII. After the Fair

The Dark-Eyed
Gentleman

To Carry Clavel

The Orphaned
Old Maid

The Spring Call

Julie-Jane

News for Her Mother

Time's Laughingstocks and Other Verses (continued)

	Female Aging and Loss of Beauty	Love's Tragic Turns	Time's Onward March	Death as Relief	The Psychology of Love	Love's Promise, Love's Inadequacy	Music and Dance	Illegitimacy	Marriage	The Local and Familial	The Failure of the Natural and Social Orders	Linking Language
The Fiddler							x		x			
The Husband's View								x	x			
Rose-Ann									x			
The Homecoming									x			
Pieces Occasional and Various												
A Church Romance										x		
The Rash Bride									x	x		
The Dead Quire										x		
The Christening								x	x			
A Dream Question											x	
By the Barrows										x		
A Wife and Another									x			
The Roman Road										x		
The Vampirine Fair									x			
The Reminder											x	
The Rambler			x									

Night in the Old Home			x	x
After the Last Breath				
In Childbed			x	x
The Pine Planters				x
The Dear				x
One We Knew			x	
She Hears the Storm		x		
A Wet Night			x	
Before Life and After	x			
New Year's Eve		x		
God's Education (His Education, TL)		x		
To Sincerity		x		
Panthera		x		
The Unborn		x		
The Man He Killed		x		
Geographical Knowledge			x	
One Ralph Blossom Soliloquizes		x		
The Noble Lady's Tale			x	
Unrealized				
Wagtail and Baby		x		
Aberdeen (Aberdeen: 1905, TL)		x		

Time's Laughingstocks and Other Verses (concluded)

	Female Aging and Loss of Beauty	Love's Tragic Turns	Time's Onward March	Death as Relief	The Psychology of Love	Love's Promise, Love's In- adequacy	Music and Dance	Illegiti- macy	Marriage	The Local and Familial	The Failure of the Natural and Social Orders	Linking Language
George Meredith (G.M., 1828–1909, TL)											x	
Yell'ham-Wood's Story											x	
A Young Man's Epigram on Existence											x	

13 Hardy and the Battle God

SAMUEL HYNES

When critics write about modern war poets, they rarely mention Thomas Hardy. In our time, just past the end of a century of wars, we take *war poet* to mean a poet who was a soldier first, who learned about war by fighting before he wrote about it. The war poems that matter are the ones that take us where we have never been, into the unimaginable experience of war. What was it like? we ask the poet. Tell us, you've been there, you know.

Hardy had not been there. He never saw a war, never heard a bullet fired in anger; the battlefields he visited were scenes of long-ago fighting, no longer battle scenes but memorials. And yet he wrote one great war epic, one poem that makes a war that was a century past when Hardy wrote about it as immediate and real as the Dorset earth. *The Dynasts* is a monstrous great poetic-drama of nineteen acts and a hundred and thirty-one scenes, too long ever to be acted straight through, too long some would say even to be read. Still, there it is, the real thing, the nearest English poetry has ever come to a war epic, and the last one we shall ever have, because it was written in the last decade in English history in which a war epic was possible.

Hardy never saw a war, but he nevertheless had a war in his head, derived not from direct experience but from memories and fictions. We all have such imagined wars, before we have real ones, wars made of whatever our time and culture give us. From such accidental stuff we construct our private myths of war. Hardy tells us in various places what the sources of his war-in-the-head were. Here is his account of his earliest reading, from *The Life and Work*:

> About this time his mother gave him Dryden's *Virgil*, Johnson's *Rasselas*, and *Paul and Virginia*. He also found in a closet *A History of the Wars* – a

periodical in loose numbers of the war with Napoleon, which his grandfather had subscribed to at the time, having been himself a volunteer. The torn pages of these contemporary numbers with their melodramatic prints of serried ranks, crossed bayonets, huge knapsacks, and dead bodies, were the first to set him on the train of ideas that led to *The Trumpet-Major* and *The Dynasts*.[1]

Later, when he was sixteen or so, he read *The Iliad* to teach himself Greek, and found another epic war.

Virgil, Homer, and a history of the Napoleonic Wars – these are predictable texts from which a bookish Dorset boy in the mid-nineteenth century might create his version of essential war. But war did not appear to him only in books. Dorchester was a garrison town, and Hardy saw a good deal of the resident troops; they walked the streets of Dorchester and Weymouth, they turned up in the neighbouring villages (as Sergeant Troy does in *Far From the Madding Crowd*), they departed for distant wars, and some of them returned. Hardy remembered their picturesque uniforms well enough half a century later to write a precise footnote to *The Dynasts* describing the look of the Hussars' sling-jackets. And he remembered their stories.

From the town's old men he heard other stories. Hardy's grandfather was dead before his grandson was born, but other local volunteers in the wars against Napoleon were still alive, still telling their tales. Hardy acknowledged his debt to these parish historians in his preface to *The Trumpet-Major*:

> The external incidents which direct [this novel's] course are mostly an unexaggerated reproduction of the recollections of old persons well known to the author in childhood, but now long dead, who were eye-witnesses of those scenes.[2]

These old persons appear in Hardy's novels and stories (Grandfer Cantle in *The Return of the Native* is one), and in early narrative poems like 'Valenciennes,' 'San Sebastian,' and 'The Alarm,' poems that carry dedication lines connecting them to actual local soldiers: 'S.C. (Pensioner),' 'Sergeant M— (Pensioner),' and 'One of the Writer's Family who was a Volunteer during the War with Napoleon' (that would be Hardy's grandfather)[3] – as though he felt a need to demonstrate that the war in his head was not altogether an invented one.

One other source was neither written nor spoken. All his life Hardy saw history as a story recorded on and below the surface of the earth – a story that preexisted its articulation in words. The earthworks of his countryside, the Roman stones of his town's walls, the bones and shards he found buried in his garden were all silent witnesses from the Dorset past. History lay everywhere around him. He makes this point in *The Trumpet-Major* preface:

> Down to the middle of this century, and later, there were not wanting, in the neighbourhood of the places more or less clearly indicated herein, casual relics of the circumstances amid which the action moves – our preparations for defence against the threatened invasion of England by Buonaparte. An outhouse door riddled with bullet-holes, which had been extemporized by a solitary man as a target for firelock practice when the landing was hourly expected, a heap of bricks and clods on a beacon-hill, which had formed the chimney and walls of the hut occupied by the beacon-keeper, worm-eaten shafts and iron heads of pikes for the use of those who had no better weapons, ridges on the down thrown up during the encampment, fragments of volunteer uniform, and other such lingering remains, brought to my imagination in early childhood the state of affairs at the date of the war more vividly than volumes of history could have done. (14)

From these silent texts Hardy got a sense not so much of the present reality of war as of its pastness: these are the materials of a myth of war such as an imaginative boy might conceive who has come along too late for the reality.

The sources of Hardy's war-in-the-head are a disparate set from which to make war poetry: Homer and Dorset village historians, a popular Victorian picture-paper, *The Aeneid*, Greek gods, an outhouse door, a green sling-jacket. But among these oddments there is material enough for the themes of war: the violence and the brutality, the dead bodies and the grieving families; and the romance – the brave uniforms and the drums and the roaring cannons; and the grandeur – great armies flowing like rivers, cities burning, dynasties falling. To understand Hardy's wars one must begin back there in the boy's imagination, with the old men's memories and the bullet-riddled door, and with the sense of a long-past time when war was epic.

The dream of a possible epic war poem runs through Hardy's journal of his novel writing years, vague at first (but always *epic*), coming at last to form and focus as *The Dynasts*. The first such entry in *The Life and*

Work is this one, from June 1875: 'Mem: A Ballad of the Hundred Days. Then another of Moscow. Others of earlier campaigns – forming altogether an Iliad of Europe from 1789 to 1815' (*LW*, 110). If you turn back a page from this passage you will find that it comes just after Hardy had visited the Chelsea Hospital in London, where army pensioners lived; the date was the sixtieth anniversary of Waterloo, and he went there to talk with survivors of the battle – seeking out, on this memorial occasion, the company of the old men and their memories.

Two years later Hardy had discarded the ballad form for drama:

> Consider a grand drama, based on the wars with Napoleon, or some one campaign, (but not as Shakespeare's historical dramas). It might be called 'Napoleon', or 'Josephine', or by some other person's name. (*LW*, 117)

A few years after that he was thinking of it again as a drama, and the following year again as a ballad, this time 'A Homeric Ballad, in which Napoleon is a sort of Achilles ...' (*LW*, 152), uncertain, here in the 1870s and 1880s, as to what form could best contain his vast ambitions. But the ambitions were never in doubt: he would write a poem of the greatest events in modern European history, an epic poem on an epic scale.

In epic poems the forces that move the universe and rule the wills of men appear as gods and goddesses; but in a modern epic set in nineteenth century historical reality such figures obviously would not do. How could the century's shaping philosophical ideas – determinism, upward evolution, the world-as-will – be given forms and voices? Hardy worried away at this problem in his journal, beginning with this 1881 note:

> Mode for a historical Drama. Action mostly automatic; reflex movement, etc. Not the result of what is called *motive*, though always ostensibly so, even to the actors' own consciousness. Apply an enlargement of these theories to, say, 'The Hundred Days'! (*LW*, 152)

No form for the ideas there yet; five years later there was:

> The human race to be shown as one great network or tissue, which quivers in every part when one point is shaken, like a spider's web if touched. Abstract realisms to be in the form of Spirits, Spectral figures, &c. (*LW*, 182)

These reflections do not come close to describing the actual philosophical machinery of *The Dynasts*; what they show is that in the 1880s Hardy was thinking of his war epic not only as modern history, but also as an expression of modern – that is, late-Victorian – ideas of the forces that move history and impel human actions, and the ironic relations between what those forces do and what men think they themselves do.

But before Hardy set himself to write his war epic he was drawn to address a different war. England's quarrel with the Boers was scarcely epic – antiepic if anything, a small discreditable colonial action fought with less than complete support from the folks at home, and with little glory in the field. The last Victorian war: why should Hardy have bothered to write a set of poems about it? Not out of patriotic enthusiasm, surely; Hardy was not a man who got excited about current events. Nor from public spiritedness; he was a reluctant public man (and wisely so, to judge from the few occasions when he attempted public poetry). Perhaps the answer is simply that he used the Boer War as a sort of trial run for his big intended war poem, an opportunity to test the elements of the war in-the-head against a real one, to see which of those elements he could use, and how.

He began, characteristically, in Wessex: three poems about the embarkation of local troops from Southampton (he rode his bicycle all the way from Dorchester to watch them depart). Then a poem about a local man, killed in the war, and later another local remembering how he killed an enemy. Writing the poems, he stressed their localness. 'Drummer Hodge' was first printed with this headnote: 'One of the Drummers killed was a native of a village near Casterbridge' (*CPW*, 1:122); 'The Man He Killed' is staged like a play – 'SCENE: The settle of the Fox Inn, Stagfoot Lane ... The speaker (a returned soldier), and his friends, natives of the hamlet' (*CPW*, 1:344; Stagfoot Lane was Hardy's name for a hamlet north of Puddletown in Dorset). These poems are like the stories the old soldiers of his youth told, war stories, but rooted in Wessex.

Of the war matter in Hardy's head he found he could use the local scene well enough, and the local dead, too – a drummer, one enemy soldier, husbands mourned by their wives, a cloud of souls of the dead, sweeping home over Portland Bill. And irony, as in poor dead Hodge, thrown uncoffined into his grave under the wheeling southern constellations, so small a corpse, so vast and strange the universe. What he could not do, yet, was *war*: he might call his set of poems 'War Poems,' but the customary trappings of war are all missing; no arms, no armies, no generals, no cannons, no drums, no trumpets, no battles, no cavalry charges, no deeds of personal heroism, no victories, no defeats. The last Victorian war poems of the last Victorian war have no war in them.

Hardy himself noted another Victorian element the poems lack: in a December 1900 letter to his friend Florence Henniker, accompanying a copy of his 'Song of the Soldiers' Wives and Sweethearts,' he wrote: 'My Soldiers' Wives' Song finishes up my war effusions, of which I am happy to say that not a single one is Jingo or Imperial – a fatal defect according to the judgment of the British majority at present, I dare say.'[4] He was right on both points: his poems were not jingoistic; and they did offend the British public, or at least that portion that wrote (and read) the London *Daily Chronicle*. Two days before Christmas, 1899, Hardy published 'A Christmas Ghost-Story,' one of his 'War Poems,' in the *Westminster Gazette*. In it a British soldier, dead and buried in South Africa like Drummer Hodge, asks:

> 'I would know
> By whom and when the All-Earth-gladdening Law
> Of Peace, brought in by that Man Crucified,
> Was ruled to be inept, and set aside?
> And what of logic or of truth appears
> In tacking "Anno Domini" to the years?
> Near twenty-hundred liveried thus have hied
> But tarries yet the Cause for which He died.'   (*CPW*, 1:121)

The *Daily Chronicle* responded with a Christmas Day leader. 'Mr. Thomas Hardy,' the *Chronicle* wrote,

> has pictured the soul of a dead soldier in Natal contemplating the battle-field, and wondering where is that peace on earth which is the Christian ideal of Christmastide. A fine conception, but we fear that soldier is Mr. Hardy's soldier, and not one of the Dublin Fusiliers who cried amidst the storm of bullets at Tugela, 'Let us make a name for ourselves!' Here is another ideal which conflicts, alas! with the sublime message we celebrate today ... [5]

There is a basic Victorian conflict in this quarrel: between the idea of moral evolution upward – Hardy called it 'evolutionary meliorism' – and its opposite, which we might call Victorian Belligerence, or perhaps Romantic Imperialism. Hardy's Boer War poems contain a good deal of the former theme; it's a Victorian commonplace, and we may take it as a sign of this delusion's popularity that even the usually pessimistic Hardy shared it. It is present as a question at the end of 'Departure,' one of the embarkation poems:

> When shall the saner softer polities
> Whereof we dream, have play in each proud land
> And patriotism, grown Godlike, scorn to stand
> Bondslave to realms, but circle earth and seas?   (*CPW*, 1:117)

And more assertively in the closing poem of the group, 'The Sick Battle-god,' which ends:

> Let men rejoice, let men deplore,
> The lurid Deity of heretofore
> Succumbs to one of saner nod;
> The Battle-god is god no more.   (*CPW*, 1:131)

That pacific view of war stayed in his mind through the decade that followed; you find it, for example, in his 1913 poem, 'His Country,' with its one-world, antiwar marginal gloss: 'He travels southward, and looks around; / and cannot discover the boundary / of his native country; / or where his duties to his fellow-creatures end; / nor who are his enemies' (*CPW*, 2:290–1).

The other view, the Victorian-Belligerent one, was also in Hardy's mind, as he confessed in a letter to Mrs Henniker:

> I constantly deplore the fact that 'civilized' nations have not learnt some more excellent & apostolic way of settling disputes than the old & barbarous one, after all these centuries; but when I feel that it must be, few persons are more martial than I, or like better to write of war in prose & rhyme. (*CL*, 2:232)

But the martial Hardy didn't get into the Boer War poems. We must take his remark in this letter not as description, but as a promise of what was still to come – an epic poem of war that would be both civilized and barbarous.

And then the next war came: The Great War, the War that Would End War, the first Modern War. Hardy's immediate response was complicated because it contained both a private and a public, 'official' element. This was a war in which, almost from the first shot, English writers were organized, recruited, drafted into literary battalions for the support of the national effort. The war was not a month old when C.F.G. Masterman, the government official in charge of propaganda, summoned principal English writers to his office in Whitehall 'for the organization of public statements of the strength of the British case and principles in the war by well-known men of letters.' (This is Hardy's formulation of the project, from his own memorandum; *LW*, 395.)

Those men of letters included Robert Bridges, Sir James Barrie, Arnold Bennett, Hall Caine, G.K. Chesterton, Arthur Conan Doyle, Anthony Hope, Maurice Hewlett, Henry Newbolt, John Masefield, John Galsworthy, and H.G. Wells. Too old for the trenches (the youngest, Masefield, was thirty-six), most of them would have supported the war with their pens, officially or not. But Hardy seems different; at seventy-four he was the oldest of the lot, and he was the most private. Left to himself he might have written 'civilized' poems of private feeling, like those he had written during the Boer War; or he might have fallen silent, as other writers did. But he was summoned by his government, and he went. And having, as it were, enlisted, he returned to Max Gate and promptly wrote an appropriate 'public' poem. 'Men Who March Away' is dated 5 September 1914 – three days after the Whitehall meeting:

SONG OF THE SOLDIERS
What of the faith and fire within us
   Men who march away
   Ere the barn-cocks say
   Night is growing gray,
To hazards whence no tears can win us;
What of the faith and fire within us
   Men who march away?

Is it a purblind prank, O think you,
   Friend with the musing eye,
   Who watch us stepping by
   With doubt and dolorous sigh?
Can much pondering so hoodwink you!
Is it a purblind prank, O think you,
   Friend with the musing eye?

Nay. We see well what we are doing,
  Though some may not see –
  Dalliers as they be! –
  England's need are we;
Her distress would set us rueing:
Nay. We see well what we are doing,
  Though some may not see!

In our heart of hearts believing
  Victory crowns the just,
  And that braggarts must
  Surely bite the dust,
March we to the field ungrieving,
In our heart of hearts believing
  Victory crowns the just.

Hence the faith and fire within us
  Men who march away
  Ere the barn-cocks say
  Night is growing gray,
To hazards whence no tears can win us;
Hence the faith and fire within us
  Men who march away. [6]

Like the Boer embarkation poems, this is a poem of military departure, marching men observed by a stationary witness. ('You may possibly have suspected,' Hardy wrote to his friend Sydney Cockerell, 'the "Friend with the musing eye" to be the author himself' [CL, 5:48].) The situation is one that is common in Hardy: a sceptical poet-watcher, motionless, observing the actions of others. Usually that watcher sees what others do not see, but here it is the other way round; the watcher doubts, but the weight of the poem is with the soldiers, who believe in their war.

Hardy was not entirely pleased with the 'official' poem he had written. He wrote to his friend Arthur Symons of these lines: 'I fear they were not free from some banalities which it is difficult to keep out of lines which are meant to appeal to the man in the street ...' (CL, 5:48). And indeed it does seem to have been written against his deepest convictions about the war, if you compare it with poems like 'Drummer Hodge' and 'The Man He Killed.'

The general critical response to 'Men Who March Away' was very favourable – at least among civilian writers such as the men of letters who gathered at Masterman's meeting; it was good propaganda, the stuff, as we say, to feed the troops. But it was not admired by young soldier-poets: they knew better. Here is a passage from a letter written by Charles Sorley – nineteen years old, not yet a war poet, not yet even in France, but already aware of what was at issue:

> Curiously enough, I think that 'Men Who March Away' is the most arid poem in the book [*Satires of Circumstance*], besides being untrue of the sentiments of the ranksman going to war: 'Victory crowns the just' is the worst line he ever wrote – filched from a leading article in *The Morning Post*, and unworthy of him who had always previously disdained to insult Justice by offering it a material crown like Victory. [7]

What Sorley expresses in this letter is more than a difference of opinion. He is giving definition to a radical division in English society, between generations, and between civilians and soldiers – a division that will split English culture into two increasingly separate and hostile parts: the men who have fought and know what war is (and are therefore the young) versus those who have not (the Old Men – profiteers and politicians and generals – and the patriotic women). Out of this sense of division will come the antiwar literature, which is the only literature of that war that we still read, and which has established itself as the continuing Modern Myth of the War. Out of it will also come postwar modernism, and the cultural mood of the 1920s. War poems by Hardy like 'Men Who March Away' are not in that modern mode; they seem to place him on the *other* side of the division, with the Old Men and the fierce women. Most of his poems of the First World War fall on that side. No doubt that is why he called them collectively not simply 'War Poems,' but 'Poems of War and Patriotism': *patriotism*, the blustering virtue, is all some of them have – that and German-hating. They do not sound like Hardy, but they are there.

Hardy recognized the contradiction between those public poems and his private feelings. 'The difficulty about the war for men at home,' he wrote in a letter in 1915, 'is that what we feel about it we must not say, & what we must say about it we seldom think' (*CL*, 5:136). But he accepted the lies that war demanded, and imposed on his sense of the war's reality the romantic falsehoods of wartime convention. He sentimentalized the death of his young nephew Frank George, who was killed at Gallipoli (to call that bloody failure of a campaign a 'Game with Death,' as he does in 'Before Marching and After' [CPW, 2:297] is gross sentimentality). And he called down curses on the Germans, whom he represented in the atrocity images of current propaganda. He could not say of these poems, as he said of his Boer War poems, that 'not a single one is Jingo or Imperial.'

It is tempting to bundle up Hardy's 'official' war poems of 1914–18 and discard them all as the works of some other, inferior sensibility – Hardy-in-Whitehall, or the sum of Masterman's committee. It was not that clear, though; Hardy carried into the First World War some of the 'martial' spirit that had been in his head since childhood, the spirit he had found in *A History of the Wars* and the stories of the old men. How else are we to explain 'Then and Now,' written in 1915, in which he repeats with obvious approval the famous daft remark of Lord Charles Hay at the Battle of Fontenoy (1745)? According to legend, Lord Charles, commanding British troops against the French, invited the French guard to fire first. The French replied: 'We never fire first: *you* fire first.' Here is Hardy's version of that exchange:

> When battles were fought
> With chivalrous sense of Should and Ought,
>   In spirit men said,
>   'End we quick or dead,
>   Honour is some reward!
> Let us fight fair – for our own best or worst;
>   So, Gentlemen of the Guard,
>   Fire first!'

(CPW, 2:299)

One cannot explain away this foolish poem simply by assigning it to Hardy's false, 'official' voice, as though he wasn't responsible for it; he really believed what he said. Here, in support of its argument is a passage from a letter dated 28 August 1914:

> As for myself, the recognition that we are living in a more brutal age than that, say, of Elizabeth, or of the chivalry which could cry: 'Gentlemen of the Guard, fire first!' (far more brutal, indeed; no chivalry now!) does not inspire one to write hopeful poetry, or even conjectural prose, but simply make one sit still in an apathy, & watch the clock spinning backwards ...
> (CL, 5:45)

There are two Hardy voices in this passage, both audible, both true. One is the martial voice in love with the old wars, the voice that yearns for a war that would be chivalrous and honourable, and so, somehow, 'civilized.' The other is the dark inward voice, passive and dejected, shocked by the horrors of the war in progress, the voice that describes the war in private letters as 'the slaughter in progress,' 'this ghastly war,' 'this brutal European massacre,' 'an accursed thing.'

The 'Poems of War and Patriotism' are not very good poems – at least as bad as the Boer War poems, but in a different way. Not bad because Hardy did not have much to say, as in 1899–1901, but because what he had to say was trite, banal, 'martial,' propagandistic, jingoist, embarrassing to an admirer of his greatest lyrics. And because we sense in them his sad admission that 'what we feel about it we must not say.' The exceptions are few: one wartime poem, one poem forty years old, and one postwar poem – none of them directly concerned with the war itself.

'A New Year's Eve in War Time' is one of Hardy's 'literally true' poems: he had stood in his doorway at Max Gate on New Year's Eve, 1915, and had heard a horse gallop by just on the strike of midnight, 'as if Death astride came / To numb all with his knock.' The poem ends:

> What rider it bears
> There is none to proclaim;
> And the Old Year has struck,
> And, scarce animate,
> The New makes moan.
>
> Maybe that 'More Tears! –
> More Famine and Flame –
> More Severance and Shock!'
> Is the order from Fate
> That the Rider speeds on
> To pale Europe; and tiredly the pines intone.   (*CPW*, 2:303)

It is another of Hardy's silent, motionless poems: the poet-watcher stands and feels, but says nothing, does nothing, because there is nothing to be said or done.

The most memorable expression of the private Hardy voice is in his shortest war poem, the exquisite little lyric 'In Time of "The Breaking of Nations."' The story of its composition is well known – Hardy told it in the *Life and Work*, how he had the experience in the Cornish countryside in 1870, while he was courting his first wife, Emma Gifford; how he watched a farm worker harrowing the arable land while in Europe the Franco-Prussian battle of Gravelotte was being fought; and how he buried that image and its emotion for more than forty years before resurrecting it in the second year of the Great War (*LW*, 82–3, 408).

> Only a man harrowing clods
>   In a slow silent walk
> With an old horse that stumbles and nods
>   Half asleep as they stalk.
>
> Only thin smoke without flame
>   From the heaps of couch-grass;
> Yet this will go onward the same
>   Though Dynasties pass.
>
> Yonder a maid and her wight
>   Come whispering by:
> War's annals will cloud into night
>   Ere their story die.   (*CPW*, 2:295–6)

An extraordinary poem – a *pastoral* war poem, so small in scale, so local, yet containing in it the fall of dynasties, the theme that informs Hardy's vast epic drama, and so reminds us of the continuing presence in his imagination of war's claim to greatness – and the universe's denial of that claim. One wants those twelve lines to contain and define the true, essential Hardy-on-war. And so perhaps they do; for they express the theme of endurance and survival and even hope, which runs through *The Dynasts* and which has the last word in the final Chorus of the Pities, and appears in lyrics like 'The Darkling Thrush' – the hope that Hardy could not justify philosophically or historically, but could not eradicate from his own heart.

In December 1918, a month after the end of the war, Hardy copied out 'Men Who March Away' for his friend Henry Newbolt, and sent it to him with a short note. 'My mind goes back,' he wrote,

> to the row of poor young fellows in straw hats who had fallen-in in front of our County Hall here – lit by the September sun, whom my rather despondent eye surveyed.

> Well, it is all over now – at least I suppose so. I confess that I take a smaller interest in the human race since this outburst than I did before. (*CL*, 5:289)

And, one might add, a smaller interest in war. The First World War was over, but hope had not triumphed over despair. There had been no epic grandeur in its devastation, no Hector and no Achilles among its troops, nor any Napoleon or Wellington or Nelson. There was no rejoicing in Hardy's message to Newbolt, and none in his heart. He had never expected much of human beings, or of the universe in which they struggled; but the war had lowered his expectations still further. And that, for him, had been its only consequence.

The great poem of this mood, and Hardy's last war poem, is, appropriately, not about the war but about the ending of it. It is titled 'And there was a great calm' (as so often, in moments of profound emotion Hardy turned to the Bible for the best phrase), and subtitled 'On the Signing of the Armistice, Nov. 11, 1918.' It is the one poem in English I know of that records the emotions of that moment with a due sense of their complexity, and the only poem of Hardy's 1914–18 war poems that has entered the canon of First World War verse – one poem among the works of the young soldier-poets by a noncombatant who was old enough to remember the Charge of the Light Brigade.

'And There Was a Great Calm' celebrates nothing. It doesn't say who won or who lost, or why they were fighting, or whether the best side triumphed. It says, rather, what Hardy had said privately at the war's beginning, that the war, simply by happening, had destroyed the dream of human progress that Hardy had believed in, in the prewar years, until the 'old hopes that earth was bettering slowly/Were dead and damned.' Rhetorically the poem begins in abstractions – Passion, Despair, Anger, Selflessness – and proceeds by emptying itself of them, until it ends in unmodified particulars – the guns silent, the horses not whipped, because the war is ended. Over the vast ruined battlefield the Spirits from *The Dynasts* hover, denying to this war the epic grandeur that Hardy found in the Napoleonic wars.

Here is the final stanza:

> Calm fell. From Heaven distilled a clemency;
> There was peace on earth, and silence in the sky;
> Some could, some could not, shake off misery:
> The Sinister Spirit sneered: 'It had to be!'
> And again the Spirit of Pity whispered, 'Why?'   (*CPW*, 2:357)

An empty earth and a silent sky, continuing misery for some, and empty fatalism for others, and an unanswered questioning of it all: Hardy had come, at the end, to the point that soldier-poets had also reached – the same bitter vision of war, and of humankind's unalterable capacity for violence against itself.

It is not surprising that those young poets admired him, and traced their poetical descent from him. The evidence is everywhere, in the poems of Sassoon, Graves, and Blunden among the survivors, and of Sorley and Edward Thomas among the dead. He was their ancestor, they were his heirs. (Sassoon and Blunden carried *The Dynasts* with them into the trenches.) What they inherited was partly the starkly formal style, in which one could talk about war without dishonesty and without high rhetoric, and partly the dark vision of existence. But there was another element, too – the Spirit of Pity; Wilfred Owen, you will remember, said of his poems: 'The poetry is in the Pity.'

The history of Hardy's poetic wars is a history of war in his lifetime – not of actual fighting, but of the evolution of ideas and feelings about war during the nearly three quarters of a century during which he wrote. In that time the romance of war receded and its epic grandeur faded. So did the hope that humankind would evolve upward, beyond the use of force against each other. Hardy's poems (including *The Dynasts*) chart those lost imaginings. They also chart a sensitive man's awareness of the sufferings that war inflicted on helpless men and women in his time, and most terribly as war became *modern* war. Hardy never got closer to actual war than the Dorchester street corner from which he watched the young men of Wessex march away; but he felt wars – as a common soldier might feel them, or a general; or a soldier's wife; or a war horse, a coney, an earthworm. And as the presiding Spirits of the universe – the Sinister Spirit, the Ironic Spirit, and the Spirit of the Pities – would feel them, if such spirits existed outside his own head.

War was an important part of the furnishings of Hardy's imagination, as it is of the imaginations of all of us. For war, like love, is a primal subject: we cannot *not* think about it, it is there in our minds because it is in our lives – changing as wars change, and as the hopes and gullibilities of people change, but there. Hardy's wars changed, too, from romantic continental battles commanded by heroes to wars that might be transcended by morally evolving humanity, to the final recognition that war is barbaric and destructive because men are, and always will be.

When Hardy dictated his autobiography to his second wife, Florence, shortly after the First World War, he described the changes that had occurred in the war in his head:

A long study of the European wars of a century earlier had made it appear to him that common-sense had taken the place of bluster in men's minds; and he felt this so strongly that in the very year before war burst on Europe he wrote some verses called 'His Country', bearing on the decline of antagonism between peoples; and as long before as 1901 he composed a poem called 'The Sick Battle-God', which assumed that zest for slaughter was dying out. It was seldom he had felt so heavy at heart as in seeing his old view of the gradual bettering of human nature, as expressed in these verses of 1901, completely shattered by the events of 1914 and onwards. War, he had supposed, had grown too coldly scientific to kindle again for long all the ardent romance which had characterized it down to Napoleonic times, when the most intense battles were over in a day, and the most exciting tactics and strategy led to the death of comparatively few combatants. Hence nobody was more amazed than he at the German incursion into Belgium, and the contemplation of it led him to despair of the world's history thenceforward. (*LW*, 394–5)

From romance, to evolutionary meliorism, to pity and despair – you can follow those imaginings in Hardy's writings about war, from the early notes for an epic through to his dark postwar despair in 'And There Was a Great Calm.' And you can see that there was one stretch of years in that arc, from the end of the last Victorian war to the middle of the first modern one, when a great poet could still write an epic of war because he could hold in his imagination at one time war's grandeur and war's pity. In those years he wrote his most monumental work and his most perfect small lyric, both war poems, and then was silenced by the reality of the war that came.

NOTES

1 Thomas Hardy, *The Life and Work of Thomas Hardy*, ed. Michael Millgate (London: Macmillan, 1984), 21. Hereafter cited parenthetically as *LW*.

2 Collected in *Thomas Hardy's Personal Writings*, ed. Harold Orel (London: Macmillan, 1967), 13–14.

3 *The Complete Poetical Works of Thomas Hardy*, ed. Samuel Hynes, 5 vols (Oxford: Clarendon, 1982–95), 1:24, 27, 46. Hereafter cited parenthetically as *CPW*.

4 *Collected Letters of Thomas Hardy*, ed. Richard Little Purdy and Michael

Millgate, 7 vols (Oxford: Clarendon, 1978–88), 2:277. Hereafter cited parenthetically as *CL*.

5 *London Daily Chronicle*, 25 December 1899, quoted in *CPW*, 1:368.

6 The quoted text is the version published in *The Times*, 9 September 1914, 9. For the version as collected in *Moments of Vision* (1917), see *CPW*, 2:289–90.

7 Charles Hamilton Sorley, *The Letters of Charles Sorley* (Cambridge: Cambridge University Press, 1919), 246.

14 Opening Time: Hardy's Poetic Thresholds

NORMAN PAGE

Broadly speaking, Hardy's ways of opening a work of fiction lean towards the traditional and the conservative, while his ways of opening a poem are often original, innovative, and – to make use of an epithet with a peculiarly Hardyan resonance – idiosyncratic. This is perhaps no more than a specific instance of the general truth, no less true for being a platitude, that he is a Victorian novelist and a modern poet; but it seems worth looking more closely at the distinctive nature of that originality, and the focus of this essay will be on the first word or words of his poem openings.

To point the contrast between his fictional and his poetic practice, however, I begin with a novelistic beginning, the first sentence of one of his mature works:

> One evening of late summer, before the nineteenth century had reached one-third of its span, a young man and woman, the latter carrying a child, were approaching the large village of Weydon Priors, in Upper Wessex, on foot.[1]

Hardy's plots have been compared to farm carts – old-fashioned and lumbering, but capable of bearing the load – and there is in this sentence something of the same creaking sense of overcoming inertia and setting out on what promises to be a long journey. In its scrupulous, almost pedantic specifying of time of day, season, period, topography or pseudotopography, and human figures and their mode of locomotion, this kind of opening looks back to Sir Walter Scott even though it is much closer in date to the modernists. There is a significant echo in this novel of the 1880s to a novel of the 1840s, Thackeray's *Vanity Fair* ('before the nineteenth century had reached one-third of its span' adapting the earlier writer's 'While the present century was in its teens'),[2] as well as a more muted echo of all those fictional narratives that present a journey, of which the most celebrated is Bunyan's *The Pilgrim's Progress*. The cunning vagueness about the identity of the three characters, whose names are not to be divulged for some time, is not at first apparent.

Nothing here, then, that anticipates the studied casualness of the novelists of the next generation – of, for instance, E.M. Forster's *Howards End* (1910) ('One may as well begin with Helen's letters to her sister')[3] – nor for that matter anything to compete with the bold experimentation of some of Hardy's Victorian predecessors, such as the one-word opening sentence of Dickens's *Bleak House* (1853), or the impassioned abruptness with which the reader is thrust into the no less bleak world, bereft of comfort and heavy with negativity, of *Jane Eyre* (1847): 'There was no possibility of taking a walk that day.'[4]

Not that Hardy would have minded this charge, or diagnosis, of traditionalism and conservatism, or had any reason to do so. But for boldness and experimentation we need to turn to the poems. Nearly all of them are short, many of them are very short, and it goes without saying that in a text of this kind there is simply no room for a leisurely, expansive exordium. But Hardy's practice often goes well beyond the requirements of directness and succinctness, and surprise – not with a Keatsian 'fine excess' but by coming at the reader from an unexpected angle.

Here is the opening line of 'He Never Expected Much' (an idiosyncratic title if ever there was one):

'Well, World, you have kept faith with me ...'[5]

The quiet audacity of the first two words is hard to match anywhere in English poetry: the first note struck is one of modest ruminativeness, immediately followed by the disclosure that the addressee is existence itself. The introductory 'Well' does not normally initiate a discourse; in, for example, a political interview or in the classroom it is a standard response to a question, sometimes a modest disclaimer, sometimes a mere playing for time. Standing as the first word of a poem, it creates in the reader the sense of something having gone before. In its way this opening is as original as that of Hemingway's *A Moveable Feast* (1964): 'Then there was the bad weather.'[6]

Hardy was not the first poet to open a poem with this kind of conversational gambit. Donne, for instance, adopts such strategies, either musingly, as in 'I Wonder by my troth, what thou, and I / Did, till we lov'd,' or peremptorily, as in 'For Godsake hold your tongue, and let me love.'[7] The musing rather than the peremptory, with its impatient imperatives, is Hardy's style, and he uses the considering 'Well ...' in two other poems: in the humorous dialogue poem 'Liddell and Scott' ('Well, though it seems / Beyond our dreams ...' [CPW, 3:176]), and the monologue 'A Philosophical Fantasy' ('Well, if thou wilt, then, ask me ...' [CPW, 3:234]), though the quasi-dramatic form of these makes its use less striking than in the more directly personal 'He Never Expected Much.'

But if the initial 'Well' produces in the reader a frisson of surprise, the collocation with the word that follows is even more unexpected. If the 'Well' opening is followed by an indication of the recipient of the response, this will normally be in the form of a proper name or some such phrase as 'my dear.' What Hardy gives us is a quite unexpected switch from the domestic to the universal: from relaxed informality to the contemplation of life itself.

A different kind of colloquial opening is represented by a group of poems in which the first word is 'Yes' or 'No.' Whatever the significance of the contrast may be, while there are seven instances of poems beginning with 'Yes' (in one case it is 'Yea'), there are thirteen that start with a negative of one kind or another ('No,' 'Not,' 'Nobody,' 'Nothing'). Hardy had a striking and well-known exemplar for the negative opening in his favourite Keats, whose 'Ode on Melancholy' begins 'No, no, go not to Lethe ...'[8] and this is perhaps consciously echoed in 'Paths of Former Time': 'No, no; / It must not be so ...' (CPW, 2:277). Hardy's is so often a poetry of absences, disappointments, and deprivations that these negatives cause no surprise, and a poem sometimes seems to take its origin from the sad reflection that something is not: 'Nobody Comes,' like 'A Broken Appointment,' is about a hoped-for event that does not happen, while another kind of failure is the starting-point for 'Places': 'Nobody says: Ah, that is the place ...' (CPW, 2:64).

Questioning and speculating are also characteristic Hardyan opening moves, and there are numerous poems that open with 'When,' 'Why,' 'If,' or similar gambits. It is not surprising that 'Why' openings are prominent in the 'Poems of 1912–13' sequence, reflecting Hardy's sense of shock and bewilderment at what he presents as a sudden and unexpected loss. In addition there are poems that, without making use of such words, open with a question, as does 'The Blinded Bird' ('So zestfully canst thou sing?' [CPW, 2:181]).

The effect produced by these colloquial or conversational openings is to suggest that the poem is in the nature of a fragment rather than a complete entity, and that the reader has, so to speak, entered a discourse already in progress. This is of course very different from the effect produced by the opening of *The Mayor of Casterbridge*, where there is a strong sense of the opening as an opening. It has been said of Tennyson that he favours in his poetic narratives the kind of conclusion in which nothing is concluded, and one may say of Hardy that he favours the kind of opening that appears to be nothing of the kind. A Hardy poem, indeed, is quite likely to open in a manner resembling a modernist novel: when Woolf writes 'Mrs Dalloway said she would buy the flowers herself'[9] there is a similar sense of something, unread and unreadable, having preceded the first line of the text. It is 'Mrs Dalloway,' as we might refer to someone already familiar and without further identification, and it is 'the flowers' – the definite article implying flowers whose nature or purpose is already known, and that have formed the topic of some discussion prior to the text itself – rather than 'flowers' or 'some flowers.'

Much more pervasive than this kind of opening gambit, however, is the use of a pronoun (or, in a few cases, its related possessive adjective) with no obvious referent. Indeed, the earliest of all Hardy's surviving poems, 'Domicilium,' opens in this manner: 'It faces west ...' (*CPW*, 3:279). There are plenty of precedents for this: Wordsworth's lyric beginning 'She dwelt among the untrodden ways' does not name the 'She' until the tenth of its twelve lines, and his 'She was a Phantom of delight' provides no identification more precise than 'a perfect Woman.' But Hardy employs this kind of opening with remarkable frequency. There are in the *Complete Poetical Works* nineteen poems beginning 'She' or 'Her,' fourteen beginning 'He,' fifteen beginning 'You' or 'Your,' thirty beginning 'We' or 'Our,' and fourteen beginning 'They.'

In a few cases, it should be said, a reference is provided by the title of the poem: thus the opening 'Not a line of her writing have I' – an archetypal Hardyan opening in its combination of pronouns and negative – is preceded by the title 'Thoughts of Phena ...' (*CPW*, 1:81). More often, however, the initial air of mystery and secretiveness remains unqualified, and sometimes the mystery remains unsolved at the end of the poem. A case in point is the haunting 'During Wind and Rain,' where the mystifying opening 'They sing their dearest songs' is followed by a line that deepens rather than clearing up the puzzle: 'He, she, all of them ...' (*CPW*, 2:239). The pronoun 'They' opens each of the poem's four stanzas but remains unexplained, and one has a sense of something intensely private, almost unspeakable.

By a very long way, though, Hardy's favourite pronoun to stand as the first word of a poem is 'I' (and, to a much smaller extent, the related 'My'). The total here is the staggering figure of 162 instances, or approximately one-sixth of all his poems, and just how remarkable this is can be seen by comparison with Wordsworth, whose collected poems provide just eleven poems beginning with the first person singular. If Wordsworth was, as Keats suggested, an example of 'the egotistical sublime,' where does this leave Hardy? A Wordsworthian poem seems much more likely to open in a declarative manner – 'There was a time ...'[10] – and his subjectivity does not take the form of the Hardyan intimacy, as if addressing a single individual and imparting some intensely private matter in confidence – or even as if talking to himself with no thought of an audience.

Moreover, the ratio of approximately one in six poems beginning with the first person singular is actually much higher if we take into account a further and considerable group of poems in which 'I,' without being the first word, occurs very early in the first line: 'The Last Signal' ('Silently I footed by an uphill road'), 'After a Journey' ('Hereto I come to view a voiceless ghost'), and 'At Castle Boterel' ('As I drive to the junction'), to cite just three very familiar examples (CPW, 2:212, 59, 63).

In a strict sense the initial 'I' might also be said to be a pronoun without a clear referent, but except for a few ballads and narrative poems, and others where the speaker is plainly not the poet himself, most readers will probably be prepared to identify the first person singular in such poems as 'The Impercipient,' 'The Darkling Thrush,' and 'I look into my glass' with the historical Thomas Hardy, and there is a sense in which his collected poems constitute an extended, albeit somewhat fragmentary, autobiography, covering his long life from infancy ('The Self-Unseeing,' 'Childhood among the Ferns') through the pains of early love ('Neutral Tones'), and the friendships and infatuations of a lifetime, to the death of Emma and old age. The favourite 'I,' therefore, can be seen as the natural mode of the autobiographer.

The total number of pronoun openings in Hardy's verse – that is, poems in which the very first word is a pronoun – is, by my count, 244, or about one in four of all his poems, and if we add to this figure the poems in which a pronoun makes its appearance in the first two or three words the number is considerably higher. I suspect it would be difficult to match this in any other English writer. For another comparison with a Romantic poet who exerted an influence on Hardy, while the Keatsian canon (157 items in a standard edition) is of course much smaller than Hardy's, it is striking that Keats's use of the initial pronoun is insignificant: just one example each of 'He,' 'You,' and 'They,' none at all of 'She' or 'We,' and, most surprising of all, only four of 'I.'

The effect of using a pronoun rather than a noun or proper name can be suggested by comparing the opening lines of two poems addressed to famous poets: Wordsworth's 'Milton! Thou shouldst be living at this hour'[11] and Auden's 'He disappeared in the dead of winter.' It might be said, of course, that the reader is left in no doubt as to the referent of Auden's initial pronoun, since above the first line stands the title 'In Memory of W.B. Yeats.'[12] Auden is not posing a conundrum, but it seems undeniable that he promotes a sense of intimacy, of closeness to both reader and subject, that is altogether absent from the Wordsworthian apostrophe, whose orotund formality creates a sense of distance and implies that great men stand apart like statues on lofty plinths.

An instructive case study for Hardy's practice is the great sequence of elegies 'Poems of 1912–13.' The present-day reader comes to these exhaustively briefed by generations of pertinacious biographical enquiry, and the life, personality, illness, and death of Emma, and Hardy's changing relationship to her and reactions to her loss, are all intimately familiar matters. But Emma's name does not appear from beginning to end of the sequence. In the first line of the first poem she is 'You,' later 'She' and even 'I,' but the reader who comes to these poems, as many of the first readers presumably did, ignorant of the poet's personal life, is left to guess. It is true that no very ingenious detective work is called for: it quickly becomes clear that there has been a death, that the dead person is a woman, and that her life has been intimately intertwined with that of the speaker, who in 'A Circular' goes so far as to identify himself wryly as her '"legal representative"' (CPW 2:58). Still, the fact – and I believe it is a revealing one – remains that Hardy bypasses the identification of his subject, and there is certainly nothing in the series' noncommittal title or the brief Latin epigraph to offer much assistance. The 'old flame' of the latter might even be misinterpreted as pointing to a long-lost lover rather than a lawful wife.

It is, at least at first, as if Hardy were quite unaware of a potential reader for the poems he regarded as very private but nevertheless did not show any great reluctance to publish. When Milton writes that 'Lycidas is dead'[13] or Shelley writes 'I weep for Adonais,'[14] these observations are clearly directed at an audience and the subject is being held at a distance. Their rhetorical tone, however, is in stark contrast to the Hardyan voice, so restrained as to be, as it were, barely audible. In many of these poems Hardy seems engaged in earnest private colloquy with the dead woman, so that the first poem opens 'Why did you give no hint ...,' the second is titled 'Your Last Drive,' and the third begins 'You did not walk with me.' It is not until we reach the fourth that the second person shifts to the third, the reader or listener enters the picture, and we find 'Clouds spout upon her,' followed by 'I found her out there' as the opening of the fifth. Thereafter there is much shifting between the dead woman as interlocutor and as subject of a confessional address to the reader: the sixth poem has 'It was your way, my dear,' and the next one 'How she would have loved / A party.' The eighth poem in the sequence begins with an unexpected pronoun, 'He': the roles are temporarily reversed and the dead woman is now addressing the survivor. But in the ninth we are back to the apostrophe, 'Woman much missed' (*CPW*, 2:47, 48, 49, 50, 51, 53, 55, 56).

The necessary points have been made and it is not necessary to lengthen this catalogue of openings in the 'Poems of 1912–13.' It is clear that pronouns dominate and produce, as they so often do elsewhere in Hardy's verse, a sense that the reader is not being directly addressed but is overhearing something very private and confidential. There was a streak of voyeurism in Hardy, and the voyeur is a recurrent figure in his fiction; but in his verse he sometimes puts the reader in the slightly uncomfortable position of being a voyeur – or, if the word can be employed in this sense, an auditeur.

'Poems of 1912–13' is Hardy's post-Victorian version of the most celebrated poem of the Victorian age, 'In Memoriam.' Tennyson, for reasons that are, psychologically speaking, of absorbing interest, initially kept the reader at bay: he first resisted the idea of finishing the poem, then performed the transparently Freudian act of mislaying the manuscript, then refused to allow the work to be published, and finally declined to have his name placed on the title page during his lifetime. But when it did at last appear in print, seventeen years after its beginning, he went as far as to identify Hallam by his initials, which form part of the title. More importantly, throughout much of the poem the dead man is a somewhat remote figure and Tennyson's sense of an audience to be moved, exhorted, and persuaded is strong. But then Tennyson, though perfectly capable of brooding introspection and coded autobiography, was for much of his career, and especially in the latter part of it, a public poet in a way that Hardy, despite occasional forays into the public sphere such as 'The Convergence of the Twain' and the war poems, was very far from aspiring to. It is true that in the poem sequences under discussion Hardy was writing much closer to the event than Tennyson, but in any case his temperament dictated a more reticent approach – one for which the pronoun-openings are an apt counterpart and vehicle.

NOTES

1 Thomas Hardy, *The Mayor of Casterbridge* (Oxford: Oxford University Press, 1987), 5.
2 William Makepeace Thackeray, *Vanity Fair*, ed. Geoffrey and Kathleen Tillotson (Cambridge, MA: Riverside, 1963), 11.
3 E.M. Forster, *Howard's End* (Harmondsworth: Penguin, 1975), 19.
4 Charlotte Brontë, *Jane Eyre* (Oxford: Oxford University Press, 2000), 7.
5 *The Complete Poetical Works of Thomas Hardy*, ed. Samuel Hynes, 5 vols (Oxford: Clarendon, 1982–95), 3:225. Hereafter *CPW*.
6 Ernest Hemingway, *A Moveable Feast* (London: Jonathan Cape, 1964), 9.
7 *The Poems of John Donne*, ed. Herbert J.C. Grierson, 2 vols (Oxford: Oxford University Press, 1966), 7, 14.
8 *The Poems of John Keats*, ed. Miriam Allott (London: Longman, 1970), 539.
9 Virginia Woolf, *Mrs Dalloway* (Oxford: Oxford University Press, 1992), 3.
10 William Wordsworth, 'Ode: Intimations of Immortality,' in *Poems*, ed. John O. Hayden, 2 vols (Harmondsworth: Penguin, 1977), 1:523. Hardy's rare declarative poetic openings – one of which, consciously or unconsciously, actually plays on the opening to Wordsworth's Ode ('A time there was' from 'Before Life and After' [*CPW*, 1:333]) – occur only in some of his 'philosophical' poems.
11 Wordsworth, 'London, 1802,' in *Poems* 1:579.
12 W.H. Auden, *Collected Shorter Poems 1930–1944* (London: Faber and Faber, 1950), 64.
13 'Lycidas,' in *John Milton*, ed. Stephen Orgel and Jonathan Goldberg (Oxford: Oxford University Press, 1990), 39.
14 'Adonais,' in *Shelley: Poetical Works*, ed. Thomas Hutchinson (London: Oxford University Press, 1968), 432.

15 Thomas Hardy and the Powyses

W.J. KEITH

John Cowper Powys's first publication, *Odes and Other Poems* (1896), contains an effusive and indifferent poem addressed to Thomas Hardy.[1] The young writer duly sent a copy to Hardy, who not only acknowledged it but invited him to visit Max Gate. At that first meeting, John Cowper was bold enough to ask Hardy and his first wife to pay a return visit to Montacute to meet his parents along with his younger siblings, and the Hardys – rather surprisingly, we may feel – accepted. The whole story is told with characteristic vitality in John Cowper's *Autobiography*.[2] So began Hardy's complex relationship with the most talented, prolific, and artistically diverse English literary family in the first half of the twentieth century, a family which, it can be argued, collectively inherited Hardy's mantle on his death in 1928.

The Powyses had a long-standing and continuing connection with the geographical area now known as Hardy's Wessex. The father, Charles Francis Powys, was born – 'like Tess of the d'Urbervilles,' as John Cowper notes (*Autobiography*, 152) – in the Vale of Blackmoor, in Stalbridge, of a long line of country clergymen. Though he served for some years as vicar of Shirley in Derbyshire, where his first five children, including John Cowper and Theodore (T.F.), were born, the family regularly spent their summer holidays in Weymouth, home of the paternal grandmother. Inheriting a small fortune on the death of his elder brother, the father chose in 1879 to accept a modest curacy at St Peter's, Dorchester, so that he could be closer to his mother during her declining years. There another three children (including Llewelyn) were born in the next six years. Coincidentally, during the last two of these years they were fairly close neighbours of the Hardys, who had rented Shire-Place Hall while Max Gate was being planned and built. There is no indisputable record, however, of any contact at this time. In 1885 the father was appointed vicar of Montacute, just over the Dorset border in Somerset, which became the birthplace of the last three children, and the Powys centre for some thirty years.

Ten of the eleven children survived infancy, most of them settling in Wessex and displaying some kind of literary or artistic talent. The best-known are, of course, John Cowper (1872–1963), Theodore Francis (1875–1953), and Llewelyn (1884–1939), and I shall be concentrating on their relationship with Hardy in the following pages. John Cowper spent only a year (1934–5) of his adult life in Dorchester between an itinerant career as travelling lecturer (mainly in North America) and his settling in Wales in his later years, but he regularly visited his brothers and sisters, and most of his novels from *Wood and Stone* (1915) to *Maiden Castle* (1936) had Wessex settings. Theodore, the most independent and reclusive of the family, farmed briefly in Suffolk before returning to Dorset, living in East Chaldon (Chaldon Herring) between 1904 and 1940, and then at Mappowder until his death. Llewelyn spent some time in the United States with John Cowper, in Kenya with his younger brother Will, and at various sanatoriums in Switzerland, but lived for a significant part of his life at the White Nose and Chydyok, both places close to Theodore and not far from Hardy at Max Gate.

Evidence for a quite considerable and enduring relationship between Hardy and the Powyses is available but widely dispersed; it will therefore be useful here to bring at least the more revealing of the scattered pieces together. A warning, however, needs to be registered at the outset. Most of this evidence depends on the testimony of the Powyses, often in the form of recollections written down or recorded long after the events in question – recollections that, while sincerely intended as truth, may have been heightened or even distorted by the passing of time. Thus comments by John Cowper towards the end of his life to the effect that Hardy had 'taught' or 'instructed' him as a boy[3] conflict with the statement in *Autobiography* (181) that he had never even heard of Hardy until leaving Cambridge in 1894. He may, in fact, have heard of him slightly earlier. Llewelyn reports how Walter Raymond praised Hardy to John Cowper 'a few years' before 1896.[4]

Besides, the Powyses were great myth-makers, many of their stories being, in words Hardy employed on another occasion, 'well-found rather than well-founded.'[5] Kate Kavanagh, in an editorial comment accompanying a recently reprinted article by David Garnett, has suggested that many of the stories circulated about Theodore were either 'invented by Theodore himself ... to see how much [Sylvia Townsend Warner] would swallow' or reflect 'Theodore and Sylvia jointly ... enjoying the creation of a character called "T.F. Powys."'[6] For example, something is clearly wrong with Theodore's claim, reported by his son Francis[7] and repeated elsewhere, that he had carved his initials alongside Hardy's on a desk in Dorchester Grammar School (which Hardy did not attend). Even Llewelyn, who mainly wrote nonfiction, tended to create literary effects poised deceptively between genuine memory and artful invention.

One must therefore step warily. Nonetheless, many records occur in letters and diaries that we have no reason to distrust, and others can be confirmed by independent reports. The following account, drawing on a wide range of sources that interconnect impressively with each other, may be accepted as generally reliable.

The relation begins, of course, with Hardy's postcard (no longer extant) inviting John Cowper to visit Max Gate in 1896. There the young man was shown the manuscript of Tess of the d'Urbervilles (Autobiography, 228), and the whole experience so impressed him that he made a personal vow 'to write a good book.'[8] The Montacute visit receives its fullest description in his Autobiography, but many of its details were later borne out by Llewelyn (Theodore was by this time farming in Suffolk). Llewelyn, indeed, added to the story by recounting his own precocious conversation with Hardy about Montacute antiquities and 'the quaint and picturesque dances that took place at our village festivals.'[9] At this point, however, it may be desirable to point out that what is probably the best-known account of this occasion within Hardy studies, in James Gibson's Thomas Hardy: A Literary Life, contains a number of inaccuracies.[10]

Llewelyn first visited the Hardys after leaving Cambridge in 1906, when he was thrilled by Hardy's telling him that he was 'occupied with The Dynasts' ('Recollections,' 65). Later, in 1913, he sent Hardy a copy of his first publication, a lugubrious essay appropriately entitled 'Death,' about which Hardy wrote the briefest of formal replies.[11] John Cowper, however, continued to write letters praising Hardy's work,[12] visited again in 1918 after Hardy's second marriage, and reported to Llewelyn that he had had 'a perfectly lovely time' with Hardy, adding: 'I rather like his little wife.'[13] By this time, indeed, he was himself listed by Hardy among 'old friends' (LW, 417). The following year, just returned from Kenya, Llewelyn paid another visit and was chagrined to discover that Hardy did not remember him,[14] though continued relations between the families are implied by Llewelyn's subsequent statement that the visit had been 'arranged' by his artist sister Gertrude ('Recollections,' 67).

This visit led to the first of two critical periods in the relations between Llewelyn and Hardy. He had written up the visit in the *Dial* in 1922, and included details that, recounted to them at second hand by Amy Lowell, annoyed the Hardys, Florence writing to the American book-collector Paul Lemperly: 'We were told he was a lion hunter from central Africa, and he proved to be a lion hunter of another type.'[15] It took a diplomatic visit from John Cowper in the summer to smooth out the contretemps (*LL*, 1:294–5). This incident led to the cancellation of Theodore's proposed visit to Max Gate ('Recollections,' 69–70) – and he refused again two years later with the Theodore-like excuse that Mrs Hardy's dogs 'might mistake me for an American'![16] But a visit did take place in 1925, after which he commented: 'What a wonderful old man. And she was kind too.'[17] John Cowper also reports visiting Hardy with Theodore, when he 'almost petrified the old gentleman by his stern aspect.'[18]

Shortly thereafter, further tension occurred when Llewelyn quoted a comment of Theodore's about Hardy in the first (American) edition of *Skin for Skin*,[19] which gave 'offence at Max Gate.' But Llewelyn wrote a letter of apology, the offending passage was omitted from the forthcoming English edition, and peace was restored.[20] Astonishingly, as late as 1926 or early in 1927 Hardy apparently even made an attempt to call upon Llewelyn and his wife Alyse Gregory when they were living in a remote coastguard cottage on open downland near the White Nose, but the long and by no means easy walk proved too much for him. Soon afterwards, however, Llewelyn and Alyse were once again guests at Max Gate ('Recollections,' 70).

After Hardy's death in 1928, the relationship between Florence and the Powyses continued. In 1930 she sent lavender from Max Gate to John Cowper while he was living in New York.[21] In 1931 Llewelyn attended the unveiling of the Hardy statue in Dorchester,[22] and in August 1932 he and his wife spent a night at Max Gate.[23] During John Cowper's stay in Dorchester, we hear of half a dozen meetings (*Dorset*, 44, 118, 145, 147, 239, 286), and also of Florence's generous assistance to all three brothers: to John Cowper in negotiations leading to Cassells accepting *Maiden Castle* and *The Pleasures of Literature* (*LL*, 2:241–2); to Theodore in similar behind-the-scenes action that resulted in a Civil

List pension; and to the ailing Llewelyn in providing a car to enable him to be present at a libel case in which he was one of the defendants.[24] John Cowper subsequently praised her as 'one of the best friends my brother Theodore and I have ever had or are likely to have.'[25]

This account of the relations between the Hardys and the Powyses should not end without reference to a further brother, Albert Reginald (A.R.), who pursued a career in architecture and became Secretary to the Society for the Protection of Ancient Buildings, an organization close to Hardy's heart. As early as 1919, the two had had a brief correspondence (CL, 5:296), and subsequently exchanged letters about the state of Stoke Poges Church and of Judge Jeffreys' lodgings in Dorchester (CL 6:207, 7:17). But the most interesting exchange (CL 6:226) concerned the church at Winterborne Tomson, which became almost an obsession with A.R. Indeed, after Hardy's death, funds for the restoration were made possible in part by the sale, appropriately enough, of 'some reports and specifications written by Hardy' for the Society, and the manuscript of 'Memories of Church Restoration,' an address originally given at a Society meeting.[26] Restoration was completed in 1932, and A.R. was buried in the adjoining churchyard four years later. Along with John Cowper, Theodore, and other members of the Powys family, Florence was present at the funeral.[27]

It seems clear, then, that mainstream literary historians have generally underestimated the strong personal connections between Hardy and the Powys family. Certainly, enthusiasm for Hardy's work is evident throughout the Powys literature; it can be found in their letters, in book dedications (John Cowper's *Wood and Stone* [1915], Llewelyn's *Thirteen Worthies* [1924]), and the numerous lectures and articles that both John Cowper and Llewelyn devoted to him. For example, when Llewelyn accompanied his eldest brother on a lecture tour to North America in December 1908, one of his first lectures was on Hardy. This was recently published in the *Powys Society Newsletter*, and Peter J. Foss (2001) later argued convincingly that it shows distinct signs of having been strongly influenced, even largely dictated, by John Cowper.[28] When Hardy died, both brothers were again in North America, and both published what were in fact obituary articles, John Cowper in *Current History* (March 1928), Llewelyn in the *New York Herald Tribune* (22 January 1928).

As literary criticism, the Powyses' discussions of Hardy's work are now, by and large, of little more than historical interest. In one respect, however, their admiration was notably in advance of its time. James

Gibson has recently written: 'Nearly seventy years after his death Hardy is being increasingly seen as one of the very greatest English writers because of his achievement in both the novel and poetry.'[29] Yet the Powyses had been well aware of this a century ago. John Cowper was lecturing on Hardy's poetry as early as 1902.[30] In 1905 Louis Wilkinson had given the young Llewelyn a copy of *Poems of the Past and the Present*,[31] and during his convalescent stay at Davos Platz (1910–11) his Aunt Dora read him Hardy's poems,[32] while Llewelyn himself read them to a girl with whom he was infatuated.[33] In 1914 Llewelyn and Will gave their sister Marian a copy of *Time's Laughingstocks*,[34] but the earlier book seems to have been a favourite with Llewelyn, who mentions 'The Souls of the Slain' in 'Portland' and discusses 'The Lost Pyx' at some length in 'Cerne Abbas.'[35] In 1924 he insists on 'the value of his poetry' in *Thirteen Worthies*,[36] and towards the end of his life, in 1938, along with Alyse Gregory, he 'often returned to Hardy's poems.'[37] In the same year, he demonstrated critical shrewdness by writing to his brother Littleton: 'It is remarkable how poetic his unpoetical crooked crabbed lines are' (*LLP*, 259).

As usual, we know little about Theodore's response, though John Cowper reports that his family was learning 'Men Who March Away' by heart at the beginning of the First World War (*LL*, 1:158). John Cowper himself shows some awareness of *The Dynasts* in his 1915 essay on Hardy in *Visions and Revisions*, and lists *Wessex Poems* in his *One Hundred Best Books* in the following year, where he praises him, in a significant order, as 'poet and novelist.'[38] In 1918, writing to Llewelyn about his visit to Hardy, he described his latest book, *Moments of Vision* (1917), as 'the very best of all,' and reports that Hardy had encouraged him to lecture on his poetry 'which he said alone interested him now' (*LL*, 1:259). Finally, by describing him as a 'Dorset-born noticer of such things,' he alludes in *Autobiography* (229) to the well-known refrain from 'Afterwards.'

The reasons for Hardy's appeal to the Powyses are now becoming evident. For John Cowper, who published verse (without great distinction) along with fiction and nonfiction throughout his life, Hardy's success in both poetry and prose must have been as encouraging as it was awesome. For all of them, his religious views seem to have been influential, and this is a topic to which I shall return. But 'Dorset-born' just quoted reveals that by far the most important reason, as might be expected, was his literary presentation of their common region, which they recognized as magisterial yet by no means exhaustive. I have suggested that the Powyses *collectively* inherited Hardy's literary mantle, and it is certainly true that each adapted and remoulded Hardy's Wessex to his own creative ends. They were at one, however, in praising him as a countryman who was a spokesman for the countryside and its people. John Cowper believed that 'only those born and bred in the country' could do justice to him (*Visions*, 162), while Llewelyn declared that he 'writes like a countryman, thinks like a countryman, has the imagination of a countryman' (*Thirteen*, 211). Only Theodore demurred somewhat, considering Hardy a writer from '*the market-town*' rather than 'the small village.'[39]

John Cowper's presentation of Wessex is the closest to Hardy's, perhaps because he was the closest to Hardy chronologically. After all, as a child in Dorchester in the 1880s he could remember William Barnes walking down the South Walk, and describes him in almost identical terms to those that Hardy used in his obituary article (*Autobiography*, 54).[40] Hardy's Wessex was, in a sense, his Wessex. In his early work he tended to set his novels, diplomatically, in areas of Wessex that Hardy had left relatively unexploited: Montacute in *Wood and Stone*; Charminster, at least in part (see *Petrushka*, 9), in *Ducdame* (1925); Sherborne, Yeovil, and Bradford Abbas in *Wolf Solent* (1929); Glastonbury in *A Glastonbury Romance* (1932). He came closer to Hardy's central region only with Weymouth and Portland in *Weymouth Sands* (1934), and 'Mai Dun' and Dorchester itself in *Maiden Castle* (1936). Perhaps significantly, only after Hardy's death did he abandon the practice of providing Hardy-like disguises for the names of his principal locations. Of course, he fills his landscapes with decidedly un-Hardyesque characters; Jeremy Hooker[41] latches helpfully onto John Cowper's own phrase, 'romantically bizarre' (*Autobiography*, 228), to highlight the transformation. Nonetheless, in its topographical and atmospheric essentials, Hardy's Wessex – albeit detemporalized – is still recognizable.

Because Theodore wrote virtually nothing that could be described as literary commentary, we are forced to deduce his awareness of Hardy's writings from the evidence of his own fiction. Fortunately, J. Lawrence Mitchell has gathered together the main facts.[42] Specific Hardy allusions are confined to the early work. 'Wessex' itself is mentioned twice, in *Father Adam*, written c. 1918–19, published 1990, and in 'Hester Dominy,' a novella of 1920 published in 1923 in *The Left Leg*.[43] The 'Isle of Slingers,' Hardy's name for Portland, is used in the early *Soliloquies of a Hermit*, while 'South Egdon' is a main location (as is the adjoining but never named 'heath') in *Mr Tasker's Gods*, his first novel written as early as 1915 but published only in 1925.[44] Such references fade out, however, as Theodore evolves his own literary region based on the countryside immediately southeast of Dorchester. Nonetheless, he follows Hardy's practice of constructing faintly disguised place names, though adapted it to his own needs. Thus he telescopes Maiden Castle and Hardy's 'Casterbridge' to produce 'Maidenbridge,' his name for Dorchester in much of his work. Similarly, though less appropriately, I suspect that he combines Weymouth with Hardy's 'Christminster' to form his own 'Weyminster.' Mitchell also shows how Theodore artfully updates the opening pages of Hardy's 'A Few Crusted Characters' at the beginning of his own *Mr Weston's Good Wine* (1927) by substituting a Ford car for the carrier van.[45]

But we can venture further than this. The savagery and sexual blatancy in village life that Theodore presents so forcefully in his early work (*Black Bryony* [1923] and *Mark Only* [1924] as well as those already mentioned) must surely derive from Hardy's darkening vision in his final novels, especially the notorious scene involving 'the characteristic part of a barrow-pig' in *Jude the Obscure*. Theodore's fictional world readily embraces what Hardy portrayed in book titles as 'satires of circumstance' and 'life's little ironies'; indeed, as one reads some of the bizarre notes and anecdotes preserved by Hardy in *The Life and Work* (e.g., 63, 160–1, 175–6, 268), one realizes the extent to which Hardy and Theodore share a similar vision.

In the last analysis, Theodore has little interest in history, or even realism. Although 'different symbolic qualities' have been found in them,[46] there are few differentiating details in his Dodders or Madders or Folly Downs. As David Gervais has cogently remarked, all Theodore's books 'are really set *sub specie aeternitatis*.'[47] Still, some teasing possible resemblances with Hardy's work continually surface. One wonders whether the conversations at the Angel Inn in *Mr. Weston's Good Wine* would have been possible without their equivalents in Warren's Malthouse in *Far from the Madding Crowd*, or whether 'The Silent Woman' of *Innocent Birds* (1926) echoes 'The Quiet Woman' of *The Return of the Native*. The woman-selling episode in *The Market Bell* (not published until 1991), with its obvious debt to *The Mayor of Casterbridge*, is also noteworthy. Moreover, Theodore's two-sided natural and human worlds, where scenes of 'quietude' are likely at any time to erupt into violence, where pastoral love making can so often turn into callous rape, may well owe something to Hardy's distinction between Talbothays and Flintcomb-Ash or The Chase. In Theodore's world, however, they overlap disturbingly.

Llewelyn's case was very different. Lacking skill in extended narrative, he concentrated on non fiction forms, especially essays based on his personal experiences and interests. Yet because the circumstances of his life led him to Africa, North America, Switzerland, and (briefly) the Holy Land, about which he wrote some of his best books, Hardy and Wessex are not always central to his work. Nevertheless, of all the Powyses Llewelyn recognized Hardy as, in J.M. Barrie's phrase, 'Historian of Wessex,'[48] an invaluable link between Wessex past and Wessex present. His essays combine his own love of rural life with nostalgic antiquarianism in the spirit, and sometimes even in the style, of Charles Lamb. Studded with quotations from medieval ballads and the old lyric poets, they focus on the historical associations of places connected with his own life (Montacute, the White Nose, etc.). And in so doing, they often, especially in *Dorset Essays*, elaborate on places better known in Hardy's work (Stinsford churchyard, Portland, the Cross-in-Hand, Weymouth Bay). Even in his writings on Hardy himself, he stresses the voice from the past that can, for instance, confirm White Nose as the original form of the place name and lament the decline of ravens in Dorset ('Recollections,' 70, 71). It is not surprising that *A Group of Noble Dames* is one of the four Hardy titles known to have been in Llewelyn's library, since he shared Hardy's delight in ferreting out legends and traditions 'buried under the brief description on a tomb or an entry of dates in a dry pedigree.'[49]

Although it is not a matter susceptible to proof, I strongly suspect that the Powyses admired Hardy for his example in the delicate area of religious belief and practice. 'Loss of faith' was, of course, a characteristic experience of Victorian intellectuals, but Hardy's personal response was unusual since it resulted in neither ostentatious abandonment nor a hypocritical outward conformity masking inner rejection. Hardy no longer believed, and made his nonbelief clear, but he maintained a love of church architecture and the details of ritual observance. He attended Sunday services with reasonable regularity throughout his life, and is on record as reading the lesson for clergyman friends. To use his own memorable phrase, he remained 'churchy' (*LW*, 407). Perhaps John Cowper best summed up the resemblances of Hardy's situation to the Powyses' own when he wrote: 'While Hardy opposes himself to Christianity, he cannot forget it' (*Visions*, 165).

Once again, however, each brother responded to the challenge in a different way. John Cowper presented himself as a sceptic, yet characteristically wrote *The Religion of a Sceptic* wherein he defends Christianity as a man-made and indispensable cultural artefact, venerating 'the familiar words of the old tradition,' especially the King James Bible, as having become part of a new secular 'ritual.'[50] Embracing a 'multiverse' rather than a universe, he also embraced – in his unique half-serious, half-clownish manner – a multiplicity of gods. The former may be seen in the personal rituals revealed in his diaries – tapping his forehead against self-designated sacred stones, reciting prayers to aspects of what we normally regard as natural phenomena. More seriously, in his fiction, we encounter the earth goddess Cybele at the conclusion of *A Glastonbury Romance* and the complex figure of Myrddin Wyllt/Cronos recognized as a 'great' god in the last lines of *Porius*.

Unlike Hardy, Theodore was never tempted to 'go and look at old churches,'[51] yet his friend Louis Wilkinson insisted that he too 'valued the Church of England as a traditional influence in English life.'[52] We know that he was a church-goer throughout his life, and regularly read the lessons at East Chaldon; typically, however, in his later years at Mappowder he attended church every day except Sundays.[53] When asked by Alyse Gregory why he went to church, he replied – only half-flippantly, one feels – that he did so because he saw Christianity as 'a survival of savagery' and because he found kneeling 'beneficial to his health.'[54] To another questioner he added a third reason: to keep the clergyman 'in full employment.'[55] Above all, of course, an empty church was a place for quiet meditation, the kind of meditation that had earlier produced *Soliloquies of a Hermit*. Here he begins with an often-quoted remark, 'A belief is too easy a road to God' (1), and concludes by propounding his death philosophy. He was unable to regard immortality as anything but 'an endless and sad ordeal' (152). This forms the basis for his series of parable-like investigations of religious issues in his fiction. One thinks of the darkest vintage in *Mr. Weston's Good Wine* (chapter 40) and the close of 'The Only Penitent' where the clergyman, hearing from him that death is final, forgives God (in the guise of Tinker Jar) for creating the world and crucifying his son, and concludes with a prayer that he will be brought 'to everlasting death.'[56] For Theodore, religion was important because it provided a much-needed preparation for death.

Llewelyn's atheistic principles are listed baldly in *Skin for Skin*: 'Christianity is not true'; 'there is no God'; 'there is no life after death' (31, 32). He is the most polemical of the brothers so far as the orthodoxies of the Christian church are concerned, writing rationalist-oriented books on the Old and New Testaments (*The Cradle of God* [1929], *The Pathetic*

Fallacy [1930]) and expressing his sense of the twentieth-century religious dilemma in his title *Now That the Gods Are Dead* (1932). For Llewelyn, a self-styled 'natural heathen,' the church-approved stories of Christ were 'incredible impossibilities.'[57] Unlike the polytheistic John Cowper, he was against all gods,[58] but they were at one in admiring Jesus and venerating the scriptures while hating the Church.[59] Indeed, whenever Llewelyn is at his most dismissive, there is always a qualification. In *The Cradle of God* the Church's arguments are false, yet Christian beliefs contain 'some invisible clue denied to ruder natures' (229); in *The Pathetic Fallacy* he rejects theological dogmatism, yet adds surprisingly: 'the essence of Christianity is true' (75). It would be a mistake to classify Llewelyn as antireligious. He is an advocate for a life-affirming religion that does not depend upon belief. He insists on the wonder of existence in a world of love and natural beauty and, while recognizing the finality of death, recommends 'adoration of life' (*Glory*, 17).

The Powyses may be said to have revered Hardy as a local cultural icon, both an example and (during his life) a wise mentor. In addition, for John Cowper, he was an imaginative inspiration, as a brief look at some of his later books will show. There are occasional and generally casual references to Hardy in many of the earlier novels, but after Hardy's death these take on a more subtle, even whimsical quality. Hardy even comes close to manifesting himself as a shadowy character within the fictions. A decidedly minor example occurs in *Weymouth Sands*,[60] when one of the main characters finds himself on a seat on the esplanade next to a young man who is reading Hardy's *The Well-Beloved*. At the level of plot, this is a gratuitous, expendable detail, but it reminds us that Portland, the 'Isle of Slingers,' had been a principal location in another novel besides the one we are reading. It is as if the spirit of Hardy, through his book, appears as an appraising presence behind the narrative.

Maiden Castle contains a more complex instance. This novel, set in the model for Hardy's Casterbridge, begins with a wife-buying and thereby establishes an immediate comparison/contrast with the wife-selling in the opening section of *The Mayor of Casterbridge*. Furthermore, John Cowper's scene takes place within sight of Maumbury Ring, the Roman amphitheatre where Michael Henchard later arranges a meeting with the wife he had once sold. But a much more equivocal effect is achieved towards the end of the novel,[61] where a scene takes place at Top o' Town at the Hardy statue, then only five years old. The scene involves a drawing of a goddess image just excavated at Maiden Castle that is being altered by the novel's protagonist, Dud No-Man, while using the back of the statue as a support. The name of No-Man's dead wife is later found scrawled uncertainly across the drawing, though no one can explain how it got there.[62] The mystery is never explained, yet once again the spirit of Hardy seems to hover intriguingly over the incident.

But the most remarkable of these scenes takes place in *Owen Glendower*, a historical novel set in early fifteenth-century Wales. In the banquet hall at Dinas Brān where some tricky English/Welsh political negotiations are under way, Thomas Fitz-Alan, Earl of Arundel and Lord of Chirk, brings in two Dorset men as his night bodyguards. Their names are Jimmy Trenchard and Tom Hardy. Trenchard is the historical Dorset name that Hardy altered to Henchard, but John Cowper uses when referring to *The Mayor of Casterbridge* – in *Maiden Castle* (255) and *Dorset* (210), for example. The two converse in John Cowper's brand of Dorset dialect, including references to Fordington (the area of Dorchester close to Max Gate) and the use of the characteristic Hardy term 'doomster.'[63] But suddenly a crisis develops. Owen Glendower, present in secret, throws off his disguise and shoots Trenchard with an arrow after the Dorset man has wounded him. Trenchard dies, and Tom Hardy promises to look after his daughter. Years later, Tom Hardy appears again, accused of dragging out of sanctuary a peasant leader with the Skeltonian name of Philip Sparrow – John Cowper is liberal with anachronistic literary reference! The 'man from Wessex,' a Wessex which we are pointedly told is 'still heathen' (907), maintains an 'unappeasable hatred' for the Welsh cause.

The allusion is obvious, its application less so. John Cowper is presumably paying a final tribute to his revered mentor by introducing one of his ancestors into fiction. I suspect, however, that he is here saying more about himself than about Hardy. He had, after all, deserted Wessex for Wales, and had abandoned the matter of Wessex for Welsh history and Welsh themes. Tom Hardy is a reminder of the tradition he had left, his hatred of the Welsh perhaps reflecting the unease that a part of John Cowper's conscience felt at the geographical and cultural shift that he underwent in the latter part of his life. John Cowper had certainly changed considerably from the aspiring Wessex author who addressed a poem to Hardy in 1896.

The Powyses, though intellectually 'modern,' continually hark back to the rural world only partly affected by industrialism into which Hardy had been born. Aeroplanes and fast-moving cars are alien objects in

John Cowper's and Theodore's villages that reflect beliefs and behavioural patterns that have changed little in the passing centuries. A temporal paradox is involved here. Hardy lived a conspicuously Victorian life, yet his work embraces a social realism that looks forward towards modernism while at the same time portraying the traditional life of rural England. The Powyses were decidedly twentieth-century in their religious attitudes and (Theodore excepted) in their sexual mores, yet their settings are remote compared with Hardy's, moving into imaginative fantasy in John Cowper or a unique brand of allegory in Theodore. Llewelyn wrote fashionably sceptical anti-Christian books while passionately adhering to the life patterns of the rural past; John Cowper 'escaped' into remote Welsh history, yet introduced into it a sensibility influenced by Dostoevsky and even modern psychology. Yet this Janus-like quality is beginning to be recognized as curiously typical of a world torn between the opposed challenges of progressivism and radical conservation. This was the world which Hardy was one of the first to experience and to explore in his disconcertingly angular poetry and fiction. His life-style – or, in John Cowper's favoured phraseology, his 'life-illusion' – was not theirs, but in him the Powyses recognized, and paid tribute to, a kindred spirit.

NOTES

1 John Cowper Powys, *Odes and Other Poems* (1896; London: Village Press, 1975), 12.
2 John Cowper Powys, *Autobiography* (1934; Hamilton: Colgate University Press, 1968), 227–30. Hereafter cited parenthetically.
3 See Glen Cavaliero, 'Recollections of John Cowper Powys,' in *Recollections of the Powys Brothers: Llewelyn, Theodore and John Cowper*, ed. Belinda Humfrey (London: Peter Owen, 1980), 253; Cavaliero, *The Powys Family: Some Records of a Friendship*, Powys Heritage Series (London: Cecil Woolf, 1999), 16; and Elizabeth Harvey, 'John Cowper Powys: A Visit,' in *Recollections*, ed. Humfrey, 260.
4 Llewelyn Powys, 'Recollections of Thomas Hardy,' in *Wessex Memories*, ed. Peter J. Foss (Gloucester: Powys Press, 2003), 60–72 (62). Shorter versions of this article appeared in *Virginia Quarterly Review* 15 (summer 1939), 425–34, and, as 'Some Memories of Thomas Hardy,' in 'Monographs on the Life, Times and Works of Thomas Hardy,' ed. J. Stevens Cox (Guernsey: Toucan Press, 1969). Hereafter cited parenthetically as 'Recollections.'

5 Thomas Hardy, *The Life and Work of Thomas Hardy*, ed. Michael Millgate (London: Macmillan, 1984), 162. Hereafter cited parenthetically as *LW*.

6 David Garnett, 'T.F. Powys' (1925), *Powys Society Newsletter* 47 (November 2002): 36.

7 Francis Powys, 'Mr. Weston's Good World,' in *Recollections*, ed. Humfrey, 124.

8 John Cowper Powys, *Petrushka and the Dancer: The Diaries of John Cowper Powys, 1929–1939*, ed. Morine Krissdóttir (Manchester: Carcanet Press, 1995), 7. Hereafter cited parenthetically as *Petrushka*.

9 Llewelyn Powys, 'Glimpses of Thomas Hardy,' *The Dial* 72 (March 1922): 287; cf. 'Recollections,' 64.

10 James Gibson, *Thomas Hardy: A Literary Life* (London: Macmillan, 1996), 89. See J[ohn] B[atten], 'The Authorized Version?' *Powys Society Newsletter* 32 (November 1997): 24–5.

11 *The Collected Letters of Thomas Hardy*, ed. Richard Little Purdy and Michael Millgate, 7 vols (Oxford: Clarendon, 1978–88), 4:266. Hereafter cited parenthetically as *CL*.

12 See Peter J. Casagrande, *Hardy's Influence on the Modern Novel* (London: Macmillan, 1987), 74.

13 John Cowper Powys, *Letters to His Brother Llewelyn*, ed. Malcolm Elwin, 2 vols (London: Village Press, 1975), 1:258. Hereafter cited parenthetically as *LL*.

14 Llewelyn Powys, 'A Visit to Thomas Hardy, 1919,' in 'Monographs on the Life and Works of Thomas Hardy,' ed. J. Stevens Cox (Guernsey: Toucan Press, 1971), 482.

15 Robert Gittings, *The Older Hardy* (London: Heinemann, 1978), 187.

16 Judith Stinton, *Chaldon Herring: The Powyses in a Dorset Village* (Woodbridge: Boydell Press, 1988), 43.

17 Ibid.

18 John Cowper Powys, *The Dorset Year: The Diary of John Cowper Powys, June 1934–July 1935*, ed. Morine Krissdóttir and Roger Peers (Bath: Powys Press, 1998), 29. Cf. 210. Hereafter cited parenthetically as *Dorset*.

19 Llewelyn Powys, *Skin for Skin* (New York: Harcourt, Brace, 1925), 112.

20 Malcolm Elwin, *The Life of Llewelyn Powys* (London: John Lane, Bodley Head, 1946), 166–7.

21 *The Diary of John Cowper Powys, 1930*, ed. Frederick Davies (London: Greymitre Books, 1987), 130.

22 Llewelyn Powys, 'At the Unveiling of the Memorial Statue of Thomas Hardy, 1931,' in 'Monographs on the Life, Times and Works of Thomas Hardy,' ed. J. Stevens Cox (Guernsey: Toucan Press, 1971), 482.

23 Elwin, *The Life of Llewelyn Powys*, 210.

24 Stinton, *Chaldon Herring*, 95–6, 117.

25 John Cowper Powys, *The Pleasures of Literature* (London: Cassell, 1938), 605.

26 F.W. Troup, 'Reminiscences of A.R. Powys and the S.P.A.B,' (1936), *Powys Society Newsletter* 38 (November 1999): 41.

27 Susan Rands, 'A.R. Powys, Roger Clark, and West Pennard Tithe Barn,' *Powys Society Newsletter* 40 (July 2000): 31.

28 'Thomas Hardy – A Lecture by Llewelyn Powys,' *Powys Society Newsletter* 39 (April 2000): 10–21. See Peter Foss, 'The Llewelyn Lecture' *Powys Society Newsletter* 42 (April 2001): 21–3.

29 Gibson, *Literary Life*, ix.

30 Paul Roberts, 'John Cowper Powys and The Cambridge Summer Meetings,' *Powys Journal* 13 (2003): 199–200.

31 Peter John Foss, *A Study of Llewelyn Powys: His Literary Achievement and Personal Philosophy* (Lewiston: Edwin Mellen Press, 1991), 367.

32 *The Letters of Llewelyn Powys*, ed. Louis Wilkinson (London: John Lane, Bodley Head, 1944), 59. Hereafter cited parenthetically as *LLP*.

33 Elwin, *The Life of Llewelyn Powys*, 79.

34 Foss, *Study of Llewelyn*, 367.

35 Llewelyn Powys, *Dorset Essays* (London: John Lane, Bodley Head, 1935), 103, 72–4.

36 Llewelyn Powys, *Thirteen Worthies* (1924; Freeport: Books for Libraries Press, 1964), 213. Hereafter cited parenthetically as *Thirteen*.

37 Elwin, *The Life of Llewelyn Powys*, 254.

38 John Cowper Powys, *Visions and Revisions: A Book of Literary Devotions* (1915; London: Macdonald, 1955), 161 (hereafter cited parenthetically as *Visions*); and *One Hundred Best Books* (New York: Arnold Shaw, 1916), 50.

39 J. Lawrence Mitchell, '"Lift up Thine Eyes to the Hills": The Visionary World of T.F. Powys,' *Powys Journal* 4 (1994): 94.

40 For Hardy's Barnes obituary, see *Thomas Hardy's Public Voice: The Essays, Speeches, and Miscellaneous Prose*, ed. Michael Millgate (Oxford: Clarendon, 2001), 66.

41 Jeremy Hooker, 'Thomas Hardy, John Cowper Powys and Wessex,' *Powys Review* 27–8 (1992–3): 26.

42 Mitchell, '"Lift up Thine Eyes to the Hills"', 94–5.

43 Theodore Powys, *Father Adam* (Doncaster: Brynmill Press, 1990), 42; and *The Left Leg* (New York: Knopf, 1923), 143.

44 Theodore Powys, *Soliloquies of a Hermit* (London: Andrew Melrose, 1918), 160; and *Mr Tasker's Gods* (New York: Knopf, 1925).

45 Mitchell, '"Lift up Thine Eyes to the Hills,"' 95.

46 Glen Cavaliero, *The Rural Tradition in the English Novel, 1900–1933* (London: Macmillan, 1977), 173.

47 David Gervais, 'Religious Comedy in T.F. Powys,' *Powys Journal* 9 (1999): 90.

48 See J.M. Barrie, 'Thomas Hardy, Historian of Wessex,' *Contemporary Review* 56 (July 1889): 57–66.

49 Thomas Hardy, *A Group of Noble Dames* (1891; London: Macmillan, 1968), 50. For Llewelyn's library, see Foss, *A Study of Llewelyn Powys*, 367.

50 John Cowper Powys, *The Religion of a Sceptic* (1925; London: Village Press, 1975), 35.

51 Theodore Powys, *Soliloquies of a Hermit* (London: Andrew Melrose, 1918), 33–4.

52 *Theodore: Essays on T.F. Powys*, ed. Brocard Sewell (Aylesbury: St Albert's Press, 1964), viii.

53 Francis Powys, 'Mr. Weston's Good World,' 126.

54 Alyse Gregory, 'The Character of Theodore,' *Recollections*, ed. Humfrey, 147.

55 Mark Holloway, 'With T.F. Powys at Mappowder,' *Recollections*, ed. Humfrey, 155.

56 Theodore Powys, *Bottle's Path* (London: Chatto & Windus, 1946), 139.

57 Llewelyn Powys, *The Pathetic Fallacy: A Study of Christianity* (1930; Thinker's Library. London: Watts, 1934), 107; and *The Cradle of God* (London: Jonathan Cape, 1929), 16.

58 Llewelyn Powys, *The Glory of God* and *Now That the Gods Are Dead* (1934, 1932; London: Bodley Head, 1949), 12. Hereafter cited parenthetically as *Glory*.

59 Llewelyn Powys, *A Baker's Dozen* (London: John Lane, Bodley Head, 1941), 13.

60 John Cowper Powys, *Weymouth Sands* (1934. London: Macdonald, 1963), 473.

61 John Cowper Powys, *Maiden Castle* (1936), ed. Ian Hughes, Cardiff: University of Wales Press, 1990), 389–90.

62 Casagrande is not justified, by the way, in stating categorically that No-Man 'writes her name across the sketch' (*Hardy's Influence*, 105).

63 John Cowper Powys, *Owen Glendower* (1941; Portway: Cedric Chivers, 1974), 376.

Selected Checklist of Hardy-Related Publications by Michael Millgate

Books

Thomas Hardy: His Career as a Novelist. London: Bodley Head; New York: Random House, 1971. 428 pp. Reissued in hardcover and paperback, with a new preface, Basingstoke: Macmillan Press, 1994.

The Collected Letters of Thomas Hardy. Volume One: 1840-1892. Coedited (with Richard L. Purdy), with an introduction. Oxford: Clarendon Press; New York: Oxford University Press, 1978. xxii + 293 pp. Reissued, with corrections, 1979.

The Collected Letters of Thomas Hardy. Volume Two: 1893-1901. Coedited (with Richard L. Purdy). Oxford: Clarendon Press; New York: Oxford University Press, 1980. x + 309 pp.

Thomas Hardy: A Biography. Oxford: Oxford University Press; New York: Random House, 1982. xvi + 637 pp. Reissued as paperback, Oxford and New York: Oxford University Press, 1985; reissued in 'Oxford Lives' series, 1987; reissued, with revisions, as a Clarendon paperback, 1992.

The Collected Letters of Thomas Hardy. Volume Three: 1902-1908. Coedited (with Richard L. Purdy). Oxford: Clarendon Press; New York: Oxford University Press, 1982. x + 367 pp.

The Collected Letters of Thomas Hardy. Volume Four: 1909-1913. Coedited (with Richard L. Purdy). Oxford: Clarendon Press; New York: Oxford University Press, 1984. x + 337 pp.

Thomas Hardy, *The Life and Work of Thomas Hardy*. Edited, with an introduction. London: Macmillan; Athens: University of Georgia Press, 1985; paperback reissued, with revisions, London: Macmillan, 1989. xxxvii + 604 pp.

The Collected Letters of Thomas Hardy. Volume Five: 1914-1919. Coedited (with Richard L. Purdy). Oxford: Clarendon Press; New York: Oxford University Press, 1985. x + 357 pp. Reissued, with corrections, 1992.

The Collected Letters of Thomas Hardy. Volume Six: 1920-1925. Coedited (with Richard L. Purdy). Oxford: Clarendon Press; New York: Oxford University Press, 1987. x + 379 pp.

The Collected Letters of Thomas Hardy. Volume Seven: 1926-1927, with Addenda, Corrigenda, and General Index. Coedited (with Richard L. Purdy). Oxford: Clarendon Press; New York: Oxford University Press, 1988. xiv + 304 pp.

Thomas Hardy: Selected Letters. Edited, with an introduction. Oxford: Clarendon Press; New York: Oxford University Press, 1990. xxvii + 433 pp.

Testamentary Acts: Browning, Tennyson, James, Hardy. Oxford: Clarendon Press; New York: Oxford University Press, 1992. x + 273 pp. Reissued as a Clarendon paperback, 1995.

Thomas Hardy's 'Studies, Specimens &c.' Notebook. Coedited (with Pamela Dalziel). Oxford: Clarendon Press, 1994. xvii + 164 pp.

Letters of Emma and Florence Hardy. Edited, with an introduction. Oxford: Clarendon Press, 1996. xxv + 364 pp.

Thomas Hardy's Public Voice: The Essays, Speeches, and Miscellaneous Prose. Edited, with an introduction. Oxford: Clarendon Press, 2001. xl + 500 pp.

Thomas Hardy: A Biography Revisited. Oxford: Oxford University Press, 2004. xii + 625 pp.

Website

'Thomas Hardy's Library at Max Gate: Catalogue of an Attempted Reconstruction': www.library.utoronto.ca/fisher/hardy (established August 2003; compiled and maintained by Michael Millgate.)

Contributions to Books

'The Making and Unmaking of Thomas Hardy's Wessex Edition.' In *Editing Nineteenth-Century Fiction*, ed. Jane Millgate, 61–82. New York: Garland, 1978.

'Thomas Hardy.' In *Victorian Fiction: A Second Guide to Research*, ed. George H. Ford, 308–32. New York: Modern Language Association of America, 1978.

'Introduction to the AMS Edition.' In Thomas Hardy, *Tess of the d'Urbervilles.* New York: AMS Press, 1984.

'Unreal Estate: Reflections on Wessex and Yoknapatawpha.' In *The Literature of Region and Nation*, ed. R.P. Draper, 61–80. London: Macmillan Press, 1989.

'Thomas Hardy and Hermann Lea' In *Hardy's Wessex Today*, by Vera Jesty, 3–5. Belper: Mellstock Press, 1990.

'The Max Gate Library.' In *A Spacious Vision: Essays on Hardy*, ed. Phillip V. Mallett and Ronald P. Draper, 139–49. Penzance: Patten Press, 1994.

'Foreword.' In *Nathaniel Sparks: Memoirs of Hardy's Cousin, the Engraver*, by Celia Barclay, 5–7. Greenwich: Cock Inn, 1994.
'Wives All: Emma and Florence Hardy.' In *Celebrating Thomas Hardy: Insights and Appreciations*, ed. Charles P.C. Pettit, 115–35. Basingstoke: Macmillan Press, 1996.
'Thomas Hardy's Wessex.' In *An Atlas of Literature*, ed. Malcolm Bradbury, 133–6. London: DeAgostini, 1996.
'Obscure Rivalry: Thomas Hardy and Henry James in Early Career.' In *Corresponding Powers: Essays in Honour of Professor Hisaaki Yamanouchi*, ed. George Hughes, 175–85. Woodbridge, Suffolk: Boydell & Brewer, 1997.
'Distracted Preacher: Thomas Hardy's Public Utterances.' In *Reading Thomas Hardy*, ed. Charles P.C. Pettit, 227–47. Basingstoke: Macmillan Press, 1998.
'Thomas Hardy: The Biographical Sources.' In *The Cambridge Companion to Thomas Hardy*, ed. Dale Kramer, 1–18. Cambridge: Cambridge University Press, 1999.
'Thomas Hardy.' In *Oxford Reader's Companion to Hardy*, ed. Norman Page, 162–5, 168–74. Oxford: Oxford University Press, 2000). Together with ten other contributions of varying lengths, amounting to some 22,000 words in all.
'The Thomas Hardy Collection of Frederick B. Adams, Jr.' In *The Library of Frederick B. Adams, Jr. Part II: Thomas Hardy*, 8–11. London: Sotheby's, 2001.
'Thomas Hardy and the House of Macmillan.' In *Macmillan: A Publishing Tradition*, ed. Elizabeth James, 70–82. Basingstoke: Palgrave, 2002.

Articles

'Hardy's Fiction: Some Comments on the Present State of Criticism,' *English Literature in Transition* 14 (1971): 230–8.
'Thomas Hardy and Rosamund Tomson' *Notes and Queries* n.s. 20 (1973): 253–5.
'Thomas Hardy: A Mystery Solved.' *Papers of the Bibliographical Society of America* 70 (1976): 406–7.
'Richard Little Purdy (1904–1990).' *Thomas Hardy Journal* 6.3 (October 1990): 41–3 (reprinted from London *Independent*).
'The "Discarded" Preface to *A Pair of Blue Eyes*.' *Thomas Hardy Journal* 13.3 (October 1997): 58–9.
'Thomas Hardy.' *Encyclopaedia Britannica* (1997 edition).
'Hardy as Memorialist.' *Thomas Hardy Journal* 15.3 (October 1999): 65–72.
'A Christmas Ghost-Story.' *The Times Literary Supplement*, 7 January 2000, 15.
'A Hardyan Pursuit, or, The Frustrations of Scholarship.' *Bancroftiana* 119 (fall 2001): 8–9.

Notes on Contributors

Pamela Dalziel is Associate Professor of English and Distinguished University Scholar at the University of British Columbia and General Editor of the Clarendon Dickens Edition. She has published numerous articles on Hardy and has edited *Thomas Hardy: The Excluded and Collaborative Stories* (Clarendon, 1992), *Thomas Hardy's 'Studies, Specimens &c.' Notebook* (with Michael Millgate, Clarendon, 1994), *An Indiscretion in the Life of an Heiress and Other Stories* (Oxford World's Classics, 1994), and *A Pair of Blue Eyes* (Penguin Classics, 1998). She is currently completing a study of the visual representation of Hardy's novels and the Clarendon edition of *Hard Times*.

Marjorie Garson, Professor of English at the University of Toronto, has published Hardy's *Fables of Integrity: Woman, Body, Text* (Clarendon, 1991) as well as articles on Swift, Keats, Austen, Scott, Dickens, Thackeray, and Munro. She has recently completed *Moral Taste: Aesthetics, Subjectivity, and Social Power in the Nineteeth-Century Novel*.

Simon Gatrell, Professor of English at the University of Georgia, is author of *Hardy the Creator: A Textual Biography* (Clarendon, 1988), *Thomas Hardy and the Proper Study of Mankind* (University Press of Virginia, 1993), and *Thomas Hardy's Vision of Wessex* (Palgrave Macmillan, 2003), with which there is an associated website, www.english.uga.edu/wessex, of material relating to Hardy's early conceptions of Wessex. He is coeditor of the Clarendon edition of *Tess of the d'Urbervilles* (1983), general editor of the World's Classics series of Hardy texts from OUP, and editor of *Tess of the d'Urbervilles* (1988), *The Return of the Native* (1990), and *Under the Greenwood Tree* (1985) in the same series. He is also editor of facsimiles of the manuscripts of *The Return of the Native* and *Tess of the d'Urbervilles* (Garland, 1986). In addition he has published numerous essays on Hardy and on other Victorian and Irish writers, including Clough, Meredith, Trollope, Gissing, Conrad, Heaney, and Johnston.

Barbara Hardy is Professor Emeritus at Birkbeck College, University of London, and Honorary Professor at the University of Wales, Swansea. Her books include critical studies of William Shakespeare, Jane Austen, Charles Dickens, the Brontës, W.M. Thackeray, George Eliot, Henry James, and Dylan Thomas; a study of poetry, *The Advantage of Lyric* (Athlone, 1977); a study of narrative, *Tellers and Listeners* (Athlone, 1975); a memoir, *Swansea Girl* (Peter Owen, 1994); a novel, *London Lovers* (Peter Owen, 1997); and *Severn Bridge: New and Selected Poems* (Shoestring Press, 2001). She is currently writing a biographical-critical study of George Eliot; a book, *Dickens and Creativity*; and a new volume of poems. She has written on Hardy in *The Appropriate Form* (Athlone, 1964), *Tellers and Listeners* (Athlone, 1975), *Tennyson and the Novelists* (Tennyson Society, 1992), and *Thomas Hardy: Imagining Imagination in Hardy's Poetry and Fiction* (Athlone, 2000). Professor Hardy is a Fellow of the Royal Society of Literature and a Vice-President of the Thomas Hardy Society.

Samuel Hynes is Woodrow Wilson Professor of Literature Emeritus at Princeton University. Author of one of the first book-length studies of Hardy's verse, *The Pattern of Hardy's Poetry* (University of North Carolina Press 1961), he is editor of *The Complete Poetical Works of Thomas Hardy* (5 volumes, Clarendon, 1982–95). Other major works include *The Edwardian Turn of Mind* (Princeton University Press, 1968), *Edwardian Occasions* (Routledge, 1972), *The Auden Generation* (Bodley Head, 1976), and *A War Imagined: the First World War and English Culture* (Macmillan, 1991). His experiences as a Marine Corps pilot are recorded in his memoir, *Flights of Passage: Reflections of a World War II Aviator* (Naval Institute Press 1988) and also inform his study of soldiers' narratives, *The Soldiers' Tale: Bearing Witness to Modern War* (Allen Lane, 1997). His most recent book is *The Growing Seasons: An American Boyhood before the War* (Viking, 2003). Professor Hynes is a Fellow of the Royal Society of Literature.

W.J. Keith was educated at the universities of Cambridge and Toronto and is Professor Emeritus at the University of Toronto. His work on

English rural literature includes *The Rural Tradition* (U of Toronto P, 1974), *The Poetry of Nature* (U of Toronto P, 1980), and *Regions of the Imagination* (U of Toronto P, 1988). He also publishes in the field of Canadian literature, including *Canadian Literature in English* (Longman, 1985), *Literary Images of Ontario* (U of Toronto P, 1992), and *Canadian Odyssey* (McGill-Queen's UP, 2002), a study of Hugh Hood's fiction. He is the author of two collections of poems, *Echoes in Silence* (Goose Lane, 1992) and *In the Beginning and Other Poems* (St Thomas's 1999). Professor Keith is a Fellow of the Royal Society of Canada.

U.C. Knoepflmacher is Paton Foundation Professor of Ancient and Modern Literature at Princeton University. Among his most recent publications are the articles 'Literary Fairy Tales and the Value of Impurity' (2003), 'Validating Defiance: From Heinrich Hoffmann to Mark Twain, Rudyard Kipling, and Maurice Sendak' (2002), and 'The Chameleon Kipling: His Rise and Fall and Rehabilitation' (2001); a book *Ventures into Childland: Victorians, Fairy Tales, and Femininity* (University of Chicago Press, 2000); and two Penguin editions, Frances Hodgson Burnett's *A Little Princess* (2002) and *The Complete Fairy Tales of George MacDonald* (1999). His work on Hardy includes 'The Return of a Native Singer: Keats in Hardy's Dorset' (1993) and 'Hardy Ruins: Female Spaces and Male Designs' (1990). He is currently finishing a memoir entitled 'Oruro: Growing Up Jewish in the Andes' and an annotated edition of Kipling's *Just So Stories*.

George Levine is Kenneth Burke Professor of English and Director of the Center for the Critical Analysis of Contemporary Culture at Rutgers University. Among his books are *The Realistic Imagination* (U of Chicago P, 1981), *Darwin and the Novelists* (Harvard UP, 1988), and most recently from University of Chicago Press, *Dying to Know: Narrative and Scientific Epistemology in Victorian England* (2002). He has edited many volumes of essays, among them, *Aesthetics and Ideology* (Rutgers UP, 1994) and *The Cambridge Companion to George Eliot* (Cambridge UP, 2001). He is also author of a book of birding memoirs, *Lifebirds* (Rutgers UP, 1995). His latest book, *Darwin Loves You*, is forthcoming from Princeton University Press.

J. Hillis Miller taught for many years at Johns Hopkins University and then at Yale University, before going to the University of California at Irvine in 1986, where is he now UCI Distinguished Research Professor.

He is the author of many books and essays on nineteenth- and twentieth-century English, European, and American literature, and on literary theory. His most recent books are *Others* (Princeton, UP, 2001), *Speech Acts in Literature* (Stanford, UP, 2002), *On Literature* (Routledge, 2002), *Zero Plus One* (Universitat de València: Biblioteca Javier Coy d'estudis nord-americans, 2003), and *Literature as Conduct: Speech Acts in Henry James* (Fordham UP, 2005). *The J. Hillis Miller Reader* was published in 2005 by Edinburgh UP and Stanford UP. Miller is a member of the American Philosophical Society.

William W. Morgan is Professor Emeritus of English at Illinois State University. He has published two coedited books on Hardy as well as Hardy-related essays in such journals as *PMLA, JEGP, Victorian Poetry, Victorians Institute Journal, Victorian Newsletter, The Thomas Hardy Journal*, and *The Hardy Review*. For ten years he wrote the annual review of Hardy scholarship for *Victorian Poetry*. He is Executive Vice-President of the Thomas Hardy Association and Director of the Association's Thomas Hardy Poetry Page. He has also published two chapbooks, *Trackings: The Body's Memory, The Heart's Fiction* (Boulder: Dead Metaphor Press, 1998), and *Sky with Six Geese* (Columbus: Pudding House Press, 2005), and over thirty poems in various journals.

Norman Page was educated at the universities of Cambridge and Leeds and is a Professor Emeritus of the University of Alberta and the University of Nottingham. His books include *Thomas Hardy* (Routledge and Kejan Paul, 1977) and *The Oxford Reader's Companion to Hardy* (Oxford UP, 2000) as well as editions of several of Hardy's novels and two selections of his verse. He has lectured on Hardy in many parts of the world, has edited the *Thomas Hardy Annual* and the *Thomas Hardy Journal*, and is a Vice-President of the Thomas Hardy Society, the Tennyson Society, and the Housman Society. He is a Fellow of the Royal Society of Canada and among other awards has held a Guggenheim Fellowship and a Leverhulme Fellowship.

Mary Rimmer is Professor of English at the University of New Brunswick. The editor of Hardy's *Desperate Remedies* for Penguin Classics, she has also published articles on Hardy, Canadian fiction, and the use of speech and dialect in Trinidadian fiction, as well as contributing to editions of three early Trinidadian novels: E.L. Joseph's *Warner Arundell: The Adventures of a Creole*, Mrs William Noy Wilkins's *The Slave*

Son, and the anonymous *Adolphus: A Tale*. She is currently writing a book on allusion in Hardy.

Jeremy Steele read Classical Mods and English at Magdalen College, Oxford. After several years as an editor in Britain, he moved to Australia, where he completed a PhD thesis, 'Hardy's Debt to the Classical World,' at the University of Sydney. He subsequently worked at Macquarie University and in educational publishing. Among his publications is the entry on classics in *The Oxford Reader's Companion to Hardy*, ed. Norman Page (2000).

Dennis Taylor is Professor of English at Boston College, and editor of the journal *Religion and the Arts*. His books include *Hardy's Poetry 1860-1928* (Macmillan, rev. ed., 1989), cowinner of the 1990 Macmillan/ Hardy Society Prize, *Hardy's Metres and Victorian Prosody* (Oxford, 1988), and *Hardy's Literary Language and Victorian Philology* (Oxford, rev. rpt, 1998). He is the editor of the Penguin edition of *Jude the Obscure* (1998), and also the editor of *Shakespeare and the Culture of Christianity of Early Modern England* (Fordham, 2003).

Keith Wilson is Professor of English at the University of Ottawa, and a Vice-President of the Thomas Hardy Association. He is the author of *Thomas Hardy On Stage* (Macmillan, 1995), editor of *The Mayor of Casterbridge* (Penguin, 1997), and coeditor (with the late Kristin Brady) of *The Fiddler of the Reels and Other Stories* (Penguin, 2003). He has published numerous articles on Hardy, as well as essays on a wide range of nineteenth- and twentieth-century writers, and on Victorian and Edwardian music hall. He is currently working on the representation of London in modern British literature.

Ruth Bernard Yeazell is Chace Family Professor of English at Yale University. She is the author of *Language and Knowledge in the Late Novels of Henry James* (U of Chicago P, 1976), *The Death and Letters of Alice James* (California, 1981), and *Fictions of Modesty: Women and Courtship in the English Novel* (U of Chicago P, 1991). Her most recent book, *Harems of the Mind: Passages of Western Art and Literature* (Yale UP, 2000) is a study of Western representations of the East from the late seventeenth to the early twentieth century. She is currently working on a study of literary realism and Dutch painting.

Index